# Manager's Survival Guide

## How to Avoid the 750 Most Common Mistakes in Dealing with People

# MANAGER'S SURVIVAL GUIDE

## HOW TO AVOID THE 750 MOST COMMON MISTAKES IN DEALING WITH PEOPLE

### ALLAN KRIEFF

**PRENTICE HALL**
Englewood Cliffs, New Jersey 07632

**Library of Congress Cataloging in Publication Data**

Krieff, Allan.
  Manager's survival guide : how to avoid the 750 most common
mistakes in dealing with people / Allan Krieff.
      p.    cm.
  ISBN 0–13–210766–X (cloth). — ISBN 0–13–210758–9 (pbk.)
  1. Communication in personnel management.   2. Communication in
management.   3. Interpersonal communication.   I. Title.
  HF5549.5.C6K748   1996
  658.3—dc20                                                              96–22264
                                                                              CIP

*Printed in the United States of America*

*10  9  8  7  6  5  4  3  2  1*

ISBN 0-13-210766-X (C)        ISBN 0-13-210758-9 (P)

**PRENTICE HALL**
Career & Personal Development
Englewood Cliffs, NJ 07632
A Simon & Schuster Company

On the World Wide Web at http://www.phdirect.com

Prentice Hall International (UK) Limited, *London*
Prentice Hall of Australia Pty. Limited, *Sydney*
Prentice Hall Canada, Inc., *Toronto*
Prentice Hall Hispanoamericana, S.A., *Mexico*
Prentice Hall of India Private Limited, *New Delhi*
Prentice Hall of Japan, Inc., *Tokyo*
Simon & Schuster Asia Pte. Ltd., *Singapore*
Editora Prentice Hall do Brasil, Ltda., *Rio de Janeiro*

**Also by Allan Krieff**

*How to Start and Run Your Own Advertising Agency*

# DEDICATION

This book is lovingly dedicated to my children, Debra and David, who so far have made few, if any, mistakes in their lives. Especially not in choosing their spouses, Matthew and Carroll. And to my grandsons, Brandon, Ryan, Donovan, Benjamin, and Truman, who so far have made no mistakes in bringing up their parents.

# ABOUT THE AUTHOR

Allan Krieff, a graduate of New York University with a B.S. in marketing, is a veteran of 39 years in advertising, marketing, and communications. Starting in the research department at Young & Rubicam Advertising in New York City in 1956, he worked on campaigns for major clients and helped establish an agency research project that was the first to pretest audience reactions to network television program pilots that agency clients were considering sponsoring.

He went on to account management at Weiss & Geller Advertising, a medium-sized New York firm known for its then revolutionary use of motivational advertising, as documented in the classic Vance Packard book, *The Hidden Persuaders*. It was here that the author, looking for unique radio and television programs for clients, decided to produce his own shows. In 1959 he and entertainer Eddie Cantor formed an association that produced TV and radio comedy and variety programs.

In 1962 he moved to Florida and established a one-man ad agency with modest billings. Krieff Advertising, based in Hollywood, Florida, grew to a full-service advertising/marketing agency with annual billings of more than $32 million and for many years has been one of the top ten agencies in south Florida. With a client roster that has included accounts in many fields, Krieff Advertising has won numerous awards for creativity and marketing and was responsible for introducing a number of innovative marketing and communications techniques now commonly used in business.

Since his book, *How to Start and Run Your Own Advertising Agency* was published in January 1993, the author concentrated on providing marketing and advertising consulting services for both large and small companies.

Anyone wishing to correspond with the author may do so at 3990 N. 32 Terrace, Hollywood, FL 33021.

# ACKNOWLEDGMENTS

Every book, including this one, is a collaboration of efforts and must go through many stages before the public gets to read it. *Manager's Survival Guide: How to Avoid the 750 Most Common Mistakes in Dealing with People* would not have been possible without the expertise and wise counsel of many people.

To begin, I'm grateful to Bert Holtje, my agent, for introducing me to Prentice Hall and at Prentice Hall to Tom Power, senior editor, and Sybil Grace, developmental editor, for their enthusiastic support and editorial suggestions; and to Ellen Schneid Coleman, who helped conceive the original idea and got the project started. I thank Jay Pasternak for his invaluable assistance and tireless research efforts; and my wife, Beth, for her patience and support over the months it took to research and write this book and for her excellent fine-tuning of the manuscript, which saved me more than a few sleepless nights and repaired more than a few little oversights.

I especially want to thank all the individuals, companies, and business associations that were willing to share their mistakes and solutions with us. We queried hundreds of managers and executives from many different kinds of companies throughout the country, as well as corporate consultants and industry associations. Though all firmly believed in the importance of the subject matter and were willing to tell us what we wanted to know, almost all asked that neither their names nor those of their companies be used. We can't say we were surprised; after all, this *is* a book about the communications mistakes businesses make, and though it also shows how the mistakes can be avoided, we understand why not everyone likes to admit, in print, that they, their company, or their clients made mistakes. However, the mistakes, the solutions and the examples in this book are all real, and actual names have been used only with permission, or in cases from public records.

# INTRODUCTION

No one is immune from making mistakes, including company managers who communicate and deal with their employees, customers, and vendors. It is important, however, to know that when you make a decision, right or wrong, the consequences are there for all to see: your boss, your peers, your customers and your potential customers, the partners or shareholders, the public, the competition, and the government. Make too many mistakes and you'll not only damage your business, you're likely to lose your position to someone just in back of you who is ready to step forward. Being knowledgeable about the mistakes that are likely to occur and knowing how to avoid making them can be a great asset to your career, no matter what business or business situation you are in.

Most communications mistakes are brought about by changes managers fail to notice, situations they don't understand and correctly respond to, and a multitude of other reasons.

This book is not about the most outrageous, humorous, or disastrous mistakes made by the titans of industry such as the Edsel, or New Coke, or how General Motors, in its infinite corporate wisdom, spent millions introducing their new Nova model in Spanish-speaking markets never realizing Nova in Spanish means "star," but when spoken aloud sounds like *no va*. Translation: "It does not go." The name was promptly changed to Caribe.

Instead, this book pinpoints, for managers, administrators, and everyone up and down the business chain of command, more than 700 of the most common business communications mistakes made by companies of every size and kind. And it shows how *any* business can correct or avoid those mistakes with solutions that are not theory, but methods, strategies, tactics, and countermeasures that have been successfully applied by businesses that learned them the hard way—through experience! Experience that can now work for you.

The mistakes and their solutions are organized in an easy-to-find, informative, to-the-point fashion to help you put them to work immediately. As you read through the three parts you will realize that they are actually three "books" in one: the most common mistakes and solutions management encounters when communicating with employees, with customers, and with vendors, professionals, government agencies, and unions.

In today's business world, we are inundated with the various elements of communication both sent by us and to us. Words, sounds, gestures, letters, electronic voice and E-mail, pictures, signals, fashion and appearance statements, facial expressions, body language, attitudes . . . the list goes on and on.

Modern business communication systems allow us to hold seminars, auctions, and videoconferences in many cities throughout the world, at the same time. A company can run a single direct-response ad on network TV, get half a million or more phone calls, and handle them all instantly and efficiently, via interactive tele-media. And during the next decade you will be interactively communicating regularly with your employees, customers, and vendors over the Internet, information superhighways of the globe, and through cyberspace, where no one can see or hear you and where your well-intended communications can easily be misunderstood, creating catastrophic results.

Today and in the years to come, being a well-informed communicator is a vital asset if you want to be successful in business.

In October 1994 the Graduate Management Admission Test, GMAT, the world's standardized entrance exam for management-education programs, was revamped for the first time in 30 years to better prepare their recruits for communicating properly in a rapidly changing business world that is influenced by culture and personal experience and shaped by events that are happening simultaneously.

Future masters of the universe will have to do more than create flow charts and electronic spreadsheets that sing and dance the praises of their company. They will also have to be proficient in communicating at all levels in a way that is concise, persuasive, and as mistake-free as is humanly possible.

How often have you heard someone say, "Hindsight is 20/20"? Or, "If only I knew what would happen, I would have done it differently." As a business person you will find *Manager's Survival Guide: How to Avoid the 750 Most Common Mistakes in Dealing with People* an essential read that you will refer to often if you are concerned with keeping your business healthy. For many companies and individuals, it will be an indispensable guide that will help you identify, correct, or avoid those mistakes that have hurt others—*before* they happen, thereby helping you achieve your goals and prosper!

*Allan Krieff*

# CONTENTS

## Chapter 3
### EFFECTIVE COMMUNICATIONS TOOLS FOR TRAINING, COACHING, AND COUNSELING WORKERS / 45

## Chapter 4
### HOW TO AVOID LOSING RESPECT AND RESULTS AS A SUPERVISOR / 73

## *Chapter 5*
### EVALUATING EMPLOYEES—THE RIGHT AND WRONG WAYS / 110

## PART 2

### THE MOST COMMON MISTAKES BUSINESSES MAKE COMMUNICATING WITH CUSTOMERS
### 279

## *Chapter 16*
### HANDLING DISGRUNTLED CUSTOMERS / 318

## *Chapter 17*
### COMMUNICATING ON THE INTERNET AND INFOHIGHWAY / 346

## *Chapter 18*
### COMMUNICATING VIA TELEMARKETING AND DIRECT RESPONSE / 370

# PART 3

## THE MOST COMMON MISTAKES BUSINESSES MAKE COMMUNICATING WITH VENDORS, PROFESSIONALS, GOVERNMENT AGENCIES, AND UNIONS
### 477

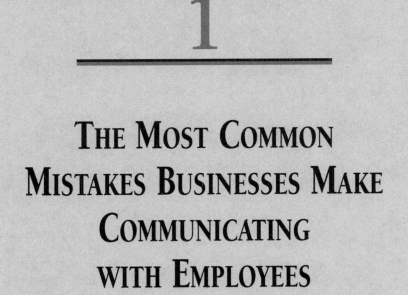

*Part*

# 1

# THE MOST COMMON MISTAKES BUSINESSES MAKE COMMUNICATING WITH EMPLOYEES

# Chapter 1

## HOW TO AVOID MISTAKES IN HIRING

Hiring mistakes can cost your company money, job interruption, high employee turnover, customers—even a lawsuit. And it could also cost you your reputation and your job.

Smart hiring—being consistent and careful in hiring the best people for the right jobs—pays back in long-term productivity and morale and will help avoid legal hassles and rehiring expenses, too.

Take for example, the Florida jury that awarded nearly $2 million to a woman injured by a salesman driving drunk on the job. The final ruling found the employer liable for her injuries because the salesman had a record of alcohol abuse when he was hired.

Though this may be an extreme example, consider this: Employee turnover has a significant cost in terms of customer relationships, training and retraining, loss of scarce skills, and reduction in efficiency. How significant, you ask? Well, many companies estimate that turnover—hiring a new employee to replace mis-hires—could cost as much as two to four times the person's salary.

### SIX COMMON MISTAKES IN FINDING THE PERSON BEST SUITED FOR THE JOB

You need to replace an employee who is leaving. Maybe you've been given two weeks' notice. Maybe not. You've placed ads, contacted the industry job banks, checked with university placement programs, and networked. Now you've got enough resumes and cover letters to wallpaper your office.

3

Whether you're hiring a chemist, a cook, or a consultant, finding the person best suited for the job may seem simple and obvious in theory, but it is not always easy in practice. Though there may be many qualified candidates in the job market, nabbing the right one takes patience and a real sense for the kind of person who could excel both in your company and in the specific job.

Not paying attention to good hiring practices can produce a multitude of problems. People hired in a rush to work in sales, for instance, may alienate customers before you discover they don't get along well with people.

## MISTAKE 1

**Hiring a warm body too quickly based on first impressions, and neglecting better candidates later on.**

### How to Avoid It

Take the time to go over all those resumes and select the most promising potential applicants. You'll need time to sell the best of the lot on the idea of working for your company and then, when they finally apply, you'll need time to make a decision on the one you want, check her out thoroughly, and negotiate a deal.

Here are some tips that will give you the time you need to hire smart:

▪ Get someone in the same department or from elsewhere within the company to fill in.

▪ Promote someone qualified from the same department. The person promoted will more than likely be happy to cover until you find someone to fill his job, giving you more time to fill the lower-salaried position.

▪ Hire a temporary until you find the right person for the job.

▪ Communicate your hiring needs to the rest of the company through the company newsletter or memos. Other employees may recruit suitable candidates. Informing other employees of hiring needs and policy creates and enforces an impression that everyone in the company is involved in the process.

## MISTAKE 2

**Hiring someone to fill a vacant job when business is slow.**

### HOW TO AVOID IT

Here are four solutions:

1. Hire temporary employees (people who perform all types of work and can fill in anywhere).

2. Hire contracted professionals (people with at least ten years' experience in their field). They can be contracted to work for a day, a week, a month, or more.

3. Use job shops (temporary help agencies that specialize in specific tasks ranging from accounting, to engineering, to stuffing and sealing envelopes).

4. Use leased labor. With staff leasing, companies unable or unwilling to provide a human-resources department simply hire a work force and turn over the personnel function to an employee-leasing operation. Or a firm may decide to discharge its employees after it contracts with the leasing company. The leasing company then hires the former employees and leases them back to the company. All employees retain their original position. The company retains supervisory control, but the leasing company is now the employer handling payroll and providing health benefits and retirement plans. Using an employee-leasing company, companies big and small can employ a work force without worrying about health plans or automatic payroll deductions. Workers, in turn, can get health coverage in jobs where benefits might never have been offered.

## MISTAKE 3

**Hiring in one's own image—hiring a candidate with the same strengths you have.**

### HOW TO AVOID IT

Think objectively about what's needed in the position. Create a checklist of all the specific skills required to do the job. This helps keep the personality out of personnel. It would be great if you get the person leaving the job to create his checklist of specific duties, physical demands, and environmental conditions. A comment such as "must be able to walk long distances repeatedly on a daily basis," will remind you of a job condition you may have forgotten about or may not be aware of, while warning the candidate of particular considerations.

## MISTAKE 4

**Bypassing background checks.**

### How to Avoid It

Call every reference and former employer the applicant gives you. Take notes during the interview and try to get the candidate to identify key people she has worked with on past jobs but might not give as a reference. Then ask the applicant to contact those people and ask them to speak freely to you. If the job is sensitive, one in which an employee deals with customers, children, or drives or handles firearms, you have to do a better-than-average background check.

Ask your local chamber of commerce for the names of firms that specialize in such checks, or look in the Yellow Pages under "Investigators."

## MISTAKE 5

**Being inconsistent in considering applicants.**

### How to Avoid It

Formalize the process. Many companies use a variety of tools to select job candidates: an application form, interviews, and reference and background checks. With a good job description, create an application that asks the questions relevant to the company and the job. Make a list of your hiring policies and procedures, and follow them religiously with every applicant.

Insisting on consistency could save you from winking at the paperwork when the applicant is the son of the best friend of the company president, and from the resulting lawsuit when he injures someone while under the influence of drugs.

## MISTAKE 6

**Not planning ahead for hiring.**

### HOW TO AVOID IT

Companies that thrive in the future must continually be active in the development of labor pools. Here are some strategies for ensuring your future work force:

- Start with your master business plan. Make provisions for reevaluating and modifying your hiring needs and procedures on a regular basis. This will allow you to make the adaptations necessary to continue to operate efficiently.

- Make recruiting awareness a way of life for all employees. Establish a reward program for those employees who do refer. This will create a constant flow of referrals and strengthen the involvement of employees with the company.

- Maintain positive employee relations, essential to the recruiting effort both inside and outside your company. Your best public relations medium is word of mouth, and the best mouths are the happy ones who work at your company.

- Take every opportunity to build company image. Circulate information about company events, programs, and community activities.

- Anticipate changes in the community's demographics that will affect its labor force.

- Be consistently aggressive and creative in your pursuit of applicants. Don't be afraid to try an unusual approach. Being different always attracts attention.

## SEVEN COMMON MISTAKES IN WRITING A CLASSIFIED AD

Today's work force is significantly different from yesterday's. Many younger workers lack the basic skills companies have traditionally looked for, and older workers lack the computer skills many employers require. As a result, employers must not only assume a greater role in employee training, they must also adapt their recruiting methods to address these changes.

Basically there are six sources most companies use to recruit external applicants for positions that are open:

1. Recruitment advertising agencies (agencies that assist companies without recruiting expertise in attracting qualified employees).

2. Employment agencies (clearinghouses for clerical, staff, and executive support).

3. College placement programs (a source for well-informed student starters and interns).

4. Public job services (services that maintain lists of candidates in your community; some are state and federally supported, others are sponsored by professional associations and civic groups).

5. Networking (spreading the word about openings through coworkers, industry acquaintances, professional groups, job clubs, on-line or Internet computer networks).

6. and the most common means of announcing job availabilities— print advertising.

There are many types of print-advertising publications: local, regional, and national newspapers; local, regional and national consumer and trade magazines; daily, weekly, and monthly business and industry journals; and so on. There are also many different places within these publications where you can place your ad. The most popular vehicle of all still remains the classified "help wanted" ad in your local newspaper.

Like any type of advertising, a classified "help wanted" ad may not always get the responses desired. First, your small ad will have to compete with hundreds of other similar ads. Second, you may not be offering as much money or sound as interesting as the ad above or below you. So just as being a strong communicator is effective for surviving in today's intensely interactive workplace, you must also be a strong communicator in your efforts to attract new and qualified employees.

## MISTAKE 7

**Not being specific about the job requirements.**

## HOW TO AVOID IT

Give as much information about the duties involved and the experience and education required as possible. Do not include the obvious. Listing duties such as typing, filing, and answering telephones for a secretarial position is redundant. If certain computer or writing skills or knowledge concerning making complicated travel arrangements are necessary, however, they should be detailed.

## MISTAKE 8

**Not using an eye-catching and descriptive headline.**

## HOW TO AVOID IT

As has been mentioned, your ad has to compete with hundreds of others in the same section, maybe even on the same page. There are, however, three good ways to bring attention to yours.

First, use white space. By purchasing two or three blank lines above and below your headline and by using white space around your logo and/or phone number at the bottom, the reader's eye will naturally go to the ad that appears easiest to read. Second, using a catchy headline that is descriptive of the position open will always make you stand out among all the others. For instance, if an advertising agency were looking for an experienced, creative copywriter they could use a headline such as "WE'RE AT A LOSS FOR WORDS." A seasoned copywriter scanning that section would instantly relate to that ad. Third, by "talking to" the applicant instead of just listing qualifications and benefits, you will make the reader relate better to your needs.

## MISTAKE 9

**Not personalizing the ad.**

## HOW TO AVOID IT

Start the ad-writing process by asking and answering the "who," "what," and "why" questions about your target readers. The more accurately you describe the applicant you are looking for, the more effective your advertising message and media placement will be. Knowing which key job features and benefits will have the greatest appeal to the applicants you seek is also an important step in getting the reader to pay attention to your ad.

One effective way of personalizing an ad is by highlighting a problem usually associated with the position and then stating your solution. ("Have you gone as far as you can go with your company?")

## MISTAKE 10

**Not knowing the industrywide going salary for the position open.**

### HOW TO AVOID IT

Often, when a position opens in a company, it involves a longtime employee who left for one reason or another. The salary he was getting may have been substantially below or above what the going rate is for the same job today at other companies. Determine the skills needed for the job you have open and the salary you can afford for someone with those skills. Then look through the classifieds for similar job offerings. Perhaps a salary range is indicated. If not you might try calling one of the advertisers to ask what the salary is, or call a few personnel agencies to find out what the going range is in your area. Try to be competitive in salary and benefits. A well-paid person with motivation is often more productive than two or three underpaid employees.

## MISTAKE 11

**Not advertising in the right section of the classifieds.**

### HOW TO AVOID IT

Look over the layout of the classified section of your daily newspaper and determine where the type of job you want to fill is best placed. Most daily newspapers divide their classified sections by types of ads (announcements, services, merchandise, residential and commercial real estate, automotive, employment, etc.). Each of those sections is then further divided into specific categories (Accounting/bookkeeping, Banking/finance, Employment—Career services, Engineering/technical, Management, Office/clerical, etc.).

There are times when an ad for a particular position could be placed in two or maybe three different categories. For example, if the position open is for a person in accounting, it might go into the "Accounting/Bookkeeping" category or into "Professional." And there are some newspapers that have catchall categories, such as "Miscellaneous" for ads that may not fit a specific category. The important thing to remember is that if your type of opening is going to be difficult to find in the classified section, you should find another place to advertise it.

Besides the classifieds, you can also advertise with display (non-classified, larger space) ads in other sections of the paper. If you are looking for a piano player for your restaurant, a small display ad in the entertainment section might do the trick. If you have openings in a bank, try a display in the financial section, possibly in an area with an editorial concerning the banking industry.

## MISTAKE 12

**Not asking for a quick response when an opening has to be filled immediately.**

### How to Avoid It

If the position to be filled is for a lower-level staff or a semi-skilled job, and the need to fill that job is urgent, it is best to put only a phone number in the ad rather than ask the applicants to write. By screening the calls, you can quickly call back those best qualified to come in for a personal interview. In most cases this will be a major time saver in that many applicants for such jobs do not have resumes anyway and would have to come in to fill out an application.

## MISTAKE 13

**Not selling the benefits of the job.**

### How to Avoid It

Sometimes, in order to save space and money, companies will place an ad that briefly lists the qualifications needed and how to answer the ad. The ad would be much more effective if it stressed why this job is so attractive, how the applicant might benefit from working here, opportunities for advancement, and quality of the work life at this company.

## FIVE MISTAKES IN EVALUATING RESPONSES

In order to hire smart and avoid wasted interviewing time and costly mishiring mistakes, you must know the most important assets and danger signals to look for in the responses that come from your ads.

When the response is a resume and cover letter, they should be neatly typed on good quality stationary, be easy to read, and should contain no grammar or spelling errors.

Unless the person responding is applying for an executive position that requires years of experience and accomplishments, the typical resume should be no longer than two pages.

Cover letters should be three or four paragraphs long and to the point. They should state what skills, experience, and accomplishments the applicant would be bringing to the position and how this will benefit the company. Is there care shown in the preparation of the letter? Is it addressed to you or to "Dear Sir"? Is it an original or one of 165 identical copies? See if there are referrals to your company instead of generic, canned phrases.

Eliminate candidates who lack the necessary criteria or whose resume raises red flags: grandiose claims; glaring typos; lengthy, unexplained gaps between jobs. Look for correspondence that demonstrates that a candidate has researched your company well.

And keep in mind that what candidates highlight on their resumes reveals a lot about what they think you are looking for.

## MISTAKE 14

**Having empathy with the respondent instead of sticking to the job criteria.**

## MISTAKE 15

**Overlooking certain shortcomings for personal reasons.**

### HOW TO AVOID THEM

Stick to formal hiring policies and procedures for all applicants. Develop a list of detailed qualifications for the position and stay completely impartial in your evaluations. You will thus avoid costly mishiring and legal problems that can arise from emotion-based decisions.

## MISTAKE 16

**Jumping to conclusions based solely on the resume.**

### HOW TO AVOID IT

All responses should be evaluated with care. If a respondent meets the criteria that have been set for the position, a personal interview should be set up. Ignoring good business sense in favor of political or personal reasons can cause serious problems.

More often than not, in their rush to get through the pressures of filling a job, evaluators will reject an applicant based on certain information on the resume they find inappropriate or personally distasteful.

An applicant for a selling position may be turned away because his major in college was Psychology. Evaluators are sometimes turned off by the sound of applicants' names, or the neighborhood they came from.

The Immigration Reform and Control Act of 1986, for example, clearly sets guidelines that specifically forbid employers from turning away applicants simply because of the sound of their name.

## MISTAKE 17

**Not having a clear picture of the position to be filled.**

### How to Avoid It

Make sure you have a complete job description for the position that identifies actual duties. Know the characteristics of your company and the department where the applicant will work. Determine what attributes the applicant needs to fit in. Determine who will be supervising the position and the other individuals the applicant will have to work with. The applicant should have attributes that will complement these people and allow her to "fit in." Look at the environment the applicant will be working in. Are there factors that have to be considered that could influence your decision to consider an individual?

## MISTAKE 18

**Hiring on the basis of amount of education rather than experience and potential.**

### How to Avoid It

Once all the criteria for the job are understood and communicated, an applicant's work experience and personal profile are the most critical information that should be considered in evaluating responses.

### *Summary for Evaluating Responses*

▍ *Track record*—resumes should exhibit successful career history, energy, strong desire to achieve, high dedication level. Look for specific work situations, initiative, results achieved, and reasons for those successes. Applicants should convince you that they can transfer these traits to the skills and characteristics necessary for the vacant position. They should show how they made a difference in past successes and why that experience sets them apart. Beware of repeated failures with "good excuses." Their recent track records should be weighed heavily.

■ *Problem-solving ability*—resumes should demonstrate logic, rationality, and objectivity in decision making. It should convey that the applicants are intelligent, resourceful, and able to solve problems as well as think in a problem-solving way. It should point out the applicants' ability to communicate what they want and expect in the job and why they think they can handle it. They should illustrate new ideas and approaches to old problems they have been faced with, the actions they took and the accomplishments made.

■ *Ambition and enthusiasm*—"doers" do not just talk, but follow through aggressively to a successful conclusion. By the language they use, and the experiences they relate, you will be able to determine whether their top priority is to make major contributions to the job or be just another worker. Look for indications that they have a desire to move up in the organization and are not afraid to compete and that working for a company like yours is exciting to them. Look for phrases such as "your product excites me," or "I've always dreamed of having a job like this," or "I'm happy with the money, benefits, and opportunities offered."

■ *Strong communications skills*—beyond basic competence in speaking and writing, they should excel in conveying information, ideas, and attitudes in a clear and persuasive way. Look for applicants' ability to communicate effectively one on one, as well as in groups. Do they have command of the language, write a well-organized resume using appropriate vocabulary, grammar, and word usage, and create the appropriate "flavor" with words such as "accomplished," "achieved," "arranged," "attended," "communicated," "conducted," "controlled," "created," "demonstrated," "directed," "established," "expedited," "facilitated," "fulfilled," "generated," "guided," "helped," "implemented," "improved," "increased," "initiated," "launched," "motivated," "organized," "participated," "proposed," "provided, " "reorganized," "resolved," "secured," "updated," "won"?

▌ *Organizational skills*—look for evidence that applicants can convert self-objectivity into self-correction and personal improvement, that they can manage, plan, and organize their own and others' work responsibilities.

▌ *Ability to work under pressure*—are they bothered by pressure or change? Can they cope effectively with complexity? Are they able to take a positive stand on an issue and stick to it? Do they show an ability to be "quick on their feet"?

▌ *Maturity*—mature applicants will highlight past experiences that demonstrate their ability to function successfully without much supervision, survive difficult times, and be willing to take on leadership. Look for their ability to retain their emotional control and productivity under pressure from competition, deadlines, personal problems and requirements by supervisors.

▌ *Team players*—Do the resumes point out applicants' willingness to cooperate with their supervisor (without being a "yes person"), and establish cohesive, collaborative relationships with peers (without being a "pushover")?

Finally, watch out for overgeneralizations—phrases such as "every time I ever suggested something, I was always totally rejected." Look out for strong feelings and beliefs. While they can be an asset for some candidates, they can also be shortcomings for others. Phrases such as "If there's anything I can't stand it's people who will do anything to get ahead!" Or, "I would never work overtime unless it were worth my while," are signs of strong beliefs. Beware of the use of "impossibility" words such as "I could never. . ." or "I can't believe. . ."

---

## FOUR BIGGEST MISTAKES MADE IN THE PRESCREENING PHONE INTERVIEW

---

It's a war out there.

Competition for jobs at all levels has grown fierce. The classified help-wanted ad you ran and the networking you did resulted in more responses than you dreamed possible. Now you're faced with a staggering amount of applications, and you've got to whittle down the list of candidates to a manageable number. How? Prescreen job candidates by phone.

There are two kinds of prescreening calls. The first kind is from you to an applicant who sent in a resume, and obviously he has some or all of the qualifications you are looking for. This kind of call will probably be the shorter of the two because you already have a lot of the basic information you need about the applicant and will not have to ask as many questions to determine whether or not you want to meet with him in person.

The second kind is from an applicant responding to the job description and telephone number you gave in your ad. You know absolutely nothing about this person and will have to ask many more questions to get a better picture of her qualifications and personality. Though this type of call may take more of your time, it can also save time because you can make an immediate evaluation and eliminate the follow-up.

In either case, the prescreening telephone interview saves both you and the applicant the trouble of an in-person interview by giving you a means of knowing if the applicant has what you're looking for and giving the applicant the opportunity to learn about the job and decide if it is what she is looking for.

---

## MISTAKE 19

Not being properly prepared to probe for and evaluate information quickly from someone who saw the ad and did *not* send a resume.

### How to Avoid It

Prepare a list of accurate job criteria and a list of probing questions that will help you quickly evaluate the prospect. Do this before placing your ad. Here are some pointers that will help:

■ Make sure your list includes all the specific duties and responsibilities, the salary and benefits, and any special physical, mental, and emotional characteristics the job may require.

■ Prepare an evaluation form that allows you to quickly summarize the applicant's experience.

■ Make a list of questions you want to ask and the answers you are looking for. For instance, "Why are you making a change?" You are looking for an answer such as "There's no room for advancement in my current job," rather than "I'm not getting along with my coworkers." Other questions you would want to ask are: "Where are you working now?" "What specific experience do you have?" "Exactly what are your duties?" "What salary are you getting now?" "What benefits or incentives are you receiving?" The answers you would expect should match the criteria and benefits of the job.

▪ Prepare a fact sheet that lists the advantages of getting the job and working for your company. Remember, the best qualified applicants will be speaking with many employers, looking for the best job and company to work for.

▪ Rehearse your "act." Being well prepared not only helps get you the information you need, it also makes a positive impression on applicants. You may want to "playact" a scenario with someone in your office, or tape-record your rehearsal and play it back a number of times to get out the kinks. Prepare yourself for questions the applicant might ask.

## MISTAKE 20

**Not preparing your staff for calls.**

### HOW TO AVOID IT

Make sure your telephone operator or receptionist and others in your office are aware of the ad running and the job that is open. Provide them with instructions on what to say and what information they should get from every applicant (name, address, telephone number at work and at home). If you have a busy switchboard, you might want to use a special phone number or extension to take those calls.

## MISTAKE 21

**Not taking notes.**

### HOW TO AVOID IT

Never trust your memory to remember all the facts applicants tell you. If you don't have time to write down their complete answers, make notes of key items. You might also want to make notes about things that disturb you, such as beating about the bush in answering a question or refusing to answer without giving a reason. You might want to take a page out of this author's book and tape-record the interviews, but you must advise callers that you are using a tape recorder and be sure you have their approval to tape the conversation.

## MISTAKE 22

**Being careless or inconsistent in the evaluation of applicants.**

### How to Avoid It

Complete each evaluation immediately or soon after the call while all the information is fresh in your mind. Be fair about the value you give to responses. An applicant who did not communicate well on the phone should not be penalized if that is not important to the job. By the same token, an applicant's ability to make quick decisions should be noted but not necessarily be given special attention.

Writing comments such as "too old" or "sounds retarded" or "seems like a real sexy swinger" could lead to legal hassles if your notes are ever reviewed. Chapters 2, 5, and 10 discuss what you legally can and can't say in more detail. Stay focused on matching the applicant to the job requirements.

## TWO COMMON MISTAKES IN GETTING YOUR COMPANY MESSAGE ACROSS ON THE PHONE

As was stated earlier, your ad is not the only ad applicants are responding to. They know their strong points and what they expect in the job and the company they will work for.

## MISTAKE 23

**Not getting all the information you need when interviewing prospects on the phone.**

### How to Avoid It

Most interviews (phone and in person) have three stages:

1. The beginning, which is devoted to getting acquainted.

2. The middle, in which you explore the applicant's credentials, work style, ideas, problem-solving abilities, strengths, and compatibility with the company.

3. The end, in which you answer questions the applicant may have and discuss details about the company and the position.

The advantage of using this method in telephone interviewing is that if a person is not qualified after you've finished stage 2, there is no need to waste time going further. The disadvantage is you may not have time to continue and may lose a good prospect because she doesn't know enough about your company.

As the saying goes, "A bird in the hand is worth two in the bush." If the person you are speaking with meets your job and personality criteria, don't risk losing him. Have your secretary or someone get the names and numbers of the other applicants waiting and take an additional two or three minutes to pitch the promising applicant on the job and the company.

## MISTAKE 24

**Not being prepared to convince an applicant that joining your company would be a winning move.**

### How to Avoid It

Anticipate questions the caller may have about your company, its employees, opportunities the job offers, and negatives she may be aware of such as high turnover or trouble meeting payroll. A smart applicant will want to know :

- Where do you see the company five years from now?
- What are the company's long- and short-term goals?
- Has the company met its past goals?
- What is the greatest threat facing the company; what is its strongest asset?
- Might this position ever be eliminated?
- Where have people who had this position gone from here?
- What would a typical day in this position be like?
- What would be the criteria for a raise or promotion in this position?
- What are the standards for rewards, and what are the rewards?

List the company's "quality of work" points on a sheet of paper—great products or service record, terrific working conditions, hours and compensation, wonderful benefits, low turnover. List any awards, special recognition, or favorable press the company has received, the company's participation in community activities, train-ing programs you offer. If you have a tuition-reimbursement policy, a college-student applicant would be happy to know about it.

Make a list of the company's negatives with notes on how you would address them if asked. A question such as "I hear you make people work long hours," can be countered with "Sometimes we get very busy and have to put in overtime. Our employees are always asked if they can work overtime. If they can, they are paid for over-time. We know there is life beyond our company and that people have personal commitments that do not always allow them to stay overtime."

Make certain the caller is treated courteously by the receptionist and that the call is properly forwarded to the person who can answer questions. If that person is not available, be sure the receptionist gets full details about the applicant and that arrangements are made for a prompt call-back. Demonstrate your integrity and desire to hire the best by following through with all the commitments you made to the applicant, such as giving your word to set up an in-person interview and sending out an application or other information you promised.

## TWO COMMON MISTAKES IN IDENTIFYING AN APPLICANT'S STRENGTHS AND MOTIVATION

Effective telephone interviewing is neither difficult nor complicated. However, you are not face-to-face with an applicant, and your time on the phone will be short, so the interview has to be deliberate. You are looking for two types of information: basic educational and work facts that will match with the job requirements and a quick indica-tion of the applicant's strengths and motives. Failure to ask the right questions means good candidates will go unrecognized.

## MISTAKE 25

**Getting sidetracked and not asking the right job-related ques-tions.**

### How to Avoid It

In general, interviewing involves the use of two different types of questions: fact-gathering (closed questions) and open-ended ques-tions. Since you may not have a resume to refer to, get the factual questions out of the way first. The answers you get will tell you whether the applicant has the education, experience, and technical ability you need, but because closed, single-answer questions suppress the opportunity to learn more about the candidate, you will not know the individual's strengths and motivation. Then the open-ended questions:

- What are your immediate and long-term career goals?
- What do you consider your most important asset?
- What is the most important feature you look for in a job?
- How did you learn about your last job?
- What was the reason you took your last job?
- What did you like (dislike) most about your last job?
- Why did you leave your last job?
- What do you look for and respect in a supervisor?
- What do you dislike most about the supervisors you have worked with?
- Why do you want to work with our company?
- Do you prefer teamwork or do you like to work alone? Why?
- If you get this job, where do you expect to be five years from now?

The answers you get will give you the ideas, aspirations, motivations, and opinions of the applicant, which brings us to the next common mistake.

## MISTAKE 26

**Not evaluating the answers to open-ended questions as they relate to the job vacancy.**

### How to Avoid It

Always remember the job you are interviewing for and consider all answers in relation to that job. It is the only way you can be assured that a candidate is right for the job. It's difficult not to be influenced by answers that are clever, interesting, and that display ambition. But to hire successfully, you must be able to separate the clever from the pertinent.

## THREE COMMON MISTAKES IN ARRANGING
## THE IN-PERSON INTERVIEW

Reading resumes or conducting limited-time telephone-screening interviews are, at best, effective ways of eliminating unqualified applicants. At worst, they are unreliable, unfocused, and shallow in the information they yield. Much of what you learn may be geared toward what a candidate thinks you are looking for. It is true, though, that even a cursory probing of a candidate's background, patterns of evolvement, achievements, and success at work, school, and in society does give the interviewer enough information to decide whether to reject the candidate or give him further consideration.

After cutting your list down to those who impressed you most, it's now time to call each applicant and set a mutually convenient date and time for the in-person interview.

## MISTAKE 27

**Not telling the applicant to bring certain things you will both need to the interview.**

### How to Avoid It

Prepare a list of items needed. If you schedule interviews by letter, include a copy of the list. You should ask for the following:

- Several copies of the resume (you may want to distribute some to other departments and don't want to be bothered making copies yourself). Also, sometimes applicants with multiple skills will prepare separate resumes, each highlighting a different skill such as bookkeeping and skills with computers.

- A list of references to contact and letters of permission to make the contacts.

- A pen and pad (so applicant can note important information about the job and company).

- A calendar of open days (in case you want to schedule additional interviews).

- Samples of their work (if showing what you've done counts).

## MISTAKE 28

**Not advising the applicant to put aside "contingency" time for unforeseen occurrences.**

### How to Avoid It

Make sure every applicant allots enough time for you to get all the information you need and won't mind canceling other appointments should a time problem arise.

## MISTAKE 29

**Not confirming the meeting.**

### How to Avoid It

Always confirm the date and time you set at least a day before the interview. Misunderstandings can occur, or an applicant may have failed to notify you of a problem she had or a last-minute change in her schedule. Likewise, you may be backed up on your interviewing schedule or you may have more promising applicants you want to see first.

# Chapter 2

# HOW TO AVOID MISTAKES
# DURING JOB INTERVIEWS

$Y$ou are finally face to face with a living, breathing, and probably nervous job candidate. Your purpose in the interview is to find out the qualifications, skills, and personal qualities of the candidate. On the other hand, the candidate wants to find out as much as possible about the position, the long-range prospects, the company, and the people with whom he may be working.

## FIVE COMMON MISTAKES IN CONDUCTING
## SUCCESSFUL DISCUSSIONS

Sometimes, an interview can become an uncomfortable face-off between the interviewer behind an imposing desk and an applicant who may be terrified. The keys to hosting a successful personal interview are creating an atmosphere that helps the applicant relax, open up, and talk candidly—and asking the right questions that will draw information out of the interviewee.

When I started writing this book, I realized that the task of interviewing and researching a work as comprehensive as this was considerable. So I put the word out for researchers who might be available to help me gather information. One of the applicants who called happened to be a young man who was my favorite waiter at a restaurant my wife and I frequented. We knew his first name but little else about him except that he was very good at his job, extremely pleasant, and had recently graduated college. When he called for an appointment, he knew he was calling one of his regular customers, but I didn't recognize his name when my secretary set up the interviewing schedule. When he walked into my office, I nearly didn't recognize him out of the restaurant environment I was familiar with. He sat down in front of my desk and seemed very uncomfortable. After all, he knew I *knew* him, but little *about* him. He knew I viewed him as a waiter, not a researcher. To break the ice, I moved the meeting from my office to the less formal conference room and told him a brief story about how I used to work at my father's gasoline station on weekends and got my first big break in business thanks to one of my father's regular customers. The young man immediately relaxed and launched into his abilities and ambitions—and I can honestly tell you that without him, this book would still be in the research stage.

## MISTAKE 30

**Not keeping it informal.**

### How to Avoid It

Friendly gestures, anecdotes, words, the phrasing of questions, seating arrangements—these are all elements that will help toward conducting an informal interview and getting the applicant to relax.

First, step out from behind your desk. Make the seating arrangement equal for both you and the candidate. Hold your calls and make sure there are no interruptions during the interview. Offer something to drink (coffee, soft drink, juice, or water), and then pour it yourself. This little gesture will make it clear that you are not someone to fear. Lead in with idle conversation about something in the applicant's resume such as "Oh, I see you worked for XYZ Company. Did you know Jim Brown?" Or you might refer to a story in the news that day, something that is nonthreatening.

Once a few laughs have lightened the mood and you feel that the applicant is relaxed, shift the conversation to telling the applicant a little about your company and the job. You don't want to get too specific about the job requirements because you may scare off an otherwise good candidate or inspire an unqualified one who will later simply repeat all the qualifications you've given.

The way you phrase a question can make a person either tense up or relax. Instead of asking, "Why did you leave your last job?" ask, "What did you like best about your last job and what did you like least?"

Give applicants some insight into what's ahead in the interview, explaining that the more you know about them the better you can judge their ability to handle the position. They should understand that you cannot accomplish this unless they are completely open and honest.

## MISTAKE 31

**Not asking the right questions.**

### How to Avoid It

Resumes, credentials, and references covering the applicant's educational and work background and technical and social skills give you only a partial picture of what you need to know. "Gut feelings," "vibes," and impressions will help make you a little more confident. But the only sure way to fill in the total picture of the applicant is to ask the right questions that will shed light on the candidate's short- and long-range goals, personal characteristics, good and bad work habits, and past work-related or personal problems.

Here are examples of wrong and right questions to ask to get the information you need about a candidate's

*Attitude about overtime work—*

WRONG:   "There is a lot of overtime. Would that be a problem?"

RIGHT:   "How did you handle your company's requests to work overtime?"

*Achievements—*

WRONG:   "What was your grade average in college?"

RIGHT:   "What was your greatest academic challenge and how did you meet it?"

*Leadership potential—*

WRONG:   "What positions of leadership have you held?"

RIGHT:   "How have you motivated subordinates?"

*Innovativeness—*

WRONG:   "How innovative are you?"

RIGHT:   "What ideas did you come up with in your last job?"

*Problem-solving ability—*

> WRONG: "What kinds of problems did you have in your prior jobs?"

> RIGHT: "Tell me about a situation you faced that demanded an unusual solution."

*Ambition—*

> WRONG: "Do you consider yourself ambitious?"

> RIGHT: "What goals have you set for yourself for the next five years?"

## MISTAKE 32

**Doing more talking than the applicant.**

## MISTAKE 33

**Not listening to the candidate.**

### HOW TO AVOID THEM

It is generally agreed among interviewing professionals and management trainers we spoke with that 70 to 80 percent of all interviewing time (especially first and second interviews) should be spent listening to the job candidates.

Encouraging them to answer open questions, recount past job and personal experiences, and ask questions will give you valuable insights you can't get from a resume. For instance, an interviewee related a story to one interviewer we spoke to about how she, on her own volition, made calls around the country to find an out-of-production part for a piece of machinery that was critical to the business of her company's client. This told the interviewer that the applicant showed initiative and responsibility and was resourceful and accomplished, which could translate to: She needs less supervision and might someday make a good supervisor. This is the kind of applicant who would probably ask, "How much responsibility will I have?" Had the same applicant instead related a story that she was the victim of problems that occurred at her previous job, it would indicate that she did not take on responsibility or accomplish as much as she could have.

A good listener also takes good notes. Jot down key words that convey the essence of the response or questions the applicants asked. One response may give you answers for a handful of specifications you are looking for.

## MISTAKE 34

**Not asking the candidate for written permission to contact references.**

### How to Avoid It

In today's "I'll see you in court" society, many companies have policies against giving out reference information on former or current employees. It will be necessary for you to get written permission from the interviewee. That does not mean, however, that you will be allowed to talk to anyone in human resources at the applicant's last job, nor does it mean that you will succeed in getting little more than confirmation dates of employment and a job title.

So why bother? Because in the majority of cases, according to the personnel professionals we spoke with, most reference sources *are* willing to give specific information on former employees (especially if they have good things to say) even though it means they are going against company policy. In fact, we have been told by almost all the people we contacted on this subject that many former bosses, in particular, feel it is moral and right to give their opinion on former employees and possibly save the next company that person applies to a lot of grief.

Though courts have been finding companies that fail to check a person's records and references *liable* for hiring bad guys, it has become a real Catch-22. While it is legal and prudent for companies to withhold information on former employees, those companies that don't check prospective employees records are vulnerable to litigation.

The same methods a good interviewer uses to draw out a candidate's pertinent background information can be used to uncover the names of former coworkers you (or the applicant) can call to check out or verify claims and references. By promising confidentiality, you can usually get the information you want as well as the names of other former coworkers to contact.

If an applicant flatly refuses to give you references or written permission to contact former employers, that should give you food for thought, but don't necessarily jump to conclusions. Ask why.

There may be a plausible reason, such as "My last supervisor dislikes me because my approach to a problem was better than his." Or, "I was unjustly accused of doing something I didn't do and since I did not want to snitch on a coworker, the company had to let me go."

## FIVE COMMON MISTAKES SHOWING DISCRIMINATION DURING THE HIRING INTERVIEW

While the ideal candidate for the job you have open may be a single, childless, healthy workaholic, chances are that person also has a private life and, with it, all the expected problems, responsibilities, and conflicts.

Though it may be tempting to ask personal questions, you must be sure and stay within the confines of the more than 400 federal laws and myriad state statutes that protect people in the United States from discrimination in hiring.

Legally, you must limit your questions to work-related qualifications. While you cannot ask about age, health, disabilities, spouses, kids, child-care arrangements, parents' backgrounds, and religious beliefs, among others, there are ways to divine the answers.

## MISTAKE 35

**Not making yourself familiar with pertinent laws against discrimination.**

### How to Avoid It

If your company has a human resources representative, ask for a list of the federal laws and a summary of interviewing questions you can and can't ask. If your company does not have a human resources person, contact the Equal Employment Opportunity Commission district office in your area and ask for their Uniform Guidelines for Employee Selection Procedures.

In addition to federal laws, individual states have their own broader, more comprehensive, and more stringent laws governing employment. You can contact your state Department of Labor and Employment Security, your state Legal Affairs Department, your state Department of Business and Professional Regulations, or your attorney and ask them to send you the information.

Besides being aware of the questions you can't ask during a hiring interview, you can defend yourself against problems by defining the job and drawing up a profile of the person you need. Then develop job-related questions that will give you the necessary information.

If your questions are limited to work-related qualifications and stem logically from the applicant's background relative to the prerequisites of the job in question, you are less likely to get into trouble for asking them.

A good way to guide yourself in asking the right questions is to create a checklist of illegal questioning areas and measure the questions you planned to ask against that list.

### Check Your Questions Against this Checklist

▮ Are your questions directly related to the job?

▮ Do any questions invade the applicant's right to privacy? (You may not ask job candidates if they are married, if they have children, or if they need time to make child-care arrangements. You cannot ask where they were born, what their spouse does for a living, if they own their own home, or if they belong to a country club.)

▮ Do any questions request information regarding racial, ethnic, or religious information? (You may not ask about an applicant's maiden name, country of origin, religion, religious customs, holidays, organization memberships, or citizenship.)

▮ Do any questions request information regarding personal activities?

▮ Do any questions request information regarding the candidate's age or information that would reveal age?

▮ Do any questions request information regarding financial status?

▮ Do any questions request information regarding physical handicaps or disabilities? Do you require a disabled candidate to have a medical exam?

## MISTAKE 36

**Asking questions that are legal but intimidating.**

## HOW TO AVOID IT

Your goal in asking any questions during an interview is to learn as much as possible about the candidate, generate enthusiasm about the position, and realistically decide if this candidate merits further consideration. However, there are many questions that are legal to ask but can be intimidating or embarrassing to the interviewee such as: "Have you ever been convicted of a felony?" "Do you anticipate any difficulties in commuting to work?" "Do you belong to any professional or business organizations that might enhance your ability to perform this job?"

There are alternatives to finding out the same information. Instead of asking:

| | |
|---|---|
| INTIMIDATING: | "This job requires physical strength. Are you able to perform all the duties?" |
| NONINTIMIDATING: | "The position you are applying for requires repeated lifting and carrying of heavy materials that could weigh 50 or 60 pounds. Will this be a problem for you?" |
| INTIMIDATING: | "Is your car in good enough mechanical shape to get you to work every day?" |
| NONINTIMIDATING: | "Do you have reliable transportation to work?" |
| INTIMIDATING: | "What are your strengths and weaknesses?" |
| NONINTIMIDATING: | "What do you like most to do?" |
| INTIMIDATING: | "Did you ever wish a supervisor or a coworker would leave so that you could have that person's job?" |
| NONINTIMIDATING: | "If you get this job, how far along do you think you'll be in a year?" |
| INTIMIDATING: | "Do you consider yourself creative?" |
| NONINTIMIDATING: | "What ideas were you responsible for at your last job?" |

## MISTAKE 37

**Being offensive instead of sensitive when interviewing candidates with physical and mental disabilities.**

## How to Avoid It

The Americans with Disabilities Act (ADA), enacted in 1992, has made a major difference in the way physically and mentally disabled job candidates may be interviewed. Often, interviewers who have not had experience with disabled people speak in ways that are offensive. Here are some don'ts and do's that will help you establish sensitivity guidelines:

Don't make generalizations about the disabled.

Don't act surprised at how "normal" the applicant acts.

Don't speak loudly to a deaf person.

Don't tell jokes or stories about disabled people you know.

Don't ask the applicants how they became disabled or the full extent of their limitations.

Don't ask disabled applicants personal questions.

Don't ask disabled applicants if they have disabilities or impairments that will affect their performance in the position for which they are applying.

Don't ask disabled applicants if they have been treated for a mental condition.

Don't ask disabled applicants how many days they were out of work last year due to illness.

Don't assume disabled applicants will not be able to handle specific tasks or that co-workers will have trouble adjusting to working with these persons.

Don't hire disabled persons only because you feel sorry for them or want to give them an opportunity. They must fit the job requirements just like any other applicant.

Do offer assistance during the interview if it is appropriate, but don't act until the offer is accepted.

Do allow for the extra time it may take a disabled applicant to fill in forms or answer questions.

Do use normal language and phrases. Blind people are used to hearing people say "nice seeing you."

Do try to stay at eye level with someone in a wheelchair.

## MISTAKE 38

**Not realizing the benefits of hiring the disabled.**

### How to Avoid It

Many business owners have found that the untapped resource of people with disabilities as employees is a gold mine. If a disabled person is given a fair chance of employment, you will benefit by getting another productive, appreciative employee. And that employee becomes a consumer, hotel guest, restaurant, and theater patron who gives back to society.

## MISTAKE 39

**Not protecting yourself against negligent hiring.**

### How to Avoid It

- Familiarize yourself and comply with all federal, state, and local discriminatory and credit-reporting laws.

- Get written permission from the applicant to check every reference given. Try to identify and contact former coworkers who were not given as references.

- Be suspicious of applicant's disclaimers, excuses, and unexplained gaps in employment.

- Document all the information given to you by the applicant and any other information you collect (licenses, certificates, diplomas).

- If the applicant served in the military, get proof of his honorable discharge.

- Be extra careful when checking the background of a candidate for a job that involves public safety, working with children, public transportation.

- If you feel the job requires it, require a physical examination (with the applicant's consent) or a criminal records investigation of the applicant.

- Be sure all test results and screening is completed and acceptable before offering employment.

And, even if an applicant is a current employee of your company desiring to move to a new position, you must still apply the same process of screening you would do with someone you don't know.

## TWO COMMON MISTAKES IN GETTING THE APPLICANT TO OPEN UP

We've talked about open questions *you* ask that give applicants a lot of room to reveal themselves. But no interview should be too one-sided.

### MISTAKE 40

**Not encouraging the applicant to ask you questions.**

#### How to Avoid It

Many candidates want to ask questions but are afraid because they think asking the wrong question could end the interview. Encourage their questions by asking, "Do you have any questions about the company, what a typical work day will be like, or what the person who formerly held this job was like?"

### MISTAKE 41

**Not following up after the interview if you realize you don't have all the information you need.**

#### How to Avoid It

After the interview is completed, if you find that there were questions you forgot to ask or responses that seemed incomplete or inconsistent, don't just forget about it and base your evaluation on what you have. Pick up the phone and tell the applicant you have a few more questions to ask.

## NINE MISTAKES IN SORTING MUST-HAVE SKILLS FROM THE HELPFUL PLUSES

Before you start the hiring process, make sure you have defined the skill requirements for the job. Instead of focusing only on a description of what has to be done, you will find that it is just as important to spend time deciding what skills are required to do the tasks. And having an understanding of the skills required for a position is as much a requirement for the person doing the hiring as it is for the applicant. If your company uses computers for word processing, graphics, presentations, cost analysis, or billing, for example, you must know the right questions to ask in order to determine if the applicant can use a computer as the job requires. If you are hiring a salesperson, you might want to ask, "What do you do to close a deal?" And then follow up with, "Can you give me the names of two people who can confirm that skill?"

In this high-tech age, employers must be critical of a candidate's technical know-how because the person's actual level of skill will directly affect company productivity. How can you protect yourself and your company from hiring applicants who claim one level of skill before being hired and demonstrate another once on the job?

No hiring method is foolproof. However, when employers specify exactly what skills are required for a position and then test applicants to make sure they have those skills, they will improve the odds of hiring smart and filling the job vacancy with a competent and promising candidate.

## MISTAKE 42

**Hiring by credentials.**

### How to Avoid It

Hiring by credentials can be an easy but sometimes expensive method of recruiting. Businesses that want to continually improve their product and market should hire people who have proven themselves to be innovative and are not encumbered by fashionable attributes that by themselves can sometimes stifle innovation.

## MISTAKE 43

**Not analyzing and categorizing all the skills and attributes the job requirements call for.**

### How to Avoid It

Make a checklist of every skill required for the job. Separate them into columns of "must have" skills, "preferred, but not absolutely necessary" skills, and as many more as you need to cover all the tasks the job requires.

## MISTAKE 44

**Not categorizing applicants and comparing their skills and attributes to the ones you're looking for.**

### How to Avoid It

Ask applicants questions that will help you sort their skills. Start with those required, then the preferred, and so on. Continue the questioning until you determine the level of all the skills each applicant has.

Now, categorize the applicants:

I Those with all the required skills.

I Those with most of the required skills.

I Those with preferred skills.

Again, create as many categories as you may need. For applicants with no required skills, it would be good public relations to write a "thank you for applying" letter. By categorizing the applicants, you will be able to see the most qualified candidates first, thus reducing your interviewing time.

## MISTAKE 45

**Not properly measuring equally qualified applicants to find the best.**

### How to Avoid It

Let's say you have six equally qualified applicants who have applied for a bank-teller position. How can you measure the skills of each before hiring? You can develop a "tellers" test that can be tailored to the position.

You might create fictitious situations and ask the applicants to complete a task.

How the test is administered is important. Ask each applicant to complete part of the assignment in your office, on your computer and under deadline. This will let you determine:

I How they handle pressure.

I How quickly they react to a situation.

I How well they process information and follow procedures.

- How much supervision they require.

- How well they know various computer and other technical applications.

- How well they fit into your working environment.

## MISTAKE 46

**Risking invasion of privacy and discrimination charges when testing for skills and aptitude.**

### HOW TO AVOID IT

Just as you risk legal hassles in the interviewing process, the same laws that govern privacy and discrimination apply to testing.

The Equal Employment Opportunity Commission (EEOC) allows employers to use any skill and aptitude tests as a form of pre-employment selection, but you must be able to prove, if challenged, that the test does not discriminate against protected classes.

## MISTAKE 47

**Not researching a test before using it.**

### HOW TO AVOID IT

The validity of using a test in one circumstance does not guarantee that it may be used in another. You must be sure the test is measuring what you want it to measure and that it will give you the specific information you are looking for.

If you create your own tests as suggested here, have them validated by an outside source following the Guidelines for Employee Selection Procedures available from the EEOC.

## MISTAKE 48

**Not having applicants sign a consent or release form for certain kinds of tests.**

### HOW TO AVOID IT

When conducting drug and alcohol screening, genetic screening, testing for AIDS and HIV, and polygraph testing, it is best to have all applicants sign a consent or release form. This procedure eliminates claims that privacy rights have been violated as well as claims that tests were conducted under duress or that permission was never given.

## MISTAKE 49

**Not keeping test results confidential.**

### How to Avoid It

No matter what the circumstance, the records of all tests must be kept confidential. Only authorized personnel should have access to these files.

## MISTAKE 50

**Not properly investigating laboratories selected to conduct drug tests.**

### How to Avoid It

Drug screenings should be conducted as part of an overall physical, not as an isolated preemployment criterion. The references, methods, accuracy, and "chain of custody" of the laboratories used to complete the tests should be thoroughly investigated.

## FOUR MISTAKES IN RECOGNIZING RED FLAGS AND RESUME INFLATORS

It is not unusual during interviews for applicants to give you certain information without realizing that they have raised a "red flag" warning signal. There are a number of such signals by which the interviewer can sense strong negative feelings coming from the interviewee and a number of ways to get more information about those feelings in order to properly evaluate the applicant for the position.

## MISTAKE 51

**Not recognizing a red flag from normal nervousness or shock; for example, feelings of anger, betrayal, and hostility as the result of previous job loss.**

## How to Avoid It

It is easy to get negative feelings from a person who is always anxious, nervous, and scared applying for a position. Follow up negative feelings with questions and try to arrive at an accurate interpretation. It may be very different from what your first impressions indicated.

---

## MISTAKE 52

**Spotting red flags and not asking for explanations.**

## How to Avoid It

Listen for and recognize red flags. When they occur, stop right then and investigate further, or make notes and go back later for the correct interpretation.

Here are some typical red-flag phrases and words to watch out for:

- "I hate to say this about him but . . ."
- "I was the only one who knew anything."
- "My last boss expected too much from me."
- "Let me tell you, those types of people . . ."
- "We always had basic differences of opinion."
- "I don't mean to generalize about certain people, but . . ."
- "It was very hard to do good work under those conditions."
- "He doesn't know what he's doing."
- "Low class. . . ."
- "Difficult. . . ."
- "Demeaning. . . ."
- "Pushy. . . ."
- "Overworks people. . . ."

---

## MISTAKE 53

**Expecting red flags to show themselves only verbally.**

## MISTAKE 54

**Not interpreting nonverbal behavior properly.**

### HOW TO AVOID THEM

Red flags show themselves in many ways other than the spoken word. Job candidates' appearance speaks volumes about how they will ultimately present themselves in a work situation. If you get the impression that certain candidates are sloppy and do not take care of themselves, these characteristics may also show up in their work.

Low energy and lack of enthusiasm are red flags. If an interviewee cannot keep up with you between the reception area and your office, the chances of that person working out in the job are small.

The interviewee's image can mean a lot. Among detrimental traits cited by veteran interviewers are excessive shyness, lack of independence, and a Pavlovian need to be praised and rewarded. If a person gives the impression of needing a title, high salary, and tangible dividends, be prepared to tell him he may be in the wrong line of work.

How applicants carry themselves is important, too. You want someone who appears confident in her demeanor and tone of voice.

When interpreting nonverbal behavior, be careful. An applicant suddenly stiffening up, shifting in his seat or crossing his arms may appear to be on the defensive, but actually may just be uncomfortable sitting in the same position for so long. However, if he suddenly gets up and leaves the interview because he does not like your line of questioning, the interpretation of this nonverbal behavior is apparent. In either case, you should ask the applicant for an explanation of his behavior and try to correct the situation.

Some other red-flag warning signals to look for:

▌ Unexplained gaps in employment.

▌ Applicants who talk around questions instead of answering them directly.

▌ Blushing.

▌ Suddenly higher or lower voice.

▌ Inappropriate use of humor.

▌ Sudden twitching, stammering, frowning, drumming fingers.

▌ Sudden use of more formal, seemingly rehearsed vocabulary.

▌ Inconsistency between words and nonverbal behavior (the applicant says, "I loved my last job," and shakes his head as if to say "No, I really didn't." The nonverbal reaction is probably the one you should go with).

▌ Sudden loss of what had been good eye contact.

▌ Speeding up or slowing down in pace.

▌ Sudden, uneasy fumbling with the person's pen or looking for gum or a breath mint.

▌ Perspiring heavily or excessive trembling of the hands.

▌ Overly involved and complex responses that seem rehearsed.

▌ Applicants who don't know when to shut up.

▌ Applicants who underestimate your knowledge or experience.

▌ Applicants who try to trip you up by asking technical questions or use one-upsmanship to put you down.

▌ Applicants who question your authority.

▌ Applicants who excessively name drop.

▌ Applicants who continually try to rephrase your questions because they are not sure of what you mean.

▌ Applicants who bring friends or family with them on an interview.

## TWO COMMON MISTAKES IN MAKING THE FINAL SELECTION

## MISTAKE 55

**Not conducting follow-up interviews.**

### How to Avoid It

No matter how thorough your interviewing may have been, there will most likely be more than one candidate left for final selection. It is important for you to call back the ones you think are best suited for the job for second and possibly third meetings before making your final decision.

Take advantage of this situation to reassess each finalist. It's your last chance to hire smart. Your last chance to avoid a costly hiring mistake.

## MISTAKE 56

**Not being sure of your final selection method.**

### How to Avoid It

If the finalists meet all or most of the job requirements, compare them against one another and make the big decision. It is wise not to settle for the best of what are inferior choices in the first place. Reject them all, review your recruiting and selecting procedures, and start looking again from scratch.

## TWO COMMON MISTAKES IN NEGOTIATING THE EMPLOYMENT AGREEMENT

The final candidate has been chosen. Unless the specific compensation was mentioned in your ad, the chances are a range was given or it was left open and depended on experience. Now it is time to call the finalist, negotiate a salary, and follow with a letter of confirmation stating the starting date and compensation agreed upon.

## MISTAKE 57

**Not preparing for negotiation.**

### How to Avoid It

Preparing for negotiation starts with writing down the top salary you can pay and whatever benefits go along with it. Add to that any incentives and bonuses tied into performance, as well as "perks," nonmonetary benefits that may be very attractive to good applicants—a title, an office, a voice in decision making, moving expenses and mortgage assistance (if applicable). Present your offer in writing. This may give an exceptional candidate the security he is looking for. Make up your mind to be strong and stick to your offer.

## MISTAKE 58

**Referring to yearly instead of weekly salaries.**

### How to Avoid It

In your ads, interviews, and negotiations, be careful not to mention anything (verbal or written) that would indicate job permanence. Merely by representing salary and/or job description in annual terms, you may be legally stuck with a mishire for that one-year period. Courts have also upheld that if you represent that there is a trial period with a review to determine future employment, the employee must be retained for at least that long.

I have found in my own hiring experiences over nearly 40 years that it is always best to mention salary in weekly terms and establish a short trial period (usually three months), with a review of the employee at the end of that period. If both parties are happy with the relationship after that time, it can then be extended for whatever period both parties agree upon.

## THREE SERIOUS MISTAKES IN HIRING FOREIGN EMPLOYEES

America has always been a haven for immigrants. They come from all parts of the globe in search of freedom, due process of law, and the right to live and work free from discrimination. Many immigrants incorrectly believe they have fewer legal rights than American-born citizens. In fact, the Constitution of the United States protects everyone, regardless of citizenship or immigration status. But suppose you want to hire a foreign employee. Should you be concerned about breaking any laws?

The answer is yes.

## MISTAKE 59

**Believing any foreigner can be hired if they have the documentation required to stay in the United States.**

### How to Avoid It

Review the Immigration and Naturalization Act of 1990 available from the Immigration and Naturalization Service (INS), 425 I Street,

N.W., Washington, DC 20507 or the U.S. Department of Labor (check the government pages of your telephone book for the nearest office). The Act sets out a complex system of quotas and preferences for determining who will be allowed to permanently live and work in the United States.

## MISTAKE 60

**Paying alien employees less than U.S. workers in cash and not withholding federal taxes.**

### How to Avoid It

Aliens are normally required to pay taxes on monies earned in the United States and are subject to normal tax withholding and reporting requirements. Aliens who are intracompany transfers and have L-1 work visas can also obtain Social Security cards, purchase property in the United States, open bank accounts, and travel freely to other countries.

## MISTAKE 61

**Expecting new employees from foreign cultures to adjust to your workplace procedures on their own.**

### How to Avoid It

Provide an American mentor for guidance. Integrate the new employees with established American or immigrant workers. Chances are they will learn by imitating their coworkers. If a foreign employee has a serious adjustment problem, recommend counseling.

## Chapter 3

# EFFECTIVE COMMUNICATIONS TOOLS FOR TRAINING, COACHING, AND COUNSELING WORKERS

You've come across the line hundreds of times—in business books and speeches, at seminars, in press releases, and in company annual reports, "People are our most important asset"—and it's true. It is also true, illogical and counterproductive as it may seem, many companies are investing in making their machinery better, instead of investing in making their employees better.

For any business to be successful, it must have an effective work force, especially in times of rapid change, stiffer competition, and a chronic shortage of skilled, sometimes even competent labor. And to have an effective work force, companies must understand the need for, and create a program for training, coaching, and counseling workers. In case you don't think it's important to implement and maintain an aggressive program in your company now, consider this: According to a finding by the National Center on Education and the Economy, if current trends continue as they are expected to, by the year 2002, 70 percent of all jobs in the United States will *not* require a college degree, and the task of training workers will become the responsibility of all businesses, no matter how large or small they may be.

## FIVE COMMON MISTAKES IN MAKING WORKERS WILLING TO LEARN

When people don't do what they are supposed to do at work, it may be because they are slow learners, have no motivation, need to sharp-

en old skills or develop new ones, or they may simply not know how
to do it.

## MISTAKE 62

**Assuming a new worker experienced at a task will know how to
perform to the standards established by your company.**

### HOW TO AVOID IT

Situations change, procedures and technology change, and yesterday's skills do not always meet today's challenges. All new employees
should be given some degree of training or you will end up with low
productivity, unsatisfactory quality, low coworker morale, and expensive rehiring. Since in most cases you will not be training groups of
people, examples given are geared to one-on-one methods. Steps to
follow are:

❚ Master your subject and prepare well for the training session.
   That includes being able to answer any questions that might be
   thrown at you.

❚ Communicate at a level appropriate with the participants' experience.

❚ Have other training personnel (who have background with the
   job), all the training aids, equipment, and materials in place
   before you start the training session.

❚ Use training aids whenever possible, and try to use them as
   effectively as possible. If you can't use them right, don't use
   them at all: manuals, audio and visual aids, charts, case studies,
   games, exercises, simulations, role plays, models, and actual
   equipment that the trainee will be using. Today we have at our
   command many advanced technological methods, techniques,
   and equipment such as computer programs and video conferencing (see Chapter 17, Communicating on the Internet and
   Infohighway), artificial-intelligence aids, and learning methods
   based on transactional analysis and gestalt, to name but a few.

❚ Make sure you will not be disturbed by others or waste time
   looking for things once you start.

❚ Make the session long enough for a trainee to absorb all the
   information, but not long enough to induce sleep.

▌ Without talking down to a trainee, explain exactly what you are doing, why you are doing it that way, and then demonstrate how you do it.

▌ Explain how doing it the way you want will satisfy you and the company.

▌ Use humor and personal experiences to make your session more interesting.

▌ When you are sure the trainee understands what to do and why, let him do it.

▌ Encourage her to ask questions about the procedure.

▌ Go through a quick summary.

▌ Make yourself available before and after sessions to answer questions and talk about important points.

▌ Monitor the employee for a week or two. Correct anything you find that the employee is doing wrong. She may be careless and is skipping some steps to get the work out faster. She may have changed the procedure because she thinks her way is better. She may be practicing bad habits that could influence other workers.

## MISTAKE 63

**Not confronting and correcting an employee who has fouled up.**

### How to Avoid It

In order to get unproductive workers up to standard operating performance and keep them motivated, you must help them change. Besides training, there are two other motivational learning techniques that can help accomplish this: coaching and counseling. These are not the same as training. Training is a technique to teach new or transferred employees how to learn and perform a task. Coaching is used when employees fail to do a task properly and you help them correct their problem. Counseling is applied when an employees' overall performance is poor and getting worse (usually because of personal problems).

One method of getting to the bottom of training-related problems (in using any or all of the three techniques), is to ask questions. If you want someone to digest and remember something, you have to get that person to think he thought of it himself. Asking "What don't you understand about the task?" and letting the person give the answer back to you can be an effective way to help him accept an idea as his own. Remember that slow learners are not necessarily stupid. Be patient. If the employee still cannot do the work, it may be best to either transfer him to a job he is capable of doing or letting him go (for more on this subject, see the section about when an employee's performance doesn't improve on page 65).

Another method many businesses are now using is showing the trainee a taped demonstration of the right way to do the job and then taping her doing the same task. The employee will better understand and will more readily accept and correct her mistake when she sees herself doing it wrong.

## MISTAKE 64

**Blaming the failings of an employee on the employee, rather than viewing it as a management weakness.**

### How to Avoid It

Steps to take:

- Clarify the job. If the task is nothing more than drawing a line on a piece of paper, tell him how long, how wide, what color, and in what direction. No matter how educated or astute a trainee may be, until he has clear information, you can't expect him to do it the way you want.

- Put it in writing as a job description. This way there can be no communications mistakes regarding what you expect from the employee.

- Unless the trainee has a point of reference for decision making on a particular task, don't expect him to think for himself at first. Without putting him down, you do the thinking for him as you go through the motions of the task. When he learns your approaches and how you think, he is on his way to becoming a good employee who fits in with your team.

- Go over the training procedure again, this time letting the employee do it. Encourage questions. Ask questions.

- If something is interfering with the person's ability or desire to do the job, you must find out who or what it is. It could be something completely beyond your control such as illness, marital or financial problems, the death of a relative or close friend, or a new hire who thinks he made a mistake in taking the job in the first place. By putting the person at ease and offering a friendly open ear, the employee will more than likely open up and discuss his problems with you. Give him whatever verbal, emotional, and other supportive help you can. You may be able to involve the employee's family or spouse in some way to add to his support. If the employee does not wish to discuss personal problems with you, you can usually get the information you need by questioning coworkers. The problem interfering with the trainee's job may be something that is within your power to correct: uncooperative coworkers, dissatisfied customers, working conditions, company policy. One way to solve these problems is by assigning the new employee to a seasoned employee who can help the trainee with orientation, coworkers, and with understanding company procedures.

▮ Follow up a week later. If the problem is not resolved, reassignment or termination may be necessary.

## MISTAKE 65

**Assigning an experienced employee—inexperienced in training— to train new hires.**

### How to Avoid It

Besides a thorough working knowledge of the job, the person doing the training should:

▮ Have the patience, flexibility, and communication skills needed for training.

▮ Be efficient and effective at the task.

▮ Feel totally secure and nonthreatened in his own job.

▮ Have been trained to train others.

▮ Have the necessary resources to perform the instruction.

▮ Have sufficient time to prepare and perform the training.

▮ Have a strong, positive attitude toward the job and the company. An unhappy trainer will only infect new trainees with her discontent.

▮ Not be expected to maintain her own job output during the training period.

After this type of training, sometimes called "Nellie and Fred training," the trainee must still be monitored and evaluated on a regular basis.

## MISTAKE 66

**Not asking suppliers to provide help with training.**

### How to Avoid It

Many training programs overlook the fact that it is in the best interest of the suppliers to make sure their equipment or products are completely understood and properly used and that suppliers are ready, willing and able to help out with your training, usually at no additional cost to your company.

## THREE COMMON MISTAKES MADE IN UPGRADING WORKERS' SKILLS

Many of the management consultants we have spoken to agree that the most significant productivity and quality gains in this age of lean production will not come from new technologies, machines, or capital investments, but from highly trained and retrained employees working smarter to make their businesses better.

## MISTAKE 67

**Not setting up a retraining program.**

### How to Avoid It

Training experts recommend that managers setting up retraining programs take these steps:

- Identify your company's specific retraining needs. Study each job to determine its tasks and the levels of skills and the knowledge required of the employee in that job. Compare the employee's evaluation reports to the job requirements. Consider any new technologies, machinery, and methods that will be used in the job. Then structure the retraining program so that employees can actually develop the skills and new knowledge they may be lacking.

▎ Try establishing a partnership with a community college or university that can help address some of your retraining requirements. They may be able to send people on their staff who can help create a customized curriculum or structured on-the-job retraining system for your firm.

▎ Check with your state and local development agencies. As worker retraining has become increasingly important in maintaining corporate competitiveness, state and local development agencies have also increased funding for training and retraining, in many cases introducing new programs intended to benefit small- and medium-sized companies. According to the National Association of State Development Agencies, states are also building more flexibility into their programs. Many more are allowing companies wider discretion in deciding where and by whom the retraining is conducted and are expanding into new areas, such as funding for ISO 9000, basic skills, and supplier training.

▎ Customize the retraining effort to your company's specific needs as well as to each employee's specific needs.

▎ Supervisors or employees who have already been retrained and have training capabilities can be used as instructors and coaches.

▎ Evaluate your retraining to determine its effectiveness. This can be done by testing employees on the new skills they have been taught.

## MISTAKE 68

**Not cross-training people in a department so that everybody can do everything.**

### How to Avoid It

Teaching people tasks that others in their department are doing makes the department more flexible, especially during emergencies, absences, or periods when you may have to downsize. At the time of hiring, advise new employees that cross-training is a company policy. Explain that though they are being hired for a specific job, knowing other jobs in their department will make them more valuable to the company. Immediate cross-training is not as effective as doing it on an as-needed basis. The quickest way to cross-train is to let people work and practice with others during their slow times. When the need does arise, they can immediately perform their new task with little or no additional help.

## MISTAKE 69

**Not looking for new approaches to update training methods.**

### How to Avoid It

When new approaches are applied, the training procedure becomes much more interesting and productive. If you've never employed video, for example, try it. Steps you can take:

■ Spend an hour or two each week (during lunch breaks, before or after work, commuting to work) reading trade-magazine articles and new books on training, listening to management, and other business tapes.

■ Attend training seminars and industry trade shows.

■ Network with friends and managers in all types of companies to find out what they are doing that is new, different, and effective. Don't hesitate to ask for information from people you don't know. Most professional people are willing and anxious to help.

■ Join a professional association in your field. Go to meetings. Chat with other members.

## THREE COMMON MISTAKES IN OVERCOMING RESISTANCE TO CHANGE

You have problems in your department. You may have to fire some longtime employees (see Chapter 11, Firing Employees) in order to cut costs or make other radical changes to survive and thrive in the constantly changing workplace. But keeping morale up and getting people to accept, cope with, and adjust to new approaches and techniques, especially those who have done it the old way for so long, can be a difficult task.

## MISTAKE 70

**Not preparing for low morale and revolt in the ranks.**

## How to Avoid It

Once you've decided what changes you are going to make and when, the first thing you want to do is stop unfounded speculation and paranoia. Get your staff together and explain the changes to be made and why. Point out that these organizational changes were anticipated and prepared for in the overall business plan for the year and that once the changes are in place, everything will be running smoothly again.

---

## MISTAKE 71

**Resorting to "Do it my way or else," methods of retraining employees.**

## How to Avoid It

There are many ways to get workers to do what you want and adjust to changes in the workplace. In pages to follow, we will cover incentives, motivation, nurturing environments, and other methods. While giving workers an ultimatum may get them to do what you want, they are not doing it voluntarily or with very much enthusiasm and care. Expect resistance from longtime employees who may resent their new boss and believe they are doing the best job they can. Steps to take:

- Gather those to be retrained and explain, first, that you are sensitive to their needs and that the retraining is not a threat to their job and, second, how it will actually help them perform their jobs better.

- Tell them you recognize the contributions they have made in the past and that you will be depending on them even more in the future.

- Assure them that you are not working against them and that you realize it may take a while for them to master the new techniques, but that once they do, their work will be easier.

- If anyone challenges you with something like: "The old way was okay all these years, why change?" throw the challenge back to her: "You're right, but times have changed. Competition is fierce. Companies that don't improve won't survive. I know you can handle this new method and get more production and better quality with less effort than you did the old way."

## MISTAKE 72

**Not recognizing anger in employees.**

### How to Avoid It

By giving employees their say, but not always their way, you are providing them with an opportunity to talk it out with the right people. You are also giving yourself an opportunity to diffuse hostility that might be building and, more important, an opportunity of understanding what your employees value and what they dislike. Systems you can set up:

- Install the good old suggestion box or create suggestion programs (with incentives) through your company newsletter.

- Initiate monthly departmental meetings.

- Encourage and help create employee-involvement teams.

- Take regular employee surveys with questions that ask for negative and positive comments about their job, the company, their supervisor, and so forth.

- Conduct one-on-one and group coaching sessions on a regular basis.

- Have a standing open invitation for employees to meet with supervisors and top executives and discuss problems.

Here are some questions to ask to determine exactly what their problems are:

- What would you do to make your job easier?

- What suggestions do you have to improve the quality of your output?

- What decisions would you like to make if you had the opportunity and authority?

- What additional responsibility would you like to have?

- What would you like to see changed?

Of course, it goes without saying, listening is not enough. You also have to act one way or another on what you have learned. Let employees know what you are doing in response to their complaints.

## THREE COMMON MISTAKES IN RECOGNIZING THE VALUE OF COMPLIMENTS AND RESPECT

Studies have shown time and again that both morale and performance are higher when the boss compliments an employee on a job well done. The compliment is a form of recognition and respect, and whether someone is adequately recognized can play a critical role in the building—or destroying—of trust in the workplace. When most employees first start working for a company, they generally extend themselves to show how ambitious they are to become a productive member of the "team" and build a lasting relationship with the company. Unless this willingness and effort is reciprocated by recognition, employees may feel hurt and betrayed and may retreat into themselves. Seasoned employees may also feel betrayed by lack of recognition. Supervisors sometimes consider a person's work effort as a commodity exchange of time for money. But many employees put more of themselves into their work than even they realize. So without recognition of that fact by supervisors and coworkers, employees tend to give less and less of their creative efforts to their jobs. Morale and production nose dives and absenteeism goes up, as do employee grievances.

There are dozens of formal and informal ways for a supervisor to recognize someone's work efforts. In the pages ahead many of these rewards and motivational techniques will be discussed. In this chapter we are talking mostly about compliments.

## MISTAKE 73

**Not taking the time to compliment employees on their work.**

### How to Avoid It

Management must do everything possible to recognize good work and treat every employee with respect as an individual. Steps to take:

■ A little praise and a pat on the back, especially in public, goes a lot further than criticizing or ignoring someone's work. The employee will feel very special; that's human nature. If you have a company newsletter, include stories about employee accomplishments (as well as birthdays, marriages, births of children, graduations of children, etc.). When workers are complimented, they feel they are working in a climate of approval rather than a climate of criticism. One company we know of uses "You Done Good" certificates that any manager or employee can send to any other employee. Does it work? You bet. Just try it and look at an employee's grievance file before and after recognition. Complimenting is also a great way to smooth over angry or belligerent employees. Just when they are all set to hate you, an honest compliment can make them love you. Express admiration for whatever the persons do well, talk about their interests, and offer helpful suggestions they can mull over that may not have occurred to them before.

■ Be sincere. Glad handing and superficial flattery won't work. People know when they are being conned. Compliments should be concrete, never left-handed put-downs. It's better to say: "It's people like you that make us all look good," rather than an insincere compliment/put-down such as: "You did a terrific job—this time."

■ Give credit when it is due. Deliver compliments on the spot as soon as you see the good behavior, and as we have mentioned, publicly in front of coworkers, if possible.

■ Send a congratulatory letter and put a copy in the employee's file.

■ Personalize the compliment and show that you recognize the individual. Know the first and last names of all your employees. It is one of the most powerful and convincing ways you can say to a person, "I recognize you as an important individual." All division heads and supervisors should know the names of all their subordinates. Some companies provide name plates for desks and ID badges for employees, not only for security reasons, but so everyone will be recognized as valued members of the company instead of faceless names or numbers on a payroll. Be careful not to forget names or mispronounce them. This will work in reverse for you.

■ Make your compliments commensurate with the importance of the accomplishment. If there were others involved in the work effort being praised, you would be exaggerating praise to an individual by saying "It could never have been done without you."

## MISTAKE 74

**Ignoring employees as individuals.**

## MISTAKE 75

**Not showing respect for employees.**

### How to Avoid Them

Besides recognition, each worker also needs something much more basic from management—something managers should recognize, but often pass by—respect. For example, we spoke with one company that refers to some of its employees as "professionals," and others as "office staff." Though "office staff" refers mostly to secretaries, clerks, and non-executives, it implies that everyone other than the "professionals" are "unprofessional." On the other hand, an airline we spoke to refers to all of its employees as "associates," which makes them all feel important and part of a team. Show respect for your employees' knowledge and skill. The truth is that they probably know more about their own individual jobs than you do.

## TWO MISTAKES IN MOTIVATING PEOPLE AND GETTING LOYALTY AND COMMITMENT

Managing people is definitely not for everyone. Just read some of the business columns and letters to the editor in your favorite trade journals and you'll discover that boss-bashing is far and away the work world's most popular sport. But employees are no picnic, either. Some have incredible talent but need constant motivation and reassurance. Others just need to be left alone to do their best work. You may have people who do wonderful things, none of which will help move your business ahead.

## MISTAKE 76

**Not recognizing the differences in employees.**

## How to Avoid It

Make an honest effort to really know your employees—as individuals. Try to get to know their attitudes, personal sensitivities and idiosyncrasies, needs and desires, likes and dislikes, what turns them on and off, what makes them different from the others. Find out what they like to talk about. What they are most proud of. What their goals are. What they complain about. What makes them laugh. Once you recognize each person's strengths and eccentricities you will be able to tease and cajole the best work out of each individual, while at the same time giving tough feedback on the areas that need improvement.

## MISTAKE 77

**Not understanding motivation and how to use it to satisfy an employee's needs.**

## How to Avoid It

Start with a definition of the word "motivation." One dictionary says, "an act or process that incites action." A good manager would say, "something you do that gets others to do what you want." I would also add, motivation is something that happens within a person that gets him to do what you want. Nearly every motivational technique falls into one of three broad categories. The following are explanations along with some don'ts and do's:

■ *Fear*—by either threat, humiliation, punishment, demotion, transfer or firing. Not many people in management will admit to using fear as a tool to get employees to do their job, but it is used quite frequently and sometimes unconsciously. Over a period of time, the use of threats and punishment as motivational tools results in employee withdrawal or hostility and does nothing to redirect the employee to do what you want. Many managers like to punish because it reinforces their authority, but it also destroys the relationship with the employee and ultimately damages the company.

Don't be tempted to threaten an employee or a group of employees by memo, letter, or verbally in public.

Do confront each individual in private, one on one, looking him right in the eye and explaining why his behavior is not right.

DON'T assume that what you consider punishment is punishment to an employee. For instance, telling someone she is suspended for a day or two without pay may seem like a vacation to her.

Do consider the laws that affect workers when doling out any form of punishment.

■ *Rewards*—stimulating people to do what you want by offering some kind of "carrot."

DON'T forget that people are human, and human nature is such that when you give someone an inch, it very quickly becomes his right—and next he'll want and expect a foot. Soon you'll run out of things to give.

Do try to use recognition as a reward.

■ *Belief building*—getting an employee to have pride and believe in himself, in his company, and in the products and services the company renders.

Do show your employees that your products and services are of the highest quality—that you refuse to put out a product that you do not believe in or can take personal pride in.

Do show employees how important your customers are—that you are always honest and fair and that you strive to serve their best interest.

Do show employees that you respect and value the relationship you have with them, and that you never regard them as objects to be used by management—that those who are so motivated can develop personally, seek advancement, and earn greater success.

Do show employees that you cooperate with the competition unless the competition practices misleading, unfair business tactics.

Do show employees that the company believes in making a fair and honest profit and in using those profits for the benefit of all employees as well as the continued building of the business.

# TWO COMMON MISTAKES IN USING COMMUNICATION TACTICS THAT GO BEYOND SALARIES AND TITLES

Employees' performance is related to the way they think. In other words, their attitude. Managers have the ability to change bad attitudes with tactics that can turn problems into opportunities.

## MISTAKE 78

**Trying to manipulate people with flattery and future promises.**

## MISTAKE 79

**Assuming that money is the sole inspiration for all employees.**

### How to Avoid Them

Consider these alternative tactics when you have to motivate people whose work is not up to par:

- *"Kill" with kindness.* Treat employees well regardless of how badly they perform or how badly they treat you. Be direct—but likable and polite.

- *Listen and respond.* Allow workers to fully express their feelings. Acknowledge that you understand the situation, reveal what you think and feel, and say what you will do about it. Tip: Don't judge ("You shouldn't do that") or generalize ("You always do that").

- *Don't take a position.* Deal with a need. Find out what the employees want, then why they want it. Once you know what motivates people you can offer alternative solutions to the problem.

- *Accept blame.* If you have played some role in bringing about the behavior you want to correct, admit what your fault is. By shouldering your share of the blame, others are more likely to own up to theirs.

- *Avoid negative and absolute statements.* Instead of "Why can't you . . ." say, "What if we . . ." Instead of "I hate it when . . ." say, "Wouldn't it be better if . . ." Instead of "It must be done this way," say, "Here's a good idea we should consider."

## FOUR COMMON MISTAKES IN EMPOWERING AUTHORITY AND RESPONSIBILITY

We've covered several kinds of motivational techniques that are used to increase worker productivity. There's another—empowering your employees with authority and responsibility. To give such empowerment to employees may upset the traditional role given to managers, but it is a highly effective, nonmanipulative technique of motivation and a great way to bolster employee self-esteem.

## MISTAKE 80

**Putting employees in the position of having to say, "I'll have to ask."**

### How to Avoid It

By empowering employees with the authority to make decisions and making them accountable for those decisions *within the guidelines you set,* each employee will be able to do the job better in her own way. Successful businesses recognize that empowering employees both bolsters their self-esteem and gives them a better hold on their job. Steps to take:

■ Enlarge the employee's responsibilities, such as: letting them issue cash refunds or credits to people who don't have receipts in hand; or deciding whether to drop freight charges or whether to hire a courier for special delivery or deliver a package themselves. Supervisors should be empowered to decide on the spot whether to pay a customer for damages; managers should be empowered to hire or fire without approval from higher-ups as long as it's legal and company policy is followed.

■ Coach them in judgment and social skills.

■ Introduce them to others in the company so they can develop connections.

■ Use your influence to persuade others to grant them more power because of their connection to you.

## MISTAKE 81

**Not being willing to give up authority.**

## How to Avoid It

There seems to be a kind of human tendency that when a person becomes a boss, she basks in the spotlight of authority and power and is reluctant to relinquish even small parts of it. With a little extra training and a set of guidelines to go by, smart managers find that it's a whole lot better to let those on the front line make the call. Besides, it does wonders for an employee's self-esteem to be the one who decides what it takes to satisfy the customer. Benefits to you:

- When you trust people enough to let them decide what's best, they'll respect you and have confidence in you.

- When you show employees you have faith in giving them authority, you'll find they need less attention and supervision from you. You'll have more time for your own work.

- The persons to whom you have given authority will be motivated to do their best for you and not let you down. They will use their imagination, initiative, and resourcefulness, which will contribute to your own success as a manager.

## MISTAKE 82

**Not giving both authority *and* responsibility.**

## How to Avoid It

Along with authority comes responsibility or accountability. One does not work without the other. The one who loses the most when an empowered employee fails is the manager; the one who gains the most when an employee performs well is the manager. So the manager must coach and assist the employee in using his authority appropriately and understanding that he will be rewarded in one way or another for making customers happy and be held accountable for mistakes, even if it means requiring him to pay a portion of any losses. When an employee is empowered with authority and responsibility, all guidelines should be very clear and in writing as part of company policy.

## MISTAKE 83

**Not putting limits on authority.**

## How to Avoid It

A major management concern in giving authority to employees is that they will "give away the store." That can be avoided by putting spending limits on their authority. For instance, it's their call up to a specified amount. Anything over that will require an okay from someone higher up.

---

# FOUR MISTAKES IN DEALING WITH SOMEONE WHO'S OVER HIS HEAD

---

Joe is a great guy whom everybody loves. He's never late for work and always tries his best. But his best is far below the performance of his coworkers and the standards of your company. Even the best interviewers cannot learn everything about an applicant during the interviewing process, and though the person's skills may have been tested, only time on the task will tell you whether or not a person can adequately handle the job they were hired for, or promoted into.

---

## MISTAKE 84

**Promoting employees to more demanding jobs because of loyalty and dependability rather than skill and ability.**

## How to Avoid It

It happens every day. A longtime employee with a good record is promoted to a more demanding job without the benefit of retraining. After a week or two, she can't hack it and coworkers must take up the slack. A potentially dangerous situation is brewing. First and foremost, this is a valued employee you don't want to lose, so get that person properly trained. If for some reason this is not possible, transfer the employee laterally to a position she can handle. Or perhaps you can create a job structured to fit the worker's abilities at the same salary level. If neither alternative is feasible, you may have to resort to demotion and risk crushing an employee's morale and loyalty. Steps to take:

■ Discuss the situation openly and frankly with the employee.

▌ Let the person know you respect her abilities and dedication, but that not everybody is suited for every job and this promotion simply was not to the job best suited for her.

▌ If it is necessary to reduce salary, explain why and give assurance that when other openings arise within her scope of expertise, she will be considered.

## MISTAKE 85

**Covering for an employee who's over his head.**

## MISTAKE 86

**Spending too much time helping less productive workers and ignoring the better ones.**

## MISTAKE 87

**Constantly supervising a less productive worker.**

### HOW TO AVOID THEM

Your time is limited, and you must use it as effectively as possible. Covering for a totally unfit employee (because you like him, feel sorry for him, feel a need for his love and respect, or can't bring yourself to confront him) is a waste of your time and your company's money. And if other workers in the same department are aware of what you are doing, serious problems could arise from the situation, including loss of respect for you and resentment of the employee you are covering for. Be a boss, not a buddy. The unfit employee may have to be transferred to a job that fits his abilities or be terminated. The time you spend on your less productive workers may be necessary; however, ignoring the good workers may make them think you don't appreciate their work. This can result in their turning in intentionally unsatisfactory work just to get your attention and recognition. Steps to take:

▌ No matter how busy you are, pay attention to and recognize the work of all your people as often as possible. Comment on their assignments, praise their accomplishments, exchange ideas.

▌ Know your employees. Some workers need more attention than others. Whether they are up to par or not, it is important that you give them the attention, recognition, and direction they need.

▌ Determine why some workers are less productive. The problem may be that the employee is a slow learner. With additional training, patience, and some experimentation, you may be able to help build their productivity. The problem might also be the person's fear of failure. You can help them overcome this by giving easier assignments that you know they can handle and praising those successes. This will build the employee's self-esteem and allow him to take on more difficult tasks with confidence.

▌ Give your less productive workers very specific assignments with time frames that must be kept. Check to make sure that the work is on schedule and praise the accomplishments.

▌ Once the workers get into the habit of doing assignments correctly and on time, extend the amount of work and time frames. It may take some time, but as workers become accustomed to this practice, they will need less and less of your time and supervision.

## FOUR COMMON MISTAKES MADE WHEN AN EMPLOYEE'S PERFORMANCE DOESN'T IMPROVE

Do you have an employee who does not follow procedure or work rules and has been behaving that way for some time? Unfortunately, you cannot always succeed in getting an employee's performance to improve. When this situation arises, you will have to resort to some kind of action that may result in termination. But termination can bring on legal problems, and as if that were not costly enough, consider the investment you already have in hiring, training, administering, and supervising that person. Efforts must be made to salvage the employee by using various disciplinary programs to help him become more productive while protecting the company from charges of unfairness and costly litigation.

## MISTAKE 88

**Not putting the responsibility for change on the person who needs it.**

## How to Avoid It

By utilizing a systematic disciplinary approach in which employees are given every opportunity to correct their problems, you can inspire an employee to change by providing:

- Reasons why she should want to change.

- Identification of behavior that needs to be changed.

- Instruction in how to change.

- An environment supportive of change.

- Positive or negative consequences, depending on his response.

## MISTAKE 89

**Not documenting confrontations.**

## How to Avoid It

Positive confrontation calls for the manager to act quickly, before the problem grows. The first time you see a deviation that could grow into something more serious, don't make a note to take care of it later, confront it immediately . . . but never in anger. Systematic disciplinary steps to follow:

- *The verbal warning*—given immediately after the offense, in private, when both manager and employee are calm. Document the warning in a departmental log in which records are kept of other matters such as attendance. It is legally best to write a memo that identifies the kind of warning given and put the memo in the employee's file. You might also want to mention it to fellow managers and make reference to them in the memo.

- *Counseling session*—when performance problems persist despite repeated warnings, conduct a more formal private counseling session. Never reprimand somebody in the presence of others. It causes bitterness and embarrassment for the offender and those who witness the reprimand. Make the employee aware what company procedures have been violated and that the matter is of serious concern to management. Focus on the problem; don't criticize the employee. Support your statements with specific facts that should be readily available to you if you have been measuring and evaluating performance. Reassure the employee that you have confidence the problem can be solved and that everyone can work together in harmony. Listen attentively and with an open mind; interrupt only to clarify. Motivate the employee to come up with ways to solve her problem rather than impose your solutions. Document the session by making a handwritten outline (on a legal pad) of what is taking place at the session and what you and the employee have agreed upon. Have the employee read it over and sign it. Give a copy to the employee and let her know you consider this a commitment.

■ *Written warning*—if the employee does not keep the commitment, document the behavior with a written warning that mentions the commitment agreed upon. This is now the third record of disciplinary action in the systematic disciplinary program.

■ *Period of probation*—gives the employee yet another chance to shape up, but firmly lets the offender know that unless the behavior is corrected within a specified period of time, punishment will follow. Probationary periods range from a few days to a month depending on union contracts, grievance procedures, company, and government and industry regulations.

■ *Suspension without pay*—for a specified period of time. This can be a sensitive action since it affects the offender's coworkers. But if systematic disciplinary action is your company's policy, it must be enforced with all people. Variations lead to setting precedents, and if you waive a rule for one, you may legally have to waive it for all.

■ *Call for reinforcements*—before giving up completely on the individual, ask yourself if someone else in or outside the company might make better headway with the individual than you can. Perhaps a psychologist, psychiatrist, or support group can accomplish what you couldn't. A friend or family member of the employee or a higher-up or peer within your company might assist. Don't be too proud to ask for help or let a new person take over.

■ *Termination of employment*—if, after you have exercised all of the preceding opportunities to help the employee improve and she doesn't, termination is the only option left. When the final decision is made, it should be carried out quickly and with consideration. Get the person in your office, close the door, and define what you are doing and why. Explain that this action is causing the company as well as coworkers who must now take up the slack to be shortchanged. Do everything you can within company policy and Equal Employment Opportunity regulations to make it easy for the person. Think about how you would like to be treated if you were in a similar position. Discuss the terms of the termination. Rather than let the person stay on and influence other employees, most of the companies we interviewed felt it is best to give them severance pay in lieu of notice and get them out as soon as possible. Find out what the employee would like others in the department to be told.

## MISTAKE 90

**Confronting a worker when you are angry.**

### How to Avoid It

If you are angry, and you know you won't handle a confrontation effectively, the responsible thing to do is keep your distance. When you display anger, it triggers the same reaction from the employee. Under these conditions, the employee will be too busy defending himself to pay attention to what you are saying. But you should not let a responsible distance become a long-standing avoidance. Take a deep breath, count to ten . . . slowly. Take time to focus your message by talking to a colleague or writing down your concern. Once you're in control of your emotions, confront!

## MISTAKE 91

**Feeling guilty about terminating an employee.**

### How to Avoid It

Have realistic expectations of what you can accomplish in changing the behavior of others. Don't accept guilt for the failings of other people; instead, leave the responsibility for change with them. Give them enough time to change, but if they don't, distance yourself mentally and physically. Give yourself credit for what you tried to accomplish (see Chapter 11, "Firing Employees").
　　Check the following list:

▐ Put problem people in proper perspective.

▐ Concentrate on constructive systematic disciplinary approach to help the individual help himself.

■ Don't avoid confrontation. Be a problem solver, not a problem evader.

■ Never confront in anger.

■ Deal directly and discreetly.

■ Visualize a positive outcome to your problem-solving efforts.

■ Document all confrontations for self-protection.

■ Be familiar with policies, procedures, and laws.

■ Be tough and supportive, straightforward and unemotional.

■ Be consistent.

■ Don't be disappointed if people don't change; don't be too proud to call in the troops for help.

■ Be gracious and don't feel guilty if your efforts result in termination.

## THREE MISTAKES IN NOT USING MINI-MEETINGS TO SOLVE BIG PROBLEMS

Problems and complaints are always present in the workplace, but they may not be reaching you because of two reasons: Your employees don't know you are available to discuss them; you are avoiding getting involved with your people and their problems.

### MISTAKE 92

**Not making yourself accessible to discuss employee complaints.**

### MISTAKE 93

**Not getting to know all the people you need to influence.**

#### HOW TO AVOID THEM

By listening to and helping employees solve their problems, you can avoid having problems yourself. Pay attention to their personal gripes and complaints, their worries and fears, and help correct a situation before it becomes dangerous and explodes. Your employees have to know that you are willing and able to listen and discuss and help solve their problems. Show your interest; keep your door open at all times for emergency problems.

You will get to know and understand better all the people you need to influence. Often, managers tend to distance themselves from employees they perceive as difficult and, as a result, don't like, and show favoritism to the others. It's a natural tendency based on personal preferences. But things are not always what they appear to be. For instance, if an employee objects to reasonable rules and regulations, he may be a troublemaker. If you know this, you are way ahead of him. If, on the other hand, his complaints are usually justified and not too frequent, he's probably a well-adjusted individual. Knowing what genuinely disturbs people should always be taken into account when you are assessing their overall value to the company. Regular mini-meetings can be a terrific way for you to know and understand each employee better, especially those you *think* you don't like.

---

## MISTAKE 94

**Not setting up regular mini-meetings to air employee complaints.**

### How to Avoid It

Mini-meetings in which employee problems can be discussed can be set up at a convenient early-morning or late-afternoon time every week or every other week. The benefits can be substantial:

▪ You'll build bridges and relationships with your workers instead of insurmountable walls. Even if the meeting is nothing more than ten minutes of small talk, it's better than no talk at all. By showing interest, paying attention, and listening in an understanding manner, you will discover one of the most effective techniques for getting along with people, putting them at ease so they will open up and talk and creating lasting friendships.

▪ You'll get the input and help you may need to solve your own problems. Yes, you are meeting with your employees to help them. But the same meetings can be used to help you when you need it. It is one thing to make demands on employees in the heat of battle; it's another to ask for their help when no conflict is involved. You will be very surprised at the cooperation you will receive and the bonds you build in the process.

Mini-meetings—steps to follow:

▪ *Make yourself easily available.*

▪ *Eliminate any worker's fear that making a complaint will antagonize you.*

▪ *Spread the word about why, when, and where regular meetings are held*—it does no good to keep your door open unless everybody knows it's open.

▪ *Put aside rules and regulations*—at least during the meetings. If you want to get to the problems and solutions in a timely manner, keep meetings plain and simple.

▪ *Practice patience and help employees voice their complaints.* You must hear out each and every complaint as early as possible, no matter how busy you may be with other things. Show your patience and understanding with workers who are unskilled at putting their problems into the right words. Make sure they know you completely understand them and are willing to help.

▪ *Ask what you can do to help*—it can turn a complaining session into a profitable one for you.

▪ *Contribute ideas.* Relevant comments from you can stimulate ideas from others that can be valuable to you.

▪ *Keep an open mind;* get rid of preconceptions. Don't block out concepts that differ from yours.

▪ *Don't make quick decisions.* Get all the facts, sort them out, verify and consider them. Wise decisions are always better than quick ones.

▪ *Take notes.* This helps you organize what goes on at the meeting and remember it all. Highlight good ideas you pick up from the conversations that take place. One good idea may be the most valuable result from holding the meeting.

▪ *Summarize.* While the meeting is still fresh in your mind, go over your notes and write or dictate a report for your files.

▪ *Announce your decisions*—when a meeting results in numerous personal employee complaints and problems, you must handle each decision on an individual basis. Tell each person your decision concerning her problem yourself and in private rather than through a secretary or a memo. It shows you have interest in the person and the problem. If the problems and complaints were of a departmental or group nature, call another meeting and inform all the workers about your decisions.

■ *Be caring or bring in some help.* Unless your employees feel and know you honestly care about their complaints and problems and really want to help them, just listening and paying attention will never be enough. If you can't bring yourself to be this way, perhaps you should ask another supervisor on your level to sit in on the meetings. This approach benefits your employees as well as the outsider, since both will hear the viewpoints of people with whom they do not usually have contact. These views may stimulate some very innovative ideas.

# Chapter 4

# HOW TO AVOID LOSING RESPECT AND RESULTS AS A SUPERVISOR

## THIRTEEN MISTAKES MADE WHEN TRYING TO IMPROVE YOUR PROFESSIONAL IMAGE WITH COWORKERS

Are you, like most of us, a little "nearsighted" when you look at yourself in the mirror? While we may not be sure about the impression we make on others, many of us have a tendency to overlook our faults and magnify our virtues.

Most of the time there is little harm in such deception, but for a manager it can be disastrous. He must see himself as others do if he is to be successful in dealing with his employees and his company.

## MISTAKE 95

**Not recognizing that image makes a difference.**

## MISTAKE 96

**Not seeing yourself objectively.**

## MISTAKE 97

**Not always looking your best.**

## How to Avoid Them

You heard it before and you better believe it, most people do "judge a book by its cover" and are more likely to react positively to someone presenting a positive image. Steps to take:

▌ Look and listen to yourself on video and audiotape. If you ask yourself, "Is that really me?" maybe you're not projecting the kind of image you want others to see.

▌ Think positive. A positive image significantly hastens the development of the trust and rapport you will have with your employees, colleagues, and superiors. They'll feel more comfortable in your presence, making it a lot easier for you to communicate effectively with them. A negative image creates roadblocks that tend to hamper effective communication.

▌ Be aware of how you look, what you say, and how you say it. From start to finish of every encounter you have with other people in the workplace (or anywhere, for that matter), your every word, gesture, expression, and impression will be evaluated, and the responses you receive will, in a way, be a measure of your success or failure in interpersonal relationships. The wrong word, a boorish action, or spaghetti sauce from lunch emblazoned on your chest could immediately turn a positive encounter into a negative one. You must be sure that the image you project in every situation is one that encourages open, honest, trusting communications. A graphic example of how image can work for or against a person was evidenced during Jack ("positive-image") Kennedy's preelection debate with Richard ("negative-image") Nixon, which turned that election in Kennedy's favor.

## MISTAKE 98

**Not making your first impression count.**

## How to Avoid It

A positive first impression makes all further communications easier and more comfortable. A negative one can turn off a relationship before it gets going. Since it is difficult to overcome negative first impressions, plan ahead carefully to be sure your first impressions will be positive. What you wear, how you're groomed, your handshake, eye contact, body posture, and voice are all factors that, taken by themselves or in conjunction with others, determine how people will initially perceive you. Here are some Dont's and Do's:

DON'T use extreme body gestures such as walking with a strut or shuffle or standing with hunched shoulders or head bowed or rocking from side to side.

DON'T sit in a slouched or unflattering position.

DO sit and walk straight and relaxed.

DON'T walk around with a deadpan, scowling, or apathetic expression.

DO smile.

Don't leave your house with dirt under your fingernails; dandruff on your jacket; rumpled, unmatched, stained, or smelly clothing; too much make-up, perfume, or jewelry; bad breath; or (please excuse this) unsightly hair protruding from your ears or nostrils.

DO wear conservative clothing that projects authority, success, and a sense of style.

DO be conservative and knowledgeable about combining complementary clothing colors, patterns, and styles.

DO make sure your clothing is clean and neat and fits you properly.

DO wear simple and functional jewelry and accessories.

DO learn to use clothing to help overcome height, weight, or age factors that might affect how and what kind of image you project. For example, tall and older-looking people can wear soft colors and textures instead of dark, overpowering clothes. Short and younger-looking people can do the opposite. Heavy people can wear dark clothing to deemphasize weight; likewise, the opposite works for thin people.

DON'T be too strong, too limp, or hold on too long when shaking someone's hand.

DO be firm and establish eye contact.

## MISTAKE 99

**Engaging in a conversation and not being familiar with the topic.**

### How to Avoid It

Knowing what you're talking about, especially when it concerns your company or particular specialty makes a difference when it concerns how people perceive and respect you. Steps to take:

▪ Continue your efforts to "keep on top" of what's going on in your company and industry, especially company policies and procedures, products, and personnel. Analyze industry trends and rate your company against the competition.

▪ Take advantage of industry seminars and company training programs that will increase your depth of knowledge and gain you the respect of your employees, peers, and bosses.

▪ Keep abreast of world happenings in general. This will help when you converse with others on matters outside your area of expertise.

▪ Keep up with world events, major sports, current movies and books.

▪ Read all the sections of your newspaper and news magazines.

▪ Watch morning and evening news coverage on TV, listen to it driving to work or while putting on your makeup. By increasing your breadth of knowledge, you can increase your circle of influence with many different types of people.

▪ Don't try to fake it. Ask questions if you are not familiar with a topic you are discussing with someone.

## MISTAKE 100

**Not adapting your behavior to fit each encounter.**

### How to Avoid It

Condition yourself to communicate and interact effectively with other people on their level. Not all people are alike, nor can they be treated alike. If they are, they will be uncomfortable, which creates tension, which causes an adverse effect on the trust relationship you are trying to establish.

Check the following Do's and Dont's:

Do slow down if you are interacting with someone who is not going as fast as you are.

Do take the time to listen more attentively and learn rather than jumping right into a situation.

Do try to communicate with others on their level.

Don't use terminology that is over their head.

Don't use examples they won't understand or relate to.

Don't continually refer to people, events, and places they are not familiar with.

## MISTAKE 101

**Not using eye and voice contact effectively.**

### How to Avoid It

Eye contact tells the person you are with, "You are important. I am talking just to you." But how you say something can be more dominant than what you say.

Use the following Don'ts and Do's:

Don't focus on the floor or ceiling or look over the head of the person you're talking to.

Do use eye contact for feedback on how you are doing with the person.

Don't speak in a monotone.

Do add variations of pitch and inflections.

Don't speak too loudly or too softly.

Don't speak too fast, too slow, or too long.

Do change your pace and use pauses.

Don't use words you don't know how to pronounce or know the meaning of.

## MISTAKE 102

**Not identifying and correcting your bad habits.**

### How to Avoid It

Most people are not aware of their bad habits that, aside from being distracting, can also be distasteful. By watching yourself on video tape or asking good friends and family, you'll get a pretty good idea of your most obvious bad habits. Once you know what they are, it's up to you to concentrate on avoiding them. Some examples:

- Biting your nails and or knuckles.
- Excessive head scratching.
- Excessive eye blinking.
- Drumming your finger on a desk top.
- Sucking your teeth.
- Chewing gum.
- Stroking your beard or (ladies) twirling your hair.
- Licking or biting your lip.
- Cracking your knuckles.
- Playing with beads, chains, or other jewelry.

## MISTAKE 103

**Not coming across sincerely.**

### HOW TO AVOID IT

Mean what you say and do. Being a sincere person means you are honest and truthful and you sincerely care about other people. When you come across as insincere, it produces feelings that you are a manipulative, self-oriented, closed-minded person and can't be trusted.

## MISTAKE 104

**Not setting an example for your employees.**

### HOW TO AVOID IT

You influence others to do what you want when you are totally consistent in what you ask them to do, as well as how you ask them to do it. Words contradicted by actions are hollow. Saying something positive to someone while unconsciously shaking your head "no," is contradictory. Try to be a smiling, happy, perennial ray of sunshine with all the people you interact with—even when you are down in the dumps yourself. When managers are happy and enthusiastic, the feeling spreads to their employees who will work harder, longer, and more accurately than those who are not happy and enthused.

## MISTAKE 105

**Not self-appraising your image periodically.**

## MISTAKE 106

**Not asking friends and associates to appraise your image.**

### HOW TO AVOID THEM

It is not easy to change the habits of a lifetime overnight, but from time to time every wise manager should stand away from himself and take a long, hard look just to see if any bad traits or stained shirts have come back to foul up your positive image. If you have the guts, you might want to ask your employees or associates how they perceive you by listing on an unsigned piece of paper the traits they admire most and least in you. The responses might give you a jolt—in the right direction.

## MISTAKE 107

**Not checking the appearance and impression of your work area.**

### HOW TO AVOID IT

Look around you and see what your employees and peers see. Is the place clean and tidy? Does it look organized and efficient? Check for barriers. A smart manager will not have a big desk as a barrier between himself and his employees. Try inviting workers, customers, whoever to sit beside your desk or at a small round table so you don't give the impression that you are on an opposite side from them.

I recall once visiting a friend in his office, and I noticed what looked like a desk plaque barely peeking out from under piles of paperwork. When I cleared the mess away, I could hardly believe what it said, "A cluttered desk is the sign of a cluttered mind." Likewise, a cluttered work area conveys a sense of disorganization and low professionalism.

## FIVE COMMON MISTAKES IN SETTING EMPLOYEE GOALS

Just when you sigh with relief that you've met this year's goals, you're back to square one for next year and you ask yourself, "Is goal setting really important?" "Does it have any effect motivating employees?"

Unless you know what you want to achieve, you cannot measure how close you are to achieving it. Goals not only give you a target to shoot for, they give you something to measure your progress against. Here are some mistakes in goal setting and ways to avoid them.

## MISTAKE 108

**Setting easy-to-measure goals that are not worth meeting.**

### How to Avoid It

It is the manager's responsibility to ensure that the goals you set for your employees are in line with what your department needs and what your company wants you to do and has empowered you to achieve. It's not how many calls an hour your phone people are capable of making, it's how many sales result from those calls. Does your motivational plan seek efficiency rather than effectiveness? Milestones instead of accomplishments? Output rather than solutions? If so, you run the risk of rewarding your employees for reaching worthless goals that actually weaken your company's performance.

## MISTAKE 109

**Judging employees on results they cannot control.**

### How to Avoid It

Nothing demoralizes workers more than being judged for the mistakes of coworkers. With rare exceptions, employees will work harder and smarter when they they are judged on their individual actions rather than on the collective actions of others in their department, but this is not always possible. Steps to take:

■ At the earliest stages of goal planning, bring together all the participants, including those from other departments.

■ Using a well-thought-out agenda, describe the goals to each employee and how they will fit into the plan, and give them the tools to help them accomplish those goals.

■ Give them the opportunity to question or comment on each stage of the project. Set interim goals for these stages.

■ Arrange for participants to intercommunicate without having to go through channels, and empower them to use their discretion to resolve minor issues.

■ Monitor progress at various stages.

■ If people get out of phase, bring them back on line quickly by showing them how their actions affect the work of others and the entire project. When people are aware of the contributions of others, they will try harder to understand and follow directions.

## MISTAKE 110

**Not making employees accountable for their actions.**

### How to Avoid It

Giving employees a stake in the outcome of a project is the best way to encourage them to accept responsibility for their own actions. It's like giving one piece of candy to two children to share with instructions that one divides it into two pieces and the other gets first choice of which piece to take. You can be assured, those two pieces will be as equal as they can possibly be. In a company, the way to accomplish this goal is to give employees end-to-end responsibility for tasks that contribute to their own success. Maybe the person who needs to have correct data in the human resources database should be the same one that gathers the data and puts them into the system. Besides eliminating finger pointing if the data are incorrect, this approach ensures that the person with the most knowledge of the results is responsible for creating the data.

## MISTAKE 111

**Not aligning departmental goals with overall corporate strategy.**

### How to Avoid It

Sometimes the goals that reward workers for individual performance work in opposition to the goals of the company. Take, for example, the introduction of a new, lower-priced product in an established product line. In order to make the new product attractive to distributors, the manufacturer offers, as a promotional gimmick, a commission double that of higher-priced products in the same line. The problem is the new line is so low priced, even double the regular commission is not enough to cover the costs of a demonstration program the distributor has to establish to sell the item and a separate accounting method needed for the sale. The result is the higher commission incentive by the manufacturer is not enough to justify the extra effort made by the distributor.

## MISTAKE 112

**Not making departmental goals meaningful enough to achieve.**

### How to Avoid It

The same consideration that goes into designing corporate goals should go into the designing of departmental goals. Suppose your compensation plan includes a bonus to each employee of up to 10 percent of their annual salaries. One third is based on company performance, one third on departmental performance, and one third on meeting individual objectives. It's a safe bet that this will not be enough to motivate employees to put in a year's worth of extra effort to reach their individual goal because there are no guarantees and there are too many factors beyond their control that could work against them.

## THREE COMMON MISTAKES IN IMPLEMENTING SELF-DIRECTED WORK TEAMS

Self-directed or self-managed work teams became staples in the workplace after World War II when other countries, especially those in Asia and Europe, discovered they could not compete with America's large industrial giants and instead created niches for themselves within the larger market with better products: radios with clearer sound; TVs with sharper pictures; smaller, fuel-efficient cars.

They created self-directed work teams by taking decision-making authority away from those in management and giving it to teams of people who did the actual work in an atmosphere of harmony and cooperation. No longer would an idea have to be proposed, studied, written up, restudied, tested, and okayed by upper management. By the time the idea traveled up and back down the hierarchal ladder of power, the market or technology had already changed and it was too late. But teams do more than save time. They also:

▪ Create more solutions and barriers to those solutions by working together than most people can working alone.

▪ Make better decisions because they know more about their tasks, and there's very little guesswork about whether any given solution will work.

▌ Train people to be leaders because team members take turns being team leaders.

▌ Increase commitment because the team makes a decision, and is responsible for its implementation, and team members are more willing to work together to succeed.

▌ Become self-policing and spread the responsibility because team members are not as individually accountable. They live and die as a unit. They examine their weakest links and give those members help. A nonproducing team member can be replaced, which effectively gives teams hiring and firing power. This also encourages them to take more risks.

▌ Exploit resources because team members challenge, communicate, inspire, debate, and bring out the best in one another.

Creating a self-directed and managed work team is not an overnight job. The process can be speeded up substantially, however, when management is willing to give the power they have over people back to those people and change the definition of the roles they play, and when employees are willing to forgo the privileges of seniority, take on more responsibility, and accept change.

## MISTAKE 113

**Thinking that if you give up your power as a manager you lose your managerial status.**

### HOW TO AVOID IT

When you bestow empowerment on a self-directed team, you are not really giving up total power, you are sharing it with the team and giving them choices within established boundaries. By sharing your power, you don't lose status, you are just changing techniques. As a facilitator, you teach, inspire, and motivate your people to use their best talents. By empowering them to make their own decisions, you build a team that is not only committed to its success and will put out the extra effort needed to make it successful, but their successes will help you become even more successful. Empowered teams come up with more and better ideas than you may have thought of alone. Workers have a lot of insight into how their jobs are done, and the views of many add to a greater whole than the input of any one person, even an experienced manager.

## MISTAKE 114

**Not convincing employees on the concept of self-directed teams.**

### HOW TO AVOID IT

Many workers feel more comfortable being told what to do and then doing their routine job in a routine way. They don't want to use their brains. They want you to adopt them. It will take a sustained effort to build the self-confidence of your workers. Steps to follow:

■ The first step is changing your role from boss to facilitator; this will encourage your employees to feel and then act as team members instead of as employees. Tell them, "You are no longer employees but team associates. I'm not your supervisor, but your team leader." Convince them that the famous Japanese slogan is true, "None of us is as smart as all of us."

■ Steer team members in how they are expected to work, how the new work methods will differ from the old, where they can go for help, and how it will pay off for them. Make all jobs interdependent. Only if all contribute can the job be completed successfully. Make sure every team member knows how to do all the jobs performed by the team. This makes each member more valuable, strengthens the team, and allows for job rotation to reduce boredom. Define all boundaries before you empower. Provide training in the areas where it is needed. Update job descriptions, create profiles of team members, and determine the technical and behavioral skills they will need for future projects. Assure them that they will not be left entirely on their own and that the ideas and concepts they come up with will be welcomed warmly by management.

■ Build teamwork with pride, recognition, and lots of enthusiasm. Get them to greet the idea of teamwork passionately. Liken it to sports teams. Make them feel that they're with a special company or institution that's worth making sacrifices for, and those sacrifices, if they're good, will come back to them a hundred times. Have members select a team name and team color. Make your people believe that they can make a difference, and let them know you will give them every opportunity to live up to that belief. Keep repeating your vision until it becomes contagious to everyone on the team. And never forget the single most important word when communicating with the team: "we."

▪ Over a period of time, give them assignments for which they will have to plan. Start with small tasks and gradually increase the complexity.

▪ Once the working team is in place, discuss specific plans for your projects. The facilitator may chair the meetings or assign a team member to preside. One or more team members may be assigned to lead specific projects. As supervisor, you can serve on teams as a member, a leader, or you can step aside and provide support and technical advice from the sidelines.

▪ Provide information resources. If you want innovation and synergistic teamwork, you can't have total control of information. Treat information and facts as friends, and let your team and stake holders get to know your friends. Keep timely, focused information within the department or in easy-to-reach places elsewhere in the company. Set up a mini-library, a computer databank, or just a file cabinet. Teach team members how to use the resources. When they bring you a problem or question that could be handled through research, refer them to a data source instead of simply answering it. If the issue requires the advice of someone in a different department, arrange for the team to have access to that individual.

▪ Create controls to measure and evaluate team performance: jobs per man hour, speed of delivery, defects per thousand units. Graph them and make them visible to your people so they can keep score. "Red flag" key indicators to initiate early problem solving. Without meaningful measurements, it is easy for teams and leaders to mistake activity and information for achievement. Consider empowering the team with the authority to evaluate itself. Ask team members to create their own criteria and measure themselves as individuals and as a team against the standards they've established.

▪ Earn and keep the trust of your team. Be there to support their efforts and understand their mistakes. Provide a safety net for legitimate mistakes. Spend time talking to your people, building worker attitude, morale, and motivation within the team network. Don't be afraid to be yourself. You will engage your team when you are authentic.

▪ Celebrate accomplishments. Give team members a sense of closure. At the completion of each project let them enjoy the feeling of a job well done. Go to lunch together; take the rest of the afternoon off. Have a party.

∎ Establish team rewards that go to the whole team as well as individual recognition that goes into an employee's file. If there are those who are not pulling their weight, peer pressure will usually bring them around. If this doesn't work, counsel the offenders. Point out how important they are to the team's success and ask what you can do to help them. If all else fails, remove them from the team. In cases in which an individual does not wish to share ideas, show that person how their contributions will be recognized.

## MISTAKE 115

**Not creating a climate of trust.**

### How to Avoid It

Self-directed work teams work well only in a climate of trust. Encouraged by their leader to question, challenge, and explore, they know that conflict is a normal part of the growing process and focus on the goals they have the responsibility and decision-making authority to achieve. Team leaders, unlike traditional managers, focus on process rather than on content, are more learners than teachers, and facilitate rather than direct. They get people involved, encourage them to do their best, foster open, honest, and direct communication, act as a resource rather than a judge, as a mentor rather than a boss, reward mutual support and cooperation, and, in general, make work fun without losing their sense of humor. When team members recognize the benefits of helping and stimulating one another to succeed, work hard to achieve their goals, and discover they don't need a leader, you know you have succeeded in establishing a good, self-directed work team.

## THE NINE BIGGEST MISTAKES IN DELEGATING WORK

If you're like many managers, you come in early and stay late while your employees are out having a good time, and you've made your staff helpless without you. Big mistakes! You may think you're preserving your sense of control, but what you're actually doing is hindering your chance for advancement. Further, refusing to delegate is the surest way to keep yourself bound to your desk.

## MISTAKE 116

**Wasting time on work that others should be doing.**

### How to Avoid It

Like team coaches who groom their assistants to one day become head coaches, the best managers empower those in their charge to grow and develop. Free from details, the best delegators can focus on becoming better at what they were hired to do: manage, supervise, lead, coordinate, mentor, and facilitate. They know that effective delegation:

- ▌ Challenges workers.
- ▌ Keeps them from stagnating.
- ▌ Demonstrates confidence and trust in them.
- ▌ Retains their loyalty and commitment.
- ▌ Expands their horizons.

## MISTAKE 117

**Not being secure enough to delegate to others.**

### How to Avoid It

Delegating means being prepared to give proper authority and responsibility without fearing loss of control or loss of credit for not completing the job yourself. If these feelings develop into major concerns they can become crippling factors that hamper your personal advancement. When you delegate, you delegate for your own good. Personal benefits to you:

- ▌ More time.
- ▌ Less stress.
- ▌ Greater productivity.
- ▌ More opportunities for growth.

## MISTAKE 118

**Having an "I can do it better" attitude.**

## How to Avoid It

Look at the bigger picture and long-range results from delegating or not delegating. Is it cost-effective to stick with the idea that each task must be performed at its absolute best only by you? Or will your success as a manager be hampered because your time will be divided between tasks anyone can do and the more involved and important tasks you should be doing as a manager? Steps to follow:

- Let your employees help you with some of the tasks you are doing.

- Determine their proficiency. Can they do it just as well as you? Satisfactorily? Better than you?

- If necessary, spend a little time training a "satisfactory" worker to be as good or better than you.

- Weigh the benefits and risks of delegating the task to the person, to you, and to the company.

## MISTAKE 119

**Lacking confidence in or not trusting your employees.**

## How to Avoid It

For some managers, delegation simply isn't worth the risk of failure, and if they've delegated in the past and gotten burned, they aren't willing to get burned again. Managers who think this way either don't understand the benefits of delegation or how to delegate successfully. The point of delegation is not who can do the job better, but rather who has the time and energy to complete the more important jobs. You have to trust others to come through without your constant coaching, and you have to be willing to give someone else a chance to succeed. Questions to ask:

- Did the person you delegated the task to understand what you wanted and expected her to do?

- Did she have the skill and temperament to complete the task you assigned?

- Did you give the proper authority to the worker along with the task?

∎ Did you point out the benefits to the worker if she completed the task properly?

## MISTAKE 120

**Not matching assignments to people.**

### How to Avoid It

Questions to ask:

∎ Does the person you delegated the task to understand what you wanted and expected them to do?

∎ Does he have the skill and temperament to complete the task you assigned?

∎ Did you give the proper authority to the worker along with the task?

∎ Did you point out the benefits to the worker if he completed the task properly?

The first step in proper delegation is knowing what tasks to delegate:

∎ *Routine tasks*—jobs you know well, even enjoy, and can easily teach someone else.

∎ *Specialty tasks*—jobs that require special skills such as writing, computer knowledge, math. Match the task with the skills of the people in your department.

∎ *Unfamiliar tasks*—tasks someone else may be much better at than you are.

Tasks you shouldn't delegate:

∎ Ceremonial tasks—funerals, retirements, banquets, award ceremonies all require your presence.

∎ Personal tasks—making decisions such as hiring, firing, and promoting, employee conflict, budget increases and decreases, employee performance appraisals or disciplinary action, decisions during periods of crises, any situation in which you risk losing face.

Steps to take to delegate:

▪ List all your duties and the time it takes to complete each one.

▪ Make a list of all the people on your staff, their best skills, and their personal preferences.

▪ Match the duties with people and specify what additional training each person may require.

▪ Motivate the person you have chosen to do a good job. Explain the benefits they will derive, anticipate any questions they might ask, be prepared to provide whatever materials, data, or training might be needed. Clarify all levels of authority and responsibility.

▪ Treat the person you have delegated as an equal. Your attitude should be one of team members working together to accomplish a goal.

▪ Explain priorities. Make sure the person you have selected knows the priorities you have set for her and what your reasons are. Employees work more intelligently when they understand both the sequence and the logic of your prescribed plan of attack.

▪ Set a timetable for completion. Be specific, such as, "by the twentieth of the month," instead of, "sometime around the end of the month."

▪ Make the delegated person a star. Introduce her to your supervisor, colleagues, and others working on the project. Make sure they all know you have delegated authority to this person and have given her the power to resolve whatever problems might arise.

▪ Solicit a firm commitment. Make sure the person knows what you want, how you want it done, and when you want it done. Shake hands on it. Put it in memo form.

▪ Let go. Once you've empowered someone else to do your task, honor it by not interfering. The task may not be done as well as you might have done it, but you'll hope people will learn from their mistakes and be better the next time. Support and confirm the wisdom of your delegation as often as possible.

▪ Accept responsibility. If your person fails, admit that you made a poor choice, expected too much, didn't provide sufficient resources, didn't follow through as you should have. Delegation is a risk that has to be taken before any benefits can be realized.

❚ Create a system to evaluate and measure employees as they work toward completion of delegated assignments.

❚ Post-delegation analysis. After the job is completed ask the person who did it:

What did you learn from this assignment? How would you do it differently the next time? What problems did you have? Should you have asked for more help? Did you use all the resources available to you? Did you enjoy and profit from your increased responsibilities? Could I have been of more help?

## MISTAKE 121

**Not minimizing your risks.**

### How to Avoid It

For those new to delegating, start small, with limited tasks such as information gathering or, perhaps, one phase of a multiphase project. Schedule frequent follow-ups so you can spot mistakes or side-tracking early and correct them. As the employee makes progress and becomes more confident, you can gradually relinquish your authority. You are ultimately responsible for the quality of the job you have delegated, so it is important to delegate carefully.

## MISTAKE 122

**Not making the time to delegate.**

### How to Avoid It

Being an effective delegator takes time. Time in planning delegation, meeting with the person you've assigned, possibly training that person, and following-up on that person. If you take the time to delegate well, it will eventually pay off in giving you more time to do more important things.

### *Considerations:*

❚ Is the task a one-time project that will take you a day to teach to a subordinate and that you could do in half a day? It may not be worth delegating this job.

▌ Is the task a monthly one and spending a day teaching it to someone will save you six days during the following year. This is a good time return on your teaching investment.

▌ Will you be helping an employee learn something new that will strengthen his overall ability to contribute?

## MISTAKE 123

**Meddling in the task you've delegated to an employee.**

### How to Avoid It

Once you've delegated a task, give the employee a fair shot at it, even if she is not doing it the way you would. Once you give authority, you should not trespass on it, take it back, or stop it short of completion. Your interference will only cause employee frustration, and it will make doing the task more difficult for her.

## MISTAKE 124

**Rushing to correct mistakes on delegated work.**

### How to Avoid It

Mistakes provide the opportunity to grow. The freedom to handle responsibility isn't worth much without the freedom to make mistakes. If you let your workers experiment with a better way, as long as it is within the framework of your rules, even if they make mistakes, they'll learn from them. You can never be sure that the work you delegate will be error-free, but that's the price of progress. Steps to take:

▌ Install monitoring controls so you can spot errors early or before they occur.

▌ Resolve mistakes with criticism that instills, not kills, the spirit to try harder. If you're angry, cool down before you approach the error. Be firm, but tactful.

▌ Stress the need for results that have to be achieved instead of details on how to achieve them.

▌ Emphasize the importance of following rules and the consequences if they are not followed.

■  Go over the guidelines for the task once more and give the person you've delegated an opportunity to figure out the solution for himself.

■  End on a note of encouragement.

## FIVE COMMON MISTAKES IN MAINTAINING CONTROL AFTER DELEGATION

As we have mentioned above, one of the elements of good delegation is installing and maintaining monitoring controls. These controls help you spot errors early or before they occur and can be essential to keeping a project on target.

### MISTAKE 125

**Not setting controls because "you just don't think it's important enough."**

#### How to Avoid It

Once a manager decides to delegate responsibility and authority, she must also exercise a certain amount of control, in the sense of coordination and knowing what is going on, otherwise she cannot respond effectively and rapidly to problems that may arise. Steps to take:

■  Understand what controls are needed and why.

■  Install them and make sure they are operated effectively.

■  Appraise them regularly to make sure they provide the information required.

■  Use the information.

### MISTAKE 126

**Not setting control points and final deadlines and not making sure they are operated effectively.**

## How to Avoid It

No matter how good communications may be between workers and management, once a delegated project is underway, problems can and probably will develop. One way to keep the job on track is to set interim control points—places at which you stop, examine what has been accomplished to that point, and—if mistakes have occurred—correct them. Without control points, errors may not be discovered until it's too late and the project is well off track. When completion time is critical, you must set exact deadlines for the job to be finished and use the control points to monitor the time on each phase. Experienced workers will know how long it takes to accomplish each phase and you can determine anywhere along the line whether or not you will meet the deadline.

## MISTAKE 127

**Forgoing controls because you feel workers will think you're "looking over their shoulder."**

### How to Avoid It

Unlike surprise inspections, everyone working on a project is aware of each control point and what should be accomplished by then. You must emphasize that while you have confidence in their ability to do the job properly, control points are designed as an aid for workers, rather than a means to check them—especially if a person is new at an assignment. As the employee gains more experience in that task, control points can be reduced accordingly.

## MISTAKE 128

**Not appraising controls regularly to ensure they provide the information required.**

### How to Avoid It

Many companies do have control systems, but they are obsolete and ineffective and may not give a true picture of what is happening. Be sure to determine if:

▮ Requirements have changed.

▮ New priority issues have to be measured.

▮ More details are needed.

## MISTAKE 129

**Not letting employees think for themselves and be individually responsible for maintaining quality standards.**

### How to Avoid It

To ensure that all delegated work meets quality standards, follow these steps:

■ Install the measuring and monitoring controls you need and *use* the information they provide.

■ Make sure your employees know exactly what is expected of them.

■ Make sure they understand the standards by which you will measure the quality of work they produce.

■ Reinforce those standards often via meetings and personal counseling.

■ When consistently high-quality work is produced, recognize and reward your workers both tangibly and intangibly.

■ Continually instill pride in the work.

## TWO COMMON MISTAKES IN CONFRONTING WORKERS WHO CROSS BOUNDARY LINES

Sometimes a poor system or the very nature of a delegated task enables and even encourages employees to try and get away with encroachment. These employees may be overeager, or they may be looking for something you're not giving them enough of—such as a chance to voice their thinking on matters that concern their work.

## MISTAKE 130

**Ignoring pushy, presumptuous, arrogant workers who pay no attention to procedures.**

### How to Avoid It

There are generally three types of people to watch out for: corner-cutters, who bend the rules and skirt the borders of acceptability; bandoleers, who flock together to ruffle feathers and subvert the chain of command; and commanders, bossy people who without authority like to order their coworkers around. Steps to take:

▮ Establish universal rules that all delegated workers on a project must have permission before they attempt any unauthorized acts.

▮ Explain that they are part of a team and that the project may be harmed and their coworkers affected if they do not follow procedures.

▮ Try to win over troublemakers by asking for their help in specific ways and showing your appreciation for their help.

▮ Talk one on one with the offender. Establish that noncompliance is a serious problem and explain what the consequences are.

▮ If the person is part of a clique, reassign him to another job or have him work in a different shift.

▮ Get the offender to "make a contract with you" outlining the steps she'll take to comply with the rules.

▮ Follow up by making suggestions and acknowledging improvement.

## MISTAKE 131

**Not paying attention to your worker's feelings.**

### How to Avoid It

Things will run smoothly if you are as dependent on your employees as they are on you and if you don't make them feel frustrated, inferior, or insecure. Steps to take:

▮ Review your management style. Establish your rules and continually check yourself to see that you treat all your workers the same.

▮ Work together to resolve the issue. Find out what you did that made him feel the way he does. Listen without interrupting and show agreement when he points out your legitimate faults. If you disagree, ask more questions.

▎ Ask for employee feedback on your behavior and act on legitimate complaints.

There will be much more on dealing with difficult employees in upcoming chapters.

## THE TWO BIGGEST MISTAKES WHEN YOU WANT TO SAY "NO"

Have you noticed how easily children say "no" to their parents, but seldom say "no" to the requests of friends? This same kind of dichotomy appears later in our business lives when many of us endure time-wasting and often unreasonable requests of both colleagues and employees simply because we are addicted to the indiscriminate "yes" and have never learned to master the art of saying "no."

## MISTAKE 132

**Not being able to say "no" without feeling guilty or losing self-esteem.**

## MISTAKE 133

**Letting others encourage you to feel guilty when you say "no."**

### How to Avoid Them

For many, saying "yes" when you really want to say "no" leads to only anger, depression, and resentment. The more confident, secure, and valued you feel, the easier it is to weigh the merits of a request and respond with an honest answer. When you feel inferior, powerless, and undervalued, you think you have no choices and say "yes" even when you want to say "no." The bottom line —if it's not worth doing, or if you can't find a good reason to say "yes," say "no." Things not worth doing divert time and energy from things that are worth doing.

Reasons why people find it difficult to say "no":

▎ Some people fear that if they assert themselves, people won't like them. They want so badly for everyone to be their pal that it embarrasses them to refuse office friends.

■ Some people enjoy being needed and contributing to others.

■ Some people can't resist the old "you're the only one who can do it" line and end up overloading themselves with more than they can handle.

■ Some people allow themselves to feel guilty (with the encouragement of others), and the moment they feel guilty, others know they'll do all kinds of things to rid themselves of the guilt.

■ Some people believe they are not carrying their fair share if they don't pitch in and comply with requests every time.

Strategies to help you learn to say "no":

■ Repeat the request to show the other party you fully understand.

■ Give a gracious, thoughtful, and firm refusal without offending. Couch your comments in terms of priorities—expressing concern about having to neglect something else that is more important. Say how much you appreciate his thinking of you.

■ If the request concerns an after-hours office function such as a party or meeting and you really don't want to go, give in and make a brief appearance. It can be important to your current and future position to show team spirit and make new contacts.

■ To escape guilt manipulation by others, be your own judge. Refuse to be tied to their view of right or wrong. Make up your own mind and be prepared to voice it.

■ Remember that the person making the request is usually more concerned with getting the work done than with who is doing it. Suggest a substitute. When someone says "Joe, you're the only one who can do it," say "I'm flattered you thought of me, but I really think Susan can do it better."

■ Don't knock yourself out trying to protect the sensitivities of insensitive time-stealers. They won't be wounded if you turn them down. They'll simply lean on someone else.

■ If you feel that a direct "no" may not be received well, offer a "no" sandwiched between two slices of compliments. If the request is, "Larry, we're having another meeting about the employees' health coverage. I know that interests you. You can find the time to squeeze in one more meeting, can't you?" your answer should be, "That's thoughtful of you to remember my interest in health plans. Unfortunately, I'm all tied up on the

XYZ project. But I'm looking forward to working with you when I'm done with the project."

▌ If the request involves something you may not be experienced in, buy some time before giving a final yes or no. Get a second opinion from someone with experience.

## FIVE COMMON MISTAKES IN KEEPING EMPLOYEES FOCUSED ON PRIORITIES

Managers who know how to set, focus on, and abide by priorities—and can help their employees do the same—have mastered one of the most valuable time-management tools of all. By helping your workers develop and cultivate a mind-set that automatically arranges thoughts, events, conclusions, plans, and actions in priority order will benefit you and the company in a number of ways. First, you'll be able to work through each day faster and more confidently than if you perpetually put out fires or operated by the seat of your pants. Second, decisions that are made will be better decisions because they deal with the crux of the matter. Third, there is more time to think out the important solutions because the lower-priority items have been postponed or discarded.

## MISTAKE 134

**Treating all tasks on the to-do list as equal.**

### How to Avoid It

Designate which tasks are most important by creating short- and long-term top priority lists. Key the really important items with numbers, letters, highlight colors, or asterisks. To determine which tasks go on which list and which ones get highlighted, subject each prospective priority to the following list of questions:

▌ Does it have a real, firm deadline?

▌ Is it an order from someone up above you can't ignore?

▌ Is it a job your employees can handle?

▌ Will it require coordinated efforts with others? If so, can I get those people started on their parts of the job immediately?

▌ If not done soon, might it create bottlenecks in your area or impede the work of other departments?

▌ Can it be combined with related work, such as writing reports, that contain similar information?

▌ Will it really matter if it's not on the priority list?

▌ Will not doing it hurt your reputation, the company, or that of your department?

If the task in question doesn't elicit a yes from any of the questions, don't put it on your priority list.

## MISTAKE 135

**Allowing employees to work on what *they* consider important rather than on what *you* consider important.**

### How to Avoid It

You have a priority problem when an employee gives you one of these reasons for not doing a high-priority task:

▌ "I didn't get a chance to do it yet."

▌ "You never told me there was a rush for it."

▌ "I was in the middle of a dozen other things."

▌ "I'll be getting to that next."

▌ "I have two hands and can only do one thing at a time."

Steps to take:

▌ If the work you assign is of multiple priorities or if the priorities change frequently, label the work according to its priority when you assign it. Explain to workers in detail why one task is a higher priority over another.

▌ If the task comes from some other source, give your employees a list of priority categories so they can prioritize the work themselves when they receive it.

## MISTAKE 136

**Changing the priority of a task without informing your employees.**

## How to Avoid It

If the priority of employees' work changes because of changing factors in their work situation:

- Give them the same general formula you use to judge the most important work from the less important.

- When work priorities change, be sure your workers are the first to know about it.

- If you frequently change the ranking of certain tasks, you must communicate these changes immediately to make certain everyone understands the new ranking and why it changed.

- Don't label everything "top-priority." Even in a hospital's ER procedures, some emergencies have higher priorities than others. Having constant panic situations in the work environment is not effective management. All it accomplishes is slowing down production and causing employee stress.

## MISTAKE 137

**Giving priorities to tasks and not to solving employee problems.**

## How to Avoid It

When you uncover employee problems in your department, you must first identify the factors contributing to them, then set priorities as to which problems get worked on first and which will be temporarily or indefinitely put aside. You may discover that some of the employees' problems are out of your domain, that others are not that serious, and that a few are both critical and within the range of your assistance. Steps to take:

- List the problems in an order that reflects how much their solutions will contribute to the workers' objectives and those of your department. Some problems are clearly more important than others and should be dealt with first.

- Distinguish between *wants* and *needs*. You may *want* to solve a particular problem first, but it's more important to take care of those you *need* to solve in order to meet important objectives first.

---

## MISTAKE 138

**Not keeping in touch with priorities in other departments.**

### How to Avoid It

Often, the priorities of other departments can have a major effect on your own priorities, so you should make it a point to be constantly aware of what is going on in your company. Take the initiative to ask your peers if their plans have changed. Confirm the status of their needs and adjust your priorities to reflect any changes.

---

## THREE COMMON MISTAKES IN BEING DEMANDING AND SUPPORTIVE

---

Managers often find themselves in the role of workplace referee, dealing with a key worker who chronically complains about team decisions or a marginal worker who constantly asks you to make exceptions for him or having to decide which of two valued employees to lay off because the company is downsizing. So how do managers balance their desire to be "nice" with the everyday necessity of maintaining a workplace that is fair to all? It isn't easy. While most of us were brought up to be sensitive, caring, and understanding of the needs of others, in today's workplace being too nice sometimes pushes managers into a trap in which they fail to hold workers accountable for their poor performance.

---

## MISTAKE 139

**Accepting the counterproductive behavior of a worker because you don't want to hurt her feelings.**

### How to Avoid It

When a valued employee is undergoing a personal crisis and the problem is not dealt with, you are creating an environment that breeds unproductive "anchors" that drag down the performance and morale of your organization. When you settle for less than acceptable performance from any of your employees, for whatever reason, you are not doing your job. By accepting instead of confronting:

■ You fail to protect people from their own incompetence.

■ You create a situation of implied contractual agreement that makes it more difficult to fire people when the time comes.

■ You lose respect with coworkers and invite others to test your limits.

Steps to follow:

■ Confront the offender.

■ Be supportive while also demanding accountability.

■ Listen to the worker's explanation, show patience, demonstrate your care and understanding.

■ Suggest directed counseling, which can often help the employee hold his own until he can turn things around and become productive again.

■ Avoid making threats or promises.

■ Provide positive feedback.

■ Be loose in the areas in which you want the person to show initiative and innovation. Create tight controls in the critical performance areas in which mistakes are costly.

■ Back up your words with appropriate action. The goal should be to retain a valuable employee by helping her solve her problem.

■ Perhaps help the employee find a more suitable position within the department or company. If you really care about the people responsible to you, consider that their difficulties might mean they are in the wrong job. They may have fallen into a position within the company that represents their level of incompetence. In the right work environment, they could come to life.

## MISTAKE 140

**Failing to keep accurate records of an employee's on-the-job performance.**

### How to Avoid It

Effective employee discipline is not meant to punish, but to inform. We've already discussed in Chapter 3 how many companies follow a course of progressive constructive discipline. Be sure that you are familiar with your company's guidelines and all the options open to you. For the first confrontation with a problem employee, an oral reprimand and a warning is appropriate. As we suggested before, you should put it in writing as a memo to yourself and place it in the employee's file. You might also want to mention it to some of your peers, just as a precaution. Each subsequent time the employee is counseled, formal documentation should be made.

▪ Specify incidents of ineffective performance or rule violation.

▪ Identify appropriate expectations for the employee.

▪ List actions taken. In many cases, the employee's knowledge that a written record exists will be all the incentive needed to get that person back on track.

## MISTAKE 141

**Failing to prevent or correct a problem and exposing yourself and your company to legal action.**

### How to Avoid It

If you know there is a problem, communicate the facts up the organization and deal with it before it deals with you. Today, courts are extending criminal statutes to the workplace. Legal precedents have been established whereby managers who fail to confront problems that might be caused by the negligence of people responsible for them can themselves be held responsible. Managers are being found guilty of their workers' negligence because they "should have known" and "had the power to prevent the violation and knowingly failed to prevent, detect, or correct the violation."

Check the following list:

▪ Care enough to confront.

▪ Document to inform, not to punish.

▪ Know your department's standards and hold your workers to it.

▪ Demand accountability while being supportive.

▪ Be consistent with all problem workers.

▪ Protect yourself and your company from legal ramifications.

## FIVE COMMON MISTAKES IN MANAGING THE STRESS/ENERGY LEVEL OF EMPLOYEES

Countless articles, books, tapes, and courses are available to help you deal with the stress caused by *your* job responsibilities. But have you stopped to think about the health and well-being of your employees whom you inadvertently may be causing to feel stress. There are many ways managers make the lives of their employees stressful. The more stress, the lower the level of energy and productivity.

## MISTAKE 142

**Not correcting poor organizational conditions.**

### How to Avoid It

Increasingly, employees are turning to workers' compensation with job-related stress claims. Some stress-preventive strategies on the organizational side are:

- Correct poor organizational style and cultural habits of the company. Its tone, priorities, and concern for individuals can cause stress or feelings of tension and anxiety among employees. The stress may come from existing conditions or recent changes. For instance, it may be company procedure to reward teamwork or cooperativeness among individuals or departments, or it may recognize and reward competition, secrecy, and one-upmanship.

- Correct poor or outdated policies; establish policies that are nonexistent.

- Make sure there are open channels of communication especially in regard to job responsibilities.

- Make employees aware of personal and professional growth or advancement opportunities.

- Correct unsafe or unattractive working conditions.

- Don't require excessive overtime.

- Keep employees interested and excited about their work. Counsel those that are bored, burned out, or have gone as far as their growth and advancement abilities are concerned.

■ Make sure there are enough resources to meet goals and responsibilities.

■ Create clear reporting relationships.

## MISTAKE 143

**Not correcting poor managerial style.**

### HOW TO AVOID IT

Workers who experience emotional distress on the job are finding the courts less willing to deal with emotional suffering than they are with discrimination issues. This puts pressure on employers, through their supervisors, to practice preventive strategies against the factors that contribute to employee stress. Some stress-preventive strategies on the managerial side are:

■ Do describe job assignments or problems fully and clearly.

■ Do be decisive.

■ DON'T be overemotional or too laid back.

■ DON'T be a nitpicker.

■ DON'T let subordinates take the blame for problems you or the company caused.

■ DON'T delegate too little or demand too much.

■ DON'T play favorites when dealing with employees.

■ DON'T be too soft or too hard on workers.

■ Do confront workers on their poor performance.

■ DON'T make a habit of having coworkers pick up a poor worker's slack.

■ Do encourage open discussions of problems and creative thinking.

■ Do treat employees as mature adults with feelings, not as if they are robots.

■ Do provide authority and rewards commensurate with responsibilities and performance.

■ Do deliver on all promises.

- Don't take credit that should go to employees.
- Do give praise or recognition for a job well done.
- Don't cheapen praise by overly praising the ordinary.

## MISTAKE 144

**Not meeting pressure head-on.**

### HOW TO AVOID IT

Many stress inducers are within your authority to change, including those that you recognize in yourself. Steps to follow:

- *Identify the cause*—take a long, hard look at the overall project and the people you have working on it. Ask them questions and get their feedback. Look for specific complaints and try to pinpoint the source of pressures they feel.

- *Take action*—minimize the pressure. Is the deadline too short? Is the staff too overworked? Are you ignoring a problem with an employee because you fear confronting the situation? Ask yourself what specific action you can take to affect positive change.

- *Accept the pressure.* There are many things we don't have control over. Take a deep breath, reprioritize the agenda, and remember, it won't last forever.

- Keep a clear perspective—look at the big picture. Mentally review the project and put the details, and pressure, in proper perspective.

## MISTAKE 145

**Not diffusing pressures.**

### HOW TO AVOID IT

Give your employees the help they need in distilling their daily work pressure. The following exercises will help:

- Encourage their talking to one another—venting their anxieties within the work environment will help alleviate stress.

- Encourage them to make a written list of their anxieties. Thoughts are often crystallized and solutions become apparent when they are put on paper, studied, and discussed.

■ Chart and post each employee's accomplishments—recognition of successes helps balance job stress.

■ Stay organized and a little ahead of things.

■ Gather information on job stress and make it available to employees to read.

■ Create a daily or weekly half-hour exercise or meditation period during which employees can walk or do aerobics or simply rest, release stress, and rejuvenate themselves.

■ Reward employees after completing a difficult assignment. Treat them to lunch or let them go home early. Reinforce the fact that pressure is temporary and worth the feeling of a job well done.

■ Keep anger down. Find a way to let employees let off steam, such as taking a five-minute walk around the office. In addition to relieving tension, this will distance the angry person from coworkers and the problem and help you restore normalcy.

■ Encourage employees to have a life after work (that goes for managers, too). Working hard and playing hard is the key to a happy, healthy, balanced life. Nobody should ever let her work life rule her.

## MISTAKE 146

**Not taking preventive steps to minimize job-stress claims.**

### How to Avoid It

The original purpose of workers' compensation laws was to quickly return employees to full productivity. Today, many believe that workers' compensation simply pays an employee not to work and actually encourages the employee to exaggerate injuries for economic gain. In general, to qualify for stress-related compensation claims, an employee merely has to subjectively believe that his job has provoked stress. Though no preventive strategy can guarantee that employees will stop bringing stress claims, the manager who takes positive steps to minimize job-stress claims is planning wisely for the future.

■ Be very selective when hiring. Screen applicants to be sure they can handle the stress of a given job. By law, you cannot ask an applicant about past compensation claims or any physical symptoms associated with stress. However, frequent job changes may reveal someone who is trying to "outrun" a performance problem.

∎ Deal with performance problems immediately. Problems such as recurring absenteeism or insubordination may be the result of an employee's inability to deal with stress. By confronting the problem promptly, administering disciplinary action, and when necessary, discharge, you may remove potential stress claimants.

∎ Develop a substance-abuse policy. If substance abusers file claims, it may be impossible to distinguish that problem from bona fide job stress. A strict drug policy (within applicable laws and employee rights) may keep this from happening. Consult your labor counselor before implementing any program.

∎ Develop stress-management strategies. Be receptive to employee complaints about stress before the employee seeks outside help (such as the courts). If a problem exists, consider transferring the employee to a less stressful job.

∎ Take an active role in processing claims. Ask questions of your insurance carrier. Don't be afraid to make suggestions when appropriate.

# Chapter 5

## EVALUATING EMPLOYEES—
## THE RIGHT AND WRONG WAYS

### NINE CRITICAL MISTAKES IN CONDUCTING
### EMPLOYEE-PERFORMANCE REVIEWS

A workplace event more foreboding than taxes lurks in practically every employee's and manager's life. Some call it the performance review, others the performance appraisal. It occurs when a manager must objectively evaluate an employee's previous 3, 6, or 12 months of work, discuss and try to solve problems that may exist, grant promotions and raises, when due, and set new objectives for the future. And though the employee's security, advancement, and income are at stake, there is no question that conducting such reviews is also the second most dreaded and difficult job a manager has to contend with—the first being firing people.

### MISTAKE 147

**The company doesn't have formal review procedures.**

### MISTAKE 148

**Reviews are a low priority because they seldom produce results.**

#### HOW TO AVOID THEM

Most workers like to know how they are doing, and managers have an obligation to keep their employees apprised of their progress, or lack of progress, on the job.

While some companies conduct formal reviews at least once a year, they should really be an informal and continuous process. A sound review system, fairly administered, can be beneficial to a company and its employees. On the other hand, one that is not properly administered can result in lower performance, greater distrust, and legal problems. Some of the benefits of regular reviews include:

■ Keeping good people from getting buried in the system and exposing nonproductive people who disrupt the system.

■ Corrections of deficiencies and improved performance.

■ Providing helpful data for promotion decisions as well as being a basis for salary and wage adjustments, bonuses, and other financial rewards.

■ Establishing a baseline against which people can measure their own progress and encouraging them to take affirmative action to work toward more challenging goals.

■ Forcing communication between manager and staff. Even if a manager does not work closely with, or get along well with an employee, he still has to sit down, interact, and decide what they are going to accomplish together in the months ahead. Because there is no way of avoiding this communication, their working relationship is likely to improve as they get to know each other better.

■ Giving managers an overview and sense of how each person is coming along. Managers get to know their staff better and establish themselves as thoughtful and interested leaders.

■ Letting people sort out problems and prevent a buildup of aggravations and disappointments.

■ Providing an opportunity for managers to ask themselves what *they* have done to improve employees' performance.

Some of the drawbacks are:

■ Reviews often smack of blatantly subjective judgments and work against the very thing we desire—improved performance.

■ Many rating systems are poorly designed and present more problems than solutions.

■ Reviews are only as good as the people administering them.

▎ They sometimes cause distrust and the assumption that the boss knows more about an employee's skills, abilities, and commitment than the employee does.

▎ The manager's task is to appraise how a person has performed in her job during the period being reviewed, then match his perception of the individual's performance with the employee's own perception. All too often, the two disagree, resulting in feelings of unfair judgment by the employee.

▎ Reviews usually conclude with vague, half-hearted suggestions on how to improve performance.

Steps to follow to set up a fair reviewing process:

▎ Determine the frequency of employee reviews during a 12-month period. Scheduling only one a year turns it into an ominous day on the calendar. It also creates the temptation to let grievances and complaints pile up. Current trends suggest every 6 or 3 months, if possible.

▎ Performance appraisals should be conducted for *all* employees, not just hourly and rank-and-file workers. When a review system is instituted, it should be applied throughout the organization.

▎ Create a rating scale that measures performance and is directly linked to the job requirements. Most companies use a five-point appraisal system. A score of five means good performance. Don't be the kind of manager who ranks everyone a three so you won't lose favor with any employees.

▎ Supervisors should be trained on proper evaluation procedures.

▎ In preparing evaluations, managers should apply consistent, explicit, and objective job-related standards. To keep bias out of the review process, work performance—not the person performing the job—should be judged.

▎ Keep the review fair and on target. Using questions as a guide gives both reviewer and employee the opportunity to approach the situation objectively.

▎ Evaluate each employee's performance achievements and problem areas on a daily or weekly basis and make notes that go in each worker's file for future referral at review time. Write comments in terms of a person's observable behavior: "Joe's meeting went well today—he did his homework and presented his ideas succinctly. He answered every question that was thrown at him directly and to the point." All notes should be specific and dated. A performance review should never be general. You should always be able to refer to specific events and dates.

■ Reviews should be held in private. The performance-appraisal dialogue should be totally, completely personal. Circulation of evaluations should be restricted to those in management having a need to know.

■ Set aside enough time not just for the "bread and butter" issues such as past performance, goals and action plans, but also for the unexpected, such as personal problems that are responsible for lower performance. You don't want to rush through personal problems.

■ Evaluations should be prepared on a timely basis and never back-dated or altered after the fact.

■ An audit system should be established to guard against inflated appraisals and to ensure that evaluations are conducted in an unbiased manner.

■ Before an evaluation is communicated to the employee, it should be reviewed and approved by another manager or someone else above. Evaluations should not be malicious. They should be truthful, candid, yet constructive. They should also hold up legally.

■ Problem areas should be detailed and documented.

■ The employee should be given the opportunity to respond to a negative performance evaluation by giving his version of the facts.

■ When an employee's performance has been appraised as substandard, specific goals, agreed upon by the employee, should be set to improve deficiency areas. Appraisals are most effective when they contain a compliance timetable and secure the worker's commitment to comply.

■ The employer should be able to prove that an employee received the evaluation, either by having the worker sign for it or by having the employee's receipt witnessed by another supervisor.

■ In considering termination based on unsatisfactory job performance, earlier evaluations should be scrutinized to determine if the employee was informed of the deficiencies and if the evaluations are consistent with the stated reasons for the employee's dismissal.

## MISTAKE 149

Feeling uncomfortable criticizing an employee's performance.

## MISTAKE 150

Avoiding making hard decisions.

## MISTAKE 151

Underrating good people in fear these workers will become competitors.

## MISTAKE 152

Overrating poor performers rather than dealing with unhappy people.

## MISTAKE 153

Being afraid that if you give clear, serious feedback relating to an employee's performance, you will also receive candid feedback on your own performance.

## MISTAKE 154

Not evaluating employees objectively.

## MISTAKE 155

Not taking into account how the review will be used.

### HOW TO AVOID THEM

Reviews should provide a nonthreatening structure for discussing sensitive topics with employees. Handling the paperwork and other bureaucratic details is usually easy—the challenge comes with the actual review. Managers may relish a review when they can heap praise on a high performer. But when they must discuss and criticize an employee's shortcomings, the process becomes a painful and emotionally laden encounter that many managers would rather not have.

The following checklist can help you avoid the pitfalls and make the session productive for both you and the employee:

▮ *Be prepared*—do your homework, and stick to the point. Go over the records you have been keeping on the person being reviewed. Note specific accomplishments and problems. Have the backup with you. Decide what points you need to make and write them down so you won't forget them. Be aware of what nervousness does to your own best intentions. Stay calm; getting excited may cause you to overstate or understate certain points, or even worse, back off and fail to say what needs to be said. Focus on what you are there to accomplish.

▮ *Schedule the review and make it private.* You might want to make it somewhere other than your office and make sure you won't be interrupted. If you do it in your office, sit on an equal level with the worker, rather than behind your desk so as not to intimidate the person with the authority your desk may symbolize.

▮ *Allow enough time.*

▮ *Support yourself*—rehearse what you want to say. Get yourself as relaxed and focused as possible before going into the review.

▮ *Prepare the employee.* If you have an agenda of topics that will be discussed, give the person a copy and allow her to participate. This enhances her self-esteem, gives her a sense of control, and underscores the idea that the review should be of mutual benefit.

▮ *Be as specific as possible*—whether you're giving praise or criticism. "Your work was great this year" is not as specific or meaningful as "You exceeded your sales goal by 25 percent, more than anyone else in the department."

▮ *Always be objective.* There are times when managers must make some subjective judgments that can lead to problems, such as grouping everyone's ratings unreasonably toward the high end of the scale, to gain favor with employees. Or allowing a favorable judgment on one quality in order to overshadow a problem. Or allowing personal bias to affect the evaluation.

▮ *Know how the review will be used* and don't let it influence your judgment. For example, if you know the results of the review will be used only to set salaries, you might unconsciously give higher ratings. By contrast, if you believe that by giving a negative evaluation it might be a way to get rid of someone you don't like, the appraisal might be harsher than warranted.

▌ *Ask smart questions.* Managers who ask smart questions get the most from performance reviews and also eliminate tension by getting the person to be his own appraiser. Asking questions forces you to plan in advance for the review and helps clarify both your thinking and your employee's. By asking questions, you talk less and therefore obtain more information. Questions put the responsibility on the other person and encourage both parties to be more objective. Remember, questions lead somewhere—accusations are a dead end.

| | |
|---|---|
| EXAMPLE OF ACCUSATION: | "You're still not doing what we discussed last week." |
| EXAMPLE OF SMART QUESTION: | "How could that have happened again? What can we do to correct it once and for all?" |

▌ *Pace yourself.* Don't be nervous and rush the review just to get it over with. Go slowly. Don't overwhelm the employee. Allow him to respond, breathe and ask questions.

▌ *Give precise steps for improvement if called for.*

▌ *Don't blame the system.* If performance is a problem, deal with it directly. If there really are problems with the review system, discuss them and how they can be changed to support this person in doing better work, but also explain why performance did not justify a better rating.

▌ *Avoid surprises.* The review should never be the first time a problem (or praise) is mentioned.

▌ *Don't dwell on negatives.* Discussion of problems need to take place during evaluations, but the overall emphasis should not be negative. Look at what you can reinforce. How can you encourage a transfer of skill and discipline from the area of success to the problem area?

▌ *Don't do all the talking.* Is there a gap between performance and expectation? Let the one being appraised explain.

▌ *Don't rely on hearsay.* No matter how reliable the source, confirm it before you embrace it as fact. Get the person providing the information to put it in writing. A willingness to go on record at least gives you something tangible to work from.

▌ *Plan for action.* Get off past events quickly and focus on the ways you can improve performance together in the future.

■ *Summarize the review.* Begin with the person's accomplishments and move on to the plans the two of you have created to improve performance. Thank the employee for engaging in the review and tell her when she will receive her evaluation.

■ *Follow up.* Reward the worker as soon as you see his performance improving and show how that improvement has helped others. Encourage continued improvement and ask how you can help him maintain the new level of achievement.

## THREE COMMON MISTAKES IN EVALUATING DIFFICULT EMPLOYEES

It has been suggested by no greater a source than Hippocrates, that just about everyone in the entire world can be divided into four personality groups. And although each of us possesses characteristics common to all four groups, one dominant trait will point to a specific group. This may very well be true. But our research shows that *difficult* people can have many dominant traits and fit into multiple groups that you are likely to encounter in the workplace, each with his or her own distinctive behaviors. For example a Super-Star can also be a Perfectionist. An Avoider can also be a Denier. A Spineless Sap can also be a Gregarious Gossip.

### MISTAKE 156

**Avoiding confrontation.**

### MISTAKE 157

**Assuming the obligations of troubled employees rather than confronting them.**

### MISTAKE 158

**Not issuing punishments, or rewards.**

#### How to Avoid Them

Your success in dealing with difficult people and motivating them to change will largely depend on your authority and how far it goes. If workers see you as the source of tangible benefits, such as pay raises, and you have the ability to hire and fire, your position is much stronger. Remember, employees (difficult or not) are individuals; some respond to the stick and some to the carrot. Steps to take:

▪ The first step is to confront as soon as possible. Don't assign other workers to cover for problem employees, and don't _you_ cover, either. Problem workers can't learn to be responsible if you assume their obligations and bail them out of their difficulties. You will end up losing the respect of good employees or overloading your own schedule—and the problem will still be there. The longer you wait, or the more you shove the problem back down to the bottom of the pile hoping it will go away, the more serious the problem can get.

▪ Look for support. Look for similar cases and find out how they were solved.

▪ Meet privately. No interruptions.

▪ Build their self-confidence. Be a friend. Show them you understand where they are coming from.

▪ Help them balance their feelings. In presenting your side, focus on their concerns, then explain the mutual benefits of resolving the situation.

▪ Help them find answers. Ask questions that get them to identify their own alternatives for resolving their difficulty.

▪ Nudge, don't push. Move slowly and gently instead of aggressively. Be sincere and honest when expressing your complaints or in issuing reprimands.

▪ Stick to the issues. Raise the level of discussion when it sinks to personal attacks.

▪ Give them an opportunity to salvage their pride and graciously save face so that they can change their ways.

▪ Encourage them to ask questions. This will give you better insight into their problems.

▪ Be crystal-clear about your expectations and be smart; document them. Supplement your verbal orders with written instructions. Demonstrate your patience and reasonableness in anticipating their getting back on track.

▪ Discuss the consequences if they don't get back on track.

▪ Help them accept responsibility. Encourage their getting outside help, if needed.

▪ Agree on a plan with specific stages and tasks that will help the workers get from point A to point B.

▪ Be prepared to issue punishments or rewards.

---

## A COMMON MISTAKE WHEN DEALING WITH A SENSITIVE EMPLOYEE WHO CRIES OR BREAKS DOWN

---

You have reprimanded Kathy for work-related problems before. Each time she listened to what you had to say, and each time her eyes welled up with tears, she began crying, and each time she went back to making the same mistakes. Now you've got to bring the situation to a head during her evaluation, but she breaks down and cries uncontrollably.

## MISTAKE 159

**Getting angry, or not handling the situation compassionately when a problem worker cries.**

### How to Avoid It

Crying may be caused by a deep-seated psychological insecurity and is often used by people to:

▪ Avoid doing things they don't want to do.

▪ Help them get out of difficult situations.

▪ Use as a tool to manipulate others.

There is little you can do to help this employee. Change has to come from within. Perhaps the crying stems from the fact that the person is very sensitive or has experienced a serious circumstance, such as the illness of a loved one. Crying can also be the result of a depressive disorder and the medication used to correct it. In any case, it is important, whenever possible, to find out the cause of the problem from coworkers or family. With this information, you can wait for a "normal" period to confront the person and show that you are concerned about her situation. Steps to take:

▌ Prepare yourself. If you know the employee is a crier, find a coworker who can give you some helpful information about the person or someone knowledgeable about emotional reactions and learn all you can about how to handle the situation before your confrontation. If this is not possible, you will have to act without knowing all you need to know, which may result in a tense time, for the employee, other employees, and you.

▌ Meet privately.

▌ When the employee starts crying, keep your cool. Do not explode or show your anger. Offer a tissue.

▌ Keep quiet and wait for the person to stop.

▌ If medical or psychological problems underlie a crying tantrum, you might suggest that the employee see a physician. If your company has an employee-assistance program, strongly suggest that she use it. Serious emotional problems are truly an illness. Regardless of how irrational and irritating a worker may seem, she may not be able to control her emotions.

▌ If the problem concerns a serious personal circumstance, hear the person out (if she is willing to talk about it). Be a friend. Express your understanding and desire to help and support. Explain that coworkers are also concerned. If the worker is not willing to talk about something so personal, you have to ask questions. Explain why you are asking these sensitive questions. By explaining why the information is necessary, the employee is more likely to see the benefit in providing you with the data. If you lay a foundation for the question before asking it, she may anticipate the question and be prepared to answer it. This helps eliminate suspicion and reduce anxiety over sensitive questions.

▌ Bear with the crying and be considerate of the person's feelings, but don't coddle the worker. Insist that she do her job properly.

▌ Document the incident and others that occurred earlier.

▌ If you consider the employee worth it, you'll have to invest more time and effort in bringing that person on track. It sometimes takes lots of time, energy, and care to grow great employees.

▌ Despite a person's emotional condition, you do not have to tolerate crying. If her actions interfere excessively with her work, you are within your rights to transfer her to a less stressful position.

## SIX MISTAKES IN DEALING WITH EMPLOYEES WHO DENY ERRORS OR THINK YOU'RE UNFAIR

Evaluations become even tougher for managers when problem workers think you are unfair or when they simply refuse to acknowledge a problem with their performance—even in the face of overwhelming evidence.

### MISTAKE 160

**Not helping your workers be honest about their mistakes.**

### MISTAKE 161

**Allowing deniers to delay meeting with you regarding performance problems.**

#### HOW TO AVOID THEM

Employees who think they are helping themselves by denying blame for their errors are really missing a chance to learn from those mistakes and improve their future performance. You can help deniers to be honest about their mistakes by:

■ Insisting on an immediate meeting with the employee as soon as you get your first negative feedback. Don't take no for an answer.

■ Don't let the denier get away with dishonesty. Otherwise, other employees will resent your lack of courage, while the denier becomes bolder.

Deniers know their manager makes the decisions on promotions and salary increases. So rather than risk looking bad in his eyes by admitting bad performance during a review, they will blame everybody and everything instead. Their typical excuses are, "Who, me?" Or, "It wasn't my fault!" Or, "It was because of budget cutbacks." Or, "My coworkers won't cooperate with me!" These are people who:

■ May lie to cover up some problem such as arguing with a coworker one minute then vehemently denying there's a disagreement.

▮ Are unrealistic about their ability to perform.

▮ Have inflated opinions about their skills.

▮ Are defensive when criticized.

▮ Don't know, care, or understand how their behavior affects coworkers.

▮ Will disagree with you about what constitutes good performance, or will disagree with you about how good performance should be measured.

## MISTAKE 162

**Allowing deniers to drag you down to their level of mud-slinging.**

### How to Avoid It

Steps to take:

▮ Don't lower yourself into a shouting match battle of accusations. Deal with clear expectations. These need to be written down to make certain both parties agree on how the job is to be done. Once the denier agrees, use them as criteria for future performance evaluations.

▮ Never call the person a liar, even if you have hard evidence. The denier won't admit to lying.

▮ Let deniers know you view honesty as important an asset as competence.

▮ Tell them you consider admitting mistakes as a sign of maturity, and give them positive reinforcement when they admit their errors.

▮ Make sure all employees know that your role is helping them do their job better.

▮ Focus on solving their problems rather than finding fault. Confront with data, not hearsay or speculation. Identify performance barriers and show why they are unacceptable.

▮ Formulate specific steps the employees can take to improve future performance.

▮ You may want to lose to win. By not refuting a denial, you can tell the denier you're "calling it a draw. That the past doesn't interest you as much as the future." Indicate your specific expectations for the future. Write them down. Give the denier a copy, put a copy in the denier's file.

## MISTAKE 163

**Being too quick to blame.**

### How to Avoid It

Don't rush to place the blame when performance problems arise. An employee's excuse may not necessarily be just an excuse; the employee may not actually be responsible (or fully responsible) for the problem. One stumbling block that appears during performance appraisals is that employees and managers have different ideas concerning poor performance and its causes. The employee may be too quick in denying responsibility, but the manager may be too quick in placing all or some of the blame on the worker.

## MISTAKE 164

**Viewing an employee's poor performance as a threat.**

### How to Avoid It

Check your own performance and attitude. Ask yourself if you're being open and fair. Poor employee performance can be the result of poor managerial supervision. Some managers faced with this problem will quickly blame employees for failures. A better approach is to make an honest assessment of the extent to which poor supervision or other factors may have played a role. Have you explained the importance of doing something a certain way? Do you turn mistakes into learning experiences for both of you?

## MISTAKE 165

**Not finding the true cause of an employee's failure.**

### How to Avoid It

It's impossible to prevent all employee failure. But when poor performance becomes an issue, it's up to you as a manager to investigate the situation objectively and determine the cause. Steps to take:

■ Look over the employee's overall record and compare it to how other employees perform the same tasks.

■ If everyone does poorly with a particular job, the task may be the problem.

■ If over a period of time the employee's record was good and then suddenly was marred by failure, look to external causes.

■ If the employee performs poorly on all tasks, you must present your evidence and identify how the performance is to be corrected in specific job-related terms.

■ Finally, identify specific corrective action that will be taken if the poor performance continues.

## A COMMON MISTAKE IN FAIRLY EVALUATING PEOPLE YOU REALLY DON'T LIKE

Just as you would want your performance to be objectively evaluated by your superiors, so do your employees.

### MISTAKE 166

**Letting personal feelings interfere with your work relationships or evaluations of a person's job performance.**

#### How to Avoid It

This is a bad management approach that not only demoralizes the employee, but causes loss of managerial respect and credibility with coworkers. Personality traits seldom have anything to do with the performance of a worker, and a good manager can't let his own personal feelings interfere with his appraisals of a worker's performance. Considering performance alone is the only fair way to evaluate a worker. Steps to take:

■ If the worker is falling short of standards, resolve your differences with a face-to-face discussion.

■ Show the employee that you are willing to put aside your personal feelings in order to get the job done right. That you are impartial and up-front about job performance, that you use the quality of a person's work as the only guideline in evaluating him.

■ Observations about the employee's work should be made directly and privately. Don't discuss what you perceive as an employee's failings with the person's coworkers. There are always people eager to spread rumors, and your remarks will eventually find their way through the workplace grapevine to the employee in question. This can be even more shattering to that person's self-esteem than the comments you make to him in private.

■ Try to set the proper tone for the meeting, otherwise it will result in bruised feelings.

■ Be specific about what steps should be taken to improve performance and how to reach those steps. If the worker claims that poor performance is based on company-related problems such as inadequate equipment or supplies, you must investigate that claim.

■ Be sure the employee knows what action must be taken once an agreed-upon standard is not met.

---

## THREE COMMON MISTAKES IN GETTING TIMID EMPLOYEES TO OPEN UP

---

While screening applicants during the hiring process can sort out potential problems, screening devices are not the final solution to a problem-free workplace. Employees who may seem "perfect" when hired can subsequently exhibit behavior they did not show during initial interviews or become involved in extremely stressful personal or workplace situations. It is important to realize that different employees react differently to criticism, no matter how constructive it may be. Timid employees, however, are more challenging than others because while they may be highly competent, they have low self-confidence and self-image. This may make your one-on-one discussions more difficult and require some additional skill in handling to help get the employee back on track.

### MISTAKE 167

**Being reluctant to confront a timid employee about poor job performance because she is difficult to speak with.**

### MISTAKE 168

**Avoiding confrontation with a timid employee because you are afraid of saying the wrong thing and making the situation worse.**

## MISTAKE 169

**Not discussing performance problems with timid employees because you're concerned about invading the employee's privacy or inquiring into areas that you're not equipped to handle.**

### How to Avoid Them

We've said it before and it's worth repeating—the long-term effects of ignoring poor performance can be much more devastating than a manager's short-term discomfort about confronting it.

When criticizing the performance of a timid person, you are likely to get two kinds of responses: the person may agree too quickly to avoid emphasis on the problem or to cover up a disagreement with the manager's viewpoint; the person may not want to enter into the conversation freely and may even hesitate at answering direct questions.

When dealing with employees with low self-confidence, managers can keep the discussion on a helpful, objective level by anticipating negative reactions and knowing how to circumvent them.

What to look for:

■ Timid people are well-meaning, good-natured, and often competent, but just don't seem to be on target.

■ They sometimes feel left out, unimportant, or simply forgotten.

■ They try to avoid confrontation with coworkers and customers and view conflict as being destructive. They are the kind of workers who are nervous and afraid to ask work-related questions in fear others will laugh at them or lose respect for them.

■ They often feel that they don't have control of situations and are searching for some kind of stability.

■ They may not be aware of the low esteem in which they are held by coworkers, superiors, or customers. Sometimes, they believe they are doing better than they actually are, regarding both their performance and their relationships with others.

■ Often, they are the objects of practical jokes that too many other coworkers go along with.

■ They don't like to hear bad or disruptive news.

■ For the sake of being liked, they will accept mediocrity, tolerate unacceptable behavior, and fail to address situations in which a decisive response might generate controversy.

The following are Don'ts and Do's with timid problem workers:

Don't laugh or in any way participate in jokes aimed at timid employees.

Do have compassion. If you show that you have interest and confidence in their doing well, that will go a long way to boosting their self-esteem.

Don't allow your discomfort with timid persons prevent you from confronting poor performance situations.

Do recognize that these persons' behavior is a reflection on your company. Until they change, this message will continue to be communicated to coworkers and customers.

Steps to take:

- Before calling a meeting with the problem worker, be sure discipline is called for, then find out as much as you can about the person in order to try and understand the cause of his lack of confidence. Hold the discussion in private.

- Don't begin your meeting with a challenge, threat, or by frightening the person with irrefutable evidence of his poor work. This will only make the person even less self-confident and make it harder for you to pry loose the information you will need to help. Emphasize the positives you see before getting to the negatives. Have clear goals for the discussion.

- Make sure the environment is relaxed. Be calm and in control of your emotions. Use open-ended questions to help draw out the possible reasons for the inadequate performance. Practice effective listening skills, being particularly careful to use pauses to encourage discussion.

- Consider possible ways you or coworkers might contribute to his problem. For example, are you an intimidating boss?

- Focus on specific behavior that the worker can change. If the person is the nervous type, put him at ease by mentioning a shared experience, a common hobby, something in the news that day.

- If the problem is that the person is in a situation he is not skilled enough to handle, put him in something he can do well. He will appreciate the gesture.

- Help the timid person to set and look forward to ambitious goals. Force him to create plans to achieve those goals. Provide coaching and counseling as he works on them.

■ Put the timid employee in a position to help someone else. This will help bolster self-confidence.

■ Link the timid person with other workers who have high self-esteem and the success that generally accompanies such self-esteem.

■ You may want to engage the timid person in self-effacing behaviors. Get him to laugh at his mistakes, admit his failures, or share his fears and weaknesses. Show him that his imperfections don't have to translate into disasters, and in fact, could become great assets.

■ Put yourself in the timid worker's shoes. Think about the possible benefits he can gain by becoming more assertive, such as pay raises, extra benefits, and other rewards.

■ Document past successes. Force the timid person to see exactly what, if anything, he did well and how it has benefited the company.

■ If you uncover a fear of failing, make it clear that in your role as manager, you will be there with your support.

■ Getting a solid commitment from the worker is essential to ensuring that any agreed-upon actions are carried out. Establish a follow-up plan.

■ If the employee overcomes his problems, show your praise.

■ End on a positive note.

## FOUR MISTAKES IN USING FEEDBACK TO TURN CLARK KENTS INTO SUPERMEN

When a missile is launched toward its target, it will most certainly go off course and never reach its goal without constant feedback. Employees are the same way. No one starts out in life to become a failure. Most people want to succeed and are willing to do what it takes to be successful. By using direct, honest feedback, you can help turn your employees with performance problems into winners who make a meaningful contribution. The result is more motivated employees who stay on course and find greater satisfaction in their work.

But effective communication between people is not always easy. It's something every manager has to work at in order for it to work at all. The proper use of questioning skills helps. Utilizing active listening helps. Sensitivity to nonverbal behavior helps. But without feedback, all of these skills are for naught. Through the effective use of feedback skills, you can create a good communications climate.

## MISTAKE 170

**Assuming you know exactly what the other person means.**

### How to Avoid It

Never assume anything in communications. If you do, you stand a good chance of being totally wrong. Never assume that you and the other person are talking about the same thing. Or that the words and phrases you are both using are automatically being understood. During interpersonal communications, it is very dangerous to assume that the other person either thinks or feels as you do at that moment. She may have her own world view, personal and professional history, value system and frame of reference that is totally different from yours. She will perceive and react according to what she believes to be true, which can be very different from your perceptions, reactions, and beliefs.

Unlike written communication, effective feedback takes place only during a two-way conversation in which both parties speak openly, listen to each other's point of view, and understand exactly what the other says and means. And that is where the problem comes in.

Interpretation of words or phrases, for instance, may vary from person to person, region to region, business to business, or society to society. Many words we use in everyday conversations have multiple meanings. The 500 most commonly used words in our language have nearly 15,000 dictionary definitions. Take the word "fast" as an example. A runner can be "fast." A promiscuous woman is sometimes considered "fast." So is a race track in good condition, a ship's mooring line, a period of noneating, or film sensitive to light. Get the idea? Assuming that you understand the meaning of an employee's communication, when in fact you really don't, leads to future misunderstandings, breakdowns in the communications process, and decreased trust.

The answer? Managers must give and get definitions. They must understand how their employees perceive events and why they act as they do. They must remain open to employees' ideas for self-improvement. When you "tell" your employees how they are doing, they miss out on valuable feedback that should be coming back to them. A manager might think poor performance is the result of the employee's carelessness, when in fact it may be the result of a problem with a particular process.

## MISTAKE 171

**Not staying current with your feedback.**

### How to Avoid It

The more immediate the information, the more useful it is to prevent a problem from mushrooming into a crisis. Give feedback when there is still time to correct the problem. Don't wait for deadlines or evaluation time before you lay on the bad news. It will result in employee resentment for "being convicted without knowing they committed the crime."

Timeliness applies to positive feedback, too. Immediate recognition of a job well done is far more appreciated than a delayed recognition. Feedback, positive and negative, should be spontaneous and given in an atmosphere of trust.

## MISTAKE 172

**Letting an employee wander off course and then not explaining why the performance is wrong and how to do it better.**

### How to Avoid It

Developing people or attempting to change their behavior requires more of you than gathering information about what the person did wrong. You must also show him why it's wrong and how to do it right. You must state your belief in the person's ability to make the change and commit to supporting the worker during the change effort.

## MISTAKE 173

**Not clarifying your intentions for feedback.**

### How to Avoid It

To evaluate workers effectively, managers must genuinely want to help them. Otherwise, the exchange will run into emotional barriers and produce uninspired ideas for improvements.

Suppose someone's poor performance disrupts your department. You get irritated, and in confronting the employee, you imply that he made you look bad, and you resent him for it. This unspoken message actually drowns out the verbal feedback that could help the person correct the problem. Steps to take:

■ Make and document observations. When employees disagree, question, or react emotionally to feedback, managers can restate the observations that initially prompted the feedback. Observations make feedback "real" for workers and give them a chance to clarify their viewpoints. If the manager thinks an employee lacks responsibility, that belief should be backed with specific instances in which the employee showed lack of responsibility. The employee might then elaborate on the circumstances, proving the real reason was because of a problem in another department. This new information should prompt the manager to revise the employee's assessment and correct the interdepartmental problem.

■ Make assessments on poor performers, but be sure to use the same behavior and performance standards for all employees. To ensure that feedback prompts desirable action, be certain that employees understand the assessment. If you tell a worker, "You're not skilled enough for this task," explain clearly what "not skilled enough" means in this context.

■ Discuss consequences. In the case of poor performers, the consequences might include transfer or termination. In the case of good performers, consequences might include promotion, bonuses, opportunities for new assignments. During feedback, the manager and employee should discuss the known or possible consequences of a given action so there won't be any mistakes about what they are. If you state consequences, you must also be able to enforce them.

■ Help your employee identify a goal for improvement and a solid plan for achieving the goal. Identify a specific result, a target date for achieving the result, and steps the employee will take to achieve the goal. Just as a manager must observe specifically what an employee's behavior lacks, she must also specify the behaviors that constitute a successful performance. Managers who can't envision a desired result can often get help by asking the employee how he might do his job more effectively. Workers often have the answers themselves. If employees disagree with your suggestions, that's normal. Explore alternatives. Let the employee feel he solved his own problem.

Managers who master the basics of effective feedback can turn losers into winners, and enjoy the peace of mind that comes with saying what they mean, meaning what they say, and helping employees perform to the best of their abilities.

## TWO MISTAKES IN RESPONDING TO AN EMPLOYEE WHO CRITICIZES YOU

Just as you care enough to criticize your employees objectively and honestly so they will learn to perform better, criticism of you by an employee is an opportunity for *you* to learn more about yourself, be a more effective manager, and identify deficiencies you may have that need correcting.

There are infinite reasons why subordinates don't always see their supervisors as supervisors see themselves. There are also infinite reasons why they will criticize you, often behind your back. They may be jealous, feel you are condescending toward them, or that you're too pushy. All of which can make the best of managers upset, frustrated, and angry.

Your objective is to clear the air and, if justified, use the criticism to your advantage. You can't allow others to make you feel diminished with their negative criticism of you. Just because you're not perfect does not mean you're not effective. Just because someone is rude or inconsiderate doesn't mean that you did or said something offensive. If you can learn to accept criticism as a vehicle for improvement, the less stressed and more motivated and effective you will become. To do this, you must think and respond differently to criticism when it's *you* on the receiving end.

## MISTAKE 174

**Getting defensive when being criticized by an employee.**

## MISTAKE 175

**Feeling guilty, incompetent, or angry when criticized by a subordinate.**

## How to Avoid Them

You must not only control the meaning you attach to criticism, you must also control how you respond to it. Here are seven tips that will help:

1. *Listen.* Don't interrupt or counterattack. Accept whatever is said that's accurate and fair. Focus on the criticism, not the criticizer.

2. *Give a positive response.* If the criticism is accurate, thank the person for bringing the matter to your attention. If it's not, thank the person anyway for taking the time and effort to make you aware of his opinion. Show you understand the criticizer's thoughts.

3. *Question the criticizer.* Your questions will lead your critic to specific answers. Use the critic's adjectives and adverbs as springboards for further questions, "What did I do, specifically, that showed you I'm uncaring?" Don't speak in a sarcastic tone, it only makes communication more difficult.

4. *Assess the validity of the criticism.* If the criticizer is right, accept the fact that you're not perfect, apologize for your mistake, promise you won't repeat it. If the criticism is invalid, ask questions that require specific answers so you can determine what your critic expects of you. She may have a false image of you or may have expected you to act in a certain way. Determine what actions you can take to correct the problem.

5. *Take responsibility for what you did, if you did it*—without putting yourself down. Admit your mistake and ask your critic for suggestions on how to improve your performance as a manager. This lets you focus on solutions instead of feeling guilty or incompetent. If the criticism is vague, acknowledge the possibility that some of the criticism may be true. Ask more questions, continue listening, and judge for yourself if your critic is accurate.

6. *Take a breather.* If the criticism is vague, unjustified, or requires a thoughtful response, take some time to think about it. Don't say something you may regret later. Give yourself time to decide how you want to respond and what action you will take. You'll be more objective with your response; your critic will be more receptive.

7. *Take action.* If the criticism is valid, don't make excuses or rationalize what you did. Actions always speak louder than words, so show your critic how serious you are about correcting and avoiding future mistakes.

## SEVEN MISTAKES SUPERVISORS MAKE WHEN PRAISING EMPLOYEES

A client of mine had a saying that he repeated to just about everybody he came in contact with, especially managers: "Criticize up, praise down." His point was, managers should make their complaints up the ladder, because sometimes it's the only way to get action. At the same time, they should praise the efforts of employees as they occur, because praise has the greatest potential to sustain improvements in performance. His philosophy was that while criticism of employees might kill pride, shatter self-esteem, and destroy desire, praising them builds new skills, stimulates self-confidence, and enriches performance. Many companies have discovered that to help people learn, praise must be specific and precise. "You did a great job," is better than no praise at all, but if you want to help an employee grow, try: "You did a great job. Here's what made it great . . ."

Unfortunately, many managers, in their relationships with subordinates, fall short of giving credit where it's due.

## MISTAKE 176

**Taking a wait-and-see attitude.**

### HOW TO AVOID IT

The timeliness of your praise is of critical importance to its influence on sustaining improvement. The longer the period of time between the actual performance and the occurrence of praise, the less influence the praise has. If someone corrects a bad behavior today, thank him face to face today rather than wait to express your appreciation a week from now, or give him a raise five months from now, or wonder if he is genuinely motivated, or if he is cooperating only to get something in return?

## MISTAKE 177

**Feeling entitled to the improved behavior.**

### How to Avoid It

Not praising someone because "they are only doing their job," is self-destructive behavior on the manager's part. Individuals are motivated by achievement and praise, not by failure or criticism. As they experience little bits of achievements and the praise that goes with it, they are motivated to try for more achievements.

## MISTAKE 178

**Not realizing the motivational power of praise.**

### How to Avoid It

Even though managers desperately want their own accomplishments to be acknowledged, they fail to empathize with the same need in others. Most people want to feel accepted, valued, and worthwhile. They want approval from others, particularly from those they respect and have to answer to. The complimentary words that a manager communicates to his employees translate to recognition of their achievements. No matter how mundane a job may be, praise makes the worker feel that her job has value and meaning. This is essential not only for a healthy and productive work force, but also for a healthy and productive company. As a manager, for instance, you may not be able to do much to change the tasks in a mail room. But with praise, you can imbue it with importance by showing the employees that tasks done properly are necessary and vital to the organization.

One of the principal tools of management is vocabulary. But many managers and companies do a poor job of communicating with their workers. So never pass up a chance to give a "thank you," for work well done—you'll find those two little words the best interpersonal motivators a manager can use to correct nonperformance problems.

## MISTAKE 179

**Not giving praise because you feel uncomfortable.**

## How to Avoid It

Overcome any feelings of getting too personal with employees or feeling uncomfortable when expressing appreciation and acknowledging someone's good work. For those times when praise is due, you should give it—and as publicly as possible. Let everyone know what a good job a particular employee did. It will not only boost his self-esteem, it will probably boost yours, too, and be a motivating force for other employees. You may have heard the saying: "Give praise publicly; keep criticism private." One successful company president we interviewed agreed, and added: "If you want to give a person credit, put it in writing and circulate it throughout the company. If you want to give him hell, do it on the phone."

## MISTAKE 180

**Qualifying or negating praise.**

## How to Avoid It

If you're giving someone praise, nothing more is necessary. There is no need or reason to add on qualifying or negative statements to the praise you give someone who is finally cooperating, such as: "Great job, Sally, too bad you didn't do it like this all along." By doing this, the good you accomplish with your praise is wiped out by the qualification.

## MISTAKE 181

**Praising the person more than the behavior.**

## How to Avoid It

When acknowledging improved performance, focus your praise on the new performance—on *what* the person has done right. Tell her why you are happy about it, and tell her how important it is for her to continue performing so well.

## MISTAKE 182

**Praising only superstars.**

## How to Avoid It

All employees who are doing their jobs well not only deserve, but require praise for both individual and teamwork accomplishments if they are expected to consistently perform at a high level. While many companies build their business on good, reliable performers, plus a few superstars, all too often it's the superstar who gets the praise and recognition while the reliable performers, who meet or exceed their quota, are taken for granted, instead of being treated like winners, too.

# Chapter 6

# KEEPING EMPLOYEES HAPPY— HINDSIGHT AND FORESIGHT

## TWO MISTAKES IN DEALING WITH EMPLOYEE RIGHTS, SALARIES, BENEFITS, AND INCENTIVES

In speaking with entrepreneurs during our research for this book, we noted that retaining key personnel was cited as a critical management problem, and two of the prime factors contributing to this problem was management's lack of fairness and recognition for the rights of employees. Dealing with valued employees who believe they have been treated unfairly or discriminated against can be a setback for any company, particularly a small business, where virtually every worker plays a pivotal role. Too often, businesses spend time and money training employees, only to have them file complaints against management and/or coworkers and eventually leave the company.

All companies, to some degree, have policies and practices that determine how employees are to be treated both by those in authority and by coworkers. Some policies are federal and state laws and regulations. Some are codified as rules in employee handbooks. Some are mandatory, others optional. And some are unwritten practices that have a profound impact on relationships within the workplace.

By accepting a job, a person also accepts the policies, practices, rules, regulations, and taboos that go along with it. This means an employee can be ordered to perform unpleasant tasks, be promoted, demoted, transferred, intimidated, fired, or laid-off without warning or explanation. Understanding the rules can help both managers and employees function efficiently in an organization. Failure to do so can result in innumerable roadblocks, frustrations, and wasted effort and time. Many rights that people enjoy and take for granted as American citizens do not exist for them in the workplace. For instance, the Bill of Rights to the U.S. Constitution protects freedom of speech, prohibits unreasonable search and seizure, and provides for due process and trial by one's peers. Yet American companies routinely penalize employees who speak their minds, routinely search their desks without a second thought of privacy, and routinely require employees to submit to tests for drugs. And even worse, workers are routinely fired without warning or having recourse within the company.

There are laws protecting employees from certain abuses regarding minimum wages, overtime pay, sexual harassment, and discrimination. There are federal and state health and safety codes, too, but for most day-to-day problems, the law offers little comfort. Employees who believe they were terminated unfairly do have the right to sue, but few workers have the time, money, and stomach to go through the process. And while union contracts can provide some measure of fairness and stability and help to make individual employees less likely to be singled out for abuse, they do little to prevent employer's abusive behavior toward all employees as a group.

## MISTAKE 183

**Not knowing or protecting the rights of your employees.**

## MISTAKE 184

**Not assuring fairness to all employees.**

### HOW TO AVOID THEM

You must recognize the vulnerability of your employees and provide safeguards to assure that they are not exploited. Here are some steps you can take to protect and keep them happy, while helping your firm retain key staff members:

■ Acquaint yourself with some of the more important federal and state laws that protect the rights of employees. Read whatever you can that's relevant. Also be sure you are aware of all the rules, regulations, and policies that your company has regarding employees. That includes job descriptions, sample forms, and particularly standard operating procedures.

▋ Stay tuned to what's going on in your department. Listen carefully and you will be able to pick up on the attitudes, concerns, and dominant values of your staff.

▋ Counter the imbalance of power between the company and the individual employee by extending rights to employees. When a company guarantees rights, it places limitations on its own power and goes a long way toward building trust in the workplace. Rights show good faith on the part of management by directly addressing the problem of employee vulnerability. Such rights are: the right to appeal decisions the employee considers unfair; the right to full and accurate information (except other employees' personnel records, plans that could be used by competitors, and sensitive financial data); the right to free speech and opinions concerning work issues without fear of retribution; the right to confront those in authority and appeal unfair treatment to others higher up without fear of retribution; the right not to participate in the "big happy family/team" if they prefer to put in their 40 hours a week working alone; the right to have other commitments besides work in their lives.

▋ Reduce class distinctions. This means not treating employees like second-class citizens and management personnel like first-class aristocrats. Many companies have, for example, an executive dining room that is off limits to most employees. If the purpose for having a dining room is to entertain customers, that's fine. However, the facility should also be available to any employee or group of employees with a good reason to use it, such as for an employee function. Executive bathrooms and parking spaces, and other perks such as stock options and "golden parachutes" also accentuate the existence of a privileged class.

▋ Examine salaries and benefits. Check the salaries you pay your workers against the competition's and according to the Fair Labor Standards Act. Without appropriate compensation, it's virtually impossible to retain your best employees. The salary structure should reflect the relative value of different jobs to the business. Employees will be resentful if they believe a coworker with less responsibility or a less important job earns more than they do. To check the fairness of your salary structure, list all positions according to their value to the company. Then see whether the salaries assigned to the jobs follow the same progression. Then check the benefits. The first "extra" employees look at is health insurance (a benefit, not a right), and the importance of other benefits varies depending on the demographics of your work force. For example, older employees will focus on pension and savings plans, while younger workers with children will put a premium on flexible working hours and child-care subsidies.

■ Avoid favoritism. This is especially important when you have friends or family members working for you. Other employees will be particularly looking for and expecting favoritism. Compensation should be based on performance, and there must be consistency throughout the company and its departments. If supervisors want to give their friends and family members more money, they should give it as a gift, not as a paycheck. (See Chapter 12—Family Members in the Same Business.)

■ Use incentive plans—especially those that link part of an employee's compensation to performance. Because each employee's needs are different, effective reward systems must be flexible. If possible, rewards should be adapted to each individual employee. By asking employees to identify their primary needs, you can work out reward mixes to match those desires. Well-designed plans improve operating results and increase worker satisfaction by demonstrating to employees that extra effort is rewarded. It also encourages them to identify more closely with the company. Incentives range from occasional bonuses, which can include rewards large enough to be worth working for, to profit sharing and employee equity. In general, it is best for incentives to cover the shortest feasible time period. A monthly or quarterly award motivates employees better than an annual one. The timing when rewards are received can be as important to an employee as the reward itself. Two or three extra days off is a welcome reward for a job well done. But saying they must be taken in the middle of the week will not be as appreciated as at the beginning or end of the week. One thing to remember: If you do offer incentives, have your plan checked out by a lawyer familiar with employment law.

■ Share information about company performance, especially when profits are low. The more employees know about the business, the more they understand what is going on. Such sharing of information also helps maintain employees' commitment.

## A COMMON MISTAKE THAT COULD RESULT
## IN GIVING THE COMPANY AWAY

The ultimate incentive for an employee is a share in company ownership through stock or stock options. While equity can help attract and retain top managers, it has pitfalls for small, closely held companies.

## MISTAKE 185

**Making employees into owners who behave like competitors.**

### How to Avoid It

While those who own a part of the company and have a stake in its success are far less likely to behave in ways that hurt productivity and profits, giving away pieces of the company does create minority-owner rights. That could be a major problem if, for example, you run the business to minimize taxable profits rather than to maximize pretax profits. In this case, a disgruntled employee/stockholder might decide to sue for breach of fiduciary obligations to minority stockholders. A successful employee-ownership program should be based on the following guidelines:

- The greater the percentage of employee ownership, the more employees should be involved in making decisions that affect their work.

- The adversarial relationship between labor and management must give way to cooperation. Everyone must learn to give a little in the interest of long-range prosperity.

- Employee ownership should be in voting stock. Unless employees can vote their stock, they aren't really owners.

- Employee owners need to realize that ownership carries with it basic responsibilities such as patience and hard work.

An alternative to making employees owners is to create a "phantom stock plan" or similar arrangement that gives key employees an opportunity to share in long-term growth. In this way, you will encourage employees to think as owners without diluting equity. These types of plans offer bonuses based, for instance, on a company's growth in value. Before instituting such a plan, make sure you are comfortable with the amount of financial information you may be required to share with employees.

Rewarding people with a piece of the action is no sure cure for poor management. But when carried out as part of a well-planned program of employee participation, it can give morale, motivation, and productivity a real boost.

## TWO COMMON MISTAKES IN GIVING EMPLOYEES ROOM TO GROW

The most effective method of retaining employees is by having them develop strong bonds with the company and identify with its success. Though workers look for financial satisfaction from their jobs, they also want to feel respected, listened to, and appreciated. They want to feel they are contributing to the company, doing work that is meaningful and growing personally.

### MISTAKE 186

**Not letting your employees know you're aware of their dissatisfactions.**

### MISTAKE 187

**Not correcting the way work is structured to make it more interesting and meaningful to the worker.**

#### How to Avoid Them

If you can change the way work is structured to make it more meaningful and enjoyable or increase advancement potential for even a few of your key workers, as long as it doesn't have an adverse effect on others, do it! Steps to take:

- Create a system of cross-training. This will allow key workers to substitute for one another, which not only helps out when you're short-handed, it also gives employees a change of normal routine that can be refreshing.

- Decentralize decision making. Involve key employees more in the decision-making process. You already have taught them how to do their jobs well. Now, instead of telling them how to do each and every thing you need done, talk to them about overall goals and leave the details up to them.

∎ Create opportunities for your employees to have direct contact with the recipients of their efforts—either within or outside the company. By seeing how their efforts benefit others, their work becomes much more meaningful.

∎ Show them you're on their side. If their jobs truly are boring and dead end, let your people know you're aware of their dissatisfactions and that you will try to make things better. Let them know that by doing a good job, you'll help them move onward and upward. If your employees think of you as an empathetic supervisor, it will be more difficult for them to imagine that you are treating them unfairly.

## THREE COMMON MISTAKES IN CREATING A NURTURING ENVIRONMENT

Letting your employees know that you are as concerned about them as you are about the success of the company will go a long way in keeping them happy and keeping them from leaving.

### MISTAKE 188

**Overlooking the value of the individual.**

### MISTAKE 189

**Not paying attention to your employees' personal needs.**

### MISTAKE 190

**Not recognizing individual differences.**

#### How to Avoid Them

You must show support for your employees through frequent two-way communication. Encourage workers to talk about what's on their minds. Listen to what they are saying and ask questions that will help "get it all out." If they have personal problems, offer coaching. If they are dissatisfied with something in the workplace, find out what, and why. Arrange for a private meeting. Discuss the employee's work, how much you appreciate the good job he has been doing, how much you like the individual personally, and how concerned you are that he is dissatisfied. In addition to finding out what's bothering him, get him to tell you his attitudes toward the company. If the motive is financial, perhaps a raise is needed. If it relates to the way he thinks he's being treated, either by management or his coworkers, discuss the situation and suggest a plan to correct it. Perhaps as a manager you are not recognizing that every worker does not fit into the same mold and that allowances have to be made for those differences to help all employees fit in. Try to resolve any problems the employee may have with the job itself and discuss any other factors that led to his dissatisfaction. Employees stay when they feel they belong and that they are cared about and listened to.

---

## TWO MISTAKES IN USING SURVEYS AND EXIT INTERVIEWS TO RETAIN EMPLOYEES

---

One of the best ways to get information that will help you create a work environment that will encourage key employees to stay is from the employees themselves. Companies large and small are using, and paying attention to, annual employee surveys and exit interviews.

### MISTAKE 191

**Not conducting surveys to get answers before they leave.**

#### How to Avoid It

Establish once-a-year employee surveys that will give you a good look at employee attitudes. Using unsigned questionnaires, it allows the employees to be frank with their answers, which in turn become more valuable to you as tools to improve their happiness.

### MISTAKE 192

**Not asking them why when they leave.**

#### How to Avoid It

An exit interview should be used when an employee leaves voluntarily. It consists of a written questionnaire and oral communications geared to get the facts and the flavor of what's behind an employee's decision to leave. Sometimes the reason is superficial. The exit interview gives you a chance not only to learn why the employee is leaving, it also gives you information about her attitude toward the job and the company that might help in reducing future turnover. Exit interviews are particularly valuable because, since they are usually taken on the employee's last day, after the final paycheck has been issued, the exiting employees have nothing to lose in being honest with their answers, and the company has everything to gain from their input. Exit interviews often show what employees value most in the workplace. These include:

❚ Recognition.

❚ Communication with one another and with management.

❚ Stability of the company.

❚ Fairness.

❚ Compensation.

Other exit comments help the company know which managers to pat on the back. Employees who are about to become free agents have every reason to tell you the truth about how they think their supervisors perform.

One particular idea that we came across in our research was creating an employee data bank that includes everyone's education, technical skills, short-term aspirations, and long-term career goals. This data bank can be used to help employees find their niche and eliminate a major reason for people wanting to leave. It also comes in handy when a position has to be filled. Before going outside to hire a new employee, managers can go to the data base and it's hoped find a company employee who has been cross-trained and would like to be transferred, or someone in another department who would be willing to take an entry-level position in a different department.

Make it your business to send all departing employees a personal letter thanking them for the job they did while employed by the company and asking for any additional comments they may have that were not mentioned during the exit interview. You want them to know, even though they have left your employment, how much you and the company appreciate them and what action you will take as a result of what you learned from them during the exit interview.

One final word on keeping employees happy—make them proud of where they work. If they are not proud, they are not happy, and you can be sure that they are not doing their best. More important, you can also be sure that they are communicating their unhappiness, in one way or another, to customers and coworkers.

# Chapter 7

## Dealing with Problem Workers—Avoiding the Deadly Sins

---

### SIX COMMON MISTAKES IN MANAGING EMPLOYEE CONFLICTS

Where there are people, sooner or later there will be conflict. Conflicts are a natural and even necessary fact of everyday business and personal life. While conflicts in the workplace are inevitable, however, it doesn't necessarily mean they are bad or that they can't be resolved easily and in a way that actually benefits all concerned. Handled properly, conflict can be an effective way to give and receive feedback, stimulate thinking, encourage contributions, spark new solutions for old problems, and build stronger business relationships. Unmanaged or handled poorly, workplace conflict can take a tremendous financial toll in a number of ways, including the time you spend dealing with it, diminished productivity, and eventually, higher personnel costs to replace workers who quit because of it.

### MISTAKE 193

**Not preventing conflict before it starts.**

#### How to Avoid It

With a little forethought and prevention, most conflicts can be nipped in the bud. Steps to take:

▌ Get to know and understand your employees better. What irritates people can be keys to their personality. People who object to reasonable rules and regulations may be malcontents and troublemakers. Learn about what makes them angry and where their "boiling points" are. Find out who are the ones with grudges and what the grudges are about. Know which employees have personalities that are easily hurt. Which ones won't back down in a situation. Knowing these kinds of things puts you way ahead of potential conflicts.

■ Watch for problems and symptoms. Alcoholism, for example, is a symptom of a larger problem. Though it is possible to stop someone from drinking, it is more difficult to eliminate the cause, which may manifest itself in some other area of the person's life.

■ Keep communication lines open. Encourage workers to be more forthcoming with their observations, opinions, and feedback for the benefit of everybody.

■ If a situation exists that might cause conflict, such as changing a procedure, determine what kind of conflict is likely, whom it will involve, and what the opposing views might be.

■ Avoid impossible situations. Don't put two obviously conflicting personalities on the same team, unless you have no alternative.

■ Avoid giving workers on the same job conflicting instructions. Be consistent in the things you say and do with all employees.

## MISTAKE 194

**Not preparing for conflict.**

### How to Avoid It

The next best thing to avoiding conflict is to be prepared for it. One of the most common causes of conflicts in any company is change or the threat of it. Anytime you know that change is coming, you can anticipate conflict coming with it. Steps to take:

■ Determine what kind of conflict is likely, whom it will involve, and what the opposing views might be.

■ The best way to be prepared is to understand that resolving conflict is not just about who's right and wrong; it's about recognizing and appreciating the differences among people. Everyone has qualities that make them special. In dealing with conflict, you must be receptive and appreciative of the qualities of each of your employees.

■ You must be ready, at all times, to preserve the dignity of anyone involved in a conflict.

■ You must be prepared to listen carefully to the conflicting views as if they were your own.

■ You must be prepared to recognize and feel each person's emotional state and remind yourself not to take a side just because it agrees with your point of view.

■ Focus on preparing for what you can say and do when a conflict arises, and accept the fact that more often than not, you're going to fail at changing someone's behavior, especially in the midst of a confrontation.

■ If you anticipate conflict, you give yourself time to find out more about the individuals involved and develop a strategy to prevent the conflict from escalating.

## MISTAKE 195

**Allowing conflict to get out of control.**

### How to Avoid It

If conflict does arise, review the information you have gathered on the people involved. It may concern a long-standing feud between individuals or even departments. As manager, you can either mediate or arbitrate. In mediation, you must listen to both sides and help them reach a meeting of the minds. As an arbitrator, you must make the decision as to what course to follow. Steps to take:

■ Listen to both sides, separately (especially if the parties don't get along). Get all the facts. Try to determine why the conflict has occurred. Evaluate what you've learned. Be sure you understand each point of view.

■ Call for a meeting.

■ Explain the rules that will be followed.

■ Ask each person to restate what the other has said to be sure both parties are talking about the same thing.

▌ Allow both parties to openly discuss their conflict.

▌ From your observations and feedback from coworkers, colleagues, and company history, see if you can spot a pattern in the conflict, such as a consistency in the way each individual behaves. This will give you some insight as to the nature of their personalities.

▌ Identify any areas of agreement they may have, put them to rest, and focus on the matters left to be resolved.

▌ Ask each person if she is open to an alternative approach to settling the difference quickly. Alternative approaches include downplaying the conflict ("What's done is done, let's get back to work"), using an external means of settling the confrontation ("Let's draw straws and settle the matter), and compromising ("Everyone has to give a little to get a little"). Though this approach is worth a shot, chances are it won't work.

▌ Use your authority and the conflict itself to reach a consensus among the conflicting individuals. Stress that your say should be considered as a view of the big picture and is of equal value to the other two views.

▌ Show both sides why the conflict and any solutions have to be seen in their proper context.

▌ Don't give in to emotional reactions you may get.

▌ Invite the parties involved to share their opinions. Work toward developing a synthesis of all the viewpoints and an agreement that both can live with. No one should get all she wants, and no one should be left empty-handed.

▌ If the conflict is not resolved at the first meeting, have a second, but encourage the parties to discuss the issues between themselves with the hope that the conflict is resolved before the next meeting.

## MISTAKE 196

**Not monitoring agreements to make sure they are carried out.**

### How to Avoid It

As conflicting employees reach a consensus, put it in writing. At the same time, everyone involved should decide on what actions should be taken if the agreement is not adhered to. Distribute the agreed-to statements to all involved and decide—with them—how, by whom, and how long it will be monitored.

## MISTAKE 197

**Overreacting to conflicts.**

## MISTAKE 198

**Caving in to conflicts.**

### How to Avoid Them

When you start getting as emotional as those in conflict, animosities develop, communications can break down, trust and mutual support can deteriorate, and hostilities can result. Steps to take:

▌ Remember that someone else's anger doesn't give you the right to be angry. The more you remain calm and matter-of-fact, the sooner you gain the confidence of those in conflict. People want to feel you're in control. That you're leveling with them. That you're not taking sides. That they can trust you. Remember that respect from others begins with self-respect.

▌ If you find yourself getting angry with the situation, or not able to handle the conflict, you have at least two options. First, you can be still or stall the action until you regain your composure. Don't let them see that you are angry over their argument or you'll lose authoritative ground that will be difficult to regain. Second, you can leave the battlefield.

## FOUR MISTAKES IN COMMUNICATING YOUR SENSE OF RIGHT AND WRONG

Today in corporate America, more and more businesses are calling for ethics and values at work and are communicating their beliefs to both employees and customers.

## MISTAKE 199

**Not having a policy for proper behavior.**

## How to Avoid It

As a business grows and adds more employees, it needs a structured approach to managing problems with workers. Companies that have policies for proper behavior, rather than relying on an instinctive sense of right and wrong, not only make it easier for managers to make appropriate decisions, these policies also help to build a company's positive image by giving employees, customers, and vendors a better picture of its values. Decisions will be made faster and more problems will be avoided when everyone involved with the company understands its values.

## MISTAKE 200

**Not defining, documenting, and communicating your company values.**

### How to Avoid It

Don't assume that all your employees think the way you do. For example, they may think that cutting corners is okay; you may not. You must articulate your stand on what's right and wrong. Steps to follow:

▌ Begin by figuring out what you stand for. What you believe in. Sure, everyone believes in profits, but what else? Break your beliefs down into categories. Values you have that concern your employees, your customers, your vendors, and the company. Questions you might ask yourself concerning employee policies are: Does the company teach employees to learn one anothers' skills? Do leadership roles rotate? Is there respect for individuality or are employees forced into molds? Is there open communication, upward, downward, sideways, outside and inside? Does the company seek feedback and encourage questions? Do employees have an opportunity to contribute, learn, grow, and advance based on merit, not politics and background? Are they treated fairly and with respect, listened to, and involved? Do they have satisfaction for accomplishments, balanced personal and professional lives, and fun in their endeavors? Values provide a common language for aligning a company's leadership and its people.

▌ Document your beliefs to help clarify your thinking. Some companies have simple written rules, regulations, and codes that are usually part of employee handbooks; others have what is called mission statements. These are documented commitments that put a company's principles into words and concern such things as product and service quality, employee behavior and development, and environmental responsibility. A statement of business ethics does not have to be a long, complicated document.

∎ Involve your employees in the policy-making process. People tend to support what they help create. Invite workers to think about what values the company should be known for such as how management and employees should behave in the workplace, how the company should act in a competitive environment, long-range goals, and so on—then hold a brainstorming session.

∎ When you have a policy worked out, post it where every employee can see it. Include it along with other company literature sent to prospective customers as well as to vendors. Once you make something public, it's less likely you'll stray from the line.

## MISTAKE 201

**Overlooking ethical conflicts.**

### How to Avoid It

The most common ethical conflicts are usually minor ones, and they are often overlooked. The example we gave earlier about cutting corners applies here. But not all such problems are minor ones. Values can't substitute for competence. Steps to take:

∎ When you have a serious problem, you must act quickly to minimize the damage that may occur.

∎ Think through all the issues and consequences; decide which of the issues is critical.

∎ Create measures to resolve the problem.

∎ If your company has made a mistake, admit it.

## MISTAKE 202

**Not monitoring your company's ethical performance.**

## How to Avoid It

You can check the progress of your company's policies by periodically checking the answers to key questions such as:

- Are you living up to your commitments to your employees?
- Are they living up to their commitments to the company?
- Are you delivering the quality you promised to your customers?
- Are you selling a product or service that is harmful to society?
- Are you honest in the way you do business with your employees, customers, and vendors?

---

# FIVE COMMON MISTAKES IN USING EFFECTIVE LISTENING TO AVOID MISCOMMUNICATIONS

---

To communicate successfully means being able to receive as well as transmit information. Unfortunately, this is not true in many businesses where communication has come to mean "tell" or "give out," not "listen" or "receive."

Listening is without a doubt the most important skill in the communication process, yet unlike reading, writing, and speaking training, virtually no formal training in effective listening is available in schools, industry, or business. Listening should not be confused with hearing. A manager with perfect hearing may hear an employee's entire message, but because his listening skills are inadequate, what he understands is not necessarily what has been said, and its meaning may be lost or distorted, making the communication incomplete. Unlike the physical process of hearing, effective listening is a process whereby a person integrates physical, emotional, and intellectual inputs in search of meaning.

No matter what techniques you use to motivate your employees, you have to be prepared to spend more of your time receiving, listening to, and digesting information than you spend giving it out. With four organs to receive, and just one to give out information, we were meant to listen more than talk. Managers who fail to receive and understand what their subordinates are trying to communicate miss out on information that may be useful in making decisions, as well as information on current or emerging problems. By not listening, their messages to employees are often inappropriate because they are addressing the wrong problems. They waste time and money on ill-conceived endeavors that might never get off the ground if they encouraged and listened to valid criticism. And they lose employee respect and cooperation. When a manager is perceived as not listening, employees feel as though they are being shut out, which fuels resistance and resentment. Managers who have learned *how* to listen—to problems as well as ideas—are the ones most likely to accurately determine employees' problems and goals, get things done right, build and enhance rapport and trust because their employees will feel understood, and recognize opportunities that other people miss.

The following are the five most common mistakes managers make when it comes to listening. See if you are guilty of any, and look at the steps to take to improve your listening abilities.

## MISTAKE 203

**Not giving the employee with a problem a chance to talk.**

## MISTAKE 204

**Listening passively and not concentrating on what the other party is saying.**

## MISTAKE 205

**Jumping to conclusions by assuming what the speaker is going to say and blocking out what he's really saying.**

## MISTAKE 206

**Shutting out ideas that are not in harmony with yours.**

## MISTAKE 207

**Not letting an employee know you're listening by showing emotions and using body language and expressions.**

## How to Avoid Them

Listening is the best way to recognize and discover facts. If you take the time to listen effectively, you can't help learning. Steps to take:

▎ Have the proper attitude that will motivate your listening. Go into the conversation with the thought that you really want to listen to the person. Understand that effective listening is a necessary skill for interactive management, as important as reading, writing, and speaking. Listening should never take a secondary position to speaking because when no one listens, it is pointless to speak. Go in knowing that employees *want* managers who understand what they have to say about their problems, and when you actively listen to them, they will reciprocate by listening to your point of view.

▎ Give full, relaxed, concentrated attention. You can't listen and do other things, like talking yourself, at the same time.

▎ Don't interrupt or rush to add your own views at the slightest pause in the conversation. Wait until the other person makes his point before expressing yours.

▎ Let the other person know you're listening. Maintain eye contact. Use gestures of acceptance such as nods and smiles of encouragement. Verbalize with an occasional "yes," or "I see," or "Is that so?"

▎ Listen for the main ideas being expressed. Specific facts are important only if they pertain to the main theme and are supported by ideas and proof that the ideas are sound. The trouble is, speakers often mix in anecdotes, irrelevancies, and empty clichés that you'll have to unscramble. If you take the main ideas out of context, there will be misinterpretation. Relate stated facts to the arguments of the speaker, and weigh the verbal evidence used.

▎ Don't assume something that has not been stated. Try to determine what the speaker's critical points are or what he's getting at before he gets to it. If you're right, your understanding is enhanced and your attention is increased. If you're incorrect, you learn from your mistake.

- Don't let your personal stumbling blocks distract you. Sometimes certain words, for instance, will bring on a negative reaction that causes a person to wander off on a mental tangent.

- Disregard side remarks and other distractions. Concentrate and tune out surrounding office noise, telephones ringing, or people passing by. Judge the content of the message, not the delivery.

- Don't show anger. Remain open to the message being conveyed. You might just try practicing listening to ideas and things you don't like.

- Listening is an active process, not a passive one. Tune in to the speaker's feelings as well as her words. Empathize. See her point of view. Appreciate the emotion behind what the person is saying more than the literal meaning of the words.

- Be aware of your own bad listening habits and change them. Don't fiddle with your pen or doodle, don't rummage through the pile of papers on your desk, make or take phone calls. Be alert and greedy to grasp new information.

- Take brief notes (using words and phrases, rather than complete thoughts) on important things that are said, how they are said, and the order in which they are said. Read between the lines, paying particular attention to what isn't said, information or ideas that aren't discussed, questions that aren't answered fully.

- Let the employee talk first. It will save time in the long run. Let him explain his situation. It may reveal valuable clues that will help you tailor your discussion to his particular needs.

- Ask open-ended questions that will allow the employee to express his feelings and thoughts. Use feedback to check your understanding of what you hear. Do not hear only what you want to hear. Ask the other person to comment or respond to what you've said.

- Listen actively as though you'll have to summarize later. Look for messages that are hidden in broader statements.

- Try not to be critical of a point of view that's different from yours. Be patient. Allow the employee time to finish his thought. Listen attentively and listen to understand.

## FIVE COMMON MISTAKES IN DEALING WITH THE WHINER, HOTHEAD, AND OTHER DIFFICULT WORKERS

Do you hear a lot of "That won't work," or "It's not my fault," or "It's impossible" from some of your employees? Do you have employees who try to intimidate you? Or who argue about decisions? Or are hostile and spread tension among their coworkers? Is there one guy who always picks a fight with one of his peers? Or a computer operator who keeps blaming the computer for not running his programs properly? Or someone who tries to sabotage procedures when they think you did them wrong? To paraphrase a line from *The Music Man,* "You've got trouble, right here in your workplace, with a capital *T,* and that rhymes with *D,* and that stands for difficult . . . difficult workers!"

While the majority of employees are self-disciplined, self-motivated, and productive, there always seem to be a few who, to put it mildly, are downright difficult. While as a manager you have a certain degree of power over your workers, they are the ones who do the work you assign, which also gives them some power over you. For things to run smoothly, you must deal with difficult people constructively and keep your workplace from being disrupted. Clever managers know that a wealth of talent can be unleashed when a so-called difficult worker is properly managed, and they are willing to invest time, money, and effort in finding and curing the cause of a person's problem and developing him into a productive worker. Other not so clever managers sometimes take one or more of three options: punishment, transferring the person to another department, or termination.

### MISTAKE 208

**Identifying people rather than behavior as the problem.**

### MISTAKE 209

**Assuming that difficult people are being difficult intentionally.**

## How to Avoid Them

Try to find a manager who has *never* encountered a problem employee. Chances are you won't. But the truth is, most managers have really encountered problem behavior, not necessarily problem employees. When unrecognized or left unattended to, problem behavior will affect the department and eventually spread to other parts of the company.

Problem behavior, especially as it relates to relationships and tasks, usually develops in childhood and becomes more pronounced by the time the dysfunctional person joins the work force. And when that person is discovered to be troublesome, management usually makes the mistake of confusing cause and effect by attacking the employee, instead of the real culprit—his behavior. "Problem employee" is really a label attached to someone who behaves badly. Steps to take:

▪ Target the behavior for change. Find out exactly what the problem is. It could be fear of being left out, unimportant, or forgotten. It may be related to change in work procedure or surroundings. The person may feel a need to control or may not be able to differentiate between good and bad, himself, coworkers, or the job. Perhaps he denies realities or feels a need for autonomy. His problem could be avoiding responsibility, or taking on too much responsibility. He may have a need to be liked, or may like to be authoritative.

▪ Once you determine what the problem is make sure it is a behavior that is harmful to the person, other employees, the company, or you, and not just an attitude that you may need to learn to live with. For example, you might think that an employee's prejudice against disabled coworkers was the problem, when the real problem was how the employee treated those coworkers. Therefore you don't want to try and change the way that person feels about disabled workers (his attitude), you want to get him to act toward them the same way he acts toward nondisabled workers (his behavior).

▪ Confront the difficult person with the specific behavior that is creating the problem, but separate that behavior from the person. For example, if you don't use the word "you," you minimize defensiveness and feelings of punishment by others and will encourage him to listen to what you have to say.

▌ Don't confront the offender in front of others. Try to confront the person when he is receptive—not angry, fearful, or upset.

▌ Have documented evidence of the damage caused, the people offended, and so forth.

▌ Explain why the behavior is wrong, such as: it's affecting the meeting of goals, or it's harming you, our relationship, or a coworker. Be as objective as you can in describing the problem. Remember that every story has two sides. As accurate as your information and perspective may be, empathize with the person and look at the issue from his perspective. Don't blame anyone. Blaming reduces the problem only to a right/wrong, good/bad, win/lose issue. Using words such as "always" and "never" can escalate the problem into a conflict as well.

▌ Explain how you feel about the problem behavior; it will increase the person's understanding of the impact the behavior is having.

▌ Give the person a chance to respond. If he doesn't, ask for a response. Make sure you have all your facts straight and that you haven't misunderstood anything.

▌ Communicate your desire to help.

▌ Be positive. Communicate your optimism about the person's ability to change.

▌ Get a commitment for corrective action. Ask the person to suggest how he would remedy the situation—"What do you think it will take to keep this from happening again?"

▌ Review *your* management style. Are you performing your job in a way that might be encouraging to difficult people? Are you, for instance, rewarding people for nonperformance? Are you equally fair with all your employees? When employees feel that they are being treated unfairly, great animosity can result. In making assignments, do you match a worker's experience and skill to the job, or do you grab anyone you can to do it? Are you a buck-passer, refusing to acknowledge and apologize for your mistakes and those of your staff? Do you operate your department at a hurried, anxiety-ridden, rush-rush pace? Establish your rules and check yourself periodically to see that you treat all your workers the same.

## MISTAKE 210

**Rewarding difficult people because they have seniority.**

## MISTAKE 211

**Not applying effective negative consequences for poor performance.**

## MISTAKE 212

**Transferring a difficult employee to another department because it's company policy.**

### How to Avoid Them

Though they may not appear related when you read Mistakes 210, 211, and 212 separately, they all concern bad management decisions that are quite common, do little to correct a difficult employee's behavior, and often serve only to encourage it.

What a manager may see as employee punishment may not be punishment to the employee at all. For example, reprimands put in a manager's file by her superior would be considered serious to the manager because managers see reprimands as punishment. A reprimand put in the file of a difficult employee may represent nothing more than another piece of paper in the file. Being told to go home for two days without pay may seem like punishment to management, but to a difficult employee, it can be considered a vacation. To make matters even worse, in many companies bad performers receive raises and choice work assignments because the company has a seniority policy.

Another common bad practice that seems baffling is managers who, rather than fire a difficult person and be the one who puts a black mark on his record, have him transferred to another department. One manager we spoke to in researching this phenomenon told us of a difficult employee who has worked for six different departments in his company, was considered very difficult to work with and a bad performer in each position, yet has been, and still is, with the company for 22 years.

Steps to take:

▌ If negative consequences do not exist in your company for employees who willfully perform inappropriately, you must try to convince management to initiate the necessary policies that will identify bad behavior (such as an ID code on a product that identifies the person who assembled, packed, or inspected it) and provide effective punishment that will deter it.

■ If an employee is doing work she likes and willfully performs badly, assign her to a job she doesn't like. The same action should be applied to difficult employees who like their work environment, or who are on expense account, or who are normally permitted to attend outside activities during work hours.

■ When employees willfully perform badly demote them and reduce their salary, or deny raises until performance improves.

■ Make sure the rules for transferring bad performers state clearly that no transfers can be made until the willful misconduct is corrected for a specific period of time. Someone performing badly for other reasons should not be transferred if the task they now perform is the same task they will be performing after transfer.

■ If willful misconduct does not improve after coaching and punishment, terminate the employee (see Chapter 11, Firing Employees—the Task Every Boss Dreads).

## THE MOST COMMON MISTAKE MADE IN COMMUNICATING THE WAY YOU WANT THINGS DONE

How many times have you said, or heard another manager say, "Why do they continue to do it wrong? They're grown, educated people; can't they get this simple task right?" The answer may have less to do with the employees and more to do with how the instructions were given or how nonperformers are treated.

### MISTAKE 213

**Not providing *all* the elements needed to get the job done right.**

#### How to Avoid It

There are many reasons why employees don't perform as you might like or expect, as covered in greater detail in Chapters 3, 4, and 5. But for purposes of showing how effective managers get what they want, here are three of the most common reasons:

∎ They don't know or understand what you want.

∎ They don't have the skill or knowledge to do the task.

∎ There are no negative consequences for performing badly, therefore no reason to change or improve.

One of your jobs as manager or supervisor is to continually strive for improved performance. Here are some steps you can take to make sure you get what you want:

∎ Tell them, in writing if possible, everything they need to know. Don't be vague or general. Employees need and deserve to know the fundamentals of their job and exactly what is expected of them. Give everyone involved in performing a particular task complete details that outline all the procedures, the results expected, any rules to be observed, all standards to be met, and examples of a properly produced finished product.

∎ Train or retrain if the task is new or changed. Just as employees need to know the fundamentals of their jobs, they also need to know whether they'll be able to perform their jobs. Don't assume an employee will automatically know or figure out how to do a job by himself.

∎ Let them know how important their input and the job is, and your employees will perform better and feel more comfortable expressing their opinions.

∎ Check out the work often and without making it seem as if you're spying. Explain in advance of starting an assignment that you will be monitoring for purposes of clarifying confusion and correcting errors in order not to jeopardize deadlines or quality. Provide whatever feedback and guidance is needed to get the job done the way you want.

∎ Be compatible. Sometimes, despite all efforts, there will be conflict or need for performance improvement. Your role as supervisor is to make sure the workers function as effectively as possible. If someone is disruptive, confront her and try to resolve the situation. If you can't, take her off the job before her actions affect everybody. If poor performance is the problem, coaching may be the answer. Show the worker what she did wrong and go over the steps needed to make it right. Don't punish or blame. Use praise and positive comments to motivate.

# THE MOST COMMON MISTAKE MADE WHEN USING HUGS AND HUMOR TO TEMPER NEGATIVE EMOTIONS

Due to the high number of divorces, single-parent families, families in which both parents work or in which one parent works two jobs, commuter marriages, and the like, employees often spend more waking hours with one another than they do with their families. As a result, the people at work, including the manager, become the "work family" or "family away from family" for many workers.

And, just as in the lives of real families, there can be personality conflicts, disagreements, and squabbles within the work family. Tempers will flare, people will blow up, rant and rave, and say things that are out of line. When this happens, the manager must provide the open communication and emotional support needed to resolve the situation.

## MISTAKE 214

**Not communicating emotional support with problem employees.**

### How to Avoid It

The success of a manager is directly related both to his relationships with the people working for him and with the people he works for. These relationships fall into two categories: business relationships and personal relationships. And it is the little emotional kind of things managers do in their personal relationships with each employee to solve problems that separate the effective managers from the ineffective ones. We call it "emotional support"; many business consultants and employees we spoke to also referred to it as "friendliness," "being a buddy," and even "love."

This doesn't mean being your employees' best friend, overlooking bad performance, understanding or involving yourself in their personal problems, lending them money, or letting them do what they want. It means giving them a sense of *belonging* in the work family, letting them know you *care* for and about them. The less people sense they're cared for by those they work for, the more time and energy they'll focus on "looking out for number one." That's something neither you, nor they, need. By investing in the personal lives of your workers, you'll make them feel like family, and they'll act like family. Absenteeism and turnover will be lower, and many new employees will come from referrals, from people who will tell their friends and relatives that your company is a good, caring place to work.

So what are some of the little emotional kinds of things you can do to make your workers feel like family? Hugs do help, especially to temper negative emotions. Problem employees who don't have loving support at home desperately need it at work. You've seen those slogans on bumper stickers, "What the world needs is a good hug."

Hugging is healthy. Many medical experts say that people want and need to be touched—and often. That hugging and touching significantly increases the hemoglobin in the blood and can lift depression and cool down hot tempers in the recipients. We read about one doctor at the U.C.L.A. pain clinic who gives hug prescriptions—"get your hug in the morning, a hug at lunchtime, one at dinner, one before bed and you'll feel better."

But many managers will tell you that they "are not the hugging kind," or that "hugging has no place in the workplace," or they fear rejection or misinterpretation of their actions. The truth is that as people become less self-conscious, they warm to the idea of being hugged, if it's done in a reassuring rather than a sexually implied manner, or in a way that does not violate the employee's personal space. They grow to like being hugged and to depend on it rather than the reverse.

Like hugging, humor is another great way to temper negative emotions, break tension that arises when productivity and the drive to excel are constantly in high gear, and to have fun and encourage friendships. The ability to find something funny in an emotionally charged situation is an important coping skill. A little humor can relieve tension and show angry employees that every problem doesn't have to be made into a federal case. Managers who can show their workers that they have a sense of humor will not be seen as overly serious, self-important, and self-righteous. But you have to be careful; wisecracking too much during a serious discussion could make matters worse.

Begin by smiling. You'll find that if you're smiling, most employees will find it difficult to continue acting negatively toward you or the situation. Next, stimulate laughter, even if it's just a chuckle. If you can do something to make an angry employee laugh, you have taken a giant step toward defeating negative, defeatist attitudes. Tips to putting humor to work for you:

▌ Try laughing at yourself when you goof.

▌ Poke fun at outmoded company and employee rituals the way comedians exaggerate the truth ("How bad was it? It was so bad that . . .").

▌ Start a humor file with short jokes and clever sayings that pertain to the workplace. Use them when they are relevant.

▌ Spend time with people who make you laugh and observe how they do it.

▌ Learn a magic trick or two; it can help break the tension and distract a person's anger.

▌ Smile at people you don't know. Watch their reactions.

Hugs and humor are two of many methods effective managers use to temper negative emotions and make workers feel cared about. Here are some more:

▌ Be polite and easy to talk to. Say "please" and "thank you."

▌ Be thoughtful and considerate of your employees.

▌ Look at people when they're talking to you and show a pleasant face.

▌ Give people a "good morning," or "good afternoon" before getting into work-related matters.

▌ Talk to your employees about their personal interests and outside activities, such as hobbies, sports, children, and the like. An effective manager will thread the "friendly stuff" in with the "business stuff."

▌ Treat workers who come into your office as guests. Ask them to sit down and be comfortable. Stop whatever work you're doing and concentrate on what they're saying.

▌ Avoid making sarcastic comments to employees.

▌ Control your emotions when you're angry. Always appear poised and friendly and you'll find that you can regain control of just about any situation no matter how hot tempered it gets.

Thinking of all your employees as extremely wealthy people who don't have to work for you if you're not nice to them, may start you acting nicer to them.

## THREE COMMON MISTAKES IN DOUSING
## A HOT OFFICE ROMANCE

Two workers in the same company but different departments are having a romance. A team leader is sleeping with a coworker. A supervisor or manager is romancing a subordinate. Two employees of your department have broken up, very messily. When men and women work together, romances may develop. Such liaisons, especially when handled badly by the company and the individuals, may cause problems that can affect business-making decisions, destroy careers, and cause conflict and tension among peers and other employees. Conversely, there are times when the effects of a romantic bond can actually work to the advantage of a company or department.

## MISTAKE 215

**Having archaic attitudes toward office romance.**

### How to Avoid It

Today, most companies are equal-opportunity employers with a work force that may be divided almost 50-50 female to male. Since people spend most of their waking hours at work, it's only logical that they are likely to find someone in the company that they are attracted to.

Romance problems among employees should not be treated as an embarrassing nonsubject that is swept under the rug. Every smart manager, vice president, and corporate head knows that human entanglements, not managed, can easily get out of hand, directly affect production, and if so, must be dealt with rapidly.

## MISTAKE 216

**Not knowing how to cope with the situation.**

### How to Avoid It

When an office romance becomes known through observation, gossip, or confession, managers are immediately placed in the position of having to make a decision. Do they do something about it or ignore it? Are there legal problems that may arise from their intervention? The final script hasn't been written yet. It is not necessary here to know what the circumstances of the romance are; however, if a performance problem does exist, it is necessary for the manager to know the following:

■ Are the employees in any kind of superior-subordinate relationship?

■ Is the relationship or breakup affecting the performance of either of the two people involved?

■ Regardless of how well the principals themselves are coping with the situation when they are at work, is the romance having a negative effect on coworkers, or is it a threatening issue to the company?

■ If so, do you expect the negative effects to be short-lived and to resolve themselves in time, or do they require your intervention now?

■ What is your company policy, if any, concerning the situation?

■ Will you be violating the participants' personal rights of privacy by intervening?

## MISTAKE 217

**Not acting quickly if an office romance is affecting work performance.**

### How to Avoid It

You are justified in involving yourself in your employees' personal lives only to the extent that what they are doing off the job affects what happens on the job, and that goes for alcoholism or any other problem an employee may have. If the two lovers throw kisses, knives, or slanderous remarks at each other when they are not at work, but are models of decorum on the job, then you have no basis for getting involved. But as soon as what's happening in their personal lives begins to affect their work performance, or that of others, you should step in firmly and swiftly. Steps to take:

■ Have private talks with both employees, together if they are still together, separately if they're not.

■ Be supportive and understanding.

■ Make certain it is clear that you have no intention of imposing any value judgments on what has happened.

■ Explain in detail the problems you've seen in their work performance.

■ Let them know you are aware of their romantic situation and
delicately inquire if that situation could be the cause of the performance problems.

■ If they deny having an affair, explain that you are concerned
enough that even the *perception* that the relationship exists is
causing problems.

■ Offer counseling, coaching, or other assistance to help them
work through the situation.

■ Make it clear that you are not concerned about their situation,
but rather the poor work performance, and you expect the performance problems to be corrected quickly.

■ Explain the effect their affair may have on their careers. Will
decisions on salaries, promotions, assignments, and career
mobility be influenced by the affair?

■ Explain the ground rules and ask them for their suggestions on
how they themselves would solve the problem. Tell them that
you don't want to lose them, but if the situation is not resolved
you will have to exercise other options.

■ Discuss the options. Suggest that the two sort out their own values and make their own choices after considering the consequences. At this point, many couples will have doubts about
what they are doing and will be grateful and relieved to talk
about it. Defusing sexual attraction early will cause the least
amount of damage.

■ If for one reason or another (such as having had a similar personal experience or bias), the manager is not comfortable discussing the problem, she should refer the matter to another
department manager or a human resources or company counselor.

■ If it's appropriate, consider offering temporary or permanent
work reassignments to allow time for the situation to be corrected. In transferring or firing employees, be warned that you
should proceed with caution so that what is an attempt to avoid
office disruption does not backfire and become even more disruptive if the employees feel that they have been discriminated
against and decide to sue. The Equal Employment Opportunity
Commission (EEOC) cautions that if you fire only one person

and do nothing to the other, you are risking liability under Title VII of the Civil Rights Act of 1964. Also, you must be consistent. For instance, if a similar situation occurred earlier and the company did nothing, it cannot suddenly issue sanctions in this case. If in the past both parties were fired as a result of a situation, the same action should be carried out in this case.

▌ If the situation seems to be affecting coworkers, observe to see whether it's the actions of the lovers that are affecting the others, or whether it's the staff's anticipation of trouble that's affecting them. If the problem has nothing to do with what the lovers are doing, you can't hold them responsible. If it is affecting performance, such as production being behind schedule, or a lot of company time is being spent on gossip, explain to the romantics what problems their situation has caused among their coworkers. Remind them of their responsibility to establish and maintain effective work relationships and see that they take whatever steps are necessary to mend relationships with the other workers.

▌ Bone up on sexual harassment laws. Keep in mind that the key language in the law's definition of harassment is "unwelcome sexual advances." Nothing is wrong when both parties are happy about an encounter. However, the problem is that if one person wants to end it and the other doesn't, it can develop into harassment. (See Chapter 9, Sexual Harassment—Costly Mistakes You'll Want to Avoid.)

▌ Finally, try to convince upper management to offer managers special training in solving the human conundrums that exist in corporate society.

## THE MOST COMMON MISTAKE IN TRYING TO IMPROVE EMPLOYEE MORALE

There can be many reasons for the lack of morale among employees. Some, such as poor physical and psychological working conditions or below standard salaries, are beyond the control of most managers. Most often, though, lack of morale is caused by departmental issues over which the manager does have control, such as problem employees who can't be fired, or racial, religious, and minority problems that are overlooked because they could trigger discrimination complaints against the company. One thing is certain, however; when employee morale is low, employee problems always rise.

## MISTAKE 218

**Treating problems that arise from poor morale with disciplinary actions and not correcting the underlying causes.**

### How to Avoid It

When some managers encounter the problems that arise from poor employee morale such as absenteeism, turnover, and low productivity, they tend to treat these situations as disciplinary problems, which provide only short-term solutions. The long-term solution lies in identifying and correcting the underlying causes.

One or two frequently absent or late employees, for example, can lower the morale of everyone in that department. Lack of guidance, trust, objectivity, and fairness by managers can lead to high employee turnover. Lack of supply information, performance feedback, and recognition of achievements can lead to low productivity. Steps to take:

■ Identify and focus on the reasons for the poor morale. Talk to your employees, observe what is going on in your department, take a look at those exit interviews and employee attitude surveys.

■ If the problem lies with you, or your predecessor, you will have to find out what is causing the discontent and promise to do your best to resolve it. Perhaps your predecessor established certain rules that have to be changed. Maybe your people think you're too negative or not appreciative enough or not tough enough with problem employees. Make sure your employees are getting the detailed direction and relevant information they need to feel in control of their environments and to give their best performance. Show your trust and respect for your workers. Give them performance feedback and responsible performance appraisals with mutually agreed-upon objectives and supportive supervision. Provide training and development opportunities, results-based rewards, and advancement based on performance, not politics. Take note of their exceptional or expected achievements and offer praise, publicly. Encourage employee ideas and involvement in putting those ideas into practice, instead of viewing them as threats.

▌ If the problem lies with difficult coworkers, counsel those that are causing the problems and try to change their attitude. Explain how their behavior is affecting everyone in the department. If your counseling doesn't work, enlist the aid of coworkers and try peer counseling. If this fails, impose disciplinary action for a limited time such as reducing benefits for a three-month period, or docking pay (for frequent latecomers or absentees). Perhaps transferring or isolating problem workers will correct the situation. Reward problem performers who become good ones.

▌ If the problem is job related or due to company policy, it may be necessary to make a full companywide commitment and a real effort to making certain changes. Job enrichment programs, for instance, are aimed at making boring jobs less boring. One method is enlarging a dull, repetitious job by adding new elements that make the procedure less dreary and more interesting, which in turn bring up the level of productivity and cut down the instances of turnover and absenteeism. Overcoming negative aspects of the work environment also goes a long way in improving poor morale. This can include redesigning jobs, changing the way work is assigned, reevaluating wages and benefits, or simply adding background music and repainting the walls.

# Chapter 8

# STRESS MANAGEMENT TIPS
# FOR THE MANAGER

Job stress has become a global epidemic and the most widespread threat to physical well-being in the U.S. workplace. Stress-related injury claims on the job account for nearly 20 percent of all occupational disease claims. The ILO, an arm of the United Nations, estimates the cost of job stress in the United States alone at over $200 billion annually and takes into account costs from compensation claims, reduced productivity, absenteeism, added health insurance costs, and direct medical expenses for related diseases such as ulcers.

The Bureau of National Affairs, a Washington, D.C., business research organization, estimates that on any given day, as many as one million Americans are absent from work as a result of job-related stress. In their research of the workplace, The National Safe Workplace Institute, along with other researchers, have found that long-term exposure to work-related stress can cause heart attacks, strokes, high blood pressure, migraine headaches, decreased immunity to viruses, skin rashes, depression and rapid mood changes, fatigue, inability to concentrate, sleep and appetite disorders, substance abuse, sexual dysfunction, various muscle pains, and even spouse and child abuse.

Managers are constantly faced with helping their workers deal with and overcome stress, but many have not learned how to manage their own stress.

## FOUR MISTAKES IN TRYING TO KEEP COOL AND NEUTRAL IN A CRAZY, STRESSFUL WORKPLACE

Stress is a fact of life. No matter who you are or what kind of work you do, you're always going to have it. Some jobs carry more stress than others. Managers and supervisors, in particular, have to deal with stress associated with the personal problems and job performance of their employees. Stress resulting from production and administrative tasks. The stress of authority, responsibility, and accountability. The stress of dealing with upper management, close deadlines, disgruntled customers and vendors, acquisitions, mergers—not to mention stresses in their personal lives.

We've all experienced good stress when we get aroused about something exciting that is happening or going to happen. Our heart rate increases, our blood pressure rises slightly, and our adrenaline starts pumping. In this state, we are happy, productive, responsive, and effective. Bad stress creates the same physical effects, only this time our body's responses work against us.

## MISTAKE 219

**Trying to control situations you have no control over.**

### How to Avoid It

Knowing there are several kinds and causes of stress is the first step to managing it. For example, there is stress that is good for you, stress that is bad for you, stress caused by things you can do something about, and stress caused by things you cannot change.

Stress you can do something about—personality conflicts, marital stress, and illness—requires that you take action. Consider the different ways you can change the situation to reduce the level of stress, then make the decision to face the stress head on. The action may simply require a little negotiation, compromise, or following doctor's orders.

Then there are the sources of stress that you cannot control or change despite your best efforts, such as a merger or buyout, a superior with personal problems, new management, new government regulations, competition, the weather, other people's behavior, death, divorce, and deadlines. Trying to control these factors will create only more stress for you.

## MISTAKE 220

**Avoiding stress or denying that stress exists.**

## MISTAKE 221

**Worrying about problems rather than facing them.**

## MISTAKE 222

**Falling apart under pressure.**

### HOW TO AVOID THEM

Avoiding stress or denying that it exists will not make it go away. When we are in the denial state, we can't recognize the impact of our choices. If others suggest that we get away for a while to renew ourselves, we feel resentful at their suggestion and usually answer, "It's easy for you to say. I can't take off, I've got a deadline to meet." Denial is characterized by feeling unappreciated, trapped, blamed, and without options. If left unattended, we can become frustrated, anxious, fatigued, irritable, worried, distracted, unproductive, and ineffective, all of which can lead to more serious physical problems. But you are not totally without power in such situations. Steps to take:

▌ Accept them for what they are. Instead of wasting your time on what you can't change, focus on what you can. Look for opportunities to take you from the status quo to the new and more effective. This is not the same as giving up. By accepting what you can't influence, you are making a choice that puts you back in control by directing your energy where you can make a difference rather than merely taking a passive role. You make a conscious decision to move past judgment, anger, and upset and face the reality of the situation.

▌ Change your thinking and learn to control your mental processing of potentially stressful information. Realize that most stress is based on your perception of something that you feel threatens you—and that you have the power to change that perception instead of distorting it by criticizing, judging, or having other negative thoughts. Step back and ask yourself what it is about the situation that threatens you and how you can see it differently. View the stressful situation as an opportunity or challenge. Recognize and accept the fact that you feel tense but don't let any negative feelings keep you down. Separate the negative aspects of the situation from the good points and direct your energy to tasks that contribute to your goals.

▌ Breathe, doodle, meditate, juggle. In times of stress, you need to stop yourself from jumping on the anxiety bandwagon. So take a few breaths of air. Sit in a comfortable position at your desk, close your eyes, inhale deeply through your nose for four seconds, and exhale through your mouth for four seconds. Repeat this exercise several times. Another exercise for staying calm under pressure is called framing. Draw a two-inch square box, and think to yourself, "I am not going to get upset." Now draw another box inside the first, and think, " There is a way to solve the problem." Continue drawing boxes within boxes and thinking positive thoughts about yourself and the situation. What looks like doodling to others is really an effective way to distance yourself from what is causing your stress. Another exercise that is effective is meditation or visualizing. Try to visualize the successful outcome of your problem without stress. Then ask yourself what you did to reach that successful outcome. Your answer is your plan for action. One consulting company offers work-weary business people a way to increase creativity, sharpen mental agility and relax through the simple art of juggling. The key to learning how to juggle three palm-sized balls is to take lots of small steps that are easy to get right. The connection between the physical mechanisms involved in learning how to juggle (hand-and-eye coordination), and the mental requirements of effectively managing seemingly unmanageable goals (patience and new techniques for containing frustration), offers managers a way to cope with business issues, release tension, and have some fun.

▌ Don't internalize. Repressing your emotions leads to disease. Thinking about what might or might not happen in the future or what might have happened in the past to cause the situation will not help the situation and will only cause you more stress. Realize that most of what you worry about simply will never happen. And while some of what you worry about will happen, most likely there's nothing you can do about it except cope, and, you'll hope, lessen the stress by taking action. Ask yourself "What is the worst that could happen?" "How likely is it that the worst will actually happen?" "Could you survive if it did happen?" "How will you cope when it does happen?"

■ Take action. Identify the source of your aggravation, develop a strategy to combat the issue, and act. Don't take the insensitive behavior of others personally. The hostility or rudeness of others is their hostility or rudeness, not yours. Be flexible. Expect the unexpected and confront it as a challenge for growth instead of an agent of destruction. Don't turn outward in revolt against whatever may be causing your stress. Don't overgeneralize situations as "always" or "never" happening, or look at things as extremes—perfect and wonderful or imperfect and awful. Don't jump to conclusions and imagine the outcome of a situation. Practice the skills necessary to avoid repeating your harmful reactions to the stressful situation; this will help build the confidence you need to handle future pressures.

■ Prioritize. Determine the order of what is important to cope with the situation and the time and energy you will need to accomplish it. By keeping your goals in sight and prioritizing what's important, you help maintain an overview of any situation. Pace yourself instead of pushing too hard. Don't constantly think about what you need to do better and faster. Make time for enjoyable activities that will take your mind off the stress.

■ Communicate with someone you trust. Let go of your frustration, anger, and pain by talking about how you feel with a peer, spouse, good friend, or counselor who may have experienced a similar stressful situation.

■ Remind yourself that this situation, like many other situations, will change.

■ Treat yourself to something nice: a movie, a workout, a gift, a dinner, whatever will make you feel better.

## THREE COMMON MISTAKES IN TRYING TO REDUCE STRESS IN THE WORK ENVIRONMENT

According to researchers, there are many job factors that can cause stress, including monotonous and boring work, excessive monitoring by management, fear of death or injury on the job, sexual harassment, insufficient control over your work situation, a heavy work-load, long working hours, lack of job security, lack of recognition and support from superiors and peers. Other very important factors often overlooked by management concern the physical conditions in the workplace that affect the mental state of employees, including managers.

## MISTAKE 223

**Not recognizing the connection between the physical office environment and the mental state of those working in the environment.**

### How to Avoid It

There are a number of ways to reduce the factors that cause stress in the work environment aside from the obvious such as sufficient and adjustable lighting, air quality, reduction of noise, a place to keep your valuables, and privacy. Here are thirteen tips:

1. Personalize your work area with photographs, memorabilia, invitations, and related items of meaning to you.

2. Exercise during your coffee, lunch, or dinner breaks. This is in addition to getting enough sleep and eating properly. If you're overweight or suffer from frequent colds and other illnesses, join a wellness program or see your doctor.

3. Chronic noise pollution is a widespread cause of stress in the workplace. In fact, more than 20 million workers are exposed to hazardous noise every year, and many of these people suffer stress as their bodies strain to adapt to the excessive stimulation. Consider playing soothing music or using white noise to block out distracting sounds or voices. Physical characteristics of buildings and premises such as odors and glare and extremes of temperature and humidity are also major causes of workplace stress that can be easily corrected.

4. Make sure you have a comfortable chair to work in, one that is ergonomic and adjustable for your height and weight.

5. If you feel exhausted or fatigued, try lying back in your chair and closing your eyes for a few minutes. If you have a couch in your office, close the door and stretch out.

6. Dress in comfortable clothes and shoes. Keep a second pair of shoes as well as an extra umbrella or raincoat to eliminate any concerns about sudden weather changes.

7. Take regular breaks even if they are only for a minute or two. Some high-stress workplaces are offering workers a trendy 15-minute acupressure upper-body massage break instead of a coffee break. Employees receive the massage while seated in a specially designed chair, in their work clothes. On-site massage therapy is supposed to leave the worker energized rather than relaxed.

8. Delegate if your workload is unrealistically heavy.

9. Follow the basic rule of effective time management—keep your priorities clear, so your stress level will be lower. By becoming more organized, you will feel confident and self-assured as you work on tasks that are important to your job.

10. Develop a positive mental attitude, since research is showing that optimists are less stressed than pessimists.

11. Consider facts versus fears, especially if you are in a profession where special precautions have to be taken for health and safety reasons such as workers in a doctor's or dentist's office, lab technicians, and nurses. The fear of getting AIDS or HIV through casual contact in the workplace is more fear than fact. Finding out the facts will lessen the fears and the stress that goes with them.

12. Don't bring your work home with you unless it is absolutely necessary. If you do, block out a specific period of time to devote to it.

13. Sometimes concern about office crime is a source of stress at work. Crimes such as burglary, robbery, muggings, and assaults in parking lots or garages are common. So is petty larceny—employees stealing other employees' wallets, jewelry, and other valuables. Most of these crimes can be eliminated or greatly reduced with additional security and screening mechanisms, private lockers, and employee and equipment IDs. Enlist the cooperation of fellow managers if buildingwide changes are necessary.

## MISTAKE 224

**Focusing on employees' reactions to stress rather than on the causes of the stress.**

## How to Avoid It

Job-related pressures and the resulting stress have been around as long as the workplace itself. But it was only recently that managers began to acknowledge negative effects of work-related stress: decreased productivity, increased absenteeism and job turnover, and rising insurance claims and premiums because of illness and workplace accidents.

Hoping to relieve job stress for their employees, many employers instituted fitness programs, or they encouraged their stressed employees to get counseling or advice for their problems.

Although well-intended, these early approaches dealt with stress only after its symptoms had appeared. Experts are now recommending that managers focus on the causes of stress rather than on employees' reactions. They feel that no matter how healthy individual employees are when they start out, if they work in dysfunctional systems, stress will get to them. Some of the newer methods now being used to reduce workplace stress are:

▪ Make communications easier between management and subordinates. By eliminating some of the layers of communication, workers can have frequent, personal contact with the person in charge, making them feel their efforts really make a difference and immediately reducing their stress.

▪ Create cohesive work teams that allow members to share common goals and accountability and help buffer one another against stress. These teams also identify business and personal concerns and make recommendations for improving the operation. Every team member has a stake in the team's success—and the company's—and every member's input is valued. In many companies, using teams may not be feasible. If that's the case in your company, there are other methods that will help you do the job.

▪ Encourage employee involvement. Two keys to keeping stress down are communication and participation. Holding regular meetings between management and employees and encouraging everyone to make suggestions to improve efficiency will accomplish that. One company we spoke with told us that when they were in the designing stage of a new facility, instead of telling the architects what management wanted, they asked their employees, who would be most affected by the facility, to give their input to the architects. The completed building had all the features that were most important to the workers, and the level of stress went down significantly. Another company used the approach of teaching their employees how to read the company's financial statements as a means of keeping them involved. When people know what is going on in their company, they naturally feel more involved in the company. Encouraging employee involvement should not end at quitting time. Many companies have frequent picnics, potluck lunches, and other opportunities for employees to enjoy recreation together and celebrate their successes.

- Don't pit workers against one another. While incentive programs that reward employee accomplishments can lead to increased sales and production, they can also lead to increased stress levels for those involved. Head-to-head competition often makes employees less likely to cooperate with one another. It also often increases the workload, and along with that, the stress levels of those who produce the products, write the orders, pack and ship the boxes, and make sure the products are paid for. Today, many companies are tying employee pay to the profitability of the company. Bonuses are given companywide. This approach gets people from different departments to talk to one another and coordinate efforts to fulfill their mutual goals.

- Be a good people manager and facilitator, not someone who just issues orders, but one who can motivate employees to work together toward a common goal. To accomplish this you will have to learn to listen to your employees. In the traditional management structure, managers set goals and enforce deadlines, which makes employees feel uncomfortable bringing up workplace problems. By maintaining an open-door policy and encouraging workers to take advantage of it for both business-related and personal problems, situations such as employee conflicts, divorce, illness, and death in the family can be discussed and the manager's skill as a facilitator can be put to use—not to tell employees what to do, but to show them a different way of looking at their problem.

- Understand that different employees react differently to stress. All good managers strive to treat all employees alike, whether they are women or men, young or old. But not all employees react to stress in the same way. Intense stress, for instance, seems to affect women more severely than men. As a result, female employees take more stress-related sick days than men exposed to the same pressures. The reverse is true when the pressure originates in the home. Men are usually less sensitive than women to the early signs of stress, and surprisingly, younger employees, who are generally exposed to more stress-causing personal changes and pressures outside the workplace than older, more stable people, bring their stress with them to work.

■ Discourage workaholism. Many managers will actively discourage drug and alcohol abuse, while encouraging, and often rewarding workaholics on their staff. The up side is that workaholics get the job done and seldom call in sick. The down side is that they often suffer acute burn out, which results in a decline in work quality, increased sick time, and stress-related claims for workers' compensation.

■ Support new employees. Nearly 50 percent of workers' comp stress claims are filed in the first six to twelve months of employment. New employees should receive good supervision, feedback, support, and a sense of personal power during this period. Make sure you provide them with access to whatever information they may need to perform their tasks.

■ Show leadership. A commitment to making a company a pleasant, productive place to work has to come from management. In all companies, particularly small ones, it is the boss who sets the tone. And if the boss does not appear to be serious about trying to reduce workplace stress, there is little likelihood that anyone else in the company will take the lead.

## MISTAKE 225

**Letting your job responsibility cause stress for others.**

### How to Avoid It

There are many ways managers make the lives of their employees stressful. The purpose of exposing them here is to cause you to do some soul-searching to determine whether you are practicing these stress-inducing activities, and if so, develop plans to change or modify your behavior and thus reduce the stress you may be causing others. Many of the following organizational and personality stress inducers are within your authority to change.

■ Company culture and climate. The style of your company, its tone, priorities, and concern for employees may cause stress or feelings of tension or anxiety. The stress may come from existing conditions or recent changes. The culture may reward cooperation and teamwork among employees, or it may encourage competition, protecting one's rear, secrecy, and one-upmanship. Poor, outdated, or nonexistent policies and an inadequate upward and downward communications system are two more factors that cause employee stress at all levels. In addition, there may be a lack of personal and professional growth or advancement opportunities, unsafe or unpleasant working conditions and environment, and problems of being bored, burned out, or having risen as far as one can go.

■ Managerial style. A boss's style may trigger feelings of unease and anxiety. Giving unclear assignments, delegating too little or too much, playing favorites, being too hard or too soft on staffers, not giving employees feedback about their performance on a timely and frequent basis, discouraging frankness or creative thinking, treating workers like robots or children, not providing authority or rewards commensurate with responsibilities and performance, not delivering on promises and agreements, taking personal credit for the work of employees, not giving praise or recognition.

■ The manager's personality. Most workers hope to be liked and respected, but sometimes a manager's personality prevents this from happening. For example, she may be indecisive, or he may make decisions others should be making or blame others for failures; she may be overemotional, too laid back, or a nit picker; he may be distrustful, demeaning, and demanding of others, showing little or no concern about the employee's work environment, problems, needs, or concerns.

---

## FOUR MISTAKES IN VENTING FRUSTRATION AND ANGER THAT CAN HURT OTHERS

---

There's probably not a manager alive who has not experienced a really bad day. Maybe your staff is talking strike—during Christmas time. Or one of your vendors is spreading rumors that your company is on the verge of bankruptcy. Or someone in shipping accidentally sent the rush Cleveland shipment by slow boat to Bosnia-Herzegovina. Whatever it is, something went terribly wrong, and there's an immediate threat to your department, your job, and possibly the entire company.

When we are faced with a situation we cannot change, disappointment can be expected. Often anger and frustration will accompany disappointment, although it is seldom helpful.

## MISTAKE 226

**Relieving your own stress at someone else's expense.**

### How to Avoid It

You may have heard of the "Bite the Cat" game. It goes like this: A person humiliates his spouse, who then yells at the oldest child, who slaps the youngest child, who kicks the dog, who then goes and bites the cat. People in business play this game with employees in a way that proves the meek will certainly not inherit the earth. What screamers like to pass off as decisiveness is really a grown-up version of a child's tantrum.

Managers must learn to go to extremes to avoid arguing. When you win an argument, you really lose, because most arguments call for one person winning and the other losing—feeling humiliated, frustrated, angry, degraded, and annoyed. When that happens, the person who lost looks for ways to get back at the guy who won.

Instead of arguing, try persuading, influencing, and negotiating to arrive diplomatically at a win-win outcome. Never relieve your stress by yelling, making humiliating comments, or mocking someone else's words or behavior.

There is a workplace truism that has been around a long time: "Be nice to people on your way up the corporate ladder, because you're going to meet some of those same people on your way down"—and they can make your life miserable.

We all try to manage our stress, but doing it at the expense of your employees can result in loss of employee trust and your reputation, at the least. This is a high price to pay for momentary relief and is sure to create new stressors after the old distressors disappear. Instead, try concentrating on giving out compliments when they are appropriate. Giving a compliment is easy to do, takes only seconds, and makes you feel good. And if that other workplace truism is correct, "What goes around comes around," when you compliment someone, both career and personal benefits may come back in return.

## MISTAKE 227

**Being a boss instead of an advocate during a crisis situation.**

## How to Avoid It

Under ordinary circumstances, you are your employees' boss. In a crisis situation, you have to change hats and become their advocate. Like a commanding officer of a unit taken prisoner, it's your job to see that your people are not abused. If the company is in immediate trouble, get the full story from top management (if the facts can legally be released), and relay it to your troops. If your department is bearing the brunt of a crisis, make sure top management is aware of your employees' special needs. If it looks as if one or some of your people are going to catch the blame for whatever went wrong, you must see to it that the innocent are protected.

## MISTAKE 228

**Rushing to put the blame on someone who caused a crisis.**

### How to Avoid It

If the crisis involves serious errors on the part of your employees, you may have to find and discipline the guilty ones. However, this should not be your first priority. When you're trying to claw your way out of a deep hole, everybody has to claw together. If you take time out to point the finger at the guilty party, you may cause division and panic in the ranks that will only make you sink deeper. During times of high-stress crisis, it is important that a sense of believability exist between labor and management and that everyone understand and believe in the company's mission statement or overall objective. If you keep in mind what your company objective is, the question of "How do we deal with this?" becomes easier to answer.

If you've communicated the company's values to your employees, and if they understand and trust the company's direction, you've gone a long way toward keeping everyone calm and effective in just about any crisis. If your employees have faith in the company, they will understand that if something goes wrong, it's only an incident—not a failure of the system.

## MISTAKE 229

**Reacting to a stressful situation with anger.**

### How to Avoid It

Anger is a secondary emotion that usually comes after first feeling hurt, fear, or powerlessness. It tends to mask these feelings that make us more vulnerable, from ourselves and from others. It does not, however, help the situation. To be able to accept the things we cannot change means we will have to come to terms with these underlying feelings. When they are protected by anger, it takes longer. Steps to take:

- Start by looking for the primary feeling. What is scaring or threatening you? Who or what hurt you? Do you feel helpless and without power? By mulling over these kinds of questions, the answer will become apparent. Often, this will be enough to dissolve the anger, because what you were trying to protect will be clearly exposed.

- If the anger is directed toward another person, you may want to express how you are feeling. Explain what situation is upsetting you. Be objective and don't place blame. Keep the discussion short, simple, and direct. Tell the person at whom you're angry the underlying feeling that caused your anger. Ask for a specific remedy to your hurt or fear. This last step can create a new avenue for communicating that might prevent the situation from recurring.

- Don't make the situation worse by behaving in a counterproductive manner such as showing resentment, threatening revenge, attacking people behind their backs, or feeling sorry for yourself.

- Learn to let go rather than hold on or add on to whatever caused your anger. Too often we hold on to the past, to things, to people, or to irrational beliefs. We add on pressures instead of setting limits. When we learn to let go, we have time to "be," to experience solitude and restore our balance. Letting go gives us a healthier body and peace of mind.

# Chapter 9

## SEXUAL HARASSMENT— COSTLY MISTAKES YOU'LL WANT TO AVOID

Sexual harassment in the workplace is one of the most explosive personnel issues of our time and can be such a costly proposition that no company, large or small, can afford to ignore it. The fact is, most large companies understand the law about sexual harassment, give their managers and employees training in the subject, have policies and procedures in place to deal with it, and do everything they can to avoid going to court over it.

It's the owners and managers of many smaller businesses, experts say, who are ignorant about the risks they face and wrongly assume that the close-knit, familylike nature of their companies offer them immunity from the problem. "Many companies haven't the slightest understanding of the sexual harassment law," one executive we spoke with said. "For them, it's a catastrophe just waiting to happen."

Right now, your employees may be keeping diaries at work and secretly planning the home of their dreams that they're going to build right after they (excuse the expression) sue the pants off your company because of some off-color remark a manager made that offended them.

And lest you think the costs of defending a sexual harassment suit can't be particularly devastating to small businesses, especially those that often don't have the infrastructure in place to deal with such problems, consider these facts: The 1991 Civil Rights Act has greatly expanded the remedies available to victims of sexual harassment in the workplace. Federal sexual harassment cases previously decided by judges are now being decided by juries, which are more likely to award the complainant large sums. In addition, these victims may also recover compensatory damages for medical and or emotional distress expenses resulting from the harassment. In cases of overly flagrant behavior, victims may also receive punitive damages, which are designed to punish companies for wrongdoing and deter future sexual harassment. Even if the company ultimately wins the case, the cost of defending such a lawsuit can add up to tens, even hundreds of thousands of dollars in legal fees, plus the costs for executive time spent in depositions and courtrooms. In addition, a firm's reputation can be damaged, employee morale lowered, and productivity slowed.

## FIVE COMMON MISTAKES—LEGALLY SPEAKING

According to guidelines issued by the federal Equal Employment Opportunity Commission (EEOC), sexual harassment is, simply stated, unwelcome, offensive behavior of a sexual nature that creates an intimidating or hostile working environment. But that's where things stop being simple.

## MISTAKE 230

**Not fully understanding the law about sexual harassment or the wide net of liability that goes with it.**

### How to Avoid It

Prevention, training, and knowledge of the law and the liabilities are your best weapons for avoiding sexual harassment problems on the job.

In 1991, the EEOC's new guidelines became effective, restating earlier civil rights legislation that declared sexual harassment an illegal form of discrimination. Federal laws offer protection against sexual harassment to employees of all public and private employers in the United States, including U.S. citizens working for U.S. companies in foreign countries.The laws also apply to labor union members and the workers they employ.

The most blatant kind of harassment takes the form of a quid pro quo: you do this for that. In this type of harassment, an employee may be offered a benefit, such as a raise or promotion, in exchange for sex. But the EEOC guidelines also prohibit more subtle sexual behavior, such as unwelcome sexual advances, verbal or physical conduct of a sexual nature, or requests for sexual favors that have the "purpose or effect of unreasonably interfering with an individual's work performance or of creating an intimidating, hostile or offensive environment."

Courts vary in their applications of these standards to specific cases and usually depend on a variety of factors, including the relationship between the parties involved and the conduct that is alleged to have occurred. In addition to the federal law, states have their own laws about sexual harassment. In California, for example, the law requires that employers distribute flyers to all employees and post notices throughout the workplace outlining both the law and complaint procedures.

Many company executives still think that sexual harassment laws apply only to male coworkers or managers harassing female workers. While it's true that these kinds of cases make up the majority, the laws also apply to women harassing men, men harassing other men, and women harassing other women.

With few exceptions, a business owner can be held liable for the sexual harassment actions of the employee's supervisors and coworkers, as well as for the conduct of outside parties who deal with the business, such as suppliers and customers, even if the owners didn't know about the conduct or if the company has a policy barring such conduct and procedures to address any complaints. In cases of one coworker harassing another, owners are liable if they knew or should have known about the harassment and didn't take prompt remedial action. If a company is held liable in a sexual harassment suit, the courts or the EEOC can, among other things:

- Order the company to reinstate or promote the plaintiff.

- Award the plaintiff back wages and job-related losses, money damages, attorneys' fees, and injunctive relief.

- Order the company to institute and abide by a written sexual harassment policy.

The forms that sexual harassment can take range from continued (more than one or two) offensive sexual innuendoes to the display of pornographic photographs to the witnessing of sexual harassment of other employees to graffiti about employees written on a bathroom wall to physical encounters, dirty jokes, and rape.

## MISTAKE 231

**Not taking steps to prevent sexual harassment in your company.**

## MISTAKE 232

**Not being willing to spend the time or money needed to investigate harassment claims or deal with the harassment issue.**

### How to Avoid Them

Employers and their managers must be fully aware of how devastating a claim of sexual harassment can be to their businesses and why they must take action necessary to prevent sexual harassment from occurring. Steps to take:

▪ Understanding and responding to the subject. It's important that supervisors, middle managers, and employees as well understand exactly what sexual harassment is and are prepared to respond to a complaint or report an incident. Should someone tell a dirty joke to another worker and a third party overhears it, that's sexual harassment. Employers should inform employees that unwarranted and unsolicited sexually related behavior that makes them feel uncomfortable and interferes with their ability to do their job is sexual harassment and that they should:

A. Confront the harasser and make it known that they are not interested and want the behavior stopped. If not, more severe measures will be taken.

B. Tell management (preferably a superior of the same sex as the offender) what has happened and ask for suggestions on how to handle the problem.

C. Keep a diary or log of what the offender has said and done, noting place, date, time, circumstances, and what the response was.

D. Confirm what's been taking place in a letter and meet with the company's EEOC representative to have the letter placed on file.

E. Keep doing their job, staying away from the offender. Tell the harassed persons not to be afraid, that they can handle the situation, that nobody has to accept anything that offends them, and that there are people in the company at every level who will help them. And make sure you tell employees that by reporting sexual harassment, they are following the law and will suffer no repercussions for reporting abuses.

F. The final step for an employee who has been harassed and is not satisfied with the results of the investigation of the claim is to file a private lawsuit under the U.S. Civil Rights Act, or what is called a tort lawsuit, which is based on civil wrongdoings that have occurred.

After informing employees of what procedures they can take, your next steps to take are:

- Communicating to employees information on their right to raise and how to raise the issue of sexual harassment under federal law. A workplace free from sex discrimination is a right guaranteed by law to all workers in the United States. Sexual harassment, like pay inequity or refusing to promote someone because of his or her sex, is a form of sex discrimination. One company we spoke to keeps its employees informed on the issues by distributing consumer and trade articles on the subject. By doing so, they help avert not just sexual harassment among its own staff members, but also inappropriate behavior toward customers. This company also instructs employees to avoid any touching that isn't necessary and also reacts immediately to any complaint by speaking with all parties concerned, determining if in fact the incident was harassment, and if not, sending out letters of apology explaining that the situation was a misunderstanding.

- Expressing strong disapproval. Besides educating themselves and employees about sexual harassment issues, business owners and managers should spread the word by way of their own behavior that sexual harassment will not be tolerated. The smaller the company, the more informal relationships tend to be, and the more workers will be aware of and influenced by management's behavior. That's why it is important that management not only say "This kind of offensive sexually related conduct is unacceptable," but *act* as though it is unacceptable. It follows that if a manager tells sexually offensive jokes or bothers subordinates for dates or sexual favors, other employees may think it's okay for them to do the same.

- Developing appropriate actions and sanctions when sexual harassment is reported (see "Hearing the Grievance," "Investigating the Claim," "Protecting the Accuser," "Confronting the Accused," and "Taking Remedial Action" in this chapter).

- Develop a written harassment policy to sensitize all concerned (see "Publishing a Sexual Harassment policy" in this chapter).

Some additional tips for managers that will help prevent sexual harassment on the job:

▮ Avoid casual flirtatious remarks in dealing with employees. What may seem to be harmless flirting to a supervisor may be interpreted as an advance by the employee.

▮ Avoid making comments about a worker's physical characteristics. What you consider a flattering remark such as "You have a beautiful bosom," or "You have the sexiest legs I've ever seen," may not be welcomed by the employee and considered harassment.

▮ Stop immediately other employees, vendors, and customers from making inappropriate remarks. Remember that anything that goes on in the workplace is the responsibility of your company. You, the manager, represent your company. It is your job to make sure all employees and visitors behave in a businesslike manner during working hours.

▮ Ignore gender-specific terms unless absolutely necessary. Though many people, particularly writers, think this practice gets a little ridiculous when it's carried too far, using gender-specific terms in the workplace can send signals that lead to problems. Try to use parallel language whenever possible ("husband and wife," instead of "man and wife"). Use words that include both sexes ("salesperson," instead of "salesman"). Avoid dividing groups of people by gender ("student," instead of "coed," "flight attendant," instead of "airline stewardess," "homemaker," instead of "housewife").

▮ Don't laugh at sexually biased jokes or innuendoes, or participate in sexually-oriented conversations that are not related to business.

▮ Don't address employees with endearing terms such as "You're a doll!"

▮ Don't use phrases that imply a relationship that extends beyond the boundaries of business such as, "Let's get together after work," or "We can work on this during dinner. I know a nice restaurant."

▮ Know your company's policy and procedures on the issue of sexual harassment, if there is a policy. If not, speak to upper management about creating one.

Managers and business owners can get more information about federal and state sexual harassment laws, as well as information about local training programs, support groups, and attorneys by contacting their local office of the EEOC and their state Fair Employment Practices agency.

## MISTAKE 233

**Using your position of supervisor to sexually harass a subordinate.**

## MISTAKE 234

**Not knowing your rights if an employee accuses you of sexual harassment.**

### How to Avoid Them

A charge of sexual harassment is justified if you made unwanted physical or verbal overtures to the employee making the complaint. Whether or not your actions or words were intended to have sexual overtones doesn't matter. What matters is that a reasonable person, objectively viewing the facts, would construe the actions or remarks as sexual in nature.

The first thing for you to do is find out the specifics of the claim that has been made against you. You are entitled to know the specific details of the charge and what evidence the accuser has in support of that charge. If specific incidents have been cited, you have the right to know all the details including dates, names, places, circumstances, and what happened.

Before responding to these allegations, think about them. Did the incidents occur as stated? If not, how do you recall what happened? If both your recollections and the accusers are essentially the same, you may realize how the accuser interpreted your actions as harassment.

You have the right to be represented in responding to the charges, which can have very serious and potentially damaging personal effects, justified or not. So before answering any questions by an investigator, make sure you are first represented by an experienced attorney or other representative and that the person is present when you answer any questions.

Confront the accuser (bring along an associate as a witness, if you can) and try to resolve the complaint before it goes further. Since the relationship is already strained, be careful of what you say and how you say it, or your efforts may end up as a new charge of reprisal later on.

Because you will be responding specifically and in detail to each charge and incident raised, get together any documents or witnesses that can support your recollection of events at the time the alleged harassment took place.

Stay as calm as you can before facing the charges. Treat your employees as you always have, fairly, impartially, and objectively. Don't intentionally avoid the accuser, but if you have an encounter, watch what you say. Sexual harassment charges are not easy to prove if there are no witnesses and no previous history of discriminatory or unethical behavior. The final decision will depend greatly on the credibility of the people involved. If you've been an honest, trustworthy manager all along, you have a good chance of refuting the charges—even without witnesses testifying on your behalf.

Of course, there's always the possibility that you actually did sexually harass your employee. If that is true, you have two choices.

First, a promise to your superiors that you will never engage in sexually harassing anyone again and that you will be particularly sensitive to how a person's actions, no matter how well-meaning, can be interpreted. Second, if you've been found to have sexually harassed the employee, intentionally or not, your effectiveness and trust as a manager will be greatly, if not entirely, diminished by the powerful stigma of sexual harassment. Your next move should be to find a new job where you can put your past mistakes behind you and start fresh.

## TWO MISTAKES MADE IN HEARING THE GRIEVANCE

No doubt it is upsetting for any business to deal with a sexual harassment complaint, but the fact that it is brought to your attention as a complaint gives you the opportunity to correct the problem before it develops into an expensive lawsuit.

## MISTAKE 235

**Ignoring sexual harassment charges.**

### How to Avoid It

When a sexual harassment charge is brought to your attention, it is the responsibility of the company, whether through the owner, a manager, or a supervisor, to offer the employee confidentiality and protection and to determine exactly what happened to provoke the charge. To fully understand the circumstances, questions will have to be asked of the accuser such as:

- ▮ "Exactly what happened? Tell me the place, the date, the time, the circumstances, and what was said."

- ▮ "Did the accused harass you verbally or physically?"

- ▮ "Has this occurred before? If so, tell me the dates and the circumstances."

- ▮ "Did you consent or encourage the behavior?"

- ▮ "Exactly how did you respond to the person who harassed you?"

- ▮ "Were there any witnesses to what happened or any documents or evidence that will support your claim?"

- ▮ "Has the person who harassed you retaliated or threatened to retaliate against you in any way? "

- ▮ "Have any of your coworkers ever told you of similar problems they had with the accused? If so, who and when?"

- ▮ "What effect has this behavior had on your ability to do your job?"

- ▮ "Do you dread or fear coming to work because of it?"

- ▮ "Are you embarrassed to be with other employees who know about the incident?"

Don't ask the complainant to sign a written complaint. It is not required, and asking for such a declaration could be considered intimidation on your part. Instead, take detailed notes during the interview or tape-record the interview.

## MISTAKE 236

**Not assessing the credibility of the complainant.**

### How to Avoid It

Your next step in hearing a grievance is to assess the credibility of the complainant. To do so, consider the following:

■ What was the complainant's reaction to the incident? If he or she was not too upset, the complaint may be trivial. On the other hand, the apparent mildness of reaction may be due to embarrassment or fear.

■ Is there any evidence that the complainant willingly participated in the horseplay or banter and now finds it objectionable?

■ What is the character of the accused? Is the person a known womanizer or excessive toucher?

■ If there is tangible evidence, such as pornographic pictures, collect the items.

■ Have there been other complaints against that person? Speak to any witnesses or other employees who may have been harassed. If the complainant does not supply the names of other workers who may have been affected, conduct a confidential investigation by speaking with your employees individually. Tell them the company has a policy against harassment and ask them if they ever had such a problem.

Managing sexual harassment grievances requires sensitivity and common sense. A proper investigation is the next phase of the procedure, and it may serve a double purpose: to dissuade a complainant from bringing suit and to discourage future harassment in your workplace.

## FOUR COMMON MISTAKES IN INVESTIGATING THE CLAIM

### MISTAKE 237

**Assuming time will heal all wounds and failing to investigate promptly.**

### MISTAKE 238

**Not taking all complaints seriously.**

## MISTAKE 239

**Not looking for patterns in personnel records.**

### How to Avoid Them

Courts seem to be in agreement that certain rules should apply to all investigations concerning sexual harassment. They are:

■ The employer is legally obliged to inquire into a complaint immediately when an employee reports being sexually harassed by a coworker. Failure to do so could make it appear that the company sanctions or ignores this kind of activity. This may cause you to lose your defense that your company vigorously enforces its sexual harassment policies and may increase your liability for the harassment. For a simple matter, you should turn your attention to the matter within 24 hours, lawyers say. A more complex situation should require about a week to research.

■ Take all complaints seriously. Often a complainant will be embarrassed or have fear of reprisal and therefore understate the incident and the resulting effects.

■ Document the investigation. Try to tape-record all interviews, if possible. This evidence may help support company action or inaction against the accused.

■ Conduct your interviews privately and maintain confidentiality during an inquiry and, if harassment is confirmed, while disciplining the harasser. Without confidentiality, the facts of what occurred may become exaggerated and people may be afraid to participate in your investigation. Discuss the investigation and its results only when necessary and only with those who need to know. The more people who know about the incident, the more you risk having a defamation claim brought against you by the accused. While these claims are rarely successful, they can be avoided by conducting the investigation in a discreet manner. In any event, the risk of such a claim is no excuse for not investigating sexual harassment allegations. Ignoring them will certainly expose you to a suit by the victim.

■ Look for patterns in the accused person's records that might indicate similar problems such as retaliation against workers who rejected sexual advances. Also look at the records of the complainant. There might be indications that the complainant has a history of making accusations or was receiving unusually positive performance evaluations because the supervisor was providing a quid pro quo: great reports in return for sexual favors.

▮ Give the accused an opportunity to refute the allegations.

## MISTAKE 240

**Assigning only one person to listen to grievances and investigate claims.**

### How to Avoid It

Employees, even in a small company, should have more than one person to report incidents to, so that they are not forced to bring their grievances to the individual who has been harassing them. If your company is small, investigations can be handled by the company owner, a manager, or a supervisor.

# THE MOST COMMON MISTAKE IN PROTECTING THE ACCUSER

## MISTAKE 241

**Not keeping the incident confidential and the claimant protected from reprisals and further harassment during your investigation.**

### How to Avoid It

As we said earlier, it is best to conduct your meetings with the accuser privately and maintain confidentiality during the inquiry. Failure to do so can cause the accuser embarrassment and cause the company additional legal problems. It is also essential to keep the accuser safe and eliminate any fear of retaliation. In most cases, protecting the accuser is as simple as limiting the instances in which harassment can occur. For instance, if the harassment was alleged to have occurred when the accuser was working on a project with the accused, change the accuser's working schedule to avoid putting the two together. However, when making such an obvious move, it is important not to make the accuser appear to be the "bad guy" by ostracizing her from the rest of the staff.

For less serious allegations, such as sexual innuendoes and jokes, it might be wise to give the accuser time off with pay while the investigation is in progress.

For more serious allegations, such as physical contact and demanding sexual favors, the harasser should be given time off with pay while you investigate the situation.

## THE MOST COMMON MISTAKE IN CONFRONTING THE ACCUSED

### MISTAKE 242

**Believing you must have absolute proof of guilt before taking action.**

#### How to Avoid It

As soon as possible after receiving sexual harassment complaints you should:

■ Confront accused parties privately and inform them of the charges.

■ Make clear that you have not yet concluded your investigation and that you want to hear their side of the story.

■ You are not required to identify the accuser, but most managers we spoke to told us they do.

■ Tell accused parties they are not to confront their accusers or retaliate in any way. If they do, you will consider that insubordination and will take appropriate action.

■ Expect an alleged harasser to give the facts from a different viewpoint or to argue that the conduct was welcomed or encouraged by the accuser. When you have to decide who is telling the truth and who is lying, you must rely on whatever facts and evidence you have, supported by witnesses and documents, if possible, and your impressions and observations of both the accused and the accuser in their daily work environment. But it is important to know that in sexual harassment claims, it is not necessary to have absolute proof of guilt in order to take appropriate action.

## TWO COMMON MISTAKES IN TAKING
## REMEDIAL ACTION

### MISTAKE 243

**Not knowing what remedial action your company policy allows.**

### How to Avoid It

If you have any questions about what your company's policy is on sexual harassment, find the answers to them immediately. The same applies if you're not sure about your own responsibilities.

### MISTAKE 244

**Not taking effective disciplinary action to resolve the problem.**

### How to Avoid It

If you're completely convinced that the alleged harassment was a misunderstanding, counsel the accused on the seriousness of the situation and explain how the behavior affected the accuser. Then get together with the accuser and see if an apology and promise not to repeat the behavior will be enough to settle the matter. If it is, get the two together and breathe a loud sigh of relief. If the accuser does not accept this remedy, but you are still convinced it was a misunderstanding, discuss the facts privately again with the accuser. If you still can't resolve the situation, advise the accuser to take whatever action he must, or suggest that the matter be resolved by the EEOC.

Should you conclude that sexual harassment has occurred, there are several actions you can take:

■ If the victim has been tangibly harmed (by being fired or denied a promotion, for example), you can reinstate or promote the employee. Try to find out what the victim wants. It may just be an apology and promise not to repeat the offense.

■ If the victim demands that you exercise discipline, your actions must be based on the facts of the situation. For instance, if women are experiencing a hostile work environment in a male-dominated workplace, you might rent a training video or hire a consultant to help male workers understand why their behavior is inappropriate. If the situation is serious and involves physical abuse as well as verbal, you must take prompt and appropriate disciplinary action. You will be acting to protect yourself and the company. In determining the punishment for one of your workers consider the following:

- The seriousness of the offense.

- The employee's work record in terms of similar prior behavior and overall performance.

- Was it clear that the harassing behavior was unacceptable in your workplace? If your company has been tolerating sexually oriented jokes for the past ten years and you just instituted a policy against them, you should treat violations of a new policy differently from violations of a standard everyone has been observing for ten years.

- If the accused is not an employee but a vendor or service person, get statements from the affected employees and talk to the vendor. Let the accused know that what is going on is disrupting work and interfering with your employees' well-being and that corrective measures must be taken. If the behavior does not stop immediately, no vendor is worth risking your business over, so take your business elsewhere, fast!

- If it's a client or customer harassing your employees, you can ask the client to stop the harassment because you don't want to work for that kind of firm or have your employees exposed to such harassment. Explain the legal ramifications that may result from the continued behavior and how it will eventually affect the quality of the work you put out. Of course, you can also assign different employees to the account or department and hope the problem will disappear. But simply replacing the target of harassment can also send the message to the client that you don't object to the harassment. Many consultants we spoke to on this matter suggested a talk with the client, and then if the harassing behavior continued, drop the client and go after his competition.

## THREE MISTAKES IN PUBLISHING
## A SEXUAL HARASSMENT POLICY

### MISTAKE 245

**Not establishing a policy because you don't think your company needs one or is too small to need one.**

#### How to Avoid It

Having a published sexual harassment policy for any business, whether large or small, serves a number of purposes:

▪ It makes it crystal clear to workers that sexual harassment will not be tolerated by management and that management will take action to deter such conduct.

▪ It lets employees know how and where they can complain about a problem, increasing the probability that the offensive behavior will be reported and that the company's management will be able to take prompt remedial action.

▪ In the event of a lawsuit, the existence of a policy may also reduce an employer's liability if, for example, the employee failed to complain through the prescribed channels or if the employer responded with prompt remedial action when the person did complain.

### MISTAKE 246

**Not knowing what is legal to include in your policy.**

### MISTAKE 247

**Establishing a policy but not distributing it to all employees.**

## How to Avoid Them

A sexual harassment policy should be prepared by an attorney familiar with federal and state discrimination laws. Many companies get copies of policies other organizations are using and tailor one for their particular business. The policy you adopt should:

- Be published and distributed to each employee as a separate document, specifically addressing the topic and informing workers that sexual harassment will not be tolerated. If possible, it should be included as part of the employee handbook, if there is one, and posted in recreational and meeting areas throughout the premises.

- Give examples of the types of conduct that will be considered sexual harassment.

- Create channels (more than one) through which workers can make a complaint without fear of retaliation and with assurances of confidentiality.

- Have provisions to accommodate employees who prefer same-gender representation.

- Provide sanctions that would be imposed against harassers.

- Inform employees that anyone who files frivolous or vindictive claims without merit will be subject to discipline or other sanctions, too.

- Include documented training and refresher counseling for managers and supervisors to ensure their familiarity with the policy and to caution them that they will be held accountable for any sexual harassment for which they are found guilty or responsible.

- Provide assurance that claims will be handled promptly and effectively.

The creation and administration of such a policy does not guarantee that a company will avoid any claims of sexual harassment. But if employees know what's expected of them and what the consequences are for violating those expectations, establishing a sexual harassment policy becomes good management.

# Chapter 10

# CONFRONTING EMPLOYEE THEFT—
# SERIOUS MISTAKES COMPANIES MAKE

Even the most familial companies can experience employee theft. And few ever recover much of what is stolen. It may be money that leaves the office in a briefcase or pocketbook or finds its way into someone's bank account in the form of a kickback from a vendor. Often, it's merchandise and equipment that goes out the back door, or valuable information and financial transactions that move out through computers and fax machines as an electronic blip.

Losses from employee theft cost U.S. businesses over $100 billion annually. Small companies are particularly vulnerable because they have neither the sophisticated security nor the accounting systems to safeguard their assets. Many small companies never report employee theft because the owner is embarrassed that an employee stole or embezzled from the firm, or for fear that bringing charges without enough proof can lead to bigger legal problems for the company.

But there are steps every company can take to avoid suffering losses at the hands of dishonest workers.

## FOUR MISTAKES IN RECOGNIZING
## THE WARNING SIGNS

### MISTAKE 248

**Not believing your employees would ever steal from you.**

## How to Avoid It

There are as many ways to steal from an employer as there are kinds of businesses. Employee theft ranges from the grocery clerk munching a candy bar taken off the shelf to the stockbroker who uses his computer to divert hundreds of thousands of dollars from clients' investment accounts.

Many businesses, particularly smaller ones, delegate certain functions to those individuals they trust. For example, you may select one person to be in charge of financial matters and another to be in charge of buying supplies and dealing with outside vendors. You hope the people you entrust with these duties will do the job well and honestly, but the sad truth is that employee theft is more fact than fiction and you should never trust anyone completely.

## MISTAKE 249

**Failing to take notice of obvious warning signs.**

## MISTAKE 250

**Hiring relatives and friends.**

## MISTAKE 251

**Accepting internal theft as an unavoidable part of fixed operating costs.**

## How to Avoid Them

Many of the signs of employee theft are painfully obvious, although managers often fail to see or recognize them. Here are some to look out for (ways to protect yourself will be given later in this chapter):

1. Start with the hiring process. Obviously, a smart manager should not hire someone with a record of stealing. But sometimes managers, in their desire to get as much employee for the money as they can, "beat" prospective hires down to a very low starting wage that can be all the inspiration an employee needs to try and "steal" what they think they're worth.

2. Hiring relatives and friends can also present problems that relate to employee theft. It is easier, for instance, to set and enforce

company policies with strangers than it is with people you know well. It is also easier to dismiss someone who is not a relative or friend. And if you have to bring charges against someone for embezzlement or theft of company property, you will be better off dealing with someone you won't have to be in contact with again in the future (See Chapter 12, "Family Members in the Same Business").

3. Unexplained inconsistencies. Often, managers would rather place blame for theft anywhere but on employees and peers. One executive we interviewed told us about his former boss who owned an electronics distributing business, who for years blamed his computers for serious inventory discrepancies. He eventually sent six employees to jail, but unfortunately the inventory losses he sustained put him out of business. A number of companies we queried on this subject gave this advice, "Don't assume employees are stealing from you, but don't ignore the possibility, either."

4. Lifestyle changes. You would certainly ask questions if your $40,000-a-year bookkeeper began driving a $60,000 Mercedes-Benz to work, wouldn't you? The partners of a law firm we spoke to came across the source of their bookkeeper's newfound wealth: She was writing company checks to phony names and endorsing them to her personal account. An investigator we interviewed told us, "There are usually lifestyle changes that will clue you in, keep your eyes and ears open, and keep an open friendly line of communication going with all employees. If an employee's lifestyle suddenly changes for the better, without explanation, chances are word will eventually get to you through the office grapevine."

5. Bad morale. Not all disgruntled employees steal, but most workplace thieves are dissatisfied with their jobs. If you know that certain employees are constantly complaining about overwork or underpay, make sure there's a system for airing and confronting those gripes, otherwise the grumblers may start trying to devise their own compensation systems.

6. Bogus and duplicate invoices. One common accounts-payable scam involves the use of bogus invoices, in which an employee submits a fictitious bill payable to a phony vendor for goods or services never provided. As part of the scam, the insider or a confederate arranges to receive and cash the check mailed to the

phony vendor. Another embezzlement technique is the dupli-cate invoice. Instead of submitting a bill from a phony vendor, the employee resubmits a legitimate invoice so that two checks are generated. The worker pockets the second check before it is mailed, then fraudulently endorses and cashes it.

7. Kickbacks by suppliers to company employees is a widespread workplace occurrence. They are not easy to detect, and they are not always in the form of cash. A kickback could be a free week-end at a resort or free tickets to a show that are given as an inducement to get your company's business, usually to employ-ees who are in a position to purchase goods or services.

8. Excessive reimbursement of expenses. Some employees identify the threshold at which a boss or bookkeeper starts paying atten-tion to expenses and files false expense vouchers below that amount.

9. Drug abuse. A good deal of theft in this country is committed to support drug habits. A workplace thief with such a problem will more than likely steal smaller items that are easy to get off the premises and that are easily resold.

10. Office romances. There have been times when confidential information was passed along to a "lover" by an unsuspecting person in another department.

11. Stealing time. The least recognized—but perhaps most costly—form of employee theft is the theft of time, some experts say. Employees who willfully waste their paid working hours are just as guilty of stealing from their companies as they would be if they took money or materials. Methods include arriving at work late, leaving work early, faking illness, claiming unwarranted "sick" days, taking long lunch hours and coffee breaks, constant socializing with other workers, making excessive personal phone calls, and creating the need for overtime by purposely slowing down during normal hours.

12. Situational pressures. There are times when honest people who are up against a lot of pressure such as heavy debts, financial reverses, or hostility toward the employer will turn to stealing just to relieve the pressure.

## TWO COMMON MISTAKES IN DEALING WITH KICKBACKS AND MISSING PAPER CLIPS

### MISTAKE 252

**Not considering taking kickbacks or bribes as employee theft.**

### How to Avoid It

As stated earlier, kickbacks are not easy to detect and are not always in the form of money. But one thing is certain; if kickbacks are being made to one or more of your employees, it probably means you are not paying the best prices for the products, supplies, or services you are purchasing or, at least, not getting the quality you are paying for.

Kickbacks usually come from vendors who want to do business with your company. The kickback represents a "bribe" the vendor pays an employee who is in a position to make a purchase. Kickbacks could possibly come from:

▮ Printing companies.

▮ Office supply companies.

▮ Travel agents.

▮ Convention and trade show managers.

▮ Vending machine operators.

▮ Office cleaning services.

Many companies have found one effective way to discourage kickbacks is to deal with more than one vendor for particular services. Always get at least three competitive bids on every order you are giving out. Keep an eye out for employees who become "chummy" with vendors. Try to change vendors on a fairly consistent basis. Set up clearly defined purchasing procedures to verify invoices. Go over vendor bills carefully. Sometimes you may spot a notation that would indicate that someone in your office is on the "take." Always check vendors' references. You may discover that they are kicking back to employees at other companies too. Discourage vendors from giving holiday gifts to your employees. You might want to make it a company policy for employees not to accept gifts from any vendors for any reason.

## MISTAKE 253

**Ignoring minor losses of office supplies and materials.**

### HOW TO AVOID IT

When it comes to employees walking off with office supplies, keep in mind that most employees do not consider taking a pen, pencil, paper clips, rolls of transparent tape, a calculator, power stapler, or box of computer disks a crime, especially if it's off their own desk. After all, nothing really big or that noticeable is missing. Still, the cost of replacing these items can be substantial when you multiply the number of items taken by the frequency and number of people doing the taking. Many companies provide lockers to safeguard employee property. These lockers may, however, be used to store stolen company property. For this reason, some companies now place clear plexiglass fronts on lockers to allow external viewing.

Periodically go over your bills for in-office supplies to see if there are any purchases that are showing up more often than they should be. Make it a part of company policy to explain to all new employees that every dollar spent replacing a lost or "acquired" office item is a dollar less that the company has to spend on raises, bonuses, better working conditions, company picnics, and other benefits to employees.

## TWO COMMON MISTAKES IN DEALING WITH ELECTRONIC THEFT

You have critical sales data and other sensitive files stored on a desktop PC in the office. One of your employees gains access, copies the files, and quickly turns the copies into cash by selling them to a rival company. Don't believe it? Try this one. During the Gulf War, hackers from the Netherlands broke into U.S. government computers containing details of troop movements and invasion plans. Still skeptical? How about the intruders who invaded the computer system at the University of California at Berkeley and installed a "sniffer" program that scooped up more than 3,000 account and password combinations in less than 24 hours. And then there are the Internet vandals who break into computer networks to eavesdrop on business deals and divert shipments of goods. They also steal merchandise, credit card numbers, and digital cash, which are "virtual" financial instruments that Internet users can swap for real goods and services

Just how snoop-proof is your business from electronic eavesdropping and computer theft?

## MISTAKE 254

**Not perceiving electronic theft as a crime.**

## MISTAKE 255

**Not installing the proper safeguards.**

### How to Avoid Them

If, like tens of thousands of other business firms, you haven't taken the most basic security precautions, your faxes, phone calls, and computer files are vulnerable to big ears and prying eyes.

Anyone can walk into an electronics store and, for less than $100, buy a scanner that picks up cordless telephone calls. It is also possible to purchase scanners (now banned by the government) that intercept cellular phone calls or get equipment that will identify and clone cellular phone numbers.

As for computer files, even though there is a Federal Computer Fraud and Abuse Act, anyone with a little cyber savvy and access to your computer for a few minutes can read, copy, and change your most intimate data. E-mail is even less secure. Typically, a letter goes through dozens of sites before it reaches its destination and at any one of them anyone could be copying your mail and selling it for beer money.

The computer has simplified the way the world does business, but it has also simplified the workplace thief's job. Employees can now embezzle with one finger, shifting numbers around, quietly fiddling with inventory records or fraudulently transferring money electronically.

And what about fax document security? How many times have you walked by the fax machine in your office and seen stacks of documents, some very sensitive and confidential, waiting to be claimed? Anyone can read them. Yet smart business people continue to fax confidential documents without safeguards and without giving a second thought as to who might be reading them.

The same technology that empowers electronic snoopers can also be used to foil them. Steps you can take to make your business more secure from electronic theft:

■ A digital cordless telephone will keep anyone short of a master snoop from listening to your calls.

■ If you're using a nondigital type of cellular phone, the only practical way to protect yourself is to be aware of its semi-public nature: Don't mention full names of companies or people. Don't give out addresses, telephone numbers, or credit card numbers. Speak in code, never go into detailed financial or personal data, and frequently remind the other party that people are listening. And they are!

■ Encryption software will stop even the CIA from reading your E-mail. They allow you to keep data secure by encoding them with passwords or pass phrases of any length. The longer the phrase, the more secure the data. With encryption software, you can sign a plain-text message with an electronic signature so the recipient can verify that it is from you and has not been tampered with. There are also systems designed to curb the theft of information such as video-on-demand, home shopping, travel and banking, and still others that provide comprehensive security for marketing and sales of economically valuable information.

■ Doing business on the Internet, with its open architecture and freewheeling culture, is a risk and may never be totally safe. But new security technologies, including a secure software interface (known as public key cryptography) for authorizing and clearing credit card transactions on the Internet, are making it much safer. Another widely used system to safeguard sensitive information on the Internet and other networks is a data-scrambling program of mathematical algorithms.

■ New software products that scramble messages with undecipherable squiggles and graphic markings allow you to use your computer to protect ordinary fax documents. However, not everybody wants or likes to use his computer to send faxes. The simplest method of faxing sensitive information to machines used by more than one person is to call the party on the telephone first, tell them what you are sending and when, and ask them to please be at their machine when your fax arrives.

The importance of secure electronic communications and protected files in the workplace can't be overemphasized.

## FOUR COMMON MISTAKES IN PROSECUTING THEFT IN THE WORKPLACE

Poor Bob. He's been with the company for 15 years. Sweet guy. Everybody likes him. There isn't anything he wouldn't do to help a fellow worker. Sure, you caught him red handed stealing money, but you can't send a guy like Bob to jail. "Maybe he'll return the money and resign," you say, "and we'll forget the whole thing."

## MISTAKE 256

**Being compassionate instead of correct.**

### How to Avoid It

Being compassionate and lenient are wonderful traits, but some experts maintain that one of the most effective deterrents to employee theft is coming down hard on those caught stealing. When you don't prosecute, you're sending a message to other employees that they can get away with ripping off the company.

Once an investigation involving employee theft is complete and all the facts are identified and substantiated the company must take action to recover its assets, correct the behavior of the employee, and reduce or deter future incidents. The action taken will depend on the offender's intent, the strength of the case, and company morale and culture. Options for action include no action at all, a verbal warning, dismissal, civil restitution, and criminal prosecution.

## MISTAKE 257

**Not making a complaint and testifying in court because it's too costly and time consuming.**

### How to Avoid It

True, it does cost money and take time to prosecute, and many managers either assume they won't be able to make criminal charges stick or they won't win a civil case. So they simply remove the worker from the payroll. This is a mistake. There are important reasons to prosecute. If you don't:

■  The thief goes unpunished.

■  You may forgo getting back what was stolen.

■  The problem goes unsolved.

■  You set a bad example for other employees.

■  Losses get charged off to consumers who will have to pay higher prices than necessary.

■  Your business may suffer serious morale problems.

■  And if you let the thieves off, they'll probably steal from you again or from their next employer.

Civil restitution is one approach to recouping losses that more and more states are legalizing. In general, it involves dropping or reducing the charges if the company and the thief can work out an arrangement for reimbursement.

## MISTAKE 258

**Not bringing charges because you're embarrassed that an employee stole or embezzled from the firm.**

## MISTAKE 259

**Not bringing charges because you're afraid of bad publicity.**

### How to Avoid Them

Prosecuting is not an easy decision, and certainly it is not appropriate for every crime, especially minor ones. It can be embarrassing to customers and devastating image-wise if you deal with the public. If the punishment is too severe, it could create resentment among your other employees as well as low morale. But in the final analysis, most of the companies we researched felt that aggressive prosecution was the most effective theft deterrent, and by taking such serious action, a company sends a strong warning to anyone else who is stealing or conspiring with others to do so.

## SIX MISTAKES IN PROTECTING YOURSELF AGAINST THEFT

The U.S. Chamber of Commerce says that monetary, merchandise, and equipment losses due to employee theft cost U.S. businesses an estimated $120 billion a year. That cost is expected to rise at least 10 percent per year and does not include the most costly form of employee theft, the theft of time.

According to specialists, there are several factors that go into an employee's decision to steal:

1. *Personal integrity.* The person is basically dishonest or predisposed to steal.

2. *Situational pressures.* The person incurred heavy debt or financial obligations.

3. *Opportunity.* The person handles money or goods without supervision. Company accounting controls are inadequate.

4. *Coercion.* The person was enticed or pressured into stealing by coworkers.

5. *Revenge.* The person felt harmed, underpaid, and overworked or otherwise taken advantage of by the employer.

These same specialists agree that reduction of theft is a much more realistic goal than attempting to stop it altogether.

## MISTAKE 260

**Not screening job applicants for trustworthiness.**

### How to Avoid It

You can greatly reduce your exposure to theft by not hiring employees who have been caught stealing in the past.

Evaluate applicants' job histories during preemployment screening for signs of strong allegiance to their employers. Ask prospective hires to sign waivers of liability so that previous employers will feel free to discuss their job histories.

Check references carefully and ask those references for the names of other references, and (if the job is a sensitive one) send them a photo of the applicant to check identification. Be sure to investigate any gaps in employment.

If you don't have the time for thorough background investigations, do your hiring through an employment agency that carefully screens the workers it provides.

Assess propensities for future theft by having applicants take written "honesty" tests. "Honesty" tests are now being used by thousands of firms nationwide, especially since the federal Polygraph Protection Act of 1988 barred the use of polygraphs (lie detectors) by most businesses. These pencil-and-paper tests predict future behavior based on the applicant's attitudes and admissions of past conduct. Applicants take the test at your company, but the test is scored by the test publisher.

## MISTAKE 261

**Not recognizing the role management plays in encouraging or discouraging theft.**

## MISTAKE 262

**Not having a company antitheft policy or communicating it to employees.**

### How to Avoid Them

Adopt and communicate a clear policy on employee theft. Inform all employees about the company's definition of theft, what will happen to employees caught stealing, and emphasize the message that theft is not acceptable behavior.

Enforce the policy equally at all levels. When sanctions are enforced, let other workers know about it, without using the names of offenders. Don't give special treatment to employees at higher levels. This will erode the fairness necessary to deter theft.

Don't hesitate to file charges and send a serious thief to jail if you catch them.

Formal and informal communication should also emphasize management's concern with this particular problem, letting workers know the company cares about both its property and its employees.

Paycheck inserts, company newsletter articles, new-employee orientations, posters in locker areas and lunchrooms, and company meetings are just some of the ways you can convey the message.

Consider using an employee incentive program as a theft-control measure. Many companies now believe in "sharing the company's savings with their employees." An incentive could be a bonus based on each department's success in meeting shortage reduction goals.

Treat employees with dignity, respect, and trust. By expecting the best of employees and treating them as honorable, trustworthy individuals, they are more likely to act as such. A positive climate can also permeate the work group and foster group norms that discourage theft.

And remember, honesty in business has to start at the top. Progress in a company's fight to reduce crime can begin only when managers at all levels regard themselves as ethical role models— avoiding conflicts of interest and clarifying the kind of business conduct expected by the company.

## MISTAKE 263

**Leaving the door open to thieves by failing to make the fullest use of auditing and tracking systems.**

## MISTAKE 264

**Not having adequate security measures to safeguard company property.**

### HOW TO AVOID THEM

Here are some steps you can take to eliminate theft opportunities:

- Use tight accounting controls that track and monitor goods and transactions against norms. Your internal controls should trace your assets as they move from raw materials or purchased products coming in the door to finished goods sold out the door. Such a system can compare expenses in various categories with the year before and show patterns of irregularity such as catching higher costs for raw materials, faster than usual inventory turnover, increased amounts of waste, and most important, declining inventories coupled with stable or falling revenues.

- If possible, separate the bookkeeping and check-preparation functions of your business. The person who handles accounts payable and processes invoices should not be the same person who approves and signs checks or who reconciles the bank account. When these functions are combined, it becomes a simple matter to generate and cover up fraudulent payments. Using computerized accounting programs, you can create safeguards against this such as requiring special authorization before certain types of data may be entered or changed.

- Have all mail sent unopened to a specified person, such as the office manager. The person who opens the mail should also distribute it and be accountable for missing checks.

■ If bogus invoices are a problem, establish strict controls over the list of vendors in your accounts-payable system. Give each vendor an ID number before a check can be issued. Vendor numbers should be printed on check vouchers and on your monthly check register. Examine checks before they are signed to ensure that the payee's name, address, and vendor number are the same as those in your vendor list.

■ If duplicate invoices are a problem, authorize payments on original invoices only, not on photocopies or faxes. Once an original bill is processed, stamp it "paid" to prevent duplication or resubmission.

■ Retail thefts usually occur at the point of sale and involve clerks underringing, passing merchandise without charging, or by fraudulent voiding of charges. In this case, closed-circuit TV or personal surveillance techniques that monitor employee behaviors, and sting operations ("mystery shoppers") that catch thieves in the act are effective measures. Many retailers also use devices that, if not detached from merchandise by a sales clerk, set off an alarm as they are taken out of the store or cause damage to the goods if they are removed outside the store.

■ Modern point-of-sale systems, the successors to cash registers, can be highly effective weapons against employee theft. Managers can use them to track overages and shortages, voided sales, cash refunds, and the frequency of a particular employee's undercharges for friends. Balance the register throughout the day, and transfer cash and checks to a bank or safe frequently.

■ Provide an alternative to theft by giving employees, whenever possible, things they might take anyway. This might include dated, partially damaged, or nonsaleable merchandise that gets thrown away. Instead of discarding it, offer it to employees. When old office equipment is replaced with new, give the old to the employees. The loyalty you gain with this simple gesture may far exceed the trade-in value of the old equipment.

■ Encourage workers to report acts of dishonesty. Employee involvement in the security, safety, and overall operation of the business can be paramount to its success. By creating an anonymous tip-line (possibly along with a reward system), employees are provided with an opportunity to report information that will rectify situations at the workplace that they know are improper.

■ Use fidelity bonds or dishonesty insurance. Bookkeepers, accountants, the company treasurer, and others with access to financial records and bank accounts should be covered by fidelity bonds, a form of insurance that pays for losses in case of dishonest acts by staff members. A fidelity bond protects in two ways. First, before the surety company bonds anyone, it does a thorough background check and weeds out unacceptable candidates. Second, once the employee is bonded, any losses, within the policy limits and deductibles, are covered by the bonding company.

■ Dishonesty insurance, usually part of a standard business insurance package, also protects the company against losses from employee theft. Before issuing such a policy, most insurance firms will check out the company's hiring procedures and theft-prevention efforts.

■ Safeguard cash. Cash is always a prime target of thieves. If not actively monitored, petty cash funds used to reimburse employees for minor expenses are ripe for picking. Have one employee responsible for such a fund. Make sure there's a receipt detailing what the refund is for before a reimbursement from petty cash is issued. Do not replenish the petty cash fund until all the money spent is accounted for. Keep large amounts of cash in a floor safe or one that is bolted to the floor. Keep the safe locked when not in use and change the combination when an employee who knows it leaves.

■ Provide assistance programs to employees with problems. Even small businesses can provide alcohol- and drug-abuse assistance through one of the growing number of such programs in hospitals and clinics. Counseling services, including financial counseling, can give a troubled employee a viable alternative to theft.

■ Provide adequate and fair compensation. You are inviting theft when your workers feel they are being compensated inequitably. Also, by giving employees job autonomy. more decision-making responsibility, a greater variety of tasks, and more opportunities to meet and work with others, less time will be spent generating theft-related activities.

■ Provide opportunities for disgruntled employees to vent their emotions. Employee surveys, informal employee-management meetings, and complaint sessions induce an emotional catharsis and provide management with important information about the operation's status. Employees will not feel a need to strike out against the company if the company is willing to listen to their gripes.

## MISTAKE 265

**Not considering the theft of time as a serious form of employee theft.**

### How to Avoid It

Time is one of a company's most valuable assets, and stealing it by coming in late and leaving early, slowing the work pace, or taking longer than allowed lunch and coffee breaks can threaten the very existence of the company. You can go a long way toward eliminating time stealing by using the following six tips:

1. Set an example and show employees the boss is the hardest worker in the company.

2. Establish clear, feasible rules and enforce them with everyone.

3. Monitor workers at various times each day, especially during breaks.

4. Spotlight top performers for special recognition to demonstrate that good work and loyal service are appreciated.

5. Involve employees in the operations of the company. Help them recognize how they can contribute to the company's success and what it potentially means to them in promotions and income.

6. Make sure workers are clear about their priorities. Communicate with employees about what they should be doing, how they should proceed, and when their deadlines will be.

# Chapter 11

## FIRING EMPLOYEES— THE TASK EVERY BOSS DREADS

You trained the employee to perform his tasks. You spoke to the employee when you first spotted his problem and on numerous occasions afterward. You provided counseling, and you reached more than a few agreements to improve the situation. You documented it all in writing many times and carefully monitored your employee's progress in changing his ways. All of your efforts have been costly and ineffective. Now comes the next dreaded step.

Whether you call it a layoff, termination, job cut, or dismissal, firing an employee spells anguish for most managers. Even if your employee expects to be fired and may actually be relieved to finally have it over with, delivering the bad news can be a manager's toughest assignment.

Although there are numerous reasons why someone could be fired, the managers we spoke to during our research cited these three as the most common reasons:

1. An employee could not perform the work regardless of how much training she had.

2. An employee could not get along with others regardless of how much counseling he had.

3. An employee's job was cut back due to company downsizing.

This chapter will cover firing employees for reasons 1 and 2. See Chapter 14, Downtime, Downsizing, and Going Out of Business, for more on reason 3.

## THREE COMMON MISTAKES IN DEALING WITH YOUR EMOTIONS

### MISTAKE 266

**Trying to spare a worker's feelings instead of doing what's best for your company.**

### MISTAKE 267

**Waiting too long to fire someone because you like the person and couldn't get up the courage to do it.**

### MISTAKE 268

**Hoping poor performers will leave on their own.**

### HOW TO AVOID THEM

There's probably not a manager alive who has not had this thought at one time or another: I know I have to do it, but I keep putting it off because firing anyone makes me emotionally upset.

You are not alone. Being fired can be a devastating emotional experience. But *doing* the firing can be just as emotionally traumatic. This is particularly true for the small-business manager or owner who has to deal with a staff that is close-knit, and terminating an employee can feel like firing a good friend or member of your family.

We have been told stories of managers who, rather than confront and fire an employee face to face, waited until the worker was on vacation and sent a termination letter in the mail. We also heard about one manager who fired an employee by fax. She wasn't in when it arrived, so all of her coworkers knew about it before she did.

One of my first jobs, many years ago, was with a medium-sized advertising agency that planned to fire a key employee who was very well liked and had been a terrific worker. Her troubles began when her mother, whom she was supporting, became ill and the worker encountered financial problems. This had a drastic effect on her job performance and attendance. In addition, she had a thing about germs. She flatly refused to be in the same room with anyone who had a cold or a sniffle. She also refused to use *any* rest room facilities that other people used, sick or not. This meant she had to walk home (she had no car), which was a mile or so away. The round trip, including the rest stop, took the better part of an hour. Multiply that by at least two trips each workday, and you'll understand why my supervisor was anxious to terminate the lady. As anxious as he was, he knew he would be removing her livelihood, and he could not get up the courage to do the firing himself. So he offered another employee in the department $20 ($20 was considered a lot of money then) if she would deliver the bad news. She accepted, but found that she couldn't get up the courage either. The offer went up to $50, then $75, but no one in the entire department was willing or able to do the downright dastardly deed. Eventually (five weeks later), a supervisor from another department did the firing.

The moral of this story is, no matter how daunting the task, when the choice is between your firm's productivity and sparing a worker's feelings, or your own, there is no choice. Do what's best for your company.

It takes skill, maturity, and thorough preparation for a manager to give an employee bad news.

First, the manager should be both honest about why the termination is happening and compassionate in the way the news is given.

Second, the news should never come as a surprise to the worker. The manager should have already documented problems and coached the employee. Documents not only protect the company against wrongful-dismissal suits, they help prepare the manager emotionally.

Documentation makes it easier for the manager to say, "You have been given every opportunity to change your behavior, and it hasn't changed. You were told what the consequences might be. You leave us with no choice but to terminate your employment. Now you will have an opportunity to find a job better suited to your skills and personality."

## THE MOST COMMON MISTAKE MADE BEFORE THE TERMINATION MEETING

## MISTAKE 269

**Not being prepared for a termination meeting.**

## How to Avoid It

Preparation won't eliminate the sting, but it can lessen the trauma for both parties. Once the decision to terminate a worker has been made, the manager should follow these tips that will help make the meeting as painless as possible:

■ Decide where and when to have the termination meeting. Preferably, schedule it in a private conference room rather than in your office. The reason for this is that sometimes an employee may become upset and try to extend the meeting with pleas for reconsideration. If matters get out of hand, you can always walk out of the conference room and leave the employee alone. It would not be a good idea to leave the discharged employee alone in your office.

■ Know what you are going to say. Write down in advance what your reasons are for terminating the employee. Focus on the facts of your employee's performance or behavior. Rely on the records you kept. Also prepare a written explanation specifying the salary continuation period, if any, severance pay, benefits and other necessary information. Having notes will deter you from saying something you could regret later. You might also want to prepare what you will be saying to the employee's coworkers. Keep it short and to the point.

■ Review any problems you had in firing other employees and decide on a plan to avoid them.

■ Ask your personnel director for guidance on company policy and procedures concerning terminating employees as well as EEOC regulations. If union or individual employee contracts are involved, consult your superiors or company attorney.

■ Schedule additional meetings the employee will need, such as with the human resources department to discuss benefits.

■ Prepare yourself emotionally. Acknowledge your anxiety. Relax before your meeting and do whatever helps you clear your mind and calm your emotions. Be sensitive to your feelings. Focus on the employee's strengths and how they might be put to better use in another job at another company. Avoid rumors by not mentioning your plans to associates or other employees. Remember that the good of the company comes first, and you need not feel guilty about this final step.

▌ Anticipate the employee's reactions. Role-play how you will deal with shock, anger, or denial. If the person argues, listen. Use preparation to keep yourself focused.

---

## SIX COMMON MISTAKES MADE AT
## THE TERMINATION MEETING

---

### MISTAKE 270

**Dismissing an employee in front of other workers.**

#### HOW TO AVOID IT

The dismissal should take place behind closed doors, so that coworkers can't hear what is being said. Always follow company policy. Never fire someone spontaneously or in front of others, especially if you're angry (see Mistake 275).

---

### MISTAKE 271

**Not having a witness present at the meeting.**

#### HOW TO AVOID IT

If you suspect the employee might be litigious, you should have a witness present at the meeting (preferably someone from human resources trained in handling terminations) and keep a record of the conversation so that the employee cannot later claim statements or promises were made that were not made. The presence of a third party inhibits both you and the subordinate from losing your tempers and saying or doing something inappropriate. The best defense against being sued is preparing the termination properly within company and EEOC regulations and having all the documentation to back it up. Most attorneys who handle this type of litigation work on a contingency basis, which means they don't get paid if they don't win. So if you are well prepared, smart lawyers won't waste their time on something they probably won't win. Some companies ask employees to sign waivers giving up their rights to sue, or guarantees that they won't go to work for a competitor for a specified period of time.

## MISTAKE 272

**Not setting a good time or time limit on the meeting.**

### How to Avoid It

While no time is a good time to fire anybody, companies differ on when they think it's the *best* time. Some of the managers we spoke with thought early in the day and early in the week was best because they could send the discharged employee home immediately after termination and the employee would have the rest of the week to find a new job. The majority of managers thought it was best to schedule the termination meeting late in the day and near the end of the week so the employee can take the evening or weekend to cool down. Everyone we spoke to agreed that, if possible, try not to fire someone on the day before her birthday or a major national or religious holiday.

Set a short time limit for the meeting, about 15 minutes, and stick to it. The longer a meeting continues, the more likely you'll say something you'll wish you hadn't, and the more emotionally exhausting the experience will be for both parties.

## MISTAKE 273

**Not being clear and honest in communicating your reasons for termination.**

### How to Avoid It

Cite the honest reasons for dismissal that you prepared earlier and express appreciation for the employee's contributions. Make your message clear and firm so that there are no misunderstandings or false hopes. Put yourself in the employee's shoes, treating him with compassion, just as you would like to be treated. Leave him with the feeling that you know he is not a total loser and can continue his career successfully along a different path, that though he may have been in the wrong job at the wrong company, you feel that he can excel somewhere else.

## MISTAKE 274

**Not protecting the employee's dignity.**

## How to Avoid It

If appropriate, ask the employee if she would prefer to resign rather than be fired. This may help the employee save face, but it will also deprive her of unemployment compensation. Because people tend to think that someone who was fired did something wrong, some companies in hopes of avoiding wrongful discharge suits use gentler terms such as layoff, staff cut, downsizing, and early retirement.

Tell the employee what you plan to say to her coworkers and ask if she has any objections. If she does, ask her what she would prefer that you say. You are not required to say anything more than you care to say or company policy dictates.

Provide the information on severance and benefits and when the last workday will be.

## MISTAKE 275

**Firing someone when you're in a rage and causing problems with coworkers.**

## How to Avoid It

Never fire someone when you're angry, especially in front of other employees. When a manager blows up, acts out an impulse, makes or takes insults, these actions can poison the morale and productivity of the employees who remain. Such action can also lead to legal problems as well as problems with coworkers who might sympathize with the terminated worker and slow down, sabotage production, or quit under protest.

## THREE COMMON MISTAKES MADE AFTER TERMINATION

## MISTAKE 276

**Not knowing what to tell other staffers when one of their coworkers has been dismissed.**

## How to Avoid It

Chances are five minutes after you've terminated an employee, everybody already knows, and unless the terminated person was the "employee from hell" whom nobody liked, morale will understandably be low. Coworkers have witnessed the employee's behavior and yours over a period of time, however, and they are aware of the disciplinary steps you have taken. Tell them their coworker has been terminated. You are not required to explain or justify your action, especially if the termination involves a union situation. Should you decide to justify your action, explain why this decision was the best one for everybody concerned. Your employees may not need to like you at this particular time, but they do need to respect you and appreciate your position. If you have been fair in your treatment of the terminated employee, the others will understand.

## MISTAKE 277

**Feeling guilty about what you just did.**

## How to Avoid It

As far as your own feelings are concerned, try to remind yourself that though being fired is a shock, you have actually done the departed worker a favor by giving him an opportunity for self-evaluation that will enable him to take a more logical direction in his work life.

After terminating the employee, be sure that all IDs, keys, and other company property the employee may have are returned. If the employee had security clearance, cancel it. Issue a final paycheck at the time of termination and send all files pertaining to the dismissed employee to personnel.

## MISTAKE 278

**Not learning from past mistakes.**

## How to Avoid It

As traumatic an experience as it may be, firing employees can also be a means toward improving your hiring practices. If done without bitterness, exit interviews, for instance, can give you some good information for the future. Don't be afraid to ask the person who is leaving a few smart questions:

"Does the department need some changes?"

"How could I have been a better manager?"

"Why do you think you could not handle the job?"

Don't be afraid to ask remaining workers similar questions. Meeting with your employees on a regular basis to discuss their productivity and gripes, as well as your expectations, allows you to keep on top of potential problems—and it's hoped to avoid the pain of having to fire someone again.

## FOUR MISTAKES MADE IN PROTECTING YOURSELF AND THE COMPANY

## MISTAKE 279

**Thinking "employment at will" protects you completely if you fire anyone, any time, for any reason.**

### How to Avoid It

Under the legal concept of "employment at will," an employer can hire or fire an employee, or refuse to hire an applicant at will, for any reason or no reason at all. It happens every day to thousands of workers. They simply receive a pink slip, a final paycheck, and an escort to the door.

To fully understand what makes this legal, you must first understand that there are no federal or state laws legalizing "employment at will." It is based on common law. So what is common law, you ask? Throughout our history, Americans have been guided by two kinds of law: legislated acts passed by Congress, the states, and local governments, and common law based on accepted practices as upheld by court decisions. Both federal and state legislation prohibits an employer from firing or refusing to hire somebody because of union activity, race, religion, national origin, age, disability, sex, and other protections. In addition, companies that have contracts with unions or individual employees agree by way of their contracts to waive their common-law rights. Violations of common law are not criminal acts; they are torts, or civil wrongs, and are dealt with as civil actions or lawsuits.

Does that mean as a manager you have the right to fire anyone, anytime, on the spot, without notice, and without encountering a wrongful dismissal suit?

According to lawyers specializing in employees' rights, depending on the situation, the employee may have the legal right to:

▌ Protection from being fired.

▌ Fair treatment during and after the firing.

▌ A positive reference to help in finding another job.

▌ Continued benefits.

▌ Monetary compensation if the firing causes the employee severe damage, or if the employer is found by the court to have wrongfully discharged the worker, breached good faith and fair dealing, breached an existing contract, or defamed the character of the employee.

An employer's use of "employment at will" termination is also restricted by federal statutes, such as EEOC regulations (covering women, minorities, older people, and disabled workers) and the National Labor Relations Act (prohibiting termination because of union activity), by a number of civil rights laws, and by various court decisions made at the state level. Managers should be aware of the specific applications concerning termination decisions in their state.

## MISTAKE 280

**Not being thoroughly trained in company policy and procedures concerning termination.**

## MISTAKE 281

**Firing someone without going through progressive discipline and documentation.**

### How to Avoid Them

It is important for managers to know and understand company policy and procedures for terminating employees because many courts consider such policies tantamount to a contract. Even though a company policy and procedures manual is not a formal, signed agreement, the company has published it, distributed it to employees, and expects the employees to abide by its rules. By the same token, management is also expected to abide by those rules. So if the procedures call for progressive discipline and documentation, for instance, and a manager doesn't follow the steps outlined in the manual, the court may find in favor of the employee. Steps to follow:

1. Properly training a worker on how to perform her tasks.

2. Confronting the employee when you first spotted a problem and on later occasions.

3. Providing counseling.

4. Reaching an agreement with the worker to improve the situation.

5. Carefully monitoring the employee's efforts to change her ways.

6. Documenting it all in writing, including your reasons for termination, and getting written statements from witnesses as to what occurred, just in case you have to prove you fired someone for just cause. If you can, get the employee to sign a statement stating your documentation is accurate.

By following the rules of progressive discipline, you will have eliminated a majority of the reasons most dismissed employees file lawsuits.

## MISTAKE 282

**Making commitments concerning tenure or other employment conditions.**

### How to Avoid It

Never make written or oral promises to new hires concerning tenure or other employment conditions. Even a flippant comment like "Do your job well and before you know it you'll be making as much as the president of the company," can get you and the company into court. Courts have ruled that oral statements such as promises of a "permanent job" are as binding as written contracts. Managers should never make oral commitments to applicants about tenure of employment. Many companies have a disclaimer on application forms stating that "employees are hired at will and no oral commitments are binding."

Tips to follow to avoid litigation:

▍ Avoid unlawful discharge claims by having solid evidence to prove your case for termination. Never terminate someone spontaneously except under special circumstances clearly delineated in the company policy such as, fighting, drinking, insubordination, or stealing on the job. Be absolutely sure of your facts and have sufficient evidence to back up your actions.

■ Avoid defamation of character claims by not publicizing an offense, naming the culprit, or specifying the cause of termination. Instead, be certain of your facts by conducting a thorough investigation. Consult your personnel and legal departments or outside attorneys. Be factual in talking with others or describing the situation in writing. Give only facts, not opinions. Tell only those who need to know. Avoid making examples of fired employees. Other employees probably know what happened, and that is usually enough to serve as a deterrent.

■ Avoid claims of "constructive discharge" (treating an employee unpleasantly so they will quit). The courts have ruled against this method, calling it termination rather than voluntary action.

■ Avoid discrimination claims. Document each disciplinary step in the same way for all employees. If you have documentation for a minority employee and nothing for a nonminority person, this alone is considered discrimination.

■ In general, employees who are fired must be paid their final check at the time of termination. In this way, you are complying with regulations, and you need have no future contact with these employees. It is not necessary to give terminated employees two weeks' notice. Employees may also be removed from the workplace immediately after dismissal.

■ If entitled, be sure to inform terminated employees of their right to continue medical coverage, how long they will be covered for benefits, and their eligibility for unemployment.

■ Ask the employee to sign a statement indicating that he has read your documents, accepted your reasons for firing him, and waives his rights to take legal action against the company. Though this is not a foolproof method of preventing a lawsuit (the dismissed employee may claim he signed under duress), and dismissed employees may balk at signing such statements, having such a statement would be better than not having it.

A final thought about firing employees. While you should do everything in your power to help underperforming workers improve, not everyone will. When you have no other choice but to terminate a poor performer, you are sending the right message to those who are giving you their all—that you appreciate their efforts and are reinforcing what's right about your company. And by sending this message, you will have performed a valuable service for everyone who is, or will ever be, an employee of your company.

## Chapter 12

---

# MANAGING UP AND ACROSS AS WELL AS DOWN THE ORGANIZATION

---

### FOUR MISTAKES IN COMMUNICATING WITH PRESIDENTS, PARTNERS, AND PEERS

You're a manager with authority, and your subordinates have to answer to you. But unless you're the CEO of your company, *you* also have to answer to a boss.

---

### MISTAKE 283

**Not using your skills to manage up and across the company as well as you manage down.**

#### How to Avoid It

Having a positive working relationship with your superiors and peers requires mastering a sensitive balance of communication, support, and conflict. And if that balance is not handled well, the effectiveness of those relationships up and across the company can be severely limited.

You must realize that in today's workplace nobody makes it completely on her own. Your superiors and your peers can make your job soft or hard, your life pleasant or miserable, your career successful or disastrous. And there are times when every manager finds herself at odds with even the best of bosses and team members—often for good reasons. The nature of lines of authority can set the stage for frustration when the boss blocks or constrains your actions, or a manager in another department causes problems in your department.

233

Nobody, including bosses and peers, likes to make mistakes. But if the bosses and peers are mature, they are concerned more with results than they are with being right. They can learn from their errors, and move beyond their jealousy and defensiveness if you can bring them to realize that such attitudes are incompatible with the goals of the company.

## MISTAKE 284

**Allowing the boss to manage you instead of your taking the initiative.**

### How to Avoid It

Effective managers do not wait for their superiors to manage them. Instead, they take the initiative in order to make work more enjoyable and productive and to maximize results for themselves and everyone in the company. To do so, they must have the fortitude and skills to confront problems up and across the lines of authority within the company. This does not mean being an apple polisher or resorting to treacherous tactics. It's a sincere, up-front way of improving the relationships with those you report to and work with, based on the premise that you are all adults with strong mutual interest in seeing to it that everyone succeeds.

## MISTAKE 285

**Not confronting authority because you are afraid of losing your reputation as a team player.**

## MISTAKE 286

**Assuming you are powerless to change or improve a difficult high-level situation.**

### How to Avoid Them

The cost of avoiding confrontation can be great. At the least, it can mean resistance, low productivity, and erosion of morale. At worst, it can lead to major problems and a potential organizational liability.

But confronting a superior without support and cooperation can be like making a milk shake with nitroglycerine. It should not be done unless you have a large insurance policy—a record of bridge building, trust, and respect that gives you the confidence to confront superiors and peers, without risking your reputation as a team player. Before you can improve a working relationship with your superior and peers you have to know their strong points, pressure points, and blind spots. You have to understand and see them as they are, not as you want or expect them to be. Do's and don'ts:

Do get to know their style of work. For instance, how do they like their oral and written information presented? Do they like detailed reports with statistical tables? Or do they prefer seeing graphs and charts rather than reading statistics? Maybe they would appreciate a short summary with backup material to study if they care to go into the matter more thoroughly? How a person dresses is another indication of his work style. If your boss wears tailored clothes and you prefer more casual wear, he may not take your suggestion as seriously as he would from someone more conservative in his choice of clothes.

Do get to know their job goals. What do your superiors and peers want to achieve in their jobs? If you can help them reach these goals, getting what you want from them will be a lot easier.

Do anticipate their needs. Through discussions and observation, you can ascertain what workplace areas most concern your boss and peers. By staying on top of what is happening in these areas, you can get the jump on potential problems and have materials and solutions ready to present when they are needed or requested.

Do build on their strengths. A good relationship with anyone is achieved by building on the best that you both have to offer and making adjustments to accommodate weaknesses. One successful strength-building tactic is finding a task in which the person you're confronting is weak and you are strong. Then volunteer your help. If your boss hates public speaking, for example, volunteer to speak for him at public functions. The more ways you can find to compliment a boss or peer, the more he will value you. As you discover other weaknesses, take steps to accommodate them. For instance, if a peer tends to be forgetful, be helpful and follow up important issues with a memo.

Don't initiate a crusade against a superior or peer or go over anyone's head. Instead, do some homework and find support for your position. Suggest how the company would benefit from following your course of action. Use diplomacy to defuse what might appear to a boss or a peer as a threat. Say something like

"I understand that you have to make the decision, and I will do everything I can to make it work. But I would appreciate it if you would think about this alternative." Such a statement will keep your assertiveness in perspective. With peers, you must understand that their position and decision to make priority judgments may be very different from yours. For all you know, their boss may have told them that their project is more important than yours. Try to get them to understand your position, for example, "I know you have priorities just as I do, but you must understand that it will be impossible for me to meet my deadline by next Monday if I don't have your input tomorrow—and if I don't, the company loses a big order." If egos, power struggles, or differences in priority get in the way of an agreement, you may have to go up the corporate ladder and get an authoritative judgment. But instead of going over the person's head, suggest that the two of you go to the boss together for a decision.

Do keep superiors and peers informed. Developing and maintaining a balanced relationship with coworkers up and across company lines means taking the initiative to keep them informed. When people don't know what's going on, they are intimidated by those who do. Intimidated people can be difficult. By keeping them informed, you remove the source of intimidation. Pass on any news, good or bad, that you think will be of interest to them. Take time to become an information broker. Scan the media for pertinent articles and information. Pass them along with a friendly note: "Thought you'd be interested in the attached article." Be prompt with your information. If you hold on to it too long, it won't be news anymore. If possible, include your support information and recommendations. If you've done your homework, your efforts will be highly appreciated.

Do strengthen your informal, personal contacts with your boss and peers. Personal contacts help build a foundation on which mutual respect can grow. Discover interests and activities you may have in common. A good personal relationship exists when you can freely discuss matters without the barrier of formal communications.

Do give your boss and peers more than their share of credit, even when it's not entirely due. A proposal with just your name on it may be doomed to failure. Even if most of the work was done by you, don't be a credit hog. Credit hogs threaten bosses and irritate colleagues. They also broadcast their lack of confidence to everyone in the organization.

Do reward superiors and peers for any positive behavior changes. You can't give your boss or peers a promotion, bonus, or piece of the business, but you can ask and look for positive behavior and reward the person for it. When you do, chances are this behavior will be repeated. You can also try an effective tactic psychologists call "shaping," which involves creating situations in which bosses and peers can behave even more as you want and reward them for that. For instance, suppose you are constantly interrupted by your boss when you are doing a task. Wait for a time when you see your boss struggling with a task and say, "You know, if I had three uninterrupted hours, I could do that task for you. Why don't you play some golf tomorrow, and I'll have it ready when you get back?" Here are eight ways to reward those who exhibit positive behavior:

1. Praise the good points of their behavior.

2. Voice public and private support for their goals.

3. Simplify their work by helping to keep them organized.

4. Volunteer to take on their routine jobs so they can focus on more important tasks.

5. Keep alert for ideas that will save time or money or improve the workplace and pass them along.

6. Offer to serve as a sounding board for their ideas or volunteer to help them solve problems.

7. Help them break in new hires by offering to show the newcomers the ropes and training them.

8. Let them know how proud and fortunate you are to have the opportunity to work for and with them.

Do know when to give up. Some superiors and peers are just never going to change their ways, even after a lot of creative trying on your part. Some will not be capable of developing a rapport with you, others will enjoy using their authority to make you feel uncomfortable. And sometimes, even with the sanest and most reasonable bosses and colleagues, your differences may be too great to be bridged. When relationships reach that stage, it may be time to transfer to another department or change jobs. No one should remain in an intolerable situation, especially if his basic integrity is being compromised.

The art of managing up and across the lines of authority in most companies is often a matter of taking the initiative to smooth out rough problems and build loyal and sound working relationships with the presidents, partners, and peers you encounter while climbing up the corporate ladder.

## ELEVEN MISTAKES IN DEALING WITH FAMILY MEMBERS IN THE SAME BUSINESS

The rivalry between two sons vying for the top spot in the family's firm is causing morale problems with the other employees. A manager is concerned that the unqualified daughter of the company president sees the family business as "a way to make a good living without having to work very hard." A college senior, who wanted to be a doctor but didn't want to hurt his parents, dropped out of medical school and joined the family business as *your* superior.

It is not unusual to hear of husbands, wives, and children not only working in the same field, but often at the same place or job. TV stations in Boston and Los Angeles have spouses that coanchor the news. There's one New York City couple we read about that became the city's first married firefighters to work in the same firehouse. And even if relatives don't start out working at the same company, it is likely that they eventually will as a result of marriage, merger, or acquisition.

It's called nepotism, originally a word that meant "favoritism to kinfolk," but now is more broadly used to describe a situation in which family members work in the same place.

Hiring family (and friends) is a common practice in many companies. In fact, in the United States there are an estimated 13 million companies, according to the Small Business Administration, in which family members influence the operation of the business through the exercise of family ties, management roles, or ownership rights. These businesses account for nearly 40 percent of the gross national product and more than half of our national employment. Because of their prevalence and significance in the work world, it is important for managers to understand the pros and cons of employing and dealing with family members.

## MISTAKE 287

**Hiring a less-qualified relative of a superior instead of a more-qualified nonrelative.**

## How to Avoid It

The practice of hiring your own relative or the relative of a superior on referral can be legally dangerous if they are not hired in the same manner as any other applicant. While it is perfectly legal to hire anyone you want, if you have 15 or more employees you must meet equal employment/affirmative action standards, and that means being consistent. It is acceptable to ask if the applicant has relatives working for the company, but your selection cannot be based on this information.

## MISTAKE 288

**Denying an applicant employment because she is married or related to another employee.**

### How to Avoid It

Some states have laws prohibiting discrimination on the basis of nepotism. This means that employment cannot be denied any applicant solely on the basis that they are related in some manner to another company employee. You can, however, prohibit that employee from working directly under the supervision of a spouse or relative.

## MISTAKE 289

**Not recognizing the potential positive and negative consequences of nepotism.**

### How to Avoid It

Though nepotism is on the increase in today's workplace, it should not be officially encouraged. If, for example, a company with a predominantly female or male labor force has a policy encouraging nepotism, it could be construed as discrimination in certain cases.

It is necessary for managers who must deal with nepotism to recognize the potential for positive and negative consequences.

Some of the arguments for nepotism are:

▮ Heightened family and company loyalty. Relatives have more of a personal interest in and are more familiar with the company because of their relationship to the person who works there. As a result, they will try harder to do a better job because they feel that the company is a part of the family.

■ While nonrelatives might just go through the motions of performing their tasks, relatives of executives have a stronger sense of mission and make more objective business decisions. They also feel more pressure to perform well because they are relatives.

■ It's easier and takes less time to train and indoctrinate relatives because you already know more about them than you do about a nonrelative, and they may know about the job, the company, and its policies.

■ Relatives working together often share common goals and values. Relatives can draw out relatives' strengths and complement their weaknesses. They can also communicate with each other more efficiently and with greater privacy.

■ Relatives who deal with customers and vendors are likely to get more respect and results than do nonrelatives, especially if they bear the company name.

■ Relatives may be willing to put in more hours without compensation knowing their efforts will be appreciated down the line. If relatives are strongly attached to the company, they can be united in their goals for it and in their willingness to contribute to it. Ultimately, this symbolism can define a sense of mission for the business that companies with anti-nepotism policies rarely match.

Some of the arguments against nepotism are:

■ Managers, peers, and employees are intimidated by subordinates who are related to executives.

■ Relatives tend to be advanced faster, usually at the expense of more competent employees. Nonrelated employees may feel there is little chance to advance very far in a company that practices nepotism.

■ Family issues and business issues can get intertwined. This is especially true when you have a high-powered husband and wife working together in the same company. Personal and office problems can get mixed up causing not only a strain on the marriage, but problems in the workplace.

■ Family rivalries can develop between relatives. It's easy to document the role that rivalry between siblings and extended relatives has played in human history. Take Cain and Abel, two belligerent boys who, as a famous comedian observed, sure didn't get in one another's face because of overcrowding in the neighborhood.

▪ Employees may feel that their privacy and confidentiality is at risk if they have to work with or around the relatives of superiors.

▪ Related employees may be under more stress than nonrelated workers because they may be made to feel that they are not meeting the expectations of other employees, or that they are there only because of family influences.

▪ The hiring of relatives brings up questions of favoritism and may have a negative influence on the morale of other employees.

▪ It is more difficult to set company and job policies and enforce those policies with people you know well than it is with strangers.

▪ Hiring someone else over a qualified relative for a position can cause friction with your peers or superiors.

▪ It is more difficult to dismiss someone who is a relative of a company executive.

▪ And as we pointed out in Chapter 10, if you have to bring charges against a relative for embezzlement or theft of company money or property, you will be bringing those charges against someone you may have to be in contact with again in the future, or at least, with their relative at work.

## MISTAKE 290

**Not having a nepotism policy.**

### HOW TO AVOID IT

Whether or not you support the practice of nepotism, your business should develop, publish, and communicate a nepotism policy that defines company hiring practices. It should apply to:

▪ Spouses of employees.

▪ Children, siblings, parents, and grandparents of employees.

▪ Extended family of employees (cousins, nieces and nephews, aunts and uncles).

▪ Employees who marry each other.

▪ Friends of employees.

## MISTAKE 291

**Not communicating policy rules to all employees.**

## MISTAKE 292

**Not applying the rules of the policy fairly.**

### How to Avoid Them

In researching the subject of nepotism policies, the majority of businesses we contacted felt that relatives of employees should meet the same job requirements (education, skills, experience) and have the same performance evaluations as all other applicants. However, in the case of family businesses in which the owners are trying to attract the next generation to the business, relatives should meet particular criteria in addition to standard qualifications before making the family business a permanent career. The criteria should include:

- Education appropriate for the job sought.

- Part-time experience in the business during high school and college to whet their appetite for the business and to learn the work ethic.

- Three to five years of outside work experience to learn their market value, receive objective performance reviews, to make mistakes away from the watchful eyes and long memories of employees in their relative's firm, and to earn the self-confidence of independent success. Outside work experience will also give them wider, more varied experience, add to their creative ability to deal with challenges, and show them that merit is more important than paternalism—all of which will give them more respect and motivation for the family's business.

- Entry into an existing, needed job with precedents for pay and performance expectations.

## MISTAKE 293

**Not having established policies to ensure against conflict of interest.**

## MISTAKE 294

**Showing favoritism to family members and causing morale problems with other employees.**

# MISTAKE 295

**Allowing family concerns to interfere with business concerns.**

## How to Avoid Them

When developing a nepotism policy, care should be taken to word it clearly and properly so as to avoid the implication of discrimination. Refusal to hire wives, for example, might be regarded as discrimination against women. Because seemingly neutral policies may have an adverse effect such as implying favoritism, which could attract the attention of the EEOC, an attorney should be consulted before the policy is published and communicated. A typical nepotism policy for family businesses or companies that practice nepotism should include:

▌ A definition of nepotism.

▌ Rules regarding the hiring, performance evaluation, promotion, and firing of relatives of employees as compared to nonrelated applicants. Include all requirements for full-time, part-time, and temporary positions, as well as company policy regarding spouses and former spouses. Relatives should not participate in the hiring of relatives. Regardless of how competent these individuals may be, allowing such a practice leaves you and the company open to charges of conflict of interest as well as other issues. These rules should also provide a system of review to determine whether unfairness or lack of ethics resulted from the relationship between two relatives.

▌ Rules for checking references. Just because a person is being referred by someone you know, don't ignore other references that may be helpful.

▌ Provisions regarding compensation of relatives. Conflict surrounding compensation issues can get especially ugly when it involves spouses and other family members who feel deprived by an inadequate or inequitable pay scale. Relatives should get the "market salary" for the position they are hired for. Favoritism, especially when it concerns compensation, could cause you major problems.

▌ Rules regarding employees who marry another employee. Should they work together in the same department or in different departments? If couples encounter problems sharing professions, the company that employs them runs into snags, too. Suppose two high-level executives marry. Should the question of firing one come up, is it fair for the other to participate in the decision? Will one quit if the other is fired? What problems will you have if there's a messy divorce and one or both want to leave?

▮ Procedures for investigation of possible nepotism during the job-screening process.

▮ Penalties for misrepresenting relationships.

▮ Rules on reporting directly to other related employees. Relatives should not supervise relatives. Once again, this could lead to conflict of interest charges.

▮ Rules on policing the behavior of relatives to ensure that they are acting in an acceptable manner toward customers, suppliers, and coworkers.

▮ Confidentiality rules concerning relatives leaving to work for a competitor.

How strict or liberal a nepotism policy may be is not as important as clear communication of the rules before they are needed and fair application of the rules when they are needed. It is important to explain the thinking that went into developing the policy and why the rules are good for relatives, other employees, and the business.

## MISTAKE 296

**Hiring the husband because it's the only way you can hire the wife.**

## MISTAKE 297

**Being reluctant to let either half go when you have married couples in positions of authority.**

### How to Avoid Them

So many husbands and wives are working together that some companies are forced into a "Hire me, hire my spouse" policy that some critics argue is the breeding ground for abuse. It happens when a job for a spouse is often the bait to lure a sought-after executive to a company (usually in another town). In many instances, the spouse is qualified and deserves the job. But more often than not, few people of equal competence have equal opportunities if one is linked to the executive the firm wants. This kind of policy has turned into disaster more than once and should not be used except in extreme cases that involve high-level positions. If a job for the spouse is being created to accommodate the person you want, be sure it won't create morale problems with other employees. Also make sure that the spouse is qualified for whatever job you assign him. One way around this would be to investigate the background and skills of the spouse and try to place her at another company in the area.

Then there are situations in which you employ a married couple and one of them has to be let go. You would naturally be reluctant to fire the problem spouse for fear of losing the good one. The best way to handle this kind of problem is to exercise extreme fairness and consistency when it comes to firing all employees. Explain your decision to both and make it clear that you must treat all employees the same. The fact that they are married cannot influence your decision if you have good reason to dismiss someone. If the other decides to leave, you will probably be better off. If they stayed on, it might result in very tense and stressful working conditions.

## Chapter 13

### Managing the Invisible— Telecommuters Who Work from Here, There, Anywhere

For many workers in the United States these days, going to work means going downstairs instead of downtown. All over America, people are replacing their designer suits with comfortable jeans, their cramped urban office cubicles with spacious suburban homes, their interoffice memos with computer bulletin boards, faxes, and E-mail. I was told by one office manager I spoke with about an employee of his in San Francisco who conducts his work while mountain climbing in Colorado. Another bank manager told me about his employees who tend their gardens, romp with their kids, run errands, or leave their desks to cook a meal—all at home—and all between handling the finances of clients from Australia to Japan.

It's called telecommuting—"open collar" employees working at home, or from any location—while linked to their offices through electronics. In addition to telecommuting, some companies help their employees enjoy more flexibility with their work and family responsibilities by allowing them to work part time at home or office, share work tasks, or have flexible work schedules. This is known as flextime employment.

With advances in telecommunications, telecommuting has become a growing revolution in the workplace. According to one New York City-based technology consulting firm, in 1997 more than 12 million Americans will be telecommuting for their companies at least part time. And that number will rise by nearly 20 percent each year as competition and lower equipment costs make electronic technology more available and affordable to all businesses.

Telecommunications gurus are even predicting that in the not too distant future, telecommuting can substantially reduce unemployment in poor rural areas by wiring up entire communities to distant corporate headquarters.

Today there are few good reasons why workers should have to spend as much as three or four hours each day preparing for work and clogging the expressways when they can commute electronically in ten seconds, be more productive at home, and attend to their personal chores without affecting the company or other employees.

---

# TEN MISTAKES IN BALANCING BUSINESS AND EMPLOYEE NEEDS

---

Telecommuting allows employees to spend all or part of the work week at home, communicating with their offices by phone, fax, and computer. Flextime allows workers to change their work hours to better fit their needs. Many employees favor telecommuting and flextime arrangements because it can save them many hours of commuting each week and give them more time to attend to personal and family needs.

But does telecommuting or flextime make sense for your company?

## MISTAKE 298

**Not considering the business reasons for initiating telecommuting and flextime programs.**

### How to Avoid It

Explore the issue with top management first to determine whether these programs make sense for your type of company and your type of employees. Does your company have a large proportion of information-oriented tasks? Does the company have a significant level of office automation? Are there trusting relationships between management and employees based on results-oriented goals?

For employers, the question of telecommuting and flextime should not be "Should we offer it?" but "Why shouldn't we offer it?" When asked about the performance of telecommuters and flextimers, the managers we interviewed for this book all reported either an increase in the employee's productivity or no change at all. None saw a decrease. Several recent studies in government and business have also found higher employee productivity. The gains were attributed primarily to better concentration on the task at home, as opposed to the normal interruptions encountered at the workplace. As we move further along the information superhighway, the reasons to have most employees clustered together at a given time no longer exists.

Besides changes in work environment and exploding technological advances on the information front, employers should also consider the following bottom-line reasons for implementing telecommuting and flextime programs:

- Companies gain by saving money on expensive office space (or making double use of desks at the office, thereby lowering overhead of space costs), insurance, taxes, and utilities. While these can be very substantial savings, it is estimated that companies can save an additional $4,000 to $20,000 annually per telecommuter in terms of reduced absenteeism and retention of workers who otherwise might leave the company. Another benefit for companies, especially those looking to cut costs by downsizing, is the use of telecommuters as part-time and contract workers who are not eligible for company benefit plans.

- Companies gain by offering customers expanded service hours.

- Companies are better able to recruit and retain skilled employees by enabling them to balance their work and family schedules.

- Company executives are better able to manage their time. They experience improved worker morale, less worker stress and turnover, and more environmental benefits.

- Companies are finding that workers who telecommute put in longer hours and are more productive than on-site workers. Research has shown that productivity of telecommuters increased by as much as 40 percent. And it is a known fact that not everybody performs best between 9 A.M. and 5 P.M. Some work best between 4 A.M. and noon or between 2 P.M. and 10 P.M., which they can do more easily if they are working from home or on a flextime arrangement.

- More and more workers who are getting their fill of rush-hour commuting and the corporate culture can save both commute time and personal costs by working at home part or all of the work week or by working off-hours. Aside from obvious savings on transportation, they also save on business clothes, meals, and day care for their children.

■ Part-time employees can set their own hours and are able to gain experience without the commitment of a full-time job.

■ Working flextime schedules, or escaping the office completely by working at home is hailed by many as the solution for employee stress, confinement, and family-care crises. Workers in these programs tend to be much happier and more fulfilled than other types of workers.

■ The federal Clean Air Act, which is taking aim at reducing air pollution and commuter-clogged roads in many states, and the Americans with Disabilities Act, which would like to meet the needs of employees with disabilities, are encouraging companies to consider the telecommuting and flextime options or be faced with penalties.

■ Natural disasters, such as earthquakes, winter storms, and floods make it difficult, if not impossible, for many people to get to their offices.

## MISTAKE 299

**Not establishing a formal procedure for selecting employees to be telecommuters or flextime workers.**

### HOW TO AVOID IT

Determine which jobs can be done out of the office, such as sales, field jobs, and other occupations with measurable functions, and which jobs can be rescheduled at off-hours. Then analyze work flow and staffing needs. Some jobs, such as those requiring interaction with customers, or teamwork require a worker's presence on-site.

Next, develop criteria for selecting telecommuters and flex-timers based on length of service, quality of work, and characteristics such as self-motivation. It follows that those employees who work best on-site will also be the best workers off-site. Telecommuting and flextime should not be considered as perks, but as one of the ways your company does business. It is important, therefore, to have objective criteria in place before making selections so that those not selected for the program cannot cry "favoritism."

The type of employee best suited for telecommuting is one with a good performance record and a reputation for loyalty and trust, who does not require much supervision, and who preferably is someone who is engaged in "knowledge work," rather than hands-on or person-to-person tasks. Some of the other factors that should be considered in selecting employees for telecommuting are:

- The employee's need to work an alternative schedule.

- Is the employee good at structuring her time?

- Does the job require seeing clients?

- Has the employee telecommuted before, and was she successful at it?

- Can the employee ignore the loss of status that usually accompanies at-home work?

- Will the telecommuter need assistants, and will the home office accommodate her?

- Will family members respect the employee's need for uninterrupted work time?

- Does the home office environment lend itself to telecommuting? Are there adequate telephone lines for the computer, fax, and E-mail? Is the lighting adequate? Are there provisions for storage and supplies? What about furniture and equipment needs? What does the homeowner's or renter's insurance cover? Is there an alarm system and fire extinguisher?

## MISTAKE 300

**Letting workers telecommute all the time instead of setting limits.**

### How to Avoid It

Many of the companies we contacted in our research of this subject felt that no employee should work at home all the time. Telecommuting should be limited to one to three days, at most, per week. While a few managers felt that it was not wise to allow Monday and Friday home days because other employees might get the idea that telecommuters were getting long weekends, a Monday, Wednesday, Friday schedule at home was recommended for top performers, with at least two days at the work place so that telecommuters could do the things that can be done only in the work place—and for interaction with other employees, peers, and customers. The telecommuting schedule should be set up on a trial basis for a given time and then evaluated before fine-tuning it and making it permanent.

## MISTAKE 301

**Not having a clearly defined telecommuting agreement.**

### How to Avoid It

Establishing a successful, clearly defined, companywide telecommuting and flextime policy that satisfies everyone isn't easy. The best way to start is with a "Work and Family Needs Assessment" survey. The anonymous survey should include questions ranging from "How much time do you spend during work hours attending to personal/family concerns?" to "If this company could make one change regarding work and family policies, what could we do to help you?" Chances are you will find your employees overwhelmingly in favor of more flexibility that would enable them to balance their jobs and their lives.

Next you must look at your computer technology. Determine the equipment that the company will have to purchase and the training that will be necessary in order to allow telecommuters to work efficiently from home. Many of your employees may already be trained in the use of computers and own home PCs and printers that are compatible with equipment used at the office.

The policy you create might offer employees several options, including:

▌ The ability to work off-site.

▌ The option to choose their own hours in a 40-hour work week.

▌ The option to work a compressed work week such as 40 hours in three or four days.

▌ Part-time or job-sharing options.

The most highly recommended way to implement a program is to have an overall policy that is amenable to both employees and managers, and to have individual agreements between telecommuters and managers. To reach that goal, present all managers with comprehensive support material that spells out the overall policy. Ask them to add their own ideas for the proposed specific arrangements:

▌ What positions are applicable to telecommuting.

▌ The terms by which the telecommuter will operate.

▌ The tasks to be completed and deadlines.

▮ In and out days.

▮ The anticipated benefits.

▮ How success would be measured.

▮ The method used to oversee off-site employees.

Give the managers two or three weeks to discuss and fine-tune the overall program and their own specifics before presenting it to everyone in the company. When it is ready, ask each employee to present a convincing case as to why he should earn the right to work an alternative schedule and how he will go about producing demonstrable results.

Other provisions that should be made a part of the policy, as mentioned earlier, are:

▮ Responsibility for liabilities.

▮ A limit for at-home days.

▮ Rules regarding regularly scheduled evaluations of compliance with the agreement.

▮ Rules regarding termination of the agreement.

The ability of any business to compete in the marketplace is determined in part by how well the company anticipates and adapts to the needs of its employees. Giving employees more flexibility with a "work/life" program not only helps boost employee morale and productivity, it will also make management more effective, as they will be forced to track results rather than spend their time keeping a close eye on workers.

## MISTAKE 302

**Not giving telecommuters a clear understanding of their responsibilities.**

### How to Avoid It

Stipulate the terms of the telecommuting and flextime arrangements in a written agreement that spells out, among other things, who is responsible for any legal liabilities that may arise from a work-at-home arrangement and how work time will be measured; for example, who will be responsible for company-owned equipment that is damaged while used at a location away from the office. Not all homeowner's and renter's insurance policies cover business equipment. Check the agreement against wage-and-hour laws to determine if your programs conform to the Fair Labor Standards Act. Increasingly popular "family friendly" flextime options include late-night to early-morning work schedules, which allow working parents to be home during the day for their children, and the 10-hour/4-day work week, which gives employees a longer weekend. As long as such employees maintain 40-hour work weeks, they earn the same benefits as all other full-time employees.

## MISTAKE 303

**Being fearful of managing employees that can't be seen and watched over.**

### How to Avoid It

Learn to trust telecommuters and flextime workers. Many managers fear implementing these types of programs because it means they must manage employees they can't see. While certain functions can be checked from afar—such as being sure vendors are paid on time—by running reports, managers cannot know how customers are being treated over the phone because they're not there to hear it. Making these programs work requires trust between management and employee. There are those managers who will be paranoid about employees working at home away from the watchful eyes of a supervisor, but managing people by their presence instead of by their productivity represents outdated thinking in today's workplace.

## MISTAKE 304

**Not properly monitoring and evaluating telecommuters and flextimers.**

### How to Avoid It

Monitor and evaluate telecommuters and flextimers periodically to ensure that the arrangement is working as per agreement. Chances are you will find that employees on these programs are so eager to cooperate they will go overboard to make the situation work well. Besides, if for some reason a program fails, the situation can be instantly corrected by asking the employee to return to the way they previously worked.

From the employees' standpoint, telecommuting and flextime have some drawbacks, but none that would prompt them to relinquish the programs. Among the few that were mentioned:

▮ Telecommuters felt that they were captives to the work because the office is right there at home and they have a tendency to work at all hours. Also, if the telecommuter lives in the East and has customers or headquarters in the West, it may require taking phone calls at all hours of the day.

▮ Telecommuters more than flextimers missed the social aspect of going to the office.

▮ Telecommuters and flextimers sensed resentment from colleagues and were worried that coworkers would think they were goofing off.

▮ Telecommuters more than flextimers worry that reduced visibility at the workplace could be a problem, that because they were out of sight, maybe they were also out of mind and managers would forget them for promotions.

▮ Telecommuters in particular encountered situations such as having a child screaming in the background while they were trying to conduct a professional conversation on the phone.

▮ Telecommuters also found that even though they were at home with their children, focusing on their tasks was more difficult, and in many cases they still needed day care for their children.

## MISTAKE 305

**Not considering the inaccessibility of key workers who, when needed in an emergency situation, are nowhere to be found.**

### How to Avoid It

Managing an invisible work force presents some real challenges. The biggest of these is trying to establish a strong corporate identity. You definitely lose that identity without face-to-face communication.

Brainstorming and creating the sense of team effort are also difficult. Individual autonomy may improve productivity, but it also inhibits the spontaneous flow of ideas. There are, however, ways of compensating. One method is by using a software system that allows more than one person to use a document at the same time. The most common (and effective) method of compensating for invisible employees is to limit their at-home days.

## MISTAKE 306

**Not considering that unsupervised workers could be making costly mistakes.**

### How to Avoid It

Ambiguity and confusion about *any* job requirements can easily destroy working relationships. Things such as not knowing what has to be done and when can mean the difference between making and missing deadlines, or doing a task right or wrong.

## MISTAKE 307

**Not having compatible equipment at the work and home sites.**

### How to Avoid It

While employees with lap-tops and PCs, modems, scanners, faxes, and cellular phones can accomplish a lot of work away from the workplace, they can share it instantly only if their equipment *away* from the work site is compatible with the equipment *at* the work site.

# Chapter 14

## Managing Downtime, Downsizing, and Going Out of Business

All companies go through up-cycles, when production and profits are on the rise and making and implementing smart management decisions seem to be a breeze. But good times, as all companies learn sooner or later, don't last.

## EIGHT MISTAKES IN COMMUNICATING BAD NEWS TO EMPLOYEES

Downsizing, rightsizing, lateralizing, reorganizing, corporate consolidating, salary freezing, benefits cutting, de-jobbing, closing—all are words you see used over and over in news stories concerning the workplace, and all have one thing in common—they are unwelcome news to employees.

### MISTAKE 308

**Providing information on good news and shielding your employees from bad news.**

#### How to Avoid It

When times are tough or when a business is going through changes, rumors fly, uncertainty and speculation are high, and even the briefest dry spell can strike terror in the hearts of everyone up and down the corporate ladder, instilling the fear that the last project, sale, meeting, or pay check may well be . . . *the last.*

256

By providing information only on good developments and failing to communicate and explain negative news to employees, you will be doing them a disservice that could damage morale. You will be doing a disservice to your company as well, by straining the management-worker relationship, which can affect production. You must communicate as much as you can as soon as you know it. When employees know the facts, even if they are unwelcome, they can respond. They are spared the anxiety that comes from not knowing, and the company gains precious productivity that might otherwise have been wasted by concerned, uninformed workers.

## MISTAKE 309

**Communicating with employees only to tell them bad news.**

## MISTAKE 310

**Being afraid that talking about bad developments will make them worse.**

### How to Avoid Them

The opposite is even worse. When management communicates with employees only to tell them bad news, that message will seem twice as bad. The effect of bad news is greatly softened when employees are communicated with during good times as well. It is to management's advantage to earn their employees' trust by communicating with them all the time.

As an example, instead of waiting until you cut medical benefits and then tell your workers, lead up to it by discussing rising health-care costs in advance of your announcement of cuts. This can be accomplished in a company newsletter or in a series of letters to employees outlining what workers can do to maintain good health. Include reprints of newspaper stories talking about rising health care costs and its effect on businesses. Some companies, cooperating with local hospitals and clinics, bring in heart, blood-pressure, cholesterol, and cataract-testing equipment on-site to plant the idea that health care is a major company concern and that the current plan is not carved in stone.

## MISTAKE 311

**Assuming employees know what is going on.**

## How to Avoid It

How management handles bad news and bad times can go a long way toward controlling the ripple effects. If handled properly, the following benefits can be derived:

- You will put rumors and speculation to rest sooner, thereby alleviating stress and keeping employee trust.

- You will reduce downtime. When bad news is in the form of rumor or speculation, employees cannot be expected to carry on as if everything is okay. They will naturally have high anxiety and more stress, which in turn will affect their morale and productivity.

- When you address the issue and provide the facts to employees as they develop, you have the advantage of putting those facts in the context that works best for you and the company.

- Managers who do not provide their workers with information during tough times are neglecting an army of communicators who can help spread the messages that will help everyone understand what is happening. For instance, by showing your employees that bad news is a fact of business life and that it must be taken in the proper context, they can learn to understand that just as good times don't last, neither do bad times.

- Sharing an experience, good or bad, tends to make employees feel as if they are trusted members of the company and part of the team.

- Communicating bad news to employees as it occurs gives them the opportunity to prepare for what may come next, and it also reduces the bitterness that often accompanies negative news. This is something they can't do if management drops a bomb. If, for example, the bad news relates to layoffs, employees can expect to be included and prepare for it, with less resentment than they would if it all came as a surprise.

- When you're open and honest and show your employees that you respect their right to know what is going on and that you care about them, they will give you their respect and trust in return.

- Your employees represent a pool of productivity, creativity, volunteerism, and other collective capabilities. Because your employees have a vested interest in the outcome of a negative situation, they can, through their collective capabilities, help bring about a solution to the company's problem.

## MISTAKE 312

**Assuming that bad news is bad news to everybody.**

### HOW TO AVOID IT

Bad news to one employee is not necessarily bad news to another. If, for example, a company decided to cut maternity benefits from their health plan, younger workers might react more strongly than older workers. The opposite would be true if the announcement concerned retirement benefits. Therefore, it is important to communicate bad news differently to different groups of employees. One way to accomplish this is to make a general announcement to all employees and follow up with special messages to different groups that further explain the reasons for the change and how those changes will specifically affect each group.

## MISTAKE 313

**Not communicating limits on changes taking place and leading employees to believe more changes are coming.**

### HOW TO AVOID IT

Employee morale can make a difference as to how you present the news. If your company is in a healthy industry and your people are happy and feeling secure, then telling them they will have to pay more for their health coverage may not affect them as drastically as it would if they were feeling insecure and morale were bad.

Workers may also feel that a particular bad-news announcement resulting from a business downturn is only the first of many more changes to come. To alleviate the fear and apprehension that comes with this feeling, you need to make strong efforts to explain the reasons for the change and to set limits on the change so that workers will know how far it will go. This can be accomplished with meetings, memos, or an explanation in the company newsletter.

## MISTAKE 314

**Not setting clear objectives on what your communication effort has to accomplish.**

### HOW TO AVOID IT

If you are downsizing the company, for example, simply making an announcement of layoffs or other cuts will not sit well with workers.

It would be more realistic and acceptable to employees, however, if they fully understood the need for a change.

You must demonstrate to employees that the change is necessary by taking them through the decision-making process that brought management to the decision. This can be done by first contacting those directly affected by the changes through group meetings or a letter from the president that not only explains what changes are being made and why, but how the company will be taking care of those who will be losing their jobs or benefits. It's important for those workers to know, for instance, that the company will continue health benefits for a limited time or that there will be severance pay or attempts to relocate displaced employees. It's also important for those remaining with the company to know what's happening. It gives employees the feeling that the company does care about people even though times are bad and the company has its own problems.

If there are no immediate plans for mass layoffs, say so; it will help the company keep its most productive people who will be anxious in the face of uncertainty.

---

## MISTAKE 315

**Not timing your communication so that your employees know first.**

### How to Avoid It

Earlier in this chapter we said you must communicate as much as you can as soon as you know it. Everyone who works for and with your company has a need (and right) to know how changes will impact them. Employees should always be considered the most important people to communicate with first; customers should be a close second. Once you are certain that some change is going to be made, some kind of information must be communicated immediately so that your employees and customers are not left feeling angry, betrayed, and the last to know.

The best-written letter announcing layoffs is worthless if everyone already read about it in the local newspaper or heard about it from internal rumors, or from a friend of a friend.

Bad timing of a negative news announcement can also affect more than employee morale and customer relations. It can affect company relationships with vendors, trade unions, and regulators, and if yours is a public company, it can have a devastating effect on the value of your stock.

## TWO COMMON MISTAKES IN TURNING
## SLOW PERIODS TO YOUR ADVANTAGE

Few businesses are immune to slow periods and the employee anxiety that accompanies them. Even owners, managers, and other top executives worry when business slacks off because they know that everyone, including their own families, are counting on them to keep the business solvent.

## MISTAKE 316

**Not reacting quickly or failing to recognize problems affecting the business.**

### How to Avoid It

In many industries, ebbs and flows are predictable. Retailers, for instance, know December will be busy and July will probably be very slow—and they can pace themselves accordingly. Home builders know they will sell more homes during certain months and fewer during others. So many builders make the off-periods vacation time for sales employees and hiring time for construction workers.

But when business slows down for two or three weeks or longer and management can't find a reason why, or management doesn't look for a reason why, or management looks at last year's comparables, which showed that business was booming during this same period, a sense of panic can easily overcome everyone involved. Employees start thinking that "maybe it will be slow forever." Executives start updating their resumes. Management starts looking at areas in which they can cut expenses.

## MISTAKE 317

**Not converting downtime into productive time.**

### How to Avoid It

Without going into the myriad reasons why a slack period may be happening, let's focus instead on how to convert downtime into productive time. Slow periods are the perfect times to do some conceptual and analytic thinking about the business. Here are some tips that will help:

■ Put the current situation in perspective to get a feeling of what your company is doing well and what it could be doing better. Meet with your peers and superiors and consider the obvious factors that exist right now. How is the business doing this quarter? This year? Where is the majority of business coming from? Have old customers been lost? Have new customers been gained? Have costs risen more sharply this period than in other periods? When business slowed down before, how long did it last and what was done to get back on track? Have the needs of the market and your customers changed? Is your company focusing on what it does best, or is it trying to be all things to all customers? Try to pinpoint possible problems and take quick action to correct them.

■ Talk with colleagues, suppliers, customers, even competitors, experts say, to determine whether the current problems are due to internal causes or are a reflection of what is happening throughout the industry. All your people may feel a lot better when they realize the slowdown is not happening just at your place.

■ Think past the lull and start planning for your next upturn. Don't sit back and wait for new business to come your way. Don't let your workers get lazy. Take advantage of the time to increase your marketing activities and get your name out. Though spending money may be the last thing you want to do during business lulls, the adage "You have to spend money to make money" still holds true, in most cases. The cost of advertising does not have to be prohibitive. A simple mailing to old customers and new prospects can cost relatively little and yet be very productive. If you have telephone salespeople who are sitting around waiting for the phones to ring, come up with a twist on your marketing approach (a private sale, a limited offer, etc.), and have them use it as a reason to make calls to prospects and old customers.

■ Use downtime to catch up on things you've been putting aside. Have your salespeople update or clean their leads and mailing lists. Get in touch with customers or vendors you haven't heard from lately. Use the time to study overhead expenses for items that can be eliminated or reduced.

■ Try not to cut your costs at the expense of your employees or customers if possible. One of the strategies companies come up with during downtime is downsizing. Their reasoning is that by shrinking into a smaller capital base, the company will have more working capital to help turn the lull into productivity. If the company is a retailer, it might decide to downsize the number of unprofitable stores and liquidate inventory to raise capital and/or pay down debt. If it's a manufacturing company, it might consolidate operations to make production more efficient and to save operating costs. Sit down and figure out the true cost of doing business, with correct margins and other figures. Many companies do not know what their actual cost of doing business is. As a result, they cannot make fully informed decisions concerning their business. If you must make cuts in benefits, for example, it is better from an employee-morale standpoint to have the employees share in the cost of the medical plan rather than cutting it out completely.

■ Concentrate on debt collection. Your own accounts receivable are a source of cash flow that can be an enormous help during downtimes.

■ Watch the store and your employees. Often when employees have job insecurity on their minds, they are not as effective in performing their jobs. You might want to double-check accounting and estimating figures, or contact your customers to make sure they are happy in their dealings with your staff. Go over your accounts payable to make sure you paid everything you owed, once! Never underestimate what seemingly rational and stable employees will do under stress. If they are people working with numbers and their minds are not on their jobs, watch out for mistakes. If they are production people working on tasks that require highly skilled techniques and they are affected by negative workplace situations, technical errors could be made that will be costly to the company.

■ Look for good deals, especially on people. Industry lulls usually mean high unemployment, and smart managers can find highly motivated and highly skilled employees at salaries these people would have rejected a year earlier. Negotiate your purchases with vendors. Chances are they are hurting, too. Don't be embarrassed to ask for discounts and favors. You'll kick yourself if you don't, because most vendors are happy to have your business at almost any cost. Lull periods are also a good time to buy the equipment you need at discounted prices. Watch the classifieds for troubled companies selling equipment.

▮ Be positive. Give employees the support and encouragement they expect (and need) from a caring employer. Try to get all workers involved in company concerns, so they won't feel alone in their fears. Encourage them to come up with positive antilull strategies. Keep the lines of communication with them open.

▮ Take care of yourself. When business slows down, meeting payroll, paying bills, coping with frightened employees, and coping with your own fears become more difficult to deal with. If you spend all your time worrying, your sleep will suffer, your personal relationships will suffer, and ultimately, so will your job. Don't blame yourself for the slowdown. Focus on healthful ways to detach yourself from the stress. Jog, play tennis or golf, work out, read, rent a lot of movies. Get your mind on other things. Remind yourself that slow times eventually end, and up to now you've been pretty good at what you do. By getting rid of your frustrations or at least tempering them, you will find that before long the waves of fear won't feel as strong, and the valleys won't seem as deep.

## NINE COMMON MISTAKES IN DOWNSIZING

Downsizing is in high gear in corporate America today. Companies are struggling to compete in an increasingly technological and global market, and the easiest costs to cut often are the jobs and benefits of employees. In 1994, corporations nationwide laid off 615,000 employees, according to *Business Week* magazine, and the pace of layoffs is accelerating by nearly 200,000 a year, with no sign of slowing down.

Downsizing, which includes restructuring and dismissals, has become one of the most complex workplace issues since the industrial revolution and has forever altered the psychological contract between management and workers. Millions of longtime employees who thought they had guaranteed lifetime jobs with a gold watch and pension at the end, now lie awake at night wondering how their company could have dismissed them after 15, 25, or 35 years of service with nothing more than two weeks notice. Many workers who have been victims of downsizing have lost all hope that companies will ever reward good work with continued employment, and as a result, they are less willing to make long-term commitments to *any* company. Generally speaking, as a result of the psychological effects of downsizing, the willingness of America's work force to sacrifice personal interests for the good of an employer seems to be fading fast.

---

## MISTAKE 318

**Expecting employees to be self-motivated during times of uncertainty.**

### How to Avoid It

As workers watch their companies shrink and their jobs disappear, many have changed their attitudes toward management. No longer do they think of the employer as caring and trustworthy. Now they are suspicious of promises and tend to be more independent by looking out for themselves. When employees are more concerned about personal satisfaction than they are about satisfying their employer, it becomes difficult for managers to motivate them. Recently, for example, employees have increasingly been resisting undesirable transfers, with many preferring dismissal rather than going somewhere they don't want to go. In general, workers have also been less willing to devote endless hours to the job, are less outspoken and aggressive, and they look more toward immediate rewards and other short-term benefits. This does not mean they are less effective in their job performance. While they might not spend as many hours on a job that may be in jeopardy, they'll put those hours to better use and get their lives in balance. And while it may seem as though work doesn't interest them as much as it once did, they know they will still need good references from their current employer in order to get a job in the future.

So how can employees be motivated when job security is uncertain? Here are some suggestions:

- From the start, acknowledge to workers that their jobs may be short-term and not exist a few years from now. The reality may appear demoralizing, but it's better than a sudden, unexpected announcement of layoffs. Some companies refer to short-term employment in their help wanted ads. One such ad we spotted was headlined "We want the next three best years of your life."

- If jobs are short-term, offer other immediate rewards besides salaries. Year-end bonuses, a leased company car, awards tied to successful completion of projects, and the like.

- Increase training programs for employees and expand opportunities for lateral transfers. Companies benefit from the additional skills of their workers. Employees also feel that these additional skills will make them more attractive in the job market. Taking employees slated to be laid off and retraining them for positions in other departments that are open saves the company money and establishes trust, concern, and loyalty between employer and employee.

∎ Encourage employees to network and keep in touch with new job opportunities elsewhere.

## MISTAKE 319

**Cutting staff first instead of last.**

### How to Avoid It

Most companies that downsize by cutting staff are forgetting that their employees are their most valuable resource, and the only way change will happen is through those employees. If people become a company's first initiative, then systems, process, and structure can flourish.

## MISTAKE 320

**Not considering the costs of layoffs.**

### How to Avoid It

Few companies, in their rush to downsize, consider the costs of layoffs. First, the company loses skilled employees, who may not be available for rehiring when the business recovers. Second, the layoffs send signals that the company does not expect an improvement in the near future. Morale sinks for employees who remain. Third, in the event a big order comes in, the company would have to pay overtime, hire temporary workers, or hire inexperienced workers who would have to go through costly training.

Another problem that occurs when downsizing takes place is that some of the employees you intend to keep may get scared and seek (and find) other employment. To avoid this, speak privately to those workers and assure them that their jobs are secure and that once the downsizing is completed, the company will be much stronger. This will give them a feeling of long-term stability as well as greater opportunities in the future.

Here are some tips on what you can do besides laying people off:

▮ Cut staff expenses without cutting staff or benefits.

▮ Freeze staff count at current levels, temporarily or permanently.

▮ Reduce temporary workers and restrict or eliminate overtime.

▮ Cut pay or benefits. Lengthen the time between pay increases for all employees or freeze increases for a specific time. Reduce executive salaries, temporarily or permanently. Reduce pay temporarily for all employees by a specific amount.

▮ Create voluntary retirement incentives.

▮ Allow employees to voluntarily reduce hours.

▮ Design job-sharing opportunities.

▮ Ask workers to volunteer to work in other departments that may be busier than yours. Retrain them instead of hiring and training new employees.

▮ Mandate companywide reduced work weeks. Cut back employees from 40 to 30 hours a week, or from five- to four-day work weeks. Shut down for a few days or a week at a time. Set up a time-off-without-pay program.

▮ Use downtime to perform maintenance or other catch-up work.

▮ Solicit and use employees' suggestions. Accelerate counseling to improve poor performers.

## MISTAKE 321

**Cutting staff and not being reassuring to those remaining.**

## MISTAKE 322

**Not recognizing or dealing with employees' "survivor sickness."**

### How to Avoid Them

Unfortunately, cutting staff has become more fashionable than it is productive. What often happens during slack periods is that work may fall off by 25 percent, but management lays off 35 percent of the workers. The remaining discontented employees have to work harder and longer hours, often under the stress of uncertainty and anxiety, to make up the difference.

For some workers, layoffs are a stimulus to work harder so they will not be among those laid off. For others, it is an opportunity to put out as little as they can get away with, especially when layoffs are based on seniority. But the majority of those remaining will feel uncertain about their future and must be reassured both about the security of their jobs and that they will not be expected to carry the work load of those laid off, at least not without getting rewarded for it.

## MISTAKE 323

**Using fear to motivate remaining workers.**

### How to Avoid It

Some companies that go through downsizing motivate their remaining workers to put out the extra effort by instilling the fear that they, too, will be laid off. Negative motivation works up to a point, especially in areas where jobs are scarce, and working harder is better than not working at all. However, a point is reached at which "survivor sickness" takes over, and stress and unhappiness undermine performance.

Instead of using fear, take the following steps:

▌ Be an enthusiastic supporter. You need to show those remaining that you know things will be tough for everyone for a while. Ask how you can help them.

▌ Share information. Discuss, don't ignore, the situation. Explain how the change will affect them, what the next steps will be, and point out the benefits to them and the company. Your enthusiasm might break through the fear and unhappiness and help the downsizing program to work better.

▌ Keep workers advised on what is happening as it happens. Don't wait for rumors to circulate.

▌ Sell those remaining on the importance of getting the work out, even if it means overtime. Make it clear to them that this is not a management problem as much as it is a problem for everyone in the company and that they are expected to cooperate. Ask for volunteers to work overtime should the need arise. If this fails, set up an overtime schedule in which everyone is required to put in a certain number of hours. If feasible, give people the opportunity to select which hours they prefer. Work along with them and show them by example that you are carrying a heavy work load also.

■ Show them the light at the end of the tunnel. Assure those remaining that every effort is being made to keep as many employees as possible. And that *if* they are selected for layoff, they will be given adequate notice, and as business picks up, laid-off workers will be the first to be rehired if they are available.

## MISTAKE 324

**Not encouraging new ways of doing things.**

### How to Avoid It

Encourage those remaining to work smarter instead of harder—to develop more efficient methods and systems. The hard facts of necessity have led to many new approaches that make work easier. Some clerical tasks, for example, may be eliminated during downsizing as people realize the paperwork is not as important as it once seemed. You need to build an environment in which employees can be creative about getting more from limited resources. One company we spoke with told us that during their downsizing period they made tremendous use of interns on the staff. The company received high-quality performance and the interns got a valuable learning experience.

## MISTAKE 325

**Not communicating that cost cutting is everyone's job.**

### How to Avoid It

If everyone would take responsibility for finding ways to save money, it might not be necessary to cut people or budgets. Cost-cutting ideas don't all have to come from the top. Your employees should be given the opportunity to help the company, and it's hoped save jobs. If you level with employees and say, "Unless we find ways to save on expenses now, we'll have to make cuts," most employees will respond.

One of the companies we researched told us they initiated a reward program for cost-cutting ideas submitted by employees. One of their secretaries, we were told, saved the company over $15,000 a year in paper and fax time by suggesting a rubber stamp for the upper right-hand corner of the first fax page to indicate who the fax went to, who sent it, date, number of pages to follow, and so forth, rather than using a separate cover page. Because the company did a lot of faxing, this simple, inexpensive idea represented significant dollar savings.

## MISTAKE 326

**Not emphasizing empowerment.**

### How to Avoid It

While many top executives we questioned agreed that their employees were the most important variable in their company's success, fewer than 30 percent considered investing in people was a "critical strategic issue."

Ironically, the fewer employees left in a firm after downsizing, the more critical their talents become. It is important, therefore, to let these employees be a "partner" with the company and share in the changes being made. This can be accomplished by empowerment.

For many people, hard times represent a chance to show their stuff and shine. Yet in most companies employees are not permitted to take the initiative to do what's best for them (see Chapter 3, "Empowering Authority and Responsibility"). But if you let workers make their own decisions without fear that a wrong decision could cost them their job, they'll come through for you and your company. If you have to ask your workers to do more with less, you need to have the right people in the right jobs, with adequate tools, training, and direction. And they need to know that you have enough trust in their abilities to give them the power and responsibility to make their own decisions.

## SIX MISTAKES IN PREPARING YOUR FIRM, AND YOURSELF, TO CLOSE SHOP

W. C. Fields once said, "If at first you don't succeed, try again. Then quit. No use being a damn fool about it."

There are dozens of reasons why companies decide to throw in the towel. Some, realizing early on that despite their best efforts the situation has grown progressively worse, decide to cut their losses as quickly as possible. Others duck the issue, invest more money, time, and energy, and try to hang on as long as possible, making the inevitable more difficult. Still others, especially small-business owners, welcome the relief that comes from shedding a burdensome and unprofitable business and look forward to new, more exciting ventures. No matter what the reason for folding a company, the process can be painful—for management, employees, and customers.

## MISTAKE 327

**Not recognizing the symptoms of failure.**

### HOW TO AVOID IT

All businesses face crisis and decline; some handle it better than others, some recover and go on to great success, some are rescued from insolvency by acquisition, buy-out or buy-in. But what brings about total failure and the destruction of a dream? As you might guess, every case is different. Yet virtually every case we researched while preparing this book confirmed three facts that were shared by all.

1. The cause of collapse was poor decision making—the failure of management to correctly handle one or more of the complex mixture of its responsibilities—and usually involved companies that were in constant crisis over a period of time.

2. The majority of companies that collapse do not collapse suddenly, without warning.

3. The signs of failure were there for anyone observant enough to see.

According to insolvency experts, the following are some of the most common signs or symptoms that eventually lead to a company's collapse (not necessarily in order of importance):

■ Poor management. Lacking professionalism by not being able to carry out fact-based analysis or understanding strategic marketing and production. Small businesses in particular often lack organizational structures, while others lack effective leadership, have a domineering executive, an unbalanced administrative team, or an uninvolved board.

■ Lack of management style and inability to adapt to changing situations in the marketplace, the physical environment, and technology.

∎ Lack of forward planning and inadequate control systems. Not knowing where you have been, not having the information needed to tell you where you are going, or how to get there.

∎ Too much internal focus. Constantly worrying about organizational structure, relative standing within the organization, and concern with company politics.

∎ Lack of financial management and overleveraging. That includes failure to collect outstanding debts, inadequate capital, and/or excess borrowed debt.

∎ Preoccupation with short-term results at the expense of long-term effectiveness.

∎ The failure and inability to involve all members of the work force in working for the success of the company.

∎ Being too dependent on a product or small number of customers.

∎ Government restraints that could tie a business down or close it down. Companies of all sizes are affected by them—whether they are economic, planning, monetary, or environmental.

∎ Too many trappings. A fish tank in the board room, the founders' statue centered in the fountain in the forecourt, a company yacht or plane, directors who use military titles, an annual report showing the CEO getting out of a helicopter. As one financial executive we spoke to put it, "Management must make the milk before they can skim off the cream."

∎ Problems relating to growth such as overexpansion, overdiversification, expansion in international markets. Failure to generate the cash flow to cover additional borrowings made to finance ambitious plans to seize new markets.

∎ Poor location—particularly in retail, the changing virtues of physical location can have a major impact on turnover and margins.

∎ Improper pricing and product competition. Not understanding costing structure and operating with an unrealistic pricing strategy.

∎ Lack of marketing effort.

∎ Bad attitudes towards controls, customers, learning, and competitors.

## MISTAKE 328

**Not being able to decide when to hold, fold, walk away, or run.**

### How to Avoid It

Being able to decide if, how, and when to cut losses—or try, try again—are all part of the larger process of knowing how to make decisions. While some people rely on gut feeling and instinct, some of the very successful businesspeople we contacted felt strongly that good decisions cannot be made unless you first understand the objective, then look at all the alternatives and their pluses and minuses, and finally consider the risk.

By following this basic process, and weighing the pluses and minuses against the risks and rewards, you will more than likely come to the conclusion that when the odds are against you, it's time to throw in the towel, salvage whatever capital remains, and try something new.

Yet watching a business collapse can be a very difficult, emotional experience that brings feelings of sadness and anger, especially if this was a venture you put money, time, and effort into.

## MISTAKE 329

**Identifying too closely with the company.**

## MISTAKE 330

**Throwing good money after bad, thinking you can recoup.**

### How to Avoid Them

Many of the business consultants we spoke to stressed the importance of employees at all levels not identifying too closely with their companies and not waiting too long to decide that enough is enough. Those in top management, for example, sometimes feel that if the business is a failure, so are they. They blame themselves for the decline of the company. Their decision making often takes on an air of desperation, especially when they take out equity loans on their homes or borrow money from family and friends to put back into the sinking business. Had they not denied the truth and called it quits early on, they would have been spared the high financial and emotional cost of a business failure.

When management can't decide whether or not to continue with their ventures, they need to admit they need advice and then seek some wise counsel—an accountant and/or lawyer, for instance. Try to find someone with a knowledge of what is involved with closing a business—the financial obligations, the legalities, someone who can reassure you that you're doing the right thing. Be careful not to rush the closing process. Maybe the business can be spruced up and sold?

## MISTAKE 331

**Fear that letting go of a business will endanger the financial future of family and employees.**

### How to Avoid It

Sometimes owners of small businesses believe their employees, especially older, longtime workers, will not be able to get comparable jobs. Or, though the owner may be ready to let go, his family members resist, fearing loss of income or status. In these situations, the decision should be to cut losses and look ahead to the problems that will be solved and the opportunities that can open up after leaving the business behind. It's time to close shop when:

■   You can't meet your business obligations.

■   Sales are stagnant, and new customers are declining.

■   Running the business is no longer a challenge.

■   Business activities aren't fun anymore.

■   Business problems are starting to affect your health or family life.

■   You feel relief at the thought of doing something new.

## MISTAKE 332

**Letting yourself get pulled under emotionally by the process of closing shop.**

### How to Avoid It

An owner or top executive who's closing the door of a company and walking away for the last time can be worn down by a flood of emotions. Shock, anger, denial, and guilt will reign before change can be accepted. You can ease the process considerably by:

▌ Acknowledging and accepting the loss.

▌ Looking at the loss in the context of a lifelong career.

▌ Recalling your successes and achievements.

▌ Evaluating your skills and strengths, finding lessons in your experience and applying them to your next venture.

▌ Nor isolating yourself. Staying in touch with colleagues, clients, and vendors and using them to network.

▌ Looking to other aspects of your life that give you a sense of self-esteem. Spending time on outside interests.

## THREE COMMON MISTAKES IN FINAL COMMUNICATIONS WITH EMPLOYEES

Each year, thousands of companies close their doors for good, and many thousands of employees—from the top of the corporate ladder on down—are permanently dismissed. Most have warning and prepare themselves, to some degree, for the inevitable. But no matter how much advance notice workers get, and no matter how much they want to move to a new beginning, when they get that final announcement, feelings of shock, betrayal, anger, confusion, and hostility are common reactions.

### MISTAKE 333

**Not delivering the final news in person.**

### MISTAKE 334

**Not expressing concern for employees.**

#### How to Avoid Them

According to John E. Whalen, senior vice president of Communispond, Inc., an international business communications consulting company, "Executives should use humane methods in their last communication with their employees." He stresses, "The most important thing is that any bad news must be delivered in person if possible, or by interactive teleconferencing if more than one office must be notified simultaneously." Mr. Whalen also advises, "First, make the message very short, about ten minutes maximum," he explains. "Tell the employees what is happening, why it's happening and what it means for them. Be up front. Second, pause. Let the information sink in. No matter how it is presented, news such as the loss of jobs is going to come across as cold and uncaring. Give the employees a chance to digest it. They aren't going to hear anything else you say immediately after such traumatic news, anyway. Third, after that brief moment of contemplation, it is time for the key element of the news—your sincere expression of concern." Some of the human resource people we contacted emphasized the importance of showing sympathy, empathy, and concern. They also thought it was equally important to listen to employees' questions and let them vent their anger.

## MISTAKE 335

**Not providing information on what the next steps will be or what rights workers have after they lose their jobs.**

### How to Avoid It

Because employees may be confused and ignorant of their legal rights, it becomes the obligation of management to provide information on what the next steps will be. All of the business communications consultants we spoke to agreed with John Whalen, "Employees will want to know whom they should see regarding severance pay, employment opportunities, and health insurance coverage." Mr. Whalen suggests that, ideally, "There should be an oral presentation, backed up by distribution of a packet of detailed information that answers critical questions such as where to obtain job-search aid or unemployment compensation; and when, where and whether final paychecks will arrive."

There are some federal, state, and local laws concerning the dismissal of employees that employers closing shop should be aware of.

Plant closing laws, which apply mostly to companies with 100 or more full-time workers, cannot prevent the closing of a worksite or the dismissing of employees. They do, however, provide for advance notice to employees (usually 60 days) that a business will be closing. Failure of a company to advise its workers of the situation can instigate some legal problems and possible penalties.

Under the 1986 Consolidated Omnibus Budget Reconciliation Act (COBRA), employers must offer dismissed workers the option of continuing to be covered by the company's group health insurance plan at the workers' own expense for 18 months (or more, under certain conditions) after employment ends.

Employers should also investigate and advise dismissed employees of various support services that may exist in their area. Many school and university alumni organizations, houses of worship, local community centers, social groups, and hospitals offer group workshops covering such subjects as writing resumes and sharpening interviewing techniques. Local newspapers usually carry calendars of such meetings and events that can be of great help and support to your employees.

*Part*

# 2

---

# THE MOST COMMON MISTAKES BUSINESSES MAKE COMMUNICATING WITH CUSTOMERS

# Chapter 15

## COMMUNICATING TO GET NEW CUSTOMERS

Getting new customers is like fishing. You need the right bait, the right equipment, and the right technique. You also have to know where and when the fish are biting.

But, it is neither as easy nor as simple as the fishing parallel makes it sound, because ever-hungry competitors are continually after just the kind of customers you are going after. And many of these competitors who may act "friendly" toward you at industry functions or through mutual vendors can be fiercely competitive when new business is at stake.

So what is the secret to getting new customers while keeping and expanding the business you already have? Two things are certain. First, few companies have the good fortune of being able to just sit back and wait for new business to come to them. Most must have an organized plan to go out and get new business, not only to grow, but to offset the business they may lose from time to time. Second, the satisfaction of your customers is the only commodity on which your business can grow and prosper. If you don't make the customer happy, your business is history. It doesn't matter what else you do.

## NINETEEN COMMON MISTAKES IN MARKETING MANAGEMENT AND COMMUNICATING WITH CUSTOMERS

This section is not just about dressing for success or using the right body language or phraseology to get and keep customers. It's primarily about marketing management and improving communications with prospects and customers. Whether you are a sales manager, a marketing or merchandising manager, or a communications, advertising, or public relations manager, in order to be effective in dealing with customers, you *must* be a strong communicator. And what you must be very skilled at communicating is image, perception, and the power of persuasion—both yours and your company's. It's crucial for teamwork, customer relations, and for surviving in our intensely interactive workplace.

## MISTAKE 336

**Not understanding the concept of marketing management.**

### HOW TO AVOID IT

Marketing management is the lifeblood of every business and involves those activities associated, in one way or another, with customer relations. It includes:

▮ Deciding which products or services to offer to prospective customers.

▮ Offering prospects the opportunity to buy the products or services of your company.

▮ Knowing how far and in what direction you want to go with your products and customers, then setting goals and spending the time, energy, and capital necessary to get there.

▮ Properly servicing customers after the sale is made.

Marketing management also includes understanding who your customers are, what they want and need, and how you can fill those needs so they feel they have received fair value for their money. When marketing tactics are effective, customers are satisfied, come back for more, spread the good word to others—and the business becomes successful.

Customer relations, which will be discussed in greater detail in the next chapter, is one of the most important elements of good marketing management and involves a number of employees in various departments including the people who make the sale, the people who service the customer, the people who deliver the order, the people who send out the bills, even the people who answer the phones.

## MISTAKE 337

**Not putting aside dollars for new business.**

## MISTAKE 338

**Relying too heavily on one major customer.**

## MISTAKE 339

**Hiring new employees in anticipation of getting new customers.**

### HOW TO AVOID THEM

If all is going well at your business, setting aside dollars for future customer development may not seem necessary. Never let your guard down—in good times or bad. You can lose a major customer and, along with it, a major source of income when you least expect it and for reasons you'd never guess. Should this happen, you will find yourself in the position of having to cut staff and expenses in order to remain in business. It's always safer to have new customers in various stages of development.

But in order to have a program for new customer development, you must have a budget for it, and that budget will stem from your marketing plan (see Creating a Feasible Marketing Plan, in this chapter). Some provision for getting new business, no matter how small the amount may seem, is better than no provision at all. Setting aside a reasonable amount of money every month or every quarter for mailers, advertising, public relations, publicity releases about your products or services, telemarketing, and the like, may well be the best investment you will ever make—because it is an investment in the development of your own business.

But just because you have a program for new customer development doesn't justify adding on payroll expenses before it is necessary. Rather than anticipate, hire those you need only when you are absolutely sure you will need them. Or, reshuffle and retrain existing personnel to help cover positions that are short.

## MISTAKE 340

**Not knowing who your customers are.**

## How to Avoid It

One of the most incredible facts that I encountered over and over during my many years in advertising, marketing, and communications was the large number of astute (and successful) business people who had little or no demographic information about their customers. I have even met business people who said, "We don't have customers," or "We don't work directly with customers." Believe me, every business has and works with customers.

The only way you can direct your selling efforts in the most efficient manner is by knowing the demographics about the people who buy your product or service.

First determine if they are businesses or individuals. If they are individuals:

- Are they male, female, or both?
- Are they married or single?
- With or without children?
- Do they own their own home, or rent?
- Do they work in a particular field?
- What is their age range?
- What is their income range?
- Where are they located in relation to your business?
- What is their reason for buying?
- What are their buying habits?
- Have they ever bought from you or your competition before?
- Are they qualified buyers?
- What are the limits of this market?

If they are businesses:

- Who are they buying from now?
- Are they within your marketing area?
- Are they too big or too small for you to handle?
- Do they pay their bills promptly?
- Are they worth putting time and effort into developing?
- Do they expect too much in the way of service?
- Who are the people you will be dealing with?

The more information you have about the customer, the easier it will be to target those potential customers that not only need your product or service, but also best fit your size and style.

Getting as much data as you possibly can on your target market and becoming as familiar as you possibly can with their needs and problems is the most effective way to get new customers.

There are a number of research sources available that can provide these data. The U.S. government's Office of Management and Budget, for example, provides information on many free-standing metropolitan areas known as MSAs (Metropolitan Statistical Areas). A good deal of information can be obtained from census reports or information available from local newspapers, broadcast stations, and chambers of commerce. Many large companies have their own research departments that continually redefine their company's market and customer base. Any company can use its current sales data as a source for new customer information. Sales data, for instance, will reveal seasonal sales patterns that may be important in scheduling promotional campaigns or hiring additional help. Sales data will also identify geographical trends or areas in which certain local factors or competitive forces play on the vitality of the product or service you are selling.

## MISTAKE 341

**Not being able to distinguish between internal and external customers.**

### How to Avoid It

Internal customers are those people, departments, or organizations served by what we do. For example, a human resources person serves employees' needs for benefits information, management's needs for staffing, and company needs for handling various legal requirements as set forth by federal and state laws.

As individuals, most of us have at least one internal customer: our boss. As managers we also have internal customers in the form of people we supervise.

The traditional use of the term *customers* refers to external customers, those individuals, departments, or businesses that are end users of your company's product or service. Depending on the kind of business involved, they can be referred to by various names other than customers. They are sometimes called clients, buyers, guests, patients, patrons, cases, franchisees, passengers, students, shoppers, purchasing agents, and so on.

A satisfied customer is one who purchases and receives value from the goods or services you offer. These customers generally have a choice concerning who they buy from. If they don't like what you offer, or your price, or your method of doing business, they can go elsewhere for similar goods or services. When they do, your company suffers. Satisfied customers mean profits, which mean success and the ability to grow.

Some companies have what are called "captive customers," customers who can get a product or service from only one source, such as utilities or license plates.

You might think, Why bother to satisfy a captive customer; they *have* to buy from us. The answer is that when a customer is displeased with service—whether it is with a for-profit company, a government agency, public utility, or a nonprofit organization—that displeasure quickly becomes animosity. And when a customer displays animosity toward the employees of these institutions, employee stress rises and often leads to more serious effects such as employee burnout and absenteeism, high turnover, expenditures to rehire and retrain, difficulty in attracting good new applicants, negative public image, lower sense of pride in the organization, and lower sense of self-worth among employees.

## MISTAKE 342

**Refusing to listen, be flexible, and respond to your customers' needs.**

### How to Avoid It

Once you have identified who your customers are, the next thing to identify is their needs.

One company we interviewed told us that their entire sales and customer relations staff is trained to ask customers "Tell us exactly what you want and need and we'll take care of it." Then they listen to what customers or potential customers say in response to that and satisfy that customer by fulfilling their needs. By using this simple, direct method, customers know you care about pleasing them. You'll build repeat, long-term business, and because customers will have invested their time in explaining what they want done—and had the opportunity to see how you deliver on your promises—they'll be less likely to switch to a competitor. This puts your company in the position of consistently challenging your competition to keep up with you.

If your employees understand that you are not in the business of just selling products or services, but rather in the business of fulfilling a customer's need, and if they follow the philosophy of "Listen, be flexible, and respond," you'll establish an image of being a customer-driven business, and you'll be well on the road to success.

## MISTAKE 343

**Going after business you can't handle or get.**

## MISTAKE 344

**Thinking bigger customers are better customers.**

### How to Avoid Them

Sometimes, people in business are not realistic. They will spend time and money soliciting customers they don't stand a chance of getting, or if they do get the business, they can't deliver the goods because the order may be too large, too small, or in an area in which they don't have servicing or distribution. Going after a new prospect who just entered into a contract with your competitor, for instance, can be a waste of time, especially if your competition provides products or services very similar to yours. But if the competitor oversold its product or service, and you know the prospect will be disappointed and ready to make a change when it discovers its mistake, you can be ready and waiting with your pitch. Whether it is the ego of the top company executive or the overenthusiasm of the company's sales manager or staff, more often than not, businesses do not see the true picture of what they have to offer a potential customer or the problems that can develop from overenthusiastic selling.

Another mistake businesses sometimes make when their customers are other businesses is going after the "biggest fish in the pond." In reality, being big today can also mean being behind, or being overextended.

Never launch a product or service by trying to sell only to big companies; often they take too long to make a decision, particularly when it involves buying a new or innovative product or service. You also risk being too dependent on a small number of large customers.

## MISTAKE 345

**Trying to be all things to all customers.**

## How to Avoid It

Trying to be all things to all customers won't work. Take a look at your strengths and weaknesses. Can you deliver on the promises you're making? Can you afford to expand people and equipmentwise as fast as you're growing saleswise? Can you get additional staff on an as-needed basis?

## MISTAKE 346

**Expanding too rapidly.**

## How to Avoid It

One of the primary reasons small businesses fail is they try to expand too quickly. It may sound strange, but sales that grow too rapidly can destroy a company, especially if safeguards are not in place to handle the growth in an orderly manner.

Before a company considers expansion, it should consider the following questions:

- Can the company handle increased overhead expenses? When hiring additional staff, you must also provide time and resources to train the new employees. Does the business generate enough profit to enable the company to pay up to six months of the new employee's salary without seeing any return on its investment? If the answer is yes, go ahead and start hiring.

- Is there working capital and cash flow to support higher amounts of inventory and accounts receivable? Before adding products or additional services, you must realize the drain on cash flow this will cause by having more of your company's cash tied up in inventory and other expenses associated with product expansion. Is your line of credit enough to carry you through cash shortages? Are suppliers willing to extend payment terms while you get your new lines up and running?

- Can you measure the productivity gains? Try to determine how the added expenses will affect the bottom line. Will you have to expand your building? Will such an expansion enable your employees to work more efficiently or give you the space you need for additional product lines? You may want to temporarily test the effect of additional space by taking a short-term (six-month) lease on nearby facilities. Analyze the results before you take on the fixed expenses of expanding what you now have.

▌ Will a different product mix make the company more profitable without the need to increase volume or expand lines?

▌ Is the staff being utilized in the most productive manner? Can current employees be cross-trained? Would current employees be willing to work overtime to meet increased demands?

▌ Can the company keep inventory levels at a minimum and ordering at optimal reorder points, to minimize storage space and high inventory carrying costs?

▌ What are the costs and the benefits of expansion? Would it make more sense to lease rather than purchase additional space? Would it make more sense to hire temporary rather than permanent workers? Are there tax benefits associated with the increased costs? What is the additional sales volume you will need to cover the costs of expansion? Does the timing of payments for additional incurred expenses work out with the receipt of anticipated additional revenues?

▌ Are there uncertainties concerning future economic conditions?

▌ How do you think your competitors will respond to your expansion? Are you ready to counter any move they might make?

▌ What are market trends in the industry? Is now the right time to expand?

It takes an analytical and intuitive perspective, as well as dealing with many missing pieces of the puzzle before these kinds of business decisions can be made. While you may not have a crystal ball to guide you in making such decisions, you can make sure you are always in control of your company's growth. Turning down potential sales is difficult for any business, especially a small business, but sometimes it's necessary in order to ensure long-term survival.

## MISTAKE 347

**Selling a mass-market product or service without a mass-market distribution or a customer service network.**

### How to Avoid It

Many good ideas for products and services are just that—good ideas. Converting a good idea into a successful business by getting the product or service to the right market takes hard work and lots of homework at every stage of the development. Miss just one link and the dream of success becomes the nightmare of failure.

First, if you are going to sell a product in volume, and in numerous markets, it is essential to have a mass market distribution system in place. This may include establishing a network of sales reps and retail outlets where the product or service can be easily purchased. Or selling through mail order or telemarketing, which may require setting up area distribution centers or drop-shipping arrangements. You will also need to have customer relations covered in each area of distribution. This may mean establishing local or regional service centers.

Second, it is necessary to determine market demand. How much would a customer be willing to pay for your product or service? Never assume what product demand will be or what a buyer would consider a fair market value for the product or service.

## MISTAKE 348

**Not staying on top of your market or in tune with your customers.**

### How to Avoid It

Every product or service has a "shelf life." You may still be marketing your product the same way you were when you first launched it, without realizing the market for your product has changed. The reason may simply be that because of day-to-day demands and consistent sales, you've been too busy or too unconcerned to notice or look for changes taking place.

By reading trade journals, attending meetings and seminars in your field, and getting feedback from suppliers, competitors, and customers, you can stay on top of your market and be aware of trends. Many companies conduct their own market audits that provide an informed and objective opinion on how much longer the market can use your product and will indicate whether or not it has become stale. There are many excellent free-lance marketing people who can conduct such an audit for a relatively reasonable fee, which may be well worth the expenditure if the information will help you save money down the line.

## MISTAKE 349

**Looking for new customers while losing touch with existing customers.**

## How to Avoid It

A major mistake that many companies make is directing all their selling and public relations efforts only toward getting new customers. When such efforts are done well, the results can be very rewarding. However, most businesses derive the bulk of their sales from existing customers, and though new customers may be marching in the front door, old proven customers with repeat business may be leaving through the back door. The reason is often because a company slips into the habit of losing touch with existing customers. This can be easily and inexpensively overcome by making occasional phone calls to find out what customers thought of their recent purchases or services, or sending out "reminder" or "sale" notices on a regular basis. Customers are pleased when a company takes the time to find out if the customer is happy, and if not, why. Chapter 16 covers this subject in more detail.

## MISTAKE 350

**Not realizing your competitive edge.**

## How to Avoid It

Why would someone choose to buy your product or service instead of a competitor's?

Just as surprised as I always am when I meet seemingly sharp businesspeople who don't know who their customers are, I'm just as amazed at all the people who haven't the slightest idea as to why their product has an edge over the competition's. Of course, there are those few celebrated products or services that are unique; the edge is obvious. But there are also many products that you see cloned in every size, shape, and color imaginable. For them, it is more difficult to become a staple that is seen and used every day, one that continues on successfully for many years.

As a business owner or a sales or promotion manager, you must find the edge that separates you from the pack and makes your product more desirable.

Ask yourself, "Why should customers choose my product or service over the competition? The answer may be price. Or service. Or packaging. Or reliability and consistency. Once you have determined your edge, the next step is to let potential customers know about it.

## MISTAKE 351

**Not establishing customer confidence.**

### How to Avoid It

Any good salesperson knows that if a potential customer lacks confidence in the product, the company, or the salesperson, the sale will probably never happen.

Customer confidence must be established and reconfirmed throughout the selling process, but especially early on. The following are some tips on prime selling opportunities that will help establish customer confidence. Each situation calls for variations of techniques.

■ Phone selling. Your objective in this situation would be to use a single item to establish enough confidence to get an order or appointment. Something like, "The XYZ Company just purchased one of our copiers. They are thrilled with its performance and efficiency. Since you are in the same business, we can show you how you will benefit from this machine. When would be a good time for you to meet with me and discuss it?"

■ Cold calling. Be as brief as possible. Try to make a strong statement that will generate interest in the first 15 to 30 seconds. The statement should focus on your edge over the competition. Once you generate interest, go for the follow-up appointment when you'll have more time to tell the whole story.

■ Making a presentation. Present your story in an orderly fashion, building one plus on top of another. Try to anticipate customer questions or doubts and be prepared with sensible answers. To help instill a sense of security and credibility, bring along any other ammunition you may have including letters from satisfied customers, PR stories, annual reports, comparison charts, and lists of longtime repeat customers.

■ On a follow-up call. Have a specific purpose for making the appointment and be sure it doesn't sound contrived or forced, otherwise the prospect may lose the confidence you worked hard to gain. Go for the order. If you get an answer such as. "Call me back in two or three weeks," chances are the confidence is gone.

■ Networking. Like the phone situation, you may have time to establish confidence with only one statement. The best kind of statement in this case would be one that refers to a sale you made to a competitor or leader in the industry. The prospect will assume that if so and so uses your product or service, he must have investigated and found you best for one reason or another.

## MISTAKE 352

**Not paying attention to a customer's buying signals.**

### How to Avoid It

Knowing when a customer is ready to buy is a matter of paying attention to questions, gestures, and statements and knowing what signals to look for. The following are typical buying signals to look for and convert into sales:

- Any statement that indicates the prospect recognizes a benefit in using your product or service.

- Questions a prospect asks concerning availability or lead time needed to order.

- Questions about price or down payment.

- Positive questions about your position with the company, the credibility of your business, and who some of your customers are.

- Statements about previous bad experiences with competitors.

- Questions relating to features, options, quality, and guarantees.

- Questions about customer service.

- Questions that seek your support in making a decision, such as "What do you think, will this take care of my needs?"

- Asking for a sample or another demonstration.

- Asking if it's okay to call satisfied customers or asking for references.

- Statements such as "Tell me more," "Really, I never knew that," or "This seems to be exactly what we've been looking for."

Once you've identified the buying signal or signals, stop selling and start closing the sale—by asking for the order. You would be surprised how many opportunities for making sales are lost only because the seller forgot to ask for the order. By asking for the order you will either get it or get a "no." Then at least you have the opportunity to find out what the obstacle is and deal with it.

## MISTAKE 353

**Not playing by the customer's rules.**

## MISTAKE 354

**Not being flexible with customers.**

### How to Avoid Them

There are companies who tell their customers how their rules work, and they rarely bend those rules to satisfy a customer. Those companies look at each customer as an insignificant individual sale that is not worth breaking rules for. There are other companies that ask their customers what they'd like the rules to be, and they will make every effort to make their customers happy. They look at every potential customer from the standpoint of what they represent in income over a long period of time. The difference in these two attitudes separates the excellent service companies from the average and poor ones. To succeed in today's highly competitive and knowledgeable marketplace, you have to play by the customers' rules, or at least be flexible enough to change a "no" situation into a "yes, this time" one. For example:

■ If your customers can shop only late, why not extend your hours to accommodate them?

■ Why can't you offer leasing as well as purchasing?

■ Why can't you deliver?

Most customers will not expect, or want you to lose money on a transaction, and will be willing to pay extra for convenience, customizing, and flexibility, as long as it meets their needs.

## THREE COMMON MISTAKES THAT HAMPER THE EFFECTIVENESS OF YOUR ADVERTISING

Statistics show that eventually nearly every business will advertise in one way or another. It could be with an infomercial on network cable, a full-color ad in a magazine, a billboard on a heavily driven highway, a bold listing in the local Yellow Pages, or something as simple as handing out a business card.

In upcoming chapters we will be covering communications mistakes made in various media such as the Interactive Superhighway, direct, voice, E-mail, telemarketing, and so on. But this topic will deal mainly with mistakes that can hamper the effectiveness of your advertising efforts.

## MISTAKE 355

**Not being knowledgeable about advertising.**

## MISTAKE 356

**Not making sure your advertising conveys the image in which you wish your business to be perceived by customers.**

### HOW TO AVOID THEM

Whatever the medium may be, creating the proper message, directing it to the proper target market, and following through with an effective advertising and marketing plan are essential. If enough of the right people aren't seeing or hearing your ads, advertising becomes just an expensive luxury. But doing everything by the book is no guarantee that your advertising will be effective for you.

It goes without saying that you must become knowledgeable about and comfortable with whatever promotional techniques you use to reach your goals. This is not to imply that you should become an expert on every subject that concerns advertising; obviously that would be a lifetime task. But there are hundreds of books (including one by this author) and college courses about art, copy, media buying, production techniques, research, and so on, that could give you the basic information you will need. Even if you use the services of an advertising or public relations firm to create, produce, and implement your campaign, you should still be knowledgeable about what you are involved with.

Take, for example, the simplest form of advertising mentioned earlier: the business card.

Any businessperson will tell you that business cards are indispensable. Your business card communicates the kind of business you are in, your name, title, address, telephone, and fax. It can also list the products or services you offer, your business hours, branch offices, and so forth. Some people even print their pictures and tiny resumes on their business cards.

When people look at your business card they get a split-second image of what you're all about. If done effectively, it can open countless doors. If not, it speaks poorly about you and your company.

So if everyone relies on business cards to tell a company's story or sell themselves, how come few people bother to learn enough about them to make them as effective as possible?

A visit to your local library or any book store will provide you with enough information to increase the effectiveness of your card. For example, we stopped in at a neighborhood library and found that:

- Business cards should correspond with the image the company is trying to portray.

- Cards should be part of a corporate logo package and correspond with the company's letterhead and stationery.

- Cards should be easy to read. Avoid tiny type or type that runs alongside the edge of the card. It might be interesting to look at, but hard to read.

- Stick to one style of type. You can add variety by using boldface, embossing, or creative spacing. Avoid using all capital letters; they're difficult to read.

- Keep the card simple, but make sure it includes the basics. Clean-looking business cards that have few tricks are most effective. Not only should address, phone and fax numbers, and a logo be included, but an individual's name and title should be prominently displayed.

- When the objective of the card is to encourage prospective customers to call, the phone number should stand out. Also, the more phone numbers listed, the larger and more impressive the business appears to be.

- Opinions differ on whether business cards should diverge from the standard 2 by 3-1/2 inch format. Cards can be cut into various sizes, such as the 4 by 3-1/2 inch card that folds in half to hold much more information, or it can be cut into various shapes to fit a Rolodex. Most people find variations from the standard format ineffective and often irritating.

- Listing key services and benefits in larger type or bold lettering highlights a company's services. "24 hours," "Same-day delivery," "Free consultation," or "Free estimates," give potential customers a reason to call. Phrases such as "In business since 1980," and "With 10 years of experience" communicate an accomplished enterprise, as do lists of professional certifications or license numbers.

▪ Use color as background or to make the type stand out. Be sure it corresponds with your business image.

▪ Different paper types can make a card stand out. Choose paper that's sturdy and durable rather than flimsy. Woven paper also can add an aura of quality.

▪ Have a realistic idea of what your budget allows. Color and quality paper will cost more than black print on simple white paper. The size, quantity, and design of the card will also affect the cost.

▪ Companies should change their business cards every four or five years to keep up with the times. A new logo, paper stock, or typeface may be all that is necessary to give the company an image boost that can draw more customers.

Though it's unlikely that a poorly designed business card will make or break your business, it should be pointed out that discovering all of the above information involved just over one hour of research and provided the knowledge needed to help create a more effective advertising tool for any business.

## MISTAKE 357

**Continually using advertising without evaluating its effectiveness.**

### How to Avoid It

If you don't advertise your business, you may never sell your product or service. If you do, you still may never sell your product or service, or at least not enough of it to cover the cost of the advertising. Most companies will choose to advertise in one form or another. And when they do, questions will come to the minds of all good sales, advertising, and marketing managers, such as: Does advertising make a difference in sales? How much difference does it make? Is one form of advertising more effective than another?

As a veteran of many years in the advertising business, I can promise you that when done properly, advertising *does* make a difference in sales. I can also tell you that it *is* possible to measure the relationship of advertising to sales. However, going into full detail would take at least another two hundred or more pages, which you don't want to read and I don't want to write, at least not at this time. So for purposes of brevity, we'll bypass the intricacies of identifying target markets, consumer buying motives, media buying, message construction and communication, and so on—and go right to a short "checklist" of ways to quickly evaluate advertising's effect on sales.

■ Inquiry, telemarketing, and mail-order evaluations. These are the three most obvious methods of measuring advertising/sales results. An inquiry advertisement asks a prospect to write or call for further information. Telemarketing and mail-order advertising asks the prospect to buy your product or service either right then while on the phone, or by mail. Sales results from these types of promotions provide a valuable measure of advertising effectiveness.

■ Consumer purchase evaluations. Such evaluations are often used in stores while products are being test-marketed in a particular area through various advertising mediums such as local newspapers and broadcast media. They provide the advertiser with information and experience needed to expand into additional markets. Prior to running the ads, a random sampling of consumers is made (either by interviewing or by giving them diaries) to determine how many bought the product prior to the advertising, how frequently they bought it, how much they have bought, and what they have on hand. This sampling is reinterviewed immediately after the ads run to determine the percentage increase (or decrease) in sales of the product.

■ Store inventory evaluations. With this method, a retailer's stock is inventoried before and after the advertising. Some companies continue to check inventories for long periods after the advertising stops, to measure the longevity of the advertising pull as well as to isolate other factors that might have been responsible for the increase in demand, such as heavy advertising by a competitor, or even the weather. One midwestern fast-food chain we interviewed told us about a limited-time coupon offer they thought would be extremely successful. They invested a sizable budget in newspapers and direct mail expecting a significant increase in sales. Unfortunately, it snowed heavily throughout the entire offering period and people could not or would not leave their homes and travel over icy roads.

▎ Keying of ads. This is a method employed by advertisers using multiple media to test the effectiveness of a particular medium. By keying or identifying each advertisement, such as coupons used in different newspapers, the advertising manager can determine which newspapers pulled best.

# EIGHT MISTAKES THAT CAN HURT YOUR PUBLIC IMAGE

All managers who deal with people outside their organization must, from time to time, deal with problems concerning their company's public image. The problem may be that your salespeople have a hard time getting in to see prospects, or your customers should be buying more from you but they aren't. Maybe you're getting bad vibes from reps, vendors, or your retail outlets. Maybe your company is losing sales because your image is out of step with the times. Or maybe, as happens at least once in every manager's career, a time comes when something goes terribly wrong and there's an immediate threat to your department, your job, and the company. It could be customers falling ill after using your product, or an environmental group targeting your company as a neighborhood health hazard, or a rumor circulating that your company is on the verge of bankruptcy.

Whatever it may be, extraordinary public relations measures have to be taken to pinpoint and deal with each problem quickly.

## MISTAKE 358

**Believing you have to hire an expensive public relations firm to get your message out to the public.**

## MISTAKE 359

**Not using free publicity to influence the public's perception of your company.**

### How to Avoid Them

Unlike advertising, which can be prohibitively expensive, especially for a small business, press coverage in newspapers and trade journals is free for the asking. And it can work wonders. Ask any experts in corporate communications and they will tell you that positive public relations and publicity can influence sales, impress suppliers and money lenders, even create the desire for people to work for you.

And all you need to get attention from the media is your imagination, common sense, persistence—and these quick tips:

- *Decide on your message.* Generally, PR concerning businesses falls into two categories: news releases about company accomplishments and feature stories on the firm itself, usually highlighting a unique aspect of the business. News releases should be short, simple, and report fresh facts of general interest, such as expansions, joint ventures, new products and services, location changes, employee promotions, special sales events, awards, and key personnel changes. One subject frequently overlooked are stories about customers, which if published puts you in a situation in which everyone wins: the company and customer both get favorable publicity, and the media gets an interesting story. The most important information should be in the first paragraph. Proofread what you write for mistakes in spelling and grammar and double-check all facts and figures you may use. Don't exaggerate, use misleading statements, or statements that criticize, especially the competition.

  Feature stories should have at least one good "angle" that the editor might think would be of interest to readers. Put yourself in the readers' shoes and think about what would be unusual or interesting to you about your company, your product or service, or your field of expertise. State this in a few straightforward sentences. Then try to relate your business to some trend or development that will affect readers' lives in one way or another.

- *Select the appropriate media.* Try to be realistic about who will want to read your story. The media selected should include local newspapers and broadcast stations, as well as trade publications. Stories should be addressed to the appropriate media editor or reporter. Directories of news-media personnel are available at your local library. Send along any photos, diagrams, and backup that substantiate and enhance the story.

- *Make the approach.* If yours is a feature story, start with a one-page letter to a news organization describing why your company merits feature coverage. Include any background, backup, and other press clippings that will support your request. Follow up with a rehearsed phone call to make sure your letter was received and to ask if there are any questions you can answer. Describe any photo possibilities. When the response is positive, follow up with another phone call or letter to arrange for an interview.

## MISTAKE 360

**Not properly preparing for an interview.**

## MISTAKE 361

**Allowing the interview to become confrontational and negative.**

## MISTAKE 362

**Not taking full advantage of positive publicity you've received.**

### How to Avoid Them

Now that you've gotten the attention of the media, the time has come for the interview. Here are some Don'ts and Do's that should be considered:

DON'T be nervous about your upcoming meeting. Interviews can and should be pleasurable. Most interviews involve cooperative communication between you, the person who has the information, and a reporter who wants that information.

Do be prepared. Have all your important points clearly in mind; be sure you state them in a positive way. If there have been previous negative stories about you or your company, try to find out *before* the interview starts if they are going to be brought up. In any case, try to be prepared to show how they have been resolved or be prepared to put off answering those questions.

Do be courteous and forthright. Have all your backup and background material handy and offer to share it with the reporter.

Do talk about what will interest the people who will see, hear, or read about the interview. Don't go off on a side track that has little or nothing to do with the subject you are discussing.

DON'T use jargon or negative statements about competition. Use simple language that can't be misinterpreted. If you use humor, make sure that it is not offensive to other companies, groups, or individuals.

DON'T panic or be evasive if you're thrown a negative question or one you can't answer. Tell the interviewer you'll have to find the answer and call back. A "No comment" reply may imply you are trying to hide something.

DO refuse to answer, in a polite way, of course, if you are asked a question that concerns proprietary business information or intrudes on your personal privacy or the privacy of others employed by your company.

DON'T make any statements you don't want to see in print. If a question requires a simple yes or no answer, don't go into a long recital that may uncover things you really don't want to talk about, such as product secrets you would rather competitors don't know about.

DO get all the mileage you can from the story. If the interview appears in a print publication, get permission to reprint it and use it as a mailing to customers, prospects, and even other media that may be interested enough to give you additional coverage.

## MISTAKE 363

**Not dealing with public attitudes concerning your company or industry.**

### HOW TO AVOID IT

Every company must deal with the attitudes of the people it does business with. Here are some tips on identifying, anticipating, and coping with them.

∎ Select one adept person in top management to keep abreast of public attitudes on matters concerning your business.

∎ Create a method of detecting, documenting, and tracking new trends and developments that affect the attitudes of groups that relate to your business.

∎ Recognize that there are various types and segments of the public, each with differences in their outlook on individual matters. Women, for example, will have attitudes about certain things different from what men will. The same is true for older and younger people, disabled and nondisabled people.

❚ Try to determine how certain people or groups are motivated and why they rationalize and react in different ways. Reasons could be frustration, resentment, envy, ambition, desire for attention, and so on.

---

## MISTAKE 364

**Undervaluing the positive effects of public relations.**

---

## MISTAKE 365

**Going into a public relations program without a plan.**

### How to Avoid Them

If your business has experienced problems relating to your public image and relations with customers, employees, competitors, governmental and environmental agencies, or the media, your company probably needs a public relations program.

When this need arises, many companies either downplay the value of public relations or plunge into it without a sound plan. Both reactions are mistakes.

According to Donald Levin, president of Levin Public Relations & Marketing, Inc., White Plains, New York, "Companies that elevate the role of communication, rather than limiting it, enjoy a decided competitive edge." He cites, as an example, one company he knew of that expanded its PR strategy by "studying attitudes of critical target audiences." This company also initiated "periodic assessment of audience opinion and other forms of communication feedback," and added programs to enhance the PR effort: "advertising, crisis preparation, ally enhancement, speech-making, and international publicity," among other things, he said.

Mr. Levin also points out that just as "you wouldn't operate an organization without a plan, you should regard your communications function the same way." He urges his clients to keep themselves educated internally as well as externally by "continually nurturing the communications channels. Staying inside the grapevine, and knowing what's going on at the top, middle, and bottom. If PR is merely external exposure," he says, "it has just begun to function."

## EIGHT COMMON MISTAKES IN HANDLING NEGATIVE PUBLICITY

How do you stay alive when the bombs start falling? How does a company caught in the wake of racial discrimination charges, for instance, rebuild its image and crippled sales? What do you do if your company is accused of price fixing, corner cutting or stock rigging? How do you handle the situation if your celebrity spokesperson, whose picture is on every ad you run and every package you sell, is accused of murder, rape, spousal abuse, or child molestation?

One thing is certain: categorically denying the charges and vowing to fight them vigorously in court will not be enough and are worthless in terms of public relations value.

## MISTAKE 366

**Not preparing for a crisis.**

### How to Avoid It

Any manager who has been involved in a crisis situation will tell you, in looking back, that dealing with it would have been a lot easier if she had been prepared for the worst that could happen. Consider possible scenarios with your peers and superiors and come up with procedures, however vague they may be, for everyone to follow. Appoint one person as the spokesperson for the company and funnel all information to and through that person. Procedures could include resources you may need to meet a crisis, the handling of reporters and cameras, and the kinds of statements made to the press. You can decide, in advance of a crisis, which questions the company can answer and, because of policy, can't answer.

## MISTAKE 367

**Not knowing or defining your objective when addressing a crisis.**

### How to Avoid It

When a crisis occurs, take a few minutes to determine your main objective. It might be to recall all defective parts or to keep things going in the face of a mass employee walkout. Your objective should boil down to one thought: What needs to get done right this minute, and what can wait? Make a list of things you have to do to meet the immediate crisis, such as informing superiors and subordinates, contacting affected customers, or recalling or replacing products or parts. Then determine what resources you might need to accomplish these things, such as extra personnel, advice from upper management, money, supplies, or liaison with other departments.

## MISTAKE 368

**Not communicating your objective clearly and consistently to everyone concerned with the crisis.**

### How to Avoid It

Communicate your objective clearly, in a forthright way, and with accurate information about the crisis. Tell the truth, the same truth, to everyone—your employees, your superiors, your customers, the general public, and the media.

## MISTAKE 369

**Allowing others to get their crisis information from sources other than you.**

### How to Avoid It

Take the initiative. Let everyone know exactly what the situation is, what steps are to be taken, and what you require of them. Make communications frequent, detailed, and honest. Your customers who are told about what's going on will be much more forgiving than those who learn about it through rumor or the media.

## MISTAKE 370

**Dealing only with external matters and not reassuring your front-line people that you're on top of things.**

### How to Avoid It

Reassure your employees that the crisis is being dealt with. This is particularly important because employees interact with customers and other crucial audiences such as the financial community. If they are misinformed or disoriented or if they have negative feelings toward the company, those feelings will be conveyed in their communications with people outside the company. Try to keep up morale as much as possible. Without making light of the problem, a little humor can go a long way in reducing stress when the going is tough. Take off your boss's hat and put on your advocate hat. Think of yourself as the commanding officer of an army unit taken prisoner. Make it your job to see that your people are not abused. If the company is in immediate trouble, make top management aware of your employees' special needs. If one or more of your employees is to blame for the crisis, protect those that are innocent.

Here are a few more tips that apply to most crisis situations that will help build bridges and protect your company's image:

■ Maintain your company's believability and stand by the company's mission statement. This can be important because in a crisis communications that nobody believes are worse than useless. By the same token, the company has to stay on course in order to survive. By keeping in mind what the company's objectives are, the question of "How do we deal with this?" becomes easier to answer.

■ Anticipate questions that will be asked by employees, customers, and the media. Prepare answers that can be backed up.

■ Know all the facts before criticizing upper management. If, for instance, your superiors do not reveal the complete truth about a situation, look into the matter before accusing them of misinforming or holding back information. There may be legal reasons for their actions.

■ Hold off finger pointing. An employee or someone else you may need to help you get out of the crisis may have caused the problem. Taking the time out to place the blame and discipline him may just make the situation worse and probably should not be your top priority at the outset.

■ When dealing with the media, be open and honest. Don't disguise important information because it's bad news. The reporter will more than likely find it and then be more suspicious of any future information you give out.

■ If there is an error in a reported story, always ask for a correction.

■ Don't rehash negative news. People tend to have short memories and will forget your crisis long before you do.

■ Seek and pay attention to public relations advice, but don't isolate yourself from direct media contact when your words can lead to better understanding. Some companies have hired what are called "turnaround marketers," people with experience in rebuilding company images after a serious crisis occurs.

■ Learn how newsrooms operate and about journalistic ethics. Refer to books that detail how news stories are assigned and edited. Don't be offended, for instance, if a reporter turns down a free sample of your product or if your statements to the press are heavily edited.

## MISTAKE 371

**Not setting business ethics guidelines to help curb misconduct and improve the corporate image.**

### How to Avoid It

Lying to supervisors, falsifying records and reports, engaging in bribery to get business, stealing files and data to get a leg up on the competition are just some of the most common unethical practices that occur daily in the workplace and often inflame public opinion.

But today, according to the Washington, D.C.-based Ethics Resource Center, many companies are setting up comprehensive ethical guidelines and programs to help clarify what constitutes misconduct and address nearly every act of unethical behavior, from sexual harassment to making personal copies on the company copy machine. Such programs typically incorporate employee training and written information to back up a company's code, and by showing that the company is operating on the side of maximum caution, go a long way in helping to put the shine back on tarnished corporate images.

In addition, companies are finding that if they can show their commitment to high ethical standards and practices and have an ethics program in operation, courts will be more lenient when handing down sentences for legal violations.

## MISTAKE 372

**Not recognizing the risks of using celebrity endorsements.**

### How to Avoid It

Using a celebrity to endorse your product or service has its rewards— by helping to break through the clutter of competitive advertising with instant recognition, credibility, and the ability to create demand. During my career I have used many celebrities to endorse the products and services of my clients. I was very lucky because all of the personalities I worked with lived up to their public images, avoided controversy in their personal lives, and retained their pulling power for long periods.

But what happens when the celebrity, who appeared to be "squeaky clean," gets into trouble, and the reputation of your product or service, and your company, is threatened by the relationship?

The first instinct is to distance the company from the personality as quickly as possible. This can sometimes create the negative impression that the company is abandoning the celebrity, especially if the allegations against the celebrity are unproven.

The answer for those companies considering celebrity endorsements is to use the celebrity to *enhance* the attributes of their products or services and not overshadow them. If companies do, they are investing major dollars in diverting both energy and image to the celebrity instead of bringing attention to the attributes of the product that, in the long run, counts for much more.

A good example is Oscar-winning actor and comedian Red Buttons. He has been the spokesperson for Century Village, four of Florida's largest and most successful adult condominium communities, since 1968 (by any measurement, a long-term relationship). Red has not only maintained his appeal with all generations of the public, but as he matured, his popularity among those of *his* generation strengthened, and his ability to bring attention to the values offered by Century Village is now greater than ever. The reasons for the success of this relationship are many and include:

■ The celebrity and product complemented each other.

■ The celebrity's fame never overshadowed the qualities of the product.

■ The product was able to stand on its own merits.

■ Red Buttons was in real life what he appeared to be in public, a nice, talented, and uncontroversial human being who related to the needs of a market.

While celebrity endorsements will always be a way for marketers to generate interest and sales, it is important to find out as much as you can about the interests of the personality in relation to the interests of your company. Keep in mind also that celebrities lead lives of unimaginable temptations, opportunities, and pressures, and more often than not, the images they project are quite different from the lives they actually lead. When a celebrity is involved in a negative situation, the appeal of the product or service he endorses could fall in direct proportion to the seriousness of the situation.

## MISTAKE 373

**Not providing for a way to void the endorsement agreement of a celebrity in trouble.**

### HOW TO AVOID IT

How can a company protect itself from negative repercussions caused by the criminal behavior of celebrity endorsers?

Like many individuals, companies often get "star struck" with celebrities. And in their rush to tie the idol up as their spokesperson, they will agree to a contract guaranteeing the personality years of work and high fees, while giving little or no thought to their star falling or their getting out of what may become a bad deal.

Like most other contracts for services, an endorsement agreement should also have some provision for the advertiser to terminate if the personality becomes involved in a situation that subjects the personality or company to ridicule, contempt, or scandal. In addition, the advertiser should be able to terminate such an agreement if performance by one party has been rendered valueless to the other party, especially in cases where the cause is the behavior of the guilty party. This might include such criminal behavior as arrest or conviction for drug use, child molestation, spousal abuse, gambling, or other crimes that would generate negative publicity and that would destroy the value of the endorser to the advertiser.

These provisions are known as morals clauses and have been used by film studios since the early 1920s when the private activities of motion picture stars negatively affected theater attendance.

Companies should insist on such a clause being a part of any agreement. If the celebrity is very powerful and the only way to obtain her endorsement is by eliminating your way out, you may want to use another method of promoting your product or, at least, another less powerful celebrity to endorse it.

# SIX COMMON MISTAKES IN CREATING A FEASIBLE MARKETING PLAN

Unlike a formal business plan, a marketing plan spells out the marketing strategies of a company and relates them to business goals and the needs of the target customer group. It describes the company, its products or services, and its customers. It details a course of action that includes market research data, as well as marketing and communications strategies and provisions for reviewing and updating the plan.

While making and keeping to a marketing plan is particularly important to a business just starting up, it is essential to the success of every company, no matter how large or small or how long it has been in business.

## MISTAKE 374

**Not having a marketing plan, or not updating the one you have.**

## MISTAKE 375

**Thinking you don't need a marketing plan because you do the same things every year.**

### How to Avoid Them

If your formal business plan is typical, it is probably riddled with rosy forecasts designed to delight loan officers and potential investors. But is your marketing plan strong enough to make those optimistic projections become reality? Does your plan take into consideration the fact that we are in an era when companies must contend with waning resources, cautious and highly sophisticated customers, increased government regulations, and other changes that can dramatically impact every business?

Top management and managers often focus their marketing plans on making the sale, but that comes only toward the end of the marketing process. Before you reach that point, prospects and customers must travel through a systematic process that involves what those in marketing call "friendly persuasion," a logical order to persuasive marketing that carries the prospect to the point of favorable action. Various authorities on the art of persuasion have advanced numerous formulas for this process, but they are all fundamentally variations on a relatively simple theory: AIDA.

The AIDA theory suggests that in order to persuade, the marketing approach must first cause changes in customers' mind-set, from ignorance of your products or services to *A*wareness of them, then *I*nterest must be created, *D*esire must be stimulated, and finally *A*ction must be taken: the purchase.

---

## MISTAKE 376

**Not knowing how to write a marketing plan or what it should include.**

### How to Avoid It

You don't have to be a marketing or advertising genius or have an MBA to prepare a marketing plan. In fact, there are a number of simplified fill-in-the-blanks computer programs available that can walk you through the planning process and tailor a plan for your specific business. These programs often ask you to answer a series of questions and then suggest language for your strategies based on your answers. There are also books, videos, college seminars, and national and local business organizations that can provide you with valuable tips and information on putting your marketing plan together.

The first step in writing a marketing plan is understanding what a marketing plan is. Stated simply, it is a systematic plan by which a business attracts the right customers and keeps them coming back for more.

Marketing plans for large companies with multiple products or services will obviously take more thought and preparation than the plan for the neighborhood dry cleaner who is mainly concerned with offering the highest quality cleaning at the lowest price.

When creating a marketing plan, decide first on how long a time period you want it to cover. A six-month or yearly period would be ideal for a small or recently organized company whose fortunes can change quickly. Once into the plan, it can then be broken down into quarterly segments. Plans that are designed for longer periods tend to serve more as a planning tool rather than as a day-to-day marketing tool. Remember, too, that successful marketing develops a cumulative effect as its results increase over time.

Here is a seven-point quick-primer for preparing your marketing plan:

1. *The title page.* Should state the date of the plan and a nondisclosure statement.

2. *Overview.* Your text should start out with a capsule overview describing your business niche in relation to a definable market need (industry category, products, services or systems, location, years in the business, areas of expertise, size of staff, equipment), its goals, its geographic trading area and target market profile, and distribution channels.

3. *Broad objectives.* This section should outline the company's long- and short-term objectives concerning market position, projected sales revenue, and specific plans for updating old or introducing new products.

4. *Research.* Now you must gather all the data you can and translate them into a description of the size and characteristics of your market and trends that have affected or may affect that market, as well as important data concerning the effects of competition and projections of changes that may occur and the resources you may need to deal with those changes.

5. *Marketing strategy.* State the attributes that differentiate your business from competitors' (quality, pricing, packaging, advertising, distribution advantages). List your specific marketing goals (projected sales volume, which is the starting point for all budgeting; customer relations efforts; and expected amount of repeat business). State your position on pricing, quality, and customer service. Describe your sales plan (training programs, territories, management, compensation, incentive and recognition programs, dealer discount policies). Itemize your marketing budget (costs for launching a new product, as well as maintaining marketplace presence; costs for self-promotion; media relations; advertising; insurance; possible interest payments on loans) and your sales promotion plan (themes for presentations, catalogs, point-of-sale displays, trade show exhibits). Maximize the plan's impact by creating programs that develop synergistic relationships. For instance, spending the bulk of your budget on a beautiful catalog is a waste of money if you don't have enough marketing dollars to attract the prospects the brochure was meant for.

6. *Communications strategy.* How you are going to communicate with your customers. Provide an outline of advertising and public relations campaigns with breakdowns showing specific budgets for each element in each media. A description of other planned communications activities such as telemarketing, direct

mail, special events, and other customer-related communications—all including budget breakdowns.

7. *The plan for implementation.* This section should detail schedules for deadlines and responsibilities for all activities, as well as procedures to measure performance and review and update the plan, if needed. It should also include, if appropriate, procedures for borrowing and repaying capital to finance the plan.

After completing your marketing plan, analyze it. Does it help you position your company with your customers and meet their needs? Will this plan help you stay ahead of the competition? Does it suggest any new approaches you might not have considered using before? Will it create a flow of new prospects and help retain your customer base? Is it too heavily budgeted in some areas and not enough in others? Is it creative—and most important, is it realistic and achievable?

## MISTAKE 377

**Preparing a plan that is creative and ambitious, but not achievable.**

### How to Avoid It

When it comes to marketing, many executives expect and sometimes demand unrealistic results even though they're unwilling to provide the budget required to reach the objectives. Try to be conservative rather than "blue sky" in your projections. Some managers we spoke with told us a general rule of thumb in preparing marketing plans is to put a great deal of time, effort, and research into forecasting sales, and after coming up with a figure that everyone agrees is very conservative, reduce it by another 15 percent—just to be sure.

## MISTAKE 378

**Failing to plan for change.**

### How to Avoid It

Many companies don't consider, until it's too late, that one of the greatest challenges they will encounter in the workplace is the challenge of change.

Examples of what can go wrong are as near as this morning's newspaper. Customers suddenly desert your product for one that incorporates new technology. A labor shortage renders you unable to fill frontline positions. A lifestyle change or federal regulation makes your services obsolete or environmentally unsafe.

Strategies for predicting and encountering change should be part of your marketing plan and should include:

■ Looking back at the trends that have affected your market in recent years.

■ Keeping abreast of emerging trends. This will put you in a better position to predict changes that could affect your marketing goals.

■ Conducting ongoing research that assesses the strengths, weaknesses, and marketing techniques of your competitors.

■ Tracking your customers' methods and their demographic and psychographic characteristics.

■ Projecting the methods of key current and future opportunities and analyzing the risks and resources involved in taking advantage of those opportunities.

■ Making budget provisions for changes, as well as for current and future opportunities.

## MISTAKE 379

**Failing to make sure that those elements you *don't* control in the marketing process are able to perform properly.**

### How to Avoid It

The best-laid marketing plans can fail because of downstream problems involving the execution of supporting functions by outside firms. I recall one advertising campaign that produced nearly 250,000 overnight inquiries for the client, a response far beyond what anyone expected. The next morning, the phones at the ad agency were ringing off the hook with congratulatory calls from various managers at the client's company. Everyone was ecstatic—for about an hour. Then the roof caved in.

The responses—mostly from TV, radio, and print—gave an 800 number. All calls were funneled to a marketing services company hired by the client's sales manager, which unfortunately was overwhelmed by the quantity and unable to effectively handle the majority of incoming responses. Many calls were lost completely, and many more had incomplete or incorrect data. The problem was magnified further by inaccurate "qualification criteria" created by another outside sales lead group hired by the client's marketing manager to identify genuine prospects. As a result, good and excellent prospects were ignored, while those with low buying potential were rated high and sent the wrong marketing literature by the outside fulfillment house, also hired by the sales manager. And, as if all this were not enough to make the client jump off the nearest bridge, it took the fulfillment house two weeks instead of the expected two days to get the material out, not that it mattered at this point.

This was a classic case of "the operation was a success, but the patient died." The advertising worked, but because of outside factors that were beyond the control of the ad agency, the client had a fiasco instead of a success.

While this example may not be typical of the things that *can* go wrong, be certain that things can go wrong. It takes only a single critical breakdown during the marketing process to sink the entire plan.

In the preceding example, the marketing plan called for various company managers to employ various vendors to perform interrelated services. And sometimes, when many people and companies are involved in such a process, things can go wrong. In this case both the sales and marketing managers should have made sure the outside support companies knew what they were doing and were capable of handling the unexpected. They also could have let the advertising agency be responsible for hiring and controlling the supporting functions.

Don't assume every big company can handle every big job. If you estimate 10,000 responses from a campaign, for example, make sure your marketing services company can handle 100,000. Know whom you are working with and what their limitations are. Build relationships with effective, talented vendors and you'll end up a hero instead of an unknowing victim.

## THREE COMMON MISTAKES IN NETWORKING FOR NEW CUSTOMERS

Every businessperson interested in getting new customers knows the value of networking. Some are experts at it. Some enjoy it occasionally. But for many, especially those less-than-adept socially, networking can make root canal work seem like a pleasurable experience.

## MISTAKE 380

**Not being willing to invest time in networking.**

### How to Avoid It

Networking to get new customers works. By creating new relationships, you will eventually, if you've done it properly, create new sales. But forming networking relationships takes time—time to show a prospect that you are credible and can deliver quality products or services consistently. And you must be willing to invest that time to get known by those who can help you reach your goals.

## MISTAKE 381

**Avoiding networking because of psychological barriers.**

## MISTAKE 382

**Not knowing where and how to network.**

### How to Avoid Them

Networking requires a willingness to venture out of your comfort zone, go to business functions disguised as social functions, and meet strangers you will have to build and nurture into long-term profitable relationships. It requires getting involved. Simply attending a networking function will not increase your accounts receivable.

Here are some tips that will help you succeed at networking for new customers:

▪ If networking, especially at group gatherings, is nerve-racking to you, work on your mind-set. Make your goals realistic. Realize that everyone involved in networking is there for the same reason as you. Remember that you are working when you are networking, so you may as well enjoy yourself. Pin your name tag near your right shoulder so that when you shake hands, your name will be in plain view. Everyone tends to forget names, so when you greet someone, say your name. If the other person does not offer his name, confess if you've forgotten it. Watch your body language. Nobody wants to work with someone who looks stiff and uncomfortable. When you're relaxed, it will be easier to walk up to someone and start a conversation. But don't overdo it. If you're a talker, control yourself, be positive rather than negative, and try to be a good listener.

- Go where your prospects are. Get there early, and don't be in a rush to leave. Pick out the individuals, groups, or organizations that are most likely to produce the results you are looking for. Ask your present customers if you can join them at their business functions. If you go to one networking function every week, you will have gone to more than 50 during the year—and probably will have had the opportunity of meeting hundreds of good prospects. You should also try to contact at least two or three people every day by phone.

- When you make contact, be prepared with name tag or business cards that you can get to easily, some subjects for small talk (the weather, compliments, current events, a few nonoffensive jokes or stories), and your appointment book. Don't forget to ask for their business cards, and ask for permission to send them some information. If you know in advance who will be there, do some background research so you'll have things in common to talk about.

- Don't push relationships too quickly. At group meetings, listen, observe, then decide how best you can relate to the individual or group. If a person seems shy or not willing to talk, don't press the situation. If the meeting is by chance or on the phone, wait at least 24 hours before following up. If you get to know and help the right people, and build solid relationships, they will go out of their way to give you their business or send others your way.

- Get the relationship to a one-on-one basis by bringing the conversation around from small talk to real issues of mutual interest. Keep in mind that though this individual may not result in a sale, if she feels you are credible, honorable, and represent a worthwhile product or service, she will recommend you to others who will become sales.

- Get involved. Attend meetings on a regular basis. Make the time to become a consistent performer and doer. Work at establishing and maintaining relationships. Volunteer for positions of leadership. Don't just be a taker. Show the group or individual that you are willing and able to work hard to help them succeed.

- Practice! Practice being relaxed. Practice smiling. Practice responding to questions. Practice becoming bolder. Practice building your communication skills. You'll find networking and meeting new people can be fun and will more than likely lead to many new customers.

# Chapter 16

## HANDLING DISGRUNTLED CUSTOMERS

"**Y**ou've got a customer for life!" "I wouldn't dream of doing business anywhere else!" "It's nice to find a company that really cares about its customers." "It seems as if all your employees go out of their way to make every customer happy."

How much would *you* be willing to pay to consistently hear your customers say these kinds of things about your company? Maybe you'd be willing to turn over your firstborn, or at least, your entire advertising and public relations budget?

Few companies can please all their customers all the time, but as more and more companies are learning, it's good business to try.

A survey by the American Management Association points out why.

▪ Sixty-five percent of an average company's business comes from repeat customers.

▪ It typically costs five times as much to acquire a new customer as to service an existing one.

▪ Most disgruntled customers never go back to a company they had a problem with.

And research conducted by Technical Assistance Research Programs Institute of Arlington, VA., concludes:

▪ Many unsatisfied customers don't even complain. In most industries, fewer than one in 20 with *major* problems complain to management or the manufacturer. Fewer than one in 50 complain about *small* problems.

▮ Each problem encountered by a customer causes, on average, a 20 percent drop in long-term loyalty. Five problems will cause a revenue loss equal to what one long-term customer would bring in.

▮ On average, the *satisfied* customer with a small problem tells 4 or 5 people; the *dissatisfied* one tells 9 or 10. The *satisfied* customer with a large problem tells 8 people; the *dissatisfied* one passes his discontent on to at least 16 others.

## TWELVE MISTAKES THAT CAN TURN CUSTOMER DELIGHT INTO CUSTOMER HASSLES

Why would customers in a restaurant pass up empty tables and wait up to an hour or more just so they can be served by a particular food server? Why do some retail customers shop only on days when their favorite salesperson can take care of them? Why are some drivers paranoid if their car breaks down and "the only mechanic in the world they trust" is on vacation? The answer is: exceptional customer service.

## MISTAKE 383

**Not believing that people don't have the time for poor service and hassles.**

## MISTAKE 384

**Not believing that customers value service more than price.**

## MISTAKE 385

**Not understanding that great customer service can set you apart from your competitors.**

## MISTAKE 386

**Not believing that good customer service builds customer loyalty and referrals that last for years.**

## How to Avoid Them

Providing exceptional service can be the most powerful tool for achieving and sustaining a competitive advantage and restoring customer goodwill.

Once you've got the customers, are you as intent on keeping them as you were on getting them? Are you aware that:

■ Today's consumers are more affluent and more time-strapped. They don't have time for poor service anymore and are more willing to pay for good service as a way to leverage their time. Hiring inefficient workers because they may cost you less may end up costing you dearly.

■ Though price holds a strong allure for most customers, it is no longer enough to keep them coming back again and again. Great service is the least expensive and surest way to build and sustain a competitive advantage. As the American Management Association survey pointed out, keeping a customer costs one fifth as much as acquiring a new one. Other research shows that customers are four times more likely to stop doing business with a company because of poor service than because they found a better or cheaper product elsewhere.

■ Great customer service is also the surest way to differentiate your business from look-alike competitors. Most department and specialty stores, office and home building supply centers, airlines, and banks, for example, offer the same products or services to the same people in the same locations. The reason one may stand out from its competitive look-alike is the quality of the people who take care of customers.

■ Happy customers are repeat customers who account for about 65 percent of your business, but in addition, they can be your best salespeople. First of all, they know you and like you. You have established rapport and have built confidence and trust. You have a history of delivery and satisfaction. They like and use your product or service. They have credit with you and have paid you in the past. While a disgruntled customer will tell nine people why they *shouldn't* do business with a company they had problems with, a happy customer will tell at least five or six why they *should*. Which makes it pretty obvious why achieving customer satisfaction is so important.

## MISTAKE 387

Putting money or profits ahead of customer service.

## MISTAKE 388

Taking your customers (and competitors) for granted.

## MISTAKE 389

Not improving service from the top down.

## MISTAKE 390

Not having measurable customer service goals.

## MISTAKE 391

Not training employees in the care and feeding of the customer.

## MISTAKE 392

Hiring for skills and training for attitude, instead of vice versa.

## MISTAKE 393

Not providing employee incentives and rewards for exceptional service to customers.

## MISTAKE 394

Not empowering employees to solve problems.

### How to Avoid Them

I am always amazed at the energy and enthusiasm some companies put into making the sale and getting the customer, and then—because of indifference, arrogance, poor follow-up, bad service, slow response, or a dozen other ridiculous reasons—lose the customer they worked so hard and spent so much to get. Based on research and various interviews with managers who have successful customer relations programs, here are seven quick tips on how to make your customer service exceptional:

1. Great customer service begins at 100 percent plus, and just plain old satisfactory customer service is no longer acceptable. Great service starts at the top and shines with those on the front line. Therefore, if you expect customer service to flourish, you cannot underpay those people in contact with customers—nor bypass training them—in an attempt to keep costs down. Customers don't want to wait in line while the improperly trained clerk on a complex electronic cash register tries to figure out which button to push and has no idea how to placate those getting more disgruntled by the minute. Companies that believe labor is cheap and replaceable, that employee turnover is inevitable, and that people will be replaced by technology may be digging themselves into a customer service grave. Ultimately, employees communicate to the customer how they feel about their jobs and employers. When your employees are happy, they are more likely to make your customers happy.

2. Never assume that customers are satisfied and that competitors aren't a step ahead of you. Stay in touch with customers and the industry. Know what your customers like about doing business with you, and what they don't like. Understand that the customer's perception is reality because the customer *must* come first, over money, profits, and policy. Always! Sometimes what makes good business sense to you, doesn't, as far as your customers are concerned. Annual surveys sent to customers, focus groups, employees talking to customers, setting up an 800 question or information line—these are all methods by which any company can find out what customers want or don't want, like or don't like. The trick is not to assume anything. Ask questions, and ask them in many ways. When customers know you really care about quality service, they'll talk to you about their small dissatisfactions—issues they'd never mention to an organization unless they are convinced it is committed to exceptional service. This also applies in business-to-business relationships. Many companies that sell to other companies assign someone in management to make "management-to-management" service survey calls on a quarterly basis. This shows the customer you care, and it helps cement your relationship, making it less likely that the customer will switch to another source.

3. Never forget that good customer service starts with those at the top. If the leader puts the customer first, the company's service programs will have a better chance of success.

4. If exceptional customer service is to be your competitive weapon, you must bring together your top people and create a game plan that spells out the level of service you intend to provide and how you will train employees to carry out the strategy. It might be something as simple as how many rings before a phone is answered. Or how quickly you respond to a customer query. Or what to say to a customer if the product fails, or how much authority to give to those servicing customers. A good service strategy should be simple, clear, and to the point.

5. Once a customer service strategy is in place, you must find the right people to execute it and come up with ways to keep the strategy alive in their minds so it influences their daily behavior. This requires paying attention to hiring. Most companies tend to hire customer contact people for skills and train for attitude when they ought to be doing it the other way around. It's a lot easier, for instance, to train someone to ring up an order than it is to teach her to smile at customers. One company that hires for attitude uses the slogan "The only thing better than friendly, courteous employees are friendly, courteous employees who know their stuff." Good interviewing skills can eliminate high-maintenance employees who require constant fixing of their mistakes and result in employees who thrive on positive reinforcement. Not only do they bring in repeat customers, they serve as role models, pushing standards ever higher. Some qualities to look for in good service employees include:

   ▌ A ferocious work ethic.

   ▌ Good disposition and love of their work.

   ▌ Seeing the world from the customer's point of view.

   ▌ Trusting customers and taking a long-term view about their relationships.

   ▌ Finding ways to do a job, not excuses to avoid doing it.

   ▌ Constantly try to improve themselves and the process.

6. Most employees get paid the same whether or not they treat the customer nicely, whether or not the customer buys, or whether they fix the problem now or a week from now. An effective way to improve customer service is to design a compensation struc-

ture that gives all employees involved with servicing customers a direct stake in the profitability of the firm if they perform well. Such incentives include pay-for-performance plans, profit sharing, cash for good ideas, promotions and job enrichment, preferred work locations (better offices, larger desks), and work scheduling flexibility. And as we pointed out repeatedly in the first section of this book, plain old recognition is always a good attitude incentive, such as compliments (spoken or written), "employee of the month" recognition, a surprise lunch, or newsletter writeups. Another type of incentive, for example, is that which some service companies impose on their repair technicians. They make it an employment condition that if technicians don't repair it right the first time, they will have to make as many return trips as necessary to solve the problem—but won't get paid for the return trips.

7. Customers judge your company by how it does business under normal conditions and how it responds when there's a problem. While some managers cringe at the thought of empowering their employees with the freedom to solve problems, they must face the fact that to provide exceptional service, employees must have the latitude to make certain decisions themselves, on the spot. It may cost more in the beginning in terms of mistakes and overly generous decisions, but it will come back many times over by eliminating misunderstandings, reducing many daily hassles, and strengthening customer loyalty.

## FIVE MISTAKES CUSTOMERS MAKE THAT CAN MAKE PROBLEMS FOR YOU

A lot of what has been written about customer relations gives the impression that poor service is the fault of the company, the manager, or the employee. Not always. Very often it's the customer who is at fault. I've noticed it myself lately, more often than I have in past years. Maybe it's the consumer's reaction to mass layoffs, downsizing, and increased competition. Maybe the business environment has become so harsh and impersonal, so profit-driven and transfixed by legalities and discounting that we have forgotten that we are all human beings working together to make a better society. Whatever the reason, it appears to us that in today's customer-oriented business atmosphere, many customers are taking advantage of the situation and demanding more in the way of services than they are entitled to. We threw this theory out to some of the businesses we were contacting for this chapter, and to our surprise, many agreed that the theory was not only true, but becoming a major concern to companies across the nation.

The responses we got identified five categories of, let's be nice and call them "mistakes by difficult customers," and some quick tips on how to handle them.

## MISTAKE 395

Being *inconsiderate*—insisting that every business transaction be a special circumstance that applies only to them, in which the rules, schedules, and pricing guidelines are waived.

### How to Avoid It

The best way to handle these customers is to be very firm about policies. Explain that all customers are treated equally and to show favoritism toward one customer over another would not be fair. However, you will do what you can to expedite their transaction.

## MISTAKE 396

Being *tyrannical*—will be abusive, abrasive, demeaning, and dictatorial during any and all transactions. They will trample your ego, interrupt whatever you're saying, assassinate your character, and tear apart your remarks.

### How to Avoid It

Identify the legitimate grievance beneath the yelling and screaming. Be firm, strong, and unemotional in your stand as you let them rant, rave, and vent their steam. When they finish what they have to say and calm down a little, rephrase their main points in your own words and explain that you are there to help them. You are not their enemy, in fact you'd like to be their friend (try to act as if you mean it). Establish the facts to reduce the complainer's tendency to exaggerate or overgeneralize. Force the complainer to suggest solutions to the problem. Try to take care of his needs quickly and get him out before he upsets other customers and employees.

## MISTAKE 397

Being a *crisis maker*—starting all encounters with moans, gasps, the need for someone to hold their hand, and because of this or that urgent situation, insist that their needs must be taken care of first, no matter what their place in line.

### How to Avoid It

Be reassuring, empathetic, and noncritical and explain that you will give their situation your personal attention and expedite it as soon as possible, but not at the expense of other customers.

## MISTAKE 398

Being a *bully*—believing they can get a better deal if they use intimidation as a weapon.

### How to Avoid It

Let them tell you what they want. Show respect for what they say to you and explain that all customers pay the same price. You might want to appease them by offering to put their name on a special list of "preferred customers" who will be the first to be notified of exceptional sales before the general public. If they are very abusive and loud, you might want to offer them a "gift" of merchandise that would relate to the product they are buying (a free blank tape if they are buying a camcorder, two free light bulbs if they are purchasing a lamp).

## MISTAKE 399

Being a *nit-picker*—taking every basic business deal down to the nth degree. They are the type who look for technical loopholes in product directions.

### How to Avoid It

Hear them out and then try to win their confidence by being reassuring, while diverting their attention to other more meaningful things such as the excellent price, exceptional product features including guarantees or warranties, the company's reputation for service, and so on.

# EIGHT MISTAKES IN RESTORING GOODWILL WITH DISGRUNTLED CUSTOMERS

We said it earlier: if you satisfy a complaining or disgruntled customer, the chances are that customer will become one of your best salespeople, and let's face it, there is no better advertising than word of mouth. The hard part is knowing how to turn a frustrated, dissatisfied customer into a cooperative one who will speak highly of you and your business.

## MISTAKE 400

**Interrupting instead of listening when a customer registers a complaint.**

### How to Avoid It

When disgruntled customers make a complaint, there are a number of techniques you can employ to appease them, but the one that produces the best result is simply to *listen*. Don't interrupt. Let the customer fully air the complaint. If you interrupt, you will appear to be argumentative. Take what she says seriously. Try to understand her problem and the reason she is upset. Because prejudice may distort what you hear, listen without prejudging. Active listening involves interpreting, so listen carefully to what is *not* said. What a person implies can be more important than what she actually says.

## MISTAKE 401

**Not apologizing or accepting responsibility for a problem.**

### How to Avoid It

After the customer gets it all out, promptly tell her you understand how she feels, empathize with her, apologize and be an ambassador for your company by telling the customer you take responsibility for the problem and will personally handle it with a sense of urgency. This will help defuse the situation to some degree because the customer probably will be expecting you to deny the blame or blame others.

## MISTAKE 402

**Totally ignoring complaints.**

### How to Avoid It

Try to solve the problem, immediately, if possible. Find some common ground other than the problem to establish some rapport. Possibly use humor; making someone laugh puts them at ease. Figure out, communicate, and agree on a way to resolve the problem. Depending on how serious the problem is, possibly the best solution is financial reparation, such a full or partial refund, or a discount on the next purchase. Another solution might be to offer to pick up or deliver goods to be replaced or repaired, or to give a gift of merchandise to repay the customer for his inconvenience. If this is acceptable, take action and follow up with a letter (or a call) of confirmation and apology.

Sometimes unhappy customers are lost because no one knew they were dissatisfied. According to one study, only 1 out of 27 discontented customers make complaints. So make it a habit (after first-time sales or on a regular quarterly basis) of following up all sales with questionnaires or phone calls to customers to find out what they liked and didn't like about what they purchased and how they found the service.

## MISTAKE 403

**Passing a complaint off to a subordinate.**

## MISTAKE 404

**Not acting on complaints immediately.**

## MISTAKE 405

**Continually promising to resolve a complaint, when intending to ignore it.**

## MISTAKE 406

**Flatly refusing to satisfy a complaint.**

## How to Avoid Them

Not responding to a complaint, passing it off to a subordinate, allowing a lot of time to pass before dealing with it, falsely promising to deal with it, or flatly refusing to satisfy it are all guaranteed ways to alienate a customer. As soon as a complaint is registered, instant communication should go into effect. Contact the customer immediately and apologize for the problem. Treat her with respect, offer a solution, and if acceptable, act on it. After righting the problem, call the customer to make sure she is now satisfied. If she is, apologize again for any inconvenience she may have been subjected to and assure her the problem will not happen again.

---

## MISTAKE 407

**Using language that customers misunderstand.**

## How to Avoid It

There are many "forbidden phrases" that sneak into workers' vocabularies that cause hassles with customers and break down attempts at restoring goodwill. Here are five of the most common, and some alternate responses that can help reduce the problems:

1. "Wait here, I'll be right back in two seconds." This is an untruth to begin with because it will take more than two seconds to find the answer you need to satisfy the customer. Instead of keeping him waiting and boiling, a better approach is, "I'm happy to help you, but it may take a while. Would you like to wait? Or if you have something else to do I'll have the information for you when you get back."

2. "I don't know." If you, the supposed expert in your field doesn't know, who does? Other similar phrases often used in place of this one are, "That's not my job." Or, "I don't work in this department." Answers such as these make you and the company look pretty stupid about your operation, and it certainly doesn't help build confidence with the customer. An alternate response is, "That's a fair question. I'd be happy to find the answer for you. If you'd like to look around or take a seat for awhile, I'll be back in a few minutes."

3. "We can't do that." A customer's normal reaction to this is to get angry and demanding. Instead try, "That may be a problem; let me see what I can do." Or, say it in a more positive way, "I see your point; here's what we can do."

4. "You'll have to . . ." Not acting on a complaint immediately, passing it off to a subordinate, or forcing the customer to go through a gamut of people and processes to solve her problem puts the customer in the position of feeling irritated, defensive, talked down to, and without options. Instead respond with something like, "Here's how we can help you with that."

5. "No!" This little two-letter word denotes total rejection. Your employees should erase it from their memories. Alternate responses should stress the positives of what can be done. "We cannot give you a refund, but we can replace the product with another or give you a credit toward another purchase."

---

## FIVE COMMON MISTAKES IN TRYING TO DO WHAT CUSTOMERS WANT

---

You've heard it said many times, "The customer is the boss." Or, "The customer is our only reason for being in business." While these may be catchy slogans, the real challenge lies in translating them into actions that convey these feelings and beliefs to the customer. And one of the problems companies run into when trying to accomplish this is the difficulty of getting their customer contact people to understand customers and then do what customers want. The problem gets trickier when those who face the customer day in and day out are the lowest paid and least trained employees.

---

### MISTAKE 408

---

**Not understanding the customer's side.**

#### How to Avoid It

Before you can do what customers want, you must understand the realities involved in dealing with them.

■ Though most customers know exactly what they want and how they want it, they may have difficulty communicating those facts to you in a way you will fully understand. Listen carefully. Be patient. Ask questions to clarify what you don't understand. When you think you do, repeat your understanding to them so everyone will be in agreement.

■ Every customer thinks he is your only customer—so make him feel important by treating him as if he were.

■ Customers are human and have problems just like the rest of us. Treat them as you expect to be treated when you are the customer.

■ Customers expect service immediately. Try to accommodate them if you can.

## MISTAKE 409

**Not paying attention to what you say and how you react.**

## MISTAKE 410

**Not having a thorough grasp of all the aspects of what it is you're selling.**

## MISTAKE 411

**Not explaining why your product or service will be of benefit to the customer.**

## MISTAKE 412

**Not giving customers a choice and then reinforcing their decision.**

### How to Avoid Them

If you don't have a clear idea of what your product or service is, what it's worth, how you charge for it and service it, and the benefits and values to the customer, sit down, map it all out, and memorize it before talking to potential customers.

Here's what the average customers want you to do:

■ Listen to what their needs are and take what they say seriously.

■ Give them the facts. Get to the main points without going through a long drawn-out story.

- Tell them the truth and show them you're ethical. If you say something they doubt or know not to be true, you're done for.

- Show and tell them why your product or service will benefit them. Why they need what you're selling, why it benefits them to buy it here and now.

- Prove what you say. Reinforce your claims with newspaper or magazine reprints, letters from satisfied customers, names of neighbors just like them who made the same purchase and are happy.

- Explain fully about the service they can expect after they buy, and show them proof. Lots of people have bought a lot of empty service promises and are wary of salespeople who promise the moon to make the sale.

- Reassure them that your price is fair. Show them that what they are buying is well worth what they are paying. Make them feel as if they're getting a deal. Many companies offer to match competitors' prices and accept competitors' discount coupons.

- Explain the methods of payment available to them. If they can't afford to pay in full, show them the alternatives and explain how they work.

- Give them a choice instead of trying to push them into a purchase. Let the decision be theirs, but make a recommendation. Tell them what you would do if it were your money.

- Reinforce their choice. Most people are unsure and nervous about making a purchase, especially a large one. Help reinforce their choice with facts that will benefit them and give them the confidence they need to justify the purchase.

Here are some Don'ts and Do's:

Don't argue with customers, even if they are wrong.

Don't make fun of a customer. Customers wearing T-shirts should not be treated any differently from those wearing suits and ties.

Don't confuse customers. The more complicated you make a situation, the more likely the customer won't buy.

Don't be negative. Customers want everything to be perfect. Don't degrade a competitor's product, a customer's trade-in, or a customer's expressed preference. Never say bad things about your company or your fellow employees.

Don't talk down to customers. Don't tell them what you think they want to hear.

Don't tell them what they did or bought is wrong. Make them feel smart. If they really did goof, be tactful and explain how many others have done the same thing.

Don't sound or act like a salesperson out to make a sale. Act like a friend trying to help. People hate being sold, but love to buy.

Don't use words and phrases that offend customers. Words such as "Honestly . . .," "Frankly . . .," "Quite frankly . . .," "And I mean that . . .," "Are you ready to order now? . . ." sound insincere and make customers suspect the person who says it.

Don't knock the competition; it only makes you look bad. As your mother may have told you, if you have nothing nice to say about someone, say nothing.

Do greet your customer like a guest in your home, and do it promptly. A prompt, friendly greeting is one of those little things that mean a lot to customers.

Do talk to customers with your eyes. Eye contact creates a bond between you and the customer. It conveys your interest in communicating further.

Do smile. Let your face show that you are glad your "guest" arrived.

Do call people by name. A person's name is her favorite sound. When appropriate, introduce yourself to customers and ask their name. You should start out calling them Mr. Jones or Ms. Smith before getting to first names. If the customers prefer being called by their first name, they will tell you.

Do listen when customers talk. They are trying to tell you what they want and are not interested in having you trying to sell them what you've got. Be patient; don't rush to make judgments. Seek clarification from customers so you fully understand their needs.

Do make customers feel special. If they are going to spend their money with you, you should make them feel good about it. Try to anticipate their needs, accommodate their urgency, help reduce any confusion.

Do get your customers involved. Take them over to the product and get them involved with it. Offer a flyer or video to review. Ask them questions such as, "How do you see yourself using this

. . ." Or, "Do you see how easy this is to operate?" Or, "What are the features *you* like best?" Or, "Why don't you test drive it?"

Do use humor. Making customers laugh puts them in a better mood, and they are more likely to buy.

Do show a personal interest in them. Not just for the sake of the sale. Ask if they live in the area, how long, what schools their kids go to; find out if they know the Smiths.

Do compliment freely and sincerely. It only takes a second and can add enormous goodwill. Safe ground is to say something complimentary about their clothing, their children, their behavior, or something they own.

Do fish for negative feedback, without being defensive. Ask them for their honest opinions and provide ways for them to tell you. You can ask, "Was everything okay?" and go further from that point. Show them their suggestions do make a difference and express appreciation for their input.

Do explain how things work. Assure your customers that the product they bought will serve them well, and should there be any problems your company and the manufacturer will stand behind it. If you are selling a service, show customers how to continue getting benefits from it. If they will receive something in the mail, tell them when. If follow-up action is necessary, explain the arrangements.

Do underpromise and overdeliver if you can. Customers love to get more than they expect. Some ways to overdeliver include:

- Providing it faster.
- Offering to deliver it personally.
- Offering to handle the transaction efficiently.
- Taking a trade-in or disposing of the old one.
- Offering to handle additional paperwork ("I'll get the license forms taken care of for you").

Do deliver what you sell, when you promised it. If you don't, it's unlikely you will get that customer back.

Do make sure your people have the tools to take care of customer complaints. A telephone in a place where it can be heard. A computer with customer records. Product information and publications. Policy statements.

## SEVEN COMMON MISTAKES MADE IN
## COMPARATIVE MARKETING

It seems that every few minutes you hear or see another company comparing their product or service with that of a competitor. Fast-food chains, soft drink companies, discount operations, and especially telephone service organizations are constantly comparing, challenging, and even bashing their competitors. While comparative selling techniques can be educationally beneficial to customers, they can also create marketing, and possible legal problems for your business. But it is impossible to conduct a comparative marketing campaign without first knowing what the competition is doing.

### MISTAKE 413

**Not having a detailed understanding of how competitors operate.**

### How to Avoid It

Without knowing in detail how competitors function, any business will operate at a disadvantage. Gathering pertinent information about the competition enables businesses to advance on several fronts.

- They can respond quickly to any move a rival may make.

- They will be in a position of being able to analyze the successes and failures of competitors.

- They will be in a better position to create sound competitive strategies and avoid ineffective ones.

- They will be in a better position to identify opportunities they might otherwise overlook.

### MISTAKE 414

**Not knowing what kind of information to gather or how or where to get it.**

### MISTAKE 415

**Not having a plan for disseminating and effectively using data about competitors.**

## How to Avoid Them

Gathering pertinent information about your competitors does not involve the use of ex-CIA agents, bugged telephone lines, or paying huge sums of money to corporate information peddlers. Much of the information you will need about the competition is available legally and inexpensively from public sources. Here are some steps to follow on collecting, storing, analyzing, and utilizing competitive intelligence:

■ Collecting information. First, you must determine exactly what you need to know about your rivals. Look closely at your own company—its structure, production, servicing, marketing and finance operations, for instance, and develop lists of the kind of information you want that will be most helpful in these areas. Contact an independent data collection company to compile and analyze the data you need. Betsy Peterson, executive director of the Marketing Research Association, Rocky Hill, Connecticut, suggests that companies contracting a study should be explicit in their instructions so that there is no guessing or different interpretations of what is expected.

■ Filing information. Create a centralized filing system to store all information you collect, such as brochures, warranty data, advertisements, and news stories concerning competitors, price lists, annual reports, information from former employees of competitors who now work for you. Assign someone to coordinate information gathering and update all files.

■ Researching. Excellent information can be obtained by questioning your own current customers through phone or mail surveys. They can tell you what types of products or services they use, what might cause them to switch to a competitor, what prices, customer services, and merchandise variety and availability the competition is offering. If you are using a phone survey (which allows in-depth questioning that often results in more honest and objective answers than does a mail survey), instruct your data collectors to ask questions linked to your own business strategy, such as, "How does our product compare with similar ones you know of in terms of features, benefits, and functions?" "If you could, what changes would you suggest to make the product better?" Other excellent sources of finding out what your competitors are doing include questioning mutual suppliers, watching the classifieds for help wanted ads a competitor may be running, clipping stories and new-product information from trade publications, clipping product ads to keep track of a rival's advertising expenditures, checking out the competitor's location (number and kinds of cars in the parking lot, new building wing), checking university and public libraries where books and articles in CD-ROM databases can be searched by company name. These facilities also have directories of public, private, and small businesses that will yield employee, marketing, and sometimes financial information. Go to industry trade shows and meet and talk with competitors and their vendors. Join a network of similar firms that exchange information on pricing and marketing techniques in noncompetitive areas.

■ Utilize the data you've collected. Once you've got the information you need about what your competitors are planning or doing, you can formulate your own strategies to meet or better theirs. This creates a healthy situation because it forces competitors to see and think about how other firms view and sell the market. However, there are some common mistakes that businesses make when they embark on a competitive marketing program.

## MISTAKE 416

**Helping a competitor by giving them free exposure in your advertising.**

## MISTAKE 417

**Creating sympathy for the product or service you are attacking.**

## MISTAKE 418

**Confusing customers and reducing the effectiveness and credibility of your marketing plan.**

## MISTAKE 419

**Not understanding the legal ramifications of inaccurate comparative marketing.**

### How to Avoid Them

Those who argue for comparative marketing believe that it can be an effective selling tool that helps show consumers the relative benefits and flaws of competing products. And without a doubt, when properly executed, honestly, fairly, and without criticizing, it does.

Those who argue against competitive marketing are quick to point out that by mentioning the competition in your selling, however, you not only diminish the image of your company by informing the customer of another source, you enhance the competition by giving them free publicity. In addition, if direct comparisons are not done in an ethical manner, you may create customer sympathy for the other company's product or service. This may also result in customer confusion that could backfire and make your company look like the bad guy. It could also result in civil litigation.

Here are some guidelines to follow to minimize the negative aspects of comparative marketing:

- Don't fabricate information. Be truthful in what you say about the competition.

- Avoid making subjective claims. Use objective claims that can be verified.

- Obtain your competitive data from reliable, independent data-collection sources.

- Document and continually update the results of your comparative selling methods.

- Be fair in your comparisons, or customers will sympathize with your rival.

- When comparing products or services, select those features that are significantly superior to the competitor's and that customers can verify for themselves.

- Make comparisons customers will believe.

- Avoid criticizing a competitor's business practices.

- Before going public with comparative selling, check out the legalities with an attorney and check your approaches against the ethical policies of your firm.

## TEN MISTAKES IN COLLECTING MONEY FROM ANGRY CUSTOMERS

Along with death and taxes, you can bet on having customers who don't pay their bills for legitimate or imagined reasons, or who intentionally pay slowly by creating disputes or excuses.

The reasons for "slow pay or no pay" of bills are endless. The customer may have a bona fide reason for holding back payment, such as failure of the product, undelivered services, or broken promises. The customer may be testing the company to see how long payment can be delayed, while using "your money" to finance other projects. They sometimes say, "Charge us interest," which translated means, "We can't get credit at the bank, so we'll use yours." The customer may not have enough money to pay the entire bill when due, but makes no attempt to make a partial payment. The customer won't accept billing without backup (usually a stalling technique) and may challenge certain items, also without offering to pay on uncontested items.

By its nature, collection work is difficult. The last thing debtors want is to be confronted by a collector's call. Consequently, hostility and rejection become stress that those responsible for collecting must cope with regularly. Add to that the frustration of record keeping and legal issues and you've got a job that demands aggressive decision making and action—a job that is definitely *not* for the faint-of-heart manager, the procrastinator, or the cockeyed optimist who believes that "the check is in the mail," or "I ran out of checks and the bank just burned down."

There are basically two types of customer collections that concern most businesses: dealing with consumers and dealing with business customers. While the collection of consumer debt is regulated by the Federal Fair Debt Collection Practices Act and by various state laws (generally aimed at preventing harassment of debtors by third-party collectors, such as collection agencies), dealing with business customers involves more in the way of prevention, customer qualification, and collection methods. Under any circumstance, collecting overdue and unpaid accounts can cost your company a great deal of time and money.

## MISTAKE 420

**Not establishing a credit policy and sticking to it.**

## MISTAKE 421

**Drawing up an agreement aimed at making the customer happy.**

## MISTAKE 422

**Not checking out a potential customer's reputation and credit history.**

## MISTAKE 423

**Not sending out clear and timely invoices.**

## MISTAKE 424

**Not acting quickly to determine the problem.**

### HOW TO AVOID THEM

Whatever the customer's reason or excuse, if your business is writing off more than 5 percent of sales in bad debt, your credit and collections controls need tightening, advises the American Collectors Association, a trade association of collection agencies in Minneapolis.

Here are some sound business practices and steps you can follow to protect yourself from these kinds of tactics:

▌ Based on the level of risk you are willing to assume, create a written credit policy that sets standards on which customers will be granted credit and which won't. Such a policy should be distributed to all employees concerned with sales and credit, as well as to customers.

▌ If the firm or individual is unknown to you, ask him to fill out a credit application, customer questionnaire, or sign a written agreement. Your credit application should ask customers for basic facts (such as address, Social Security number, and driver's license number) that will be helpful later in tracking down those who don't pay. It should also explain the terms of payment and all charges (including those for late payment) that will appear on a customer's bill.

▌ If you are drawing up a specific agreement to cover the purchase of a product or service, have your attorney check it out *before* you offer it to the customer for review and approval. Too often, businesspeople, anxious to make a sale, have a tendency to be as flexible or congenial as possible in order to make the customer happy, only to be sorry later. Written agreements should include exactly what both parties expect to achieve, all the terms of the agreement such as when invoices will be sent, when payment is due, inclusion of legal costs if litigation is needed to collect, and it should also request the names of the customer's accounts-payable officers. Don't forget early termination clauses and customer penalties for canceling before delivery, if applicable.

▌ Check out the customer's reputation and credit history. On your credit application, request references from at least two firms that have given the customer its highest lines of credit. Contact credit-reporting services for information on the credit histories of business customers. Some companies check with their agency that collects state sales tax to see if the customer's business is paid up. State incorporation records tell you how long a business has been in existence.

▌ Once you've delivered the goods, follow up with a call immediately asking, "How did you like it?" Then you know right away if there's a complaint or a payment problem and can act on resolving the situation. Often customers have a complaint about your product or service that can be easily resolved. Others want to pay, but simply need time or help in allocating income to cover various debts. You may be able to work out a schedule of payments.

▌ If there is no problem or if the complaint has been satisfied, prepare your invoice and send it out quickly. Check it over to make sure it is error-free.

▌ If payment is late, immediately send out another copy of the outstanding bill with the notation "past due" or "second notice" stamped on the front. If this does not bring payment, contact the customer immediately by telephone (which forces an immediate response from the debtor), using a friendly, courteous tone. Once you are sure he has received the first two invoices and that there are no problems concerning his ability to pay, remind him of the amount owed and push to set a deadline for payment. A dispute over individual items in an invoice may result in nonpayment of the entire invoice. Should this occur, try to persuade the customer to pay the undisputed portion of the bill in the meantime. If you're dealing with a business customer and can't get action from subordinates, go to the top.

## MISTAKE 425

**Being too naive and believing customer excuses.**

## MISTAKE 426

**Feeling guilty when asking for money.**

### How to Avoid Them

Feeling guilty about pressuring for payment and buying customers' excuses because you want to believe them, only prolongs the time you are out your money. And as more and more time passes, collection becomes more difficult. You have to be realistic, not naive. There are people out there who don't care about you, your company, your payroll, your debts, or contracts they have agreed to. They want something for nothing—and if you aren't realistic about the procedures and actions you must take, they will try to take advantage of you.

Some of your customers may be totally immune to polite and gentle approaches. If this seems to be the case, advise the debtor that her reputation and credit rating may be damaged. Up to this point, you have done your best to maintain consideration and respect for the customer's situation; now it's time to give this customer up and take the measures required to collect the money owed you. You can, for instance, look for and notify other creditors of the customer to put a damper on her receiving further credit extensions elsewhere. We found one company that sent a sight draft to the customer's bank with instructions to pay the amount owed them. The bank, of course, needed the debtor's consent to do this, but in many cases, when the bank calls the debtor for consent, the debtor may approve payment just to avoid embarrassment with the bank. Small claims court is an inexpensive and informal method of recovering monies owed. But often, receiving a favorable judgment doesn't guarantee you'll get payment.

## MISTAKE 427

**Chasing delinquent customers yourself instead of using a professional collection agency.**

## How to Avoid It

For many businesses, especially smaller ones, it is not cost-effective to spend time chasing delinquent customers. If you have a large volume of such accounts, a collection agency may be able to do a more efficient job. While a collection agency will take a substantial percentage of any monies collected, it is better than writing it off as a total loss, or subjecting yourself and your staff to the stress involved in doing it yourself.

## MISTAKE 428

**Procrastinating on a collection and then discovering the customer has filed for bankruptcy.**

## How to Avoid It

As more and more companies and individuals find themselves in deep financial trouble and file for bankruptcy, more and more businesses find themselves stuck with bad debts and the possibility of collecting little or none of what they are owed.

The two most widely used bankruptcy provisions for businesses that need this help are Chapter 7 of the bankruptcy law, under which a firm's assets are sold to pay creditors, and Chapter 11, which permits a company to do business while paying its debts under court supervision. Steps to take as a creditor:

- ▪ File a proof-of-claim form with the court in order to be eligible for payment. Submit any other documents that show the size of the debt, such as receipts, invoices, and contracts. If the debtor has listed you among its creditors in its court filing, the court will send you a proof-of-claim form. If you don't receive one, call a bankruptcy court (listed in the white pages under U.S. government).

- ▪ Respond immediately because deadlines for filing proof-of-claims forms are strictly enforced, and you must meet them in order to recover anything. Forms for Chapter 7 filings are due within 90 days of the first date set by the court for a meeting of all creditors. During that meeting, a trustee may be selected by the creditors, or as is more common, by the U.S. Trustee's Office. Officials of the debtor company are required to be present and to answer all creditors' questions under oath.

■ You must now wait for the trustee to locate and distribute the debtor's assets. Secured creditors, such as lenders holding mortgages, and the debtor's lawyers and accountants are paid first. Suppliers and other trade creditors share whatever is left. When the money runs out, most remaining debts are "discharged" or legally forgiven.

■ The deadline for filing forms for Chapter 11 cases is set by the court. The debtor company, which remains in business while restructuring its operations, may offer to renegotiate the terms of its debt to you. Should you fail to renegotiate, the court may eventually impose a settlement. However, do not enter into renegotiating a debt without your attorney being present.

## MISTAKE 429

**Not protecting yourself from international "no pays."**

### How to Avoid It

Few companies, or individuals, for that matter, like to pay cash in advance or by letter of credit for merchandise they have not yet received and inspected. This is especially true of customers who are ordering goods from outside the United States. So how do you allow your foreign buyers to pay on delivery while still protecting yourself so that the shipment will not be delivered until payment is assured?

Using a method referred to as draft collection, the buyer does not have to pay until the goods arrive, while the seller is assured that the goods can't be obtained until payment is established.

The key to this is the "order of shipper," a transportation bill of lading by any surface method of shipment that is written to consign the goods to the "order of shipper." In its simplest form, this type of consignment instructs the carrier that your goods are still your property and can be delivered to your consignee only against the order of shipper.

By showing the merchandise as consigned to "order of shipper," you are in effect instructing the carrier not to hand over the goods until release instructions are received from you ordering the carrier to do so.

The concept is similar to a claim check or a laundry ticket. No ticket, no laundry! The order bill of lading is exactly the same. If your buyer does not have the order bill of lading, then the carrier cannot deliver the shipment. Delivery is based on the recipient being able to turn over the bill of lading to the carrier to get the goods.

To achieve the objective of not delivering until payment is received, you attach a "collection instrument" to the shipment. The most common is the sight draft, which uses the bank system as the collecting arm of the shipper.

A sight draft is a demand for payment from the shipper on the buyer for the value of the invoice, including all freight and insurance charges, if any.

This sight draft is, in fact, a promissory note that the shipper makes and passes on to the buyer's bank overseas with instructions to collect the amount of the note or sight draft. Obviously, an agreement must be reached between buyer and seller before the sale is closed so that this method of payment is satisfactory to your customer.

Most commonly, the draft is sent from the United States by the seller's bank with instructions to collect the amount of the draft through the buyer's bank overseas. The buyer agrees to pay this draft "at sight," as soon as the bank overseas requests payment. The money collected is remitted to your bank, where it is credited to your account (see Chapter 23 on global marketing.).

# Chapter 17

## COMMUNICATING ON THE INTERNET AND INFOHIGHWAY

Are you ready to manage the twenty-first century? You'd better be; it's here now. And if you are going to play electronic commerce in the arena called cyberspace, there are two things you must know: the name of the game is communication, and information is the currency of the new economy.

Thanks to the explosion of affordable and versatile communications technology during the last decade, cybermanagers at businesses of every kind are not only conducting electronic commerce on the Internet, the government-spawned "network of networks," they are also gathering and dispensing voice, print, and action data on the Information Superhighway, the multimedia link between telephone, computer, and television.

The Internet—long the private preserve of academics, government agencies, and researchers—has opened a new world of opportunities for businesses to increase production, be more flexible in the way they run their operations, and improve their communications with customers. For example, with today's technology:

- On-line information is customized to meet a company's specific needs.

- Machines talking to machines free up our time and reduce paperwork.

- Strategic decisions that once took days or weeks of negotiation and data gathering can be accomplished in hours or minutes.

346

■ Companies and individuals can tap new sources of on-line information, equipment, and services from anyplace they can plug in their computers, akin to searching through the Yellow Pages of every city on earth.

■ New business alliances can share expertise and exploit global marketplace opportunities.

Eventually, everyone will be connected to everyone and everything by worldwide satellite networks, wireless communication systems, and a growing infrastructure (information highway) that will know no political or geographic boundaries.

But as more and more companies connect to online e-mail, computer databases, and the Internet, the work location becomes more and more irrelevant. Businesses are discovering it is possible to operate efficiently from offices without walls, where nearly everyone can do his job from anywhere.

## FIVE MISTAKES MANAGERS MAKE IN SUPERVISING AND COMMUNICATING WITH REMOTELY LOCATED EMPLOYEES

Tomorrow's office is here; where is everybody?

While improved technology has greatly increased the pace of business, many managers are finding that supervising and communicating with remotely located employees is very different from getting people together in a room and talking, arguing, and coming up with the results.

Mobile managers now have the ability to stay in constant contact with colleagues and customers from anywhere. Armed with cellular phones and beepers, powerful portable computers with intelligent software and built-in fax/modems, access to voice and electronic mail, scanners, copiers, printers, and databases of every kind imaginable—all tied to a ubiquitous communications network—they are running their companies from cars, planes, hotel rooms, or while relaxing in their backyards at home.

## MISTAKE 430

**Not being able to recognize and react and adapt to change.**

## MISTAKE 431

**Not being sensitive to the nuances of communication in the new, "smarter" workplace.**

### HOW TO AVOID THEM

Companies are finding that the new workplace is changing so rapidly, their ability to recognize, understand, react to, and adapt to those changes is one of the most crucial challenges confronting management.

Today, when executives or employees in the new "virtual" workplace say, "I'm at work," more often than ever before, they are referring to what they are doing—not where they are. The result can mean better work coming from happier workers at substantially lower costs.

Executives who thrived on daily meetings and administrative assistants will have to learn how to work effectively with no face-to-face interaction, absence of support staff, and isolation from other members of the management team. Here are some more changes they will have to cope with:

▌ The integration of all aspects of office life.

▌ Portability and miniaturization of everything, from computers to copiers. Advances in microprocessor technology now allow you to virtually carry around your office with you in your wallet. For example, high-powered, battery-operated notebook computers with built-in modems have replaced laptops and can communicate digitized data in any medium—voice, data, image, or video—anytime, to anywhere, from literally any place.

▌ Just as virtual office technology allows workers to keep up with tasks while they are outside the office, life inside the virtual office has changed also. For example, employees in different locations can work on the same document simultaneously, see the changes as they are done, and have verbal communication at the same time. It is also possible to set up conference calls with full-motion video. When a telecommuter does come into the office, his notebook computer interfaces easily with office systems in seconds, eliminating the need to copy disks or otherwise transfer files. Workers are also more mobile within the office. Work space has become nonterritorial, with employees traveling from workstation to workstation. The information they need is stored in computerized databases they can access from any workstation or telephone.

▌ Customers are able to interact with the new office in new ways. Interactive voice-response systems enable businesses to dispense and receive more information with less manpower. A business can conduct a customer-satisfaction survey, for instance, by allowing customers to call a toll-free number. The customer responds to specific automated questions by using the telephone key pad. The responses are continually processed, providing management with up-to-date customer likes, dislikes, and trends. The same technology applied to a fax-on-demand system enables a salesperson on the road or in a customer's office to call the base and by just using the telephone key pad pull up a specific product data sheet from the company database and automatically fax it to the customer. The telephone has become an indispensable and multifaceted office tool that helps in improving the relationship between company and customer. Applications such as "Caller ID" permit customer service or sales representatives to have a customer's file on a computer display terminal even before they answer the phone. Desktop screen or video phones combine voice and video capabilities that allow callers to see each other, transfer bank funds, make travel reservations, send and receive e-mail, and get on-screen directory assistance.

▌ In the virtual office, activation by speech is replacing keystroke control. To transfer a call, for example, simply ask the computer to, "Transfer this call to so and so," or "Fax this letter to that person," or "Show me or read me my voice mail."

▌ In the virtual office, companies automatically order, and pay for, inventory and supplies without filling out or mailing purchase orders or invoices. Supermarkets, for example, are using a Continuous Replenishment Program (CRP), which ties together retailers, wholesalers, and marketers in a program that uses computer-generated information to track product movement, forecast inventory requirements, and create orders almost immediately. CRP replaces the traditional replenishment process driven by distributor-generated purchase orders with a timely, accurate, paperless information flow that results in smooth, continual product movement matched to consumption. The key is that all of the participants in the supply chain have to become "intimate partners" who are willing to work together and trust one another by electronically joining forces, communicating, and sharing information. When they do, the results can be significant. A report by the Grocery Manufacturers of America and the Food Marketing Institute notes that with the Continuous Replenishment Program, retail/warehouse inventory levels can be reduced by 10 to 60 percent, reducing the pressure for retailers to build additional warehouse space to house the more than 3.2 million items an average supermarket must stock. CRP also reduces store handling costs while increasing inventory turns, which means fresher products at lower prices for consumers. And it allows for consolidating the smaller orders of many stores into larger, more cost-efficient orders, with those savings also passed on to consumers.

■ The mouse and keyboard are giving way to digitized pads where data is input via pen, finger, or scanner.

■ Copiers now translate and fax text.

■ PCs with sound and video capabilities allow preparation of documents while simultaneously watching broadcast programs.

■ Artificial intelligence, such as optical character-recognition software, speech-recognition systems, and voice-text annotation greatly improves accuracy, allows users to control functions with simple voice commands, and allows readers to insert comments on documents by recording them within a document, instead of printing out a hard copy and jotting a note in the margin.

■ Presentations and reports are delivered on floppy disks rather than on hard-copy printouts. The recipients can review the report, complete with elaborate color graphs, charts, and photographs on their desktop or laptop PCs.

## MISTAKE 432

**Assuming productivity will soar because of advanced technology.**

## MISTAKE 433

**Not creating a period of adjustment to adapt new tasks to new tools.**

## MISTAKE 434

**Caring more about using new technology to increase control of employees rather than about using it to expand their knowledge.**

### How to Avoid Them

The most important changes to learn to cope with are the overall changes in the work ethic. Managers will have to learn how to pay attention to what employees produce, and less to where and when they produce it. They'll also have to understand that while new programs and technology are constantly making it easier and cheaper to maintain professional standards, there will be employees who will use those programs and technology, employees who won't need it and won't use it, and employees who will need more than what you have given them to work with. In other words, don't assume that just because you're equipped for working in tomorrow's office that productivity will rise because of it.

Here are five ways for managers to reinvent themselves so they can better adapt to the new workplace:

1. Define the company's ambition in relation to the technology available. Think in terms of radical improvement of product, efficiency (cost and time savings), communication enhancement, employee and customer relations, service, marketing and distribution, and of course, profitability.

2. Communicate all technological and operating changes up, down and across the corporate ladder, as well as to those you deal with outside.

3. Motivate your employees. In an era of self-managed workers, executives need employees to accept and be energized by the changes taking place. This takes persuasion and a compelling picture of future results.

4. Empower. With the changing of the workplace comes a change in the nature of supervision and control. The workers upon which today's managers rely are considerably different from those whom previous generations of executives faced. Aside from cultural and gender differences, workers are educated and trained (or retrained) to perform multiple job functions. They must be able to work with less direction while making more

decisions on their own. Therefore, managers with fewer, but more skilled employees must increase their dependence on their workers by empowering them with the authority to make more decisions. Work must also be redesigned so people can exercise all their skills fully.

5. Measure results in terms of the customer by inviting feedback.

## EIGHT COMMON MISTAKES IN PLUGGING INTO ELECTRONIC COMMERCE

Since its inception in the mid seventies as a U.S. Defense Department experiment, access to the Internet, with its highly complex operating system, was limited to large corporations, government agencies, and universities. Now the Internet (also known as the World Wide Web, the Web, and the Net) is open to everyone and has become the fastest-growing on-line global network. Consumers and businesses, through Internet Service Providers (ISPs), are connecting up by the millions so they can browse through the thousands of sites of information the Internet has to offer.

### MISTAKE 435

**Believing that doing business on the Internet is no different from traditional marketing.**

### MISTAKE 436

**Rushing to buy and sell goods and services in a vast marketplace you don't fully understand.**

### MISTAKE 437

**Not conducting safe transactions.**

### MISTAKE 438

**Not protecting your product from infringement.**

## How to Avoid Them

Though the Internet has been around for many years, the phenomenon of conducting *safe* electronic commerce is so new and different from other ways of doing business that many of the traditional rules and regulations do not or cannot apply in cyberspace.

Before you can conduct safe and successful electronic commerce, you must first understand what the term "electronic commerce" means. In simplified terms, it can be defined as "the changing of business procedures that will enable companies connected to the Internet and online services to go beyond normal commercial boundaries and interact freely with customers, suppliers, distributors, and others in a global electronic trading community."

When done successfully, electronic commerce will automate internal and external business processes and enable companies to improve their productivity and communication with customers and other businesses on a scale never before possible. One example concerning benefits in inventory management mentioned earlier was the Continuous Replenishment Program used by supermarkets. An example of benefits in money management that we came across concerned an overnight courier company that employed 250 people to process some 60,000 checks it received daily. Now, linked to an electronic receivables system, only two people are needed.

Many companies that have already invested in information technology to automate their key internal processes such as purchasing, invoicing, and other similar functions and have the technical infrastructure in place think all they have to do is simply "connect to the Net" to engage in electronic commerce. But watch out—doing business on the Internet is very different from traditional methods that are tried and true.

First of all, consider the fact that you are linking electronically to a "global flea market" with more than 50 million individuals and companies buying and selling everything from cookie recipes to sex advice. While this fact makes the Internet so appealing to users, it also makes it dangerous to use.

Unlike closed commercial online services such as Prodigy or America Online, no one company runs the Internet, which links disparate computers and networks with varying standards and capabilities. Some of the problems to watch out for are:

- Find an Internet provider to link you to the network and establish and maintain your presence. When you do engage a provider, establish an agreement detailing its rights and obligations, especially those concerning its reliability. If people come knocking on your door and find no one home—that is, the system is down and not responding—you might as well have never been on the Internet at all. Your agreement, therefore, should guarantee a minimum level of reliability and allow you to cancel if the service does not meet those standards.

- If you hire someone to design and maintain your site for you, you must establish clearly who owns the product and that all rights to the design and look of your Internet site belong to you.

- Since you will be continually updating the content, establish how often updates will be done and how long it will take after you have submitted the updated material.

- What you put on your site is up to you, but whatever it is, make sure you own all the rights to use it. That includes pictures of people and products, news from wire services, graphics created by outside companies, slogans, musical scores, copyrighted jokes, recipes, and so forth.

- Be sure you protect your product or service, as well as corporate integrity and identity, against infringement by others by posting an on-screen copyright notice.

- Determine the appropriate distribution channel for your digital message. Consider services that offer interactive multimedia elements that will give you the capability of doing business on the Internet with a variety of applications that will attract attention and stimulate the senses.

- Don't attempt to exchange data unless participating parties have compatible data formats, otherwise information can be lost in cyberspace or received and interpreted incorrectly.

- One downside of selling products on the Internet is the fact that cybercriminals are able to intercept merchandise orders or customer credit card numbers. Therefore, using hardware and software defenses (also known as "firewalls") to authenticate the identities of purchasers and keep data such as credit card numbers private is of prime importance when conducting electronic transactions on the Internet. Credit card encryption is one security method widely used, but this is not foolproof. Using a technique called "spoofing," computer hackers are able to fool a computer into thinking that another, friendly computer is requesting access. The result can be high-level computer "hijacking." Another recently introduced method is an electronic-cash ("digital" cash) software system that offers security and anonymity to consumers and retailers in cyberspace. Consumers are able to download the software free on the Internet, register their credit card number and password online, then download cash from their credit card onto their hard drive, where it will be protected from hackers. Another European company offers a system that allows consumers to carry up to $1,000 in a digital "purse." Consumers can exchange currencies in moments over any phone line, with one another or with merchants with complete anonymity.

## MISTAKE 439

**Substituting new technology for traditional marketing channels.**

### How to Avoid It

Don't rely on technology alone to sell your product or service. It's fine to make ads, brochures, and other information available online, but remember the medium is only a supplement to, not a substitute for, traditional marketing channels such as radio, TV, and direct mail. Even when posting messages online, make sure to include your phone number.

## MISTAKE 440

**Expecting customers to visit your site just because you are there.**

## MISTAKE 441

**Not giving prospective customers a reason for visiting you in cyberspace.**

### How to Avoid Them

Opening a storefront on the Internet may be the last word in high-tech retailing, but don't cancel your lease at the local mall just yet. While millions of prospective buyers are out there shopping (or surfing the Net), they won't visit your site without a reason. Just like in the old-fashioned nonelectronic world of retailing, you can get the attention of prospective cybercustomers by using promotions, give-aways, double coupons, even online rock concerts if you can afford them. One of the easiest ways to boost your online profile is to cre-ate a "mini billboard," essentially an online business card. On the Internet, they are known as signature files, or "sig files," which are short identifiers at the bottom of your e-mail message or bulletin-board posting. They state your name, company, postal address, e-mail address, phone and fax numbers, and, often, a few words about your company. People who read your posting and like what they see can contact you for information on your company's products and services. Unlike printing business cards, there's no charge to create a sig file, which can be an effective way to get new customers. Many companies are not relying on demographic trends to support their presence on the Internet. They are instead educating their target customers on how to go online through seminars and demonstra-tions and by free giveaways of diskettes containing online access software.

When marketing on the Internet, think globally, not locally. Consider diluting your costs by using noncompeting sponsorship messages stripped across the top or bottom of your page. On the Internet, unlike the commercial online services, online time is cheap or free, and users don't mind a few ads in return for access to all sorts of cool information, graphics, sounds, and video.

## MISTAKE 442

**Not being aware of the legal problems associated with marketing on the Net.**

### How to Avoid It

Be aware of legal problems that can arise from doing business on the Internet. For instance:

▪ Never resell Internet consumer data without the express permis-sion of the user. Unlike commercial services, where it is clearly understood that data generated through consumer interaction are being sold to marketers, Internet data should remain the pri-vate property of the user.

▪ Conduct consumer research only with the consumer's full con-sent.

▌ When selling products through promotions, be sure the consumer has full disclosure about rules, guidelines, and parameters of the event before they commit.

▌ Don't use Internet communications software that hides concealed functions, such as the ability to scan users' hard drives for text that appears to be an address.

## FOUR COMMON MISTAKES THAT CAN MAKE ELECTRONIC MAIL SHOCKING

The simplest form of corporate e-mail is passing messages back and forth internally among employees with computers connected as a network. But expand that network through a gateway to include other businesses in other cities and countries, and e-mail becomes a powerful, efficient, and time-saving means of communication.

Much has been written about the pros and cons of e-mail. For distribution of mail to multiple sites and for transmitting computer files, there are few alternatives to e-mail. E-mail makes it as easy to send the same message to 5,000 people as it is to one, paying nothing other than your monthly Internet access fee. You can communicate in writing with people and not have to wait weeks for a reply or have to pay for postage. The system is always ready to accept your messages, to deliver accumulated messages, and to store your messages for later reference. The advantage to the recipient is that the information is already in a computer-readable form.

Beyond person-to-person correspondence, e-mail is used for a powerful new way of communicating known as "mailing lists." These mailing lists are creating communities around special interests.

Anyone can subscribe to mailing lists. First, you must get a copy of the List of Lists, a compendium that catalogs each mail list, its address, the rules for subscribing, and topics covered. Then, after deciding which list you want to be on, they simply e-mail your name and electronic address to a Listserv, a computer that automatically handles that e-mail list. Any message sent to the Listserv bounces out to all the members of the list. So if someone on a list about, say, dogs, sends a question to the Listserv asking why does my dog chase his tail, the question would go out to everyone. Chances are someone knows why and will send a reply back to the list.

Some other advantages of this computer-based postal system are that it eliminates telephone tag, speeds up decision making, shortens the communication cycle time, and flattens corporate hierarchy—factors that professionals consider when trying to improve productivity.

But e-mail has its downside, too.

## MISTAKE 443

**Not knowing or having company guidelines concerning e-mail monitoring.**

## MISTAKE 444

**Assuming e-mail messages are private.**

## MISTAKE 445

**Assuming that when you delete a message it's gone forever.**

## MISTAKE 446

**Assuming only you can send e-mail messages in your name.**

### How to Avoid Them

If you're like many of the millions of people who use e-mail in the workplace every day, you may assume that only you have access to your mailbox and its messages, especially as you have a password known only to you. You may also assume that when you delete a message, you've wiped out any trace of it. These assumptions, unfortunately, are wrong. Consider these facts:

■ E-mail messages can be accessed, intercepted, rerouted, and altered on most computer networks.

■ E-mail messages, including those you've deleted, are stored on most company systems for days, weeks, or even years.

■ Some employers look at stored messages to resolve technical problems, monitor an employee's performance, or check out suspicious behavior. Some employers go through an employee's stored messages after that employee has been terminated.

▮ If you leave your workstation while you're logged on to your e-mail, anyone can stop by and access your messages or send one in your name.

Under the federal Electronic Communications Privacy Act of 1986, e-mail gets most of the same protections as letters and phone conversations from "outside" interception by a third party—such as an individual, the government, or police—without proper authorization (such as a search warrant). But the law does not cover "inside" interception, such as bosses reading their employees' e-mail.

The fact is no absolute privacy exists in a computer system, even for the boss. System administrators need to have access to everything in a computer in order to maintain it. Moreover, every piece of e-mail leaves an electronic trail in backup tapes or hard drives.

There are many pending court cases, as well as pending federal workplace-privacy legislation that may help define the legal rights of employers and employees concerning e-mail and other types of electronic communication, such as video conferencing. But regardless of their outcome, it's clear that technology has created new opportunities for the old-fashioned office snoops to peek at everything from confidential performance evaluations to the intimate details of an office romance without ever getting out of their own chairs. It's clear, too, that everyone using e-mail needs to be cautious. Here are ten steps to take to help protect yourself and your company:

1. If your company is going to be accessing the e-mail of its employees, it needs to have a stated policy to that effect. Know your company's current e-mail monitoring policy. If it hasn't been circulated or established, get to work on it immediately. Without an e-mail policy, employers could be setting themselves up for litigation that will be costly even if they win. In some instances, such as violations of safety rules, illegal activity, suspicion that an employee is exposing confidential business information, racial discrimination, or sexual improprieties, it may be proper for an employer to monitor e-mail. Companies may also need to access business information if, for instance, an employee is out sick or has left the company. The key is to make your computer-privacy policies explicit and part of other company rules and regulations. The following elements should be included:

   ▮ A statement that electronic communications systems are company assets, and all communications to, from, or stored in these systems are company property.

▍ A statement that company electronic communications systems are provided for company business purposes only.

▍ A statement that while the company is committed to privacy, electronic communications may be monitored by the company at its discretion and that any messages sent that are not related to business are being sent at the employee's risk.

▍ A statement about how passcodes are assigned and under what circumstances.

▍ A form for employees to sign acknowledging that they have read and understood the company's policy regarding e-mail.

2. Change your e-mail password monthly or quarterly. Choose a combination of letters and symbols you can easily remember. Don't use an obvious word like your name.

3. Log off your e-mail when you leave your desk for an extended period so no one can retrieve your incoming messages or send one out in your name.

4. Scramble your messages with encryption codes. There are many software systems available. In fact, as this book is being written, the U.S. Postal Service is considering a plan for providing "postmarks" for electronic mail. Under the plan, when a person sends an e-mail message he would click an onscreen icon that would affix an encrypted bar code or signature by which the post office could assure the recipient that the sender was authentic.

5. Keep your messages businesslike. Never use e-mail to send jokes, complaints, gossip, or confidential information.

6. Don't put anything in writing that you wouldn't want other people to read, such as personal information or a note to another manager discussing the possible dismissal of an employee.

7. Avoid using unnecessary adjectives, for example, referring to a "weird" project or "stupid" subordinate. It's much more difficult to communicate the tone you intend when writing than when speaking to someone. Also avoid words that can be misinterpreted, such as "I resent the letter" when you mean, "I re-sent the letter."

8. Think carefully before attaching sensitive documents, such as spreadsheets, to an e-mail message.

9. Be wary if you can't get into your e-mail with your password. Your superiors may have changed your password in order to access your mail.

10. When all else fails, just pick up the phone, or better yet, stroll down the hall and have a good old-fashioned face-to-face conversation.

## THREE MISTAKES IN MAKING E-MAIL E-FFECTIVE AND E-FFICIENT

In the right hands, an e-mail address on the Internet can be a valuable tool. For too many users, however, it's an open-ended invitation to waste time on the job or at home because of the all-you-can-eat-for-free nature of e-mail and the unfettered ability to window shop everywhere. Managers at more than a few companies we researched were terrified of opening access to the Internet because of the productivity-sucking effect that takes place when workers log on.

Managers were also fearful of managing e-mail overload. E-mail traffic on the Internet—or even on internal networks, for that matter—has reached unmanageable proportions. There's too much mail, from social and business messages to junk messages and e-mail bombs (time-wasting messages that are "exploded" through unsuspecting networks into your personal mailbox).

And as more and more techno-tyros log on and as more companies attempt to exploit the e-mail networks commercially, whole work patterns are changing. One manager told us each morning after turning on his computer he went through an average of 200 messages, a lot of it junk and a lot of it hidden, which is dangerous because you might delete something important accidentally. By the time he was finished responding to the important ones, it was nearly 2 P.M. with little time left to tackle other tasks. As a result, he was forced to answer most of his e-mail messages from home after work. Which meant his 8-hour workday became 13 hours. That didn't leave very much time for family and personal needs.

Of course, you could ignore the bulk of your messages, but then you would always have that nagging fear that if you don't read every message immediately, you'll miss the important one from your boss.

---

## MISTAKE 447

**Believing e-mail is a time saver compared to telephoning or faxing.**

---

## MISTAKE 448

**Not communicating effectively via e-mail.**

### How to Avoid Them

While e-mail does solve the telephone tag problem and does allow you to communicate at your convenience and does encourage you to think quickly and express yourself precisely—it definitely is not a time saver when compared to the phone or fax.

Think about it. You've got to sit down at your computer, log into your e-mail system, compose a letter, type it out, address and send it. The recipient has to log into his e-mail (maybe hours or days later), find what you sent, read it, compose and type out the response, and send it. And then you both have to spend time on the phone clarifying and understanding the message you could have phoned in the first place.

In the many conversations we had with managers on the subject of what constitutes effective, efficient e-mail, there were 12 elements that most agreed were necessary:

1. Never be intrusive. No one should receive a message they haven't either asked to receive, need to receive, or want to receive.

2. Identify the people and organizations outside your company with which you need to communicate. Use a tone of address that's appropriate to each recipient.

3. Always be clear and action-oriented in what you write. Never use words that can be misunderstood.

4. Be security conscious. Data traveling over networks are fair prey for eavesdroppers. Never forget that the illusion of privacy you get when working at your computer is nothing more than an illusion. While you may be working alone in your office on the same computer you use every day, it's natural to feel a sense of comfort and confidentiality. But once you transport your work and thoughts into e-mail, you have entered a very public arena.

5. Never discuss private, nonbusiness matters, classified company information, reprimands, or personal reviews of other employees.

6. Consider the necessity of sending graphics, spreadsheets, and formatted documents as these take more time and effort to send than simple typed messages.

7. Make your message brief and to the point. Lead the message with the most important information. Whenever possible, use acronyms that your recipient is familiar with, such as LOL for Laughing Out Loud, or ROTFL for Rolling On The Floor Laughing, or IMHO for In My Humble Opinion, or MOTOS for Member Of The Opposite Sex.

8. Use subheads, such as "Action requested," or "Steps to take," to break up long messages.

9. Always be courteous and tactful. If there's any doubt that e-mail is the right medium for your message, use another form of communication.

10. Put a "smiley" or two into everything you write to convey the winks, grins, and grimaces of ordinary conversations and then send your message out into stone-cold cyberspace.

11. If you write a message when you're upset, let it sit for awhile, then reread it before you send it.

12. Deliver all emotion-laden ("flame") messages as well as negative feedback in person or over the telephone. Until the time e-mail technology advances to the point where it will offer the option of delivering multimedia messages via voice, sound bites, or video clips, it's too easy to misconstrue or misrepresent your feelings or position, or even more so, someone else's, in a written format.

## MISTAKE 449

**Spending too much time on e-mail and not enough on more important work.**

### How to Avoid It

On the subject of spending too much time on e-mail and not enough on more important work, our research turned up these suggestions:

▪ If your problem is e-mail overload, you can always change your address or insist that your correspondents label their messages to software that can automatically put them in different files. This allows you to filter out the junk, put it in a pile at the end of the day, and delete, delete, delete.

▮ Install e-mail software that lets you program the mail system to perform tasks if certain events occur, such as if you receive a message from your superior. You simply make a selection from the menu such as "Notify me if I receive a message from the boss," or "Store messages older than January 8th." When a message from the boss comes in, the system checks the sender's name and subject heading. If it's from the boss, the computer sounds a bell. These software programs are also capable of keeping private messages confidential, rather than forwarding them to someone else, and they automatically filter noncritical messages.

▮ By automating responses that you normally type repeatedly, you can save a great deal of time. For example, if a customer wants to return a product for repair, the e-mail system automatically sends the customer the requirements you need to process the repair order. This allows the customer to get an immediate response, it allows the company to repair the unit more quickly, and it gives you that much more time to work on other tasks. The system can also be programmed to notify anyone sending you e-mail that you are out of the office for an extended period of time and whom they should contact in your absence.

## FOUR MISTAKES IN USING VIDEOCONFERENCING

Meetings are essential to the successful operation of every business. Simply defined in workplace terms—a meeting is getting all the right people together to discuss and successfully get a specific task done. Sounds easy, doesn't it? But what if all the right people are in different parts of the country and can't attend in person? In these days of telecommuting employees and "virtual" workplaces, videoconferencing (and audioconferencing, both sometimes referred to as teleconferencing), may be the answer.

Sophisticated advances in telecommunications technology along with greater affordability have made marketing tools such as videoconferencing more available to companies wanting to build sales, speed product development and boost customer service. In fact, many users of videoconferencing have found this type of meeting considerably more effective and often less expensive than in-person meetings.

## MISTAKE 450

**Using audioconferencing when the meeting calls for videoconferencing.**

### How to Avoid It

Often, when meetings require getting people in different locations together, most companies set up an audioconference—a relatively inexpensive telephone conference call tying in all members of the meeting.

This method of teleconferencing is effective when meetings are short, the number of participants is small, and the material to be communicated does not require visuals. But when a meeting involves people huddled around speakerphones, wading through lengthy, detailed discussions with questions, answers, and opinions going back and forth in "cavelike" hollow sounds, without the benefit of the participants' seeing each other, there is a tendency to lose focus on the important issues.

Videoconferencing, on the other hand, instantly improves communication through visually amplified images and spontaneous discussions and is particularly effective when a meeting involves:

▎ Top executives speaking with subordinates or customers.

▎ The use of demonstrations or visual aids.

▎ The importance of seeing the expressions, gestures, and emotions conveyed by the interpretation of what is being discussed.

▎ Keeping everyone's attention focused on the agenda.

One example of the effectiveness of videoconferencing concerns a company that was building an addition to its manufacturing facility.

The project required close coordination between design engineers, contractors, various subcontractors, and company executives, many of whom were located in different cities.

By linking up, on an as-needed basis, with an AT&T high-speed multilocation videoconferencing system during planning meetings, all parties were simultaneously visually apprised of the project's progress. After the completion of the project, the company estimated savings of approximately 30 percent as compared to what it would have cost in time and expenses to hold those same meetings in person.

In another example of how effective and flexible this form of communication can be, the dean of the engineering college of a university in Florida is successfully using videoconferencing to communicate face to face with high school guidance counselors in numerous cities to promote the college's degree programs and to recruit potential engineering students.

## MISTAKE 451

**Treating a videoconference as a presentation rather than a meeting.**

### How to Avoid It

Many managers, we have found, do not fully understand the difference between a presentation and a meeting. As a result, they tend to apply the same tools and techniques they use in presentations to meetings, which is not altogether bad (see Chapter 20 for more about sales presentations). However, there are significant differences between presentations and meetings, and knowing how meetings work will help to make them work more effectively.

One major difference is that even the most interactive presentation is mostly a one-sided event that requires preparation and delivery of information by the presenter and little more than attention by the audience. A meeting, however, works best when everyone involved comes prepared with information, opinions, arguments, and documentation relevant to the discussion, and when everyone stays focused on the topics.

## MISTAKE 452

**Not preparing for the videoconference.**

### How to Avoid It

Since meetings, such as videoconferences, function as an important mechanism for regulating management work flow, and since the per-minute cost of running a videoconference can be relatively high, careful planning and preparation become the most important elements in putting together a smooth-running, productive, and enjoyable session that sets the agenda and pace for information gathering, analysis, and decision making.

"Conference originators," according to Kevin R. Daley, president and CEO of Communispond, Inc., management consultants in business communication, "have all the technological problems to worry about—and that should be enough, for electronic meetings are seldom trouble-free," he says. But there are other considerations that could also develop into problems. "The camera," as Mr. Daley points out, "never lies. If anything, it accentuates our weaknesses. If you're good, you look better. If bad, you look worse." He suggests, however, that "before the cameras roll, you can take many steps to assure a successful teleconference."

Many managers who regularly run successful videoconferences create and meticulously follow checklists that include points such as:

■ Deciding on the kind of equipment you are going to use, where the teleconference will originate from, and where the participants will participate from. Equipment to consider includes two-way video and audio systems that allow participants to talk back and forth, even full-motion "follow-me" video that provides a professional-looking, person-to-person transition of video pictures individually controlled by keypads held by each participant. With the "follow-me" concept, the key pad acts as a camera director. When an off-camera individual starts to speak, she simply presses the keypad and the camera quickly and automatically locates her and magnifies her gestures, whether she is sitting and talking, conducting a demonstration, or walking to a graphic. Compact, integrated rollabout systems have made group videoconferences possible for users who don't have the budget or space for full-scale videoconferencing rooms. Rentable videoconferencing facilities are as close as the nearest Kinko's or office products superstore.

■ Set a firm starting time.

■ Set a firm ending time.

■ Organize and rehearse the topics to be discussed with local participants or, if possible, with all participants. If you are not videocasting from your own facilities, get a layout of the conference center you will be working from so you can map out the camera movement to focus on the decision makers as well as on the point of view on each topic. Also determine the placement and lighting of graphics. Try to keep things uncomplicated.

■ Set a general time frame for each speaker to present his information and set general time frames for discussions.

## MISTAKE 453

**Not taking full advantage of the visual benefits offered by video-conferencing.**

### How to Avoid It

A picture is worth a thousand words, so think visually about each subject.

In an article he wrote for *Teleconferencing News,* "What to Do Before the Teleconference," Kevin R. Daley, of Communispond, Inc., noted, "Human beings have five senses that bring information to the brain. But one is dominant: eighty percent of all the information stored in the brain comes through the eyes. That means that visual aids are important tools when making a presentation, especially during a teleconference."

Mr. Daley suggests that "visuals should be well thought out, clear in concept and execution," and "They should be a 'quick read.'" He offers these guidelines used by companies in the forefront of tele-conferencing:

- Prepare your visuals well in advance of your videocast so you have time for changes and for rehearsals.

- Don't rely exclusively on "bullet-point visuals." Words make dull visuals.

- Plan visuals that add a new dimension to your spoken words, that illustrate your message vividly and memorably.

- Limit each visual to just one thought, one fact, one point of view. Cluttered visuals result in confused viewers.

- Be especially careful when presenting sales figures or other statistics. Edit out the unimportant data. Don't get carried away with bar graphics and charts showing "pieces of pie." Today, with computer graphics, much more imaginative illustrations are within your grasp.

- Keep the number of words per visual to a minimum. Generally, the less there is to read, the better.

Some final suggestions from other veteran videoconference experts:

▮ Visuals and demonstrations should enhance the information being discussed, not overpower it.

▮ Consider visuals in terms of possible lighting problems. Flip charts, for example, have great flexibility, and unlike using slides, they do not require the dimming of room lights.

▮ Remember, the participants are visual aids themselves. Encourage them to use their faces, arms, hands, and fingers to illustrate what they are saying. Show them that by using action verbs, color words, touch and feeling words they can stimulate pictures and extend and embody their message.

▮ If possible, have all the members attending the session pretape themselves on video so that you will have a chance to see how they come across and how their chemistry interacts. You will be better able to recommend ways for them to improve their performance, if necessary.

# Chapter 18

# Communicating via Telemarketing and Direct Response

Legend has it Alexander Graham Bell once said he'd never have a telephone in his house. If that legend is true, it's probably because he never imagined that his creation would evolve into a medium for telemarketing, hooking up to computer modems and connecting callers interactively to advertising, entertainment, enormous databases, all sorts of knowledgeable and interesting people, and an incalculable range of global services.

Utilizing much of the same creativity and strategic thinking that goes into traditional marketing programs, telemarketing and direct-response techniques present marketers with unique point-of-sale and instant-response opportunities, especially with target audiences who are hard to reach through traditional media.

With breakthrough applications in merging-voice, computer, and video technology, expertise in the use of this competitive marketing tool has brought telemarketing to the point of being an everyday technique that has changed the way both businesses and customers interact.

## FIFTEEN MISTAKES CONCERNING TELEPHONE TACTICS, TECHNOLOGY, AND TAG

Whether you are making or taking calls, you and your employees will have frequent contact with customers and with most people, for that matter, via the phone. And how effectively the phone is used as a marketing tool can determine whether you create business—or lose it.

## MISTAKE 454

**Making wasted calls on poor prospects.**

## MISTAKE 455

**Wasting time on incoming calls because your don't have all the right customer information.**

## MISTAKE 456

**Not identifying the caller's needs.**

## MISTAKE 457

**Not being prepared before making a sales call.**

### HOW TO AVOID THEM

There are several different kinds of customer calls every business encounters, including incoming calls for orders, information, service, and complaints, and outgoing sales, service, and information calls. Consider these steps to improve your tactics with both and turn every telephone contact into an image-boosting, positive impression for your company:

▪ Always qualify the prospect you're calling or identify the caller's needs. Knowing what the prospect wants or the caller needs before the communications process starts is essential. Screening incoming calls can be helpful. Ask callers for their names and the names of the companies they represent and how you can be of help to them. Accessing quality leads from a current database of qualified targets is the best way to avoid making wasted calls and increase sales.

▪ Be prepared. Know as much as you can about the people you are speaking with (especially those you are calling) and the companies they work for. Enhanced market identifiers—using various kinds of information, all arranged in easy-to-read sections—give you and your sales team an instant overview of your prospect. If the callers are company customers, chances are you can get the same kind of information from your own database. The more you know, the more ways you have of influencing them.

---

## MISTAKE 458

**Not presenting a professional image on the phone.**

### How to Avoid It

Invite callers to get to the point of their call. Use questions such as "How can I assist you?" or "What can I do for you?" Before making a call, make sure your message is clear in your mind. Use a script if you have to.

Answer incoming calls quickly. Answering within three rings, for example, will be more pleasing and impressive to callers than if they have to wait for nine or ten rings before someone picks up. When a customer calls and no one answers, or the line is busy, it's like telling the customer that "you're sorry, but we are much too busy, so please take your money elsewhere." By giving callers the impression that you are efficient, they will be more disposed to trust you to handle their needs quickly and efficiently.

Return phone calls as quickly as possible. The best time to catch callers is immediately after they have called. If you wait too long, the caller may have left her office or home. People like their calls returned quickly and resent not having calls returned at all or having them returned after a long period.

Identify yourself to incoming callers just as you would in a face-to-face situation. If you are making the call, state your name and company before being asked and be friendly to whomever picks up the phone. Anticipate what the other party will ask, such as the nature of your call.

---

## MISTAKE 459

**Giving up on a sales call when you can't get through to your target the first time.**

### How to Avoid It

Don't be stopped by the first block when making a call. If your first listener is someone screening calls, ask for his help. You have something that is going to make life better for everyone at his company and you don't want them to miss the opportunity to learn about it. If the person you want is out, ask the screener when it would be convenient to call back or if there is someone else you could talk with. Try to get a direct line to that person if possible. If a screener is particularly hostile to your cold call, remember that he probably works nine to five and takes an hour for lunch. Decision makers, on the other hand, often come in early, stay late, and have their lunch brought in. So it stands to reason you will have a better chance of reaching them when the screener is not there.

## MISTAKE 460

**Spending unnecessary time on prolonged calls.**

### How to Avoid It

Mind your time on the phone. Your time is important to you, and the other party's time is just as important to her. Find a polite way to cut a prolonged conversation short, such as, "I've taken up so much of your time. Thanks again," or "Let's hold that for when I call back tomorrow," or "I'd like to talk longer, but I'm needed at a meeting in a few minutes. I'll speak to you again soon."

Avoid putting people on hold. Unless there is an emergency or some other good reason, it is unprofessional and inconsiderate to leave people hanging. If you have to put a call on hold to look up information, don't leave him there for more than 30 seconds without checking back on him. By telling him that his call is important and what you plan to do to help him, you give the party on the other end a sense of confidence and control. If putting someone on hold will take longer than a few minutes, ask if you can call him back. Make sure that you make note of the commitment to call back and put it in a place where you won't forget about doing it.

## MISTAKE 461

**Not listening to what the party on the other end is saying.**

### How to Avoid It

Pay attention to what the other party is saying, but listen to more than the words. Since you can't see the person's facial expressions or body language, you want to be especially sensitive to voice inflection, innuendo, and possible hidden agendas. That is hard to do, especially if you're doing other things while you're talking.

## MISTAKE 462

**Not taking notes as you talk.**

## How to Avoid It

Take notes. Write down all callers' names and use them repeatedly in the conversation that follows. Make note of the reasons they are calling. Here are some additional tips:

▌ If you're forwarding a message, make sure the information you take is accurate and complete. Get the caller's name, company, and phone number. Make sure you have the correct spelling of the name. If it's a difficult-to-pronounce name, write it out phonetically. The date and time of message is also important. Consider noting the caller's mood. Finally, be sure you put your own name on the message in case the recipient needs clarification.

▌ If you have to transfer a call, be sure to give the caller the name and number of the person you are transferring him to in case there is a problem with the switch. If you can, stay on the line to make sure the transfer goes smoothly.

▌ Don't interrupt. Your impatience will be seen as an indication of how your company treats its customers. If a caller is especially long-winded and you have no choice but to interrupt, ask a question that will help identify the direction the party wants to go in. Long-winded people don't mind interruptions if they can continue to talk about themselves.

▌ Provide positive feedback. Show the other party you understand her needs or problem with affirmations such as "Yes," "I see," and "I understand." Show your concern, ability to empathize, and willingness to help.

▌ Using friendly, tactful, sincere words is the key to building trust and establishing a relationship with both prospects and customers. Let your voice fluctuate in tone, rate, and loudness so the other party knows he is not talking to an automated prerecorded system. You hold people's attention by putting life into your voice. Express honest reactions in expressive ways. Never accuse a caller or confuse a prospect. Never talk above or down to anyone on the phone or act as though you are doing her a favor by talking to her. Always show respect.

▌ Smile into the phone. Somehow, people have a way of "hearing" a smile and knowing that you are enjoying helping them. Some telephone professionals look into a mirror as they speak on the phone.

# MISTAKE 463

**Not being able to handle rejection on the phone.**

## How to Avoid It

If an incoming caller is angry or makes a complaint, remember that he is not angry with you, he is just taking his anger out on you. Relax, stay calm, give the caller the impression that you are confident and experienced. Let him get everything he wants to say out before you respond. Encourage him to say more than he hoped to with sympathetic statements such as "I understand," "That never should have happened," and "That's terrible; I can see why you're so upset." Be on his side even if he is wrong. Call him by name and go over the problem to make sure you're both on the same wavelength. You should also:

- Make a commitment. Get your caller or prospect to agree with you. Tell the party you are speaking with specifically what you will do and when you will do it ("I'll check out the billing problem, Mr. Smith, and get back to you within an hour. Will that be convenient?" or "I'm sorry this happened. We'll deliver a replacement by tomorrow. What time would be best for you?").

- Provide alternatives. Give the other party the sense of being in control. If for example, the person you are calling is unavailable, ask if calling back in ten minutes or the next morning would be more convenient.

- Expect objections. Few sales or complaints are finalized without objections, and everything you've done up to this point should give you most of what you need to handle objections effectively. Your first response to an objection should be to remain calm. Then answer by tailoring the response to the person's needs.

- End the conversation by either closing the sale or by solving the problem when you sense the other party is ready. For instance, if a prospective customer asks "How long will it take for delivery?" chances are she is convinced enough to place an order, so answer her question and ask for the order. Reviewing benefits and solutions as they pertain to the person's needs helps reinforce her acceptance. Once you've made your closing statement, try not to say anything more. Let the pressure of your silence bring its full force to bear. To talk further at this point is overkill and will only serve to make her think twice about her decision.

Thank her for listening or calling and tell her you will confirm the outcome of the conversation.

## MISTAKE 464

**Promising anything to get a sale or get a complaining customer off the phone.**

### How to Avoid It

Never lie, resort to hype or sob stories, or make impossible promises to get a sale or satisfy a disgruntled customer. After the party hangs up and thinks about what transpired, chances are the order will be canceled or the complaint will be called in again.

## MISTAKE 465

**Not keeping up with new technology.**

### How to Avoid It

It is important for every business to keep abreast of what is available now or will be available soon to aid in product planning, gathering market intelligence, and enhancing sales and customer service.

While there are many innovative telecommunications tools that have been around for some time and are affordable to even the smallest of companies, there are still many that continue to do business using old-fashioned methods. Maybe it's because they are antagonized by or afraid of new technology. These kinds of companies will shy away from using even such taken-for-granted tools as speakerphones and conference calls, which enable several people to exchange information and perhaps come to a decision without having to make many time-consuming and expensive individual calls.

Portable cellular phones have become necessities for many people. They are great time-savers. You can have calls forwarded to your portable or your car cellular. You can return calls immediately by checking your voice mail. You can use it to dictate messages to your assistant. If you're lost, you can call for directions. If you're running late, you can call to inform the other party what's happening. If your car breaks down, you can summon help and avoid danger.

See Chapter 17 for more detailed information about many of the sophisticated and affordable capabilities that exist right now and those that will be arriving soon.

## MISTAKE 466

**Playing telephone tag instead of talking with anyone else.**

### How to Avoid It

You call and leave a message. The person you called returns your call and leaves you a message. You return the returned call and find that once again, the person is not there. Telephone tag is one of the most frequent barriers to business communication, and it's a game in which no one wins.

Often the answer you need can be found elsewhere, possibly with an assistant or someone close to the situation. If the person you're calling back is out, get the person who answers the phone to help you by pointing out an advantage such as, "So we won't play telephone tag, I wonder if you might help me? Do you know what Mr. Smith was calling me about?"

## MISTAKE 467

**Calling people at the wrong time.**

### How to Avoid It

Avoid calling at "dead times." You are less likely to find people available to talk on the telephone between 11:45 A.M. and 2:30 P.M., after 4:45 P.M., and on Friday afternoons. If you are trying to reach a decision maker, you will be more likely to reach him by calling at 8:30 A.M. or 5:30 P.M., Monday through Thursday. If your party is not available to take your call, ask the person you are speaking with to recommend a good time to call back. Secretaries can often answer this question, and they know they are on the hook if their boss is not available when the call is returned.

Answer any questions when you return a call—even when none are asked. Let the person you are speaking with know the best time for the other party to call you back. For example, "If Ms. Jones needs updated information, I will be in my office between 2 and 4 this afternoon." In many cases this strategy will eliminate the need for a return call. If you were the original caller and still have not reached your party, try leaving a summary of your purpose for calling.

## MISTAKE 468

**Not using alternative methods to reach your party.**

HOW TO AVOID IT

Instead of making a call, send a fax or e-mail. This is especially effective when you have statistics or other detailed information to convey. You will be able to say almost everything you need to say in a fax or e-mail and, often, your contact will be able to review your message before calling you back. This streamlines your communication. You might also try to reach your party on her cellular phone or beeper.

---

## EIGHT MISTAKES THAT CAN HANG YOU UP ON AUTOMATED VOICE MAIL SYSTEMS

An increasing number of companies are using automated voice mail systems to make their businesses more efficient, and I, for one, have fully accepted the fact that the days of speaking, selling, exchanging ideas, arguing, or even telling a joke to someone person to person on the phone are disappearing fast.

Today, when you call someone to get some simple information you get a voice-mail message that informs you of a menu of eight numbers to pick from. After listening to a recorded explanation of each of the options and how to reach them, you hesitatingly press what you hope is the right touchtone button and you hear yet another voice mail message that gives you more choices and more buttons to push. If, after ten minutes of listening to different messages and pressing buttons, you happen to press the wrong one, you have to hang up, call back, and start the whole process again—without ever having spoken with another human.

---

## MISTAKE 469

**Not using voice mail because you don't trust or understand the technology or simply don't like the concept.**

HOW TO AVOID IT

Some people don't like to be anonymous. They want their faces and voices to be recognized. They feel that if we went to all the trouble to create communications technology that can get us to anyone's desk anywhere in the world, someone should be there to take our call. Others love the feeling of conducting private business and not having to talk to anyone. Whatever your feelings about voice mail may be, it *is* an economical, time-saving customer-relations tool designed to better aid businesses and their customers by accurately taking and dispensing information without the need to have a human answer the phone. And as far as productivity is concerned, it virtually does away with time constraints. A lot of companies now have 24-hour lines with 800 numbers, so they can do business anytime, anywhere, and at no cost to the customer.

To better relate to the benefits of automated phone systems, it is necessary to first understand them. There are three basic types, which are often combined:

1. The *automated attendant,* which gives the option of pressing a touchtone pad and then being transferred to the right person. In a perfect world, it's designed to handle overflow, rather than replace an operator.

2. The more advanced *voice messaging* or *voice mail* gives the caller directions to a location and has the ability to retrieve information with a password, without speaking to another person.

3. The most sophisticated is the *interactive voice response* system often associated with a database of information. It is commonly used for bank transactions, airline bookings, and virtually anything that can be programmed onto a database.

Smaller businesses can get linked to voice mail through service bureaus that buy the equipment and sell phone numbers in lots of five or more numbers.

## MISTAKE 470

**Not properly explaining to customers how to use your system.**

### How to Avoid It

No matter how good a system may be, if the customer can't understand it, the customer won't use it. Many companies have a live operator on hand to explain the procedure, others send instruction brochures to customers explaining how to operate their voice-mail systems. Most problems arise because of unclear or incomplete instructions. For instance, if you call someone and encounter his voice-mail message, you might be instructed to leave a message "after the tone." What it didn't tell you in advance is that you may first have to press 1, or you may have only one or two minutes of message time when you need four or five. As new technology is added, the challenge to make sure these systems are easy to use increases.

## MISTAKE 471

**Not installing security measures or not having a voice-mail policy.**

### How to Avoid It

Using voice mail does not mean that someone can't monitor your calls. The question of whether conversations recorded in electronic voice-mail boxes are granted the same confidentiality protections as are live telephone calls or postal mail is being fought in courtrooms across the nation. Also in question is how far an employer can go in eavesdropping at work for "quality assurance" or other business reasons.

The American Civil Liberties Union argues that covert electronic monitoring generally should be avoided. The U.S. Chamber of Commerce counters that employers should not be restrained in trying to ensure their telephones, computers, and other property are used strictly for business.

Company policies that cover use of other office equipment should apply to the use of voice mail. When necessary, stricter security measures should be employed. Banks, for instance, use changeable personal I.D. numbers (PINs) and passwords.

## MISTAKE 472

**Using a computer-simulated voice instead of a personalized message on your voice mail.**

## MISTAKE 473

**Having too long a menu for callers to work through.**

## MISTAKE 474

**Using a greeting that is too long, too complicated, and not informative.**

## MISTAKE 475

**Not asking for information you will need.**

## MISTAKE 476

**Not using voice mail to screen calls.**

## How to Avoid Them

Used correctly, voice mail can eliminate errors in communication and save time in dozens of ways. With voice mail, it's no longer necessary to talk in real time. Some people deliberately call when the other party is likely to be out in order to leave a short voice-mail message. If the person is there, they know the call will probably take longer. Here are some tips you can follow to make your voice-mail system customer-friendly:

▌ Use a personalized message on your voice mail instead of a computer-simulated voice, which tends to turn off callers.

▌ Don't give the caller a long up-front menu to work through. At most, have three or four options such as "If you are calling to place an order, press 1 . . . if you are calling about your account balance or for assistance in making a payment, press 2 . . . if you need to speak to a living, breathing person, press 3." If it's too long and complicated, the caller will become annoyed and frustrated and hang up.

▌ Keep your greeting short and informative. Give your callers information about where you are, when you will return, or how soon you will pick up your messages. For instance, "I'm in the office but away from my desk right now. Please leave a message at the tone and I'll get back to you within the hour." Or, "I'm out of town until Thursday, June 12th, but I'll be calling in for my voice mail every day." A typical greeting should run about 30 seconds and should include asking callers for the information you need such as their name, number, time of call, reason for calling (as detailed as possible so you can be prepared to return their call), and the best time for you to call back. Be sure to let callers know how much message time they have so they won't get cut off in the middle of leaving their message.

▌ Use voice mail to screen calls as a time management technique. If you are hiring, for instance, you can use voice mail to take applications. Verbal resume voice mail packages are available that allow the applicant caller to "fill out" the form orally. Voice mail can also be used to give priorities to your messages. Using a feature called *nonsimultaneous communications,* outsiders can reach a person directly by phone, but employees use the voice-mail system unless there's an emergency. The employee calls can then be returned at the employer's convenience.

▌ Use voice mail to give directions, instructions, and business hours.

▌ Never prevent a caller from reaching a real person. Some companies require a code or extension number before allowing callers to reach their party directly. Always have a mechanism to get the caller back to an operator or other employee such as by dialing zero or by holding.

## EIGHT COMMON MISTAKES IN INTERACTIVE TELEMARKETING

Reaching customers and prospects by telephone has long been an effective way to market products. It is more personal than mailings because a real person, or a recorded message, is actually interacting with the prospect.

Using 800 lines that are toll-free to the prospect, computerized message machines, and touchtone voice response, it is possible to reach your targets at home or in their place of work, give them a sales pitch over the phone, or take their orders 24 hours a day, without the use of "live" operators.

## MISTAKE 477

**Not considering the telephone as part of a well-rounded media mix for selling.**

### How to Avoid It

There is no doubt that the telephone has become an integral part of the marketer's media mix. 800 and 900 telephone numbers, fax, telemarketing, computer, and other information activities over telephone lines have impacted virtually every facet of the marketing/advertising industry, complementing campaigns in traditional media and serving as the centerpiece of innovative product promotions, contests, and electronic couponing and rebate programs.

## MISTAKE 478

**Not considering the telephone an effective medium for selling.**

## How to Avoid It

In a competitive environment, with marketers demanding tighter targeting and more accountability, interactive telemarketing emerges as an effective advertising medium that goes beyond the bounds of ordinary mass media. Here are some of the reasons why:

▪ Interactive telemarketing is much more personal than other media that simply address mass audiences. Also, with database knowledge of a caller's demographic characteristics, telemarketing is capable of directing a "personalized" message to that caller.

▪ 900 interactive telemarketing is less costly than traditional media because the consumers pay to participate. In addition, since it employs automated voice information services, it is less costly than using live phone operators.

▪ Customer reaction time to an offer is faster, because people have a reason and a way to react on impulse to telemarketing promotions. The responses can also be instantly measured.

▪ Telemarketing, unlike other mass media, provides quality interaction with customers. Callers receive personalized information merely by pressing touchtone selections on their telephone. Callers also have the opportunity to express their opinions in many promotions.

▪ Interactive telemarketing adds an additional and personal dimension to campaigns in other media.

▪ Interactive telemarketing generates and qualifies consumer leads.

▪ It builds databases of prospects by profiling customers.

▪ It helps promote long-term customer loyalty.

▪ Telemarketing has been successful in getting competitive users to switch brands.

▪ Telemarketing allows consumers to respond to advertising around the clock, as long as they are close to a telephone.

---

## MISTAKE 479

**Not properly targeting prospects for telemarketing.**

## How to Avoid It

Once you've decided to use interactive telemarketing as part of your overall marketing campaign, you will first have to decide whether to use it locally or on a wider basis.

The decision, among other reasons, depends on your product or service, your target market and their needs, and the purpose of the telemarketing campaign.

If your product or service is being offered locally or regionally, for instance, you wouldn't want to use a national (800 or 900) response number unless you are interested only in getting a database for future sales in other markets.

Another reason for using local telemarketing is if you are running a test program in one of several major markets.

Two methods that are commonly used to qualify and target prospects and customers are through use of a database of detailed information about prospects and customers gathered from service bureaus or through customer and prospect data in the company's own database. This information is often obtained through interactive telecommunications systems that gives the marketer the ability to:

▮ Analyze, profile, and qualify prospects or customers.

▮ Identify the most profitable segments within the total audience and then from the demographic information on that segment,

▮ Determine the most important product benefits and the right appeal and message that will stimulate purchase through a telephone call.

Collecting databases in this automated interactive manner can be less expensive than other methods of information gathering because live operators are not necessary and information can be gathered at any and all times. Large savings can also be realized from follow-up direct selling and promotional efforts.

As an example of using database information to create a sales approach that will satisfy the prospects' reasons to purchase and motivate them to respond, suppose you are a builder selling condominiums to the senior market. Your database information shows a primary reason for many seniors not buying at this particular time is because they can't sell the home they are in. Your creative sales approach could address this problem head-on with a number of alternative marketing plans that would allow a potential buyer to feel better about buying now. A "you buy ours, we'll buy yours" approach is one. A "buy now, don't make payments for three months" program is another.

By calling people who have visited your sales office before, you can get even more personal in your approach. Since they have been there, they are familiar with the products and have met the staff.

## MISTAKE 480

**Not motivating the target to respond.**

### How to Avoid It

When people learn of a product or service that interests them, they usually act on impulse and want to buy it quickly, much the way they do in stores. They also want as much information about this product as they can get, and that information should be available while the interest is at its highest point. Information such as:

▋ The benefits of the product or service.

▋ How much it costs.

▋ How they can order the advertised product.

▋ How quickly they can get delivery.

If calls are coming back in response to an advertisement, telemarketing personnel should know what questions to ask callers, or the interactive system should be programmed to ask the right questions. They should encourage an order or visit and get as much personal information as possible: "Are you interested in a condominium just for you, for you and your spouse or for a friend or relative?" " Do you live in a home or rental apartment now?" "What price range are you interested in?" "How many bedrooms do you want or need?" "Do you own a car or have a pet?" "Are you interested in recreational and social amenities—what kind?" "Do you know anyone who already lives here?" "How did you hear of us?" "How soon do you need occupancy?"

Looking at the information gathered as a whole, you'll see how it can be broken down into a number of segments, each motivated by different reasons for purchase. For example, those potential condominium buyers who are now renting don't have to worry about selling a home. In future campaigns that address that problem, that segment of the database can be eliminated or sent a different message.

Whether you are selling condos, cars, or cruises, by feeding the responses from your campaigns back into your database and continually updating each prospect's or customer's information, you can not only track and qualify leads, you can also establish loyal, ongoing relationships and communicate with them as individuals—not just as names on a customer list.

## MISTAKE 481

**Not having good security measures in place when taking orders over the phone.**

### How to Avoid It

Direct-mail companies and retailers, whose direct-marketing business is done mainly through catalogs and print ads touting toll-free phone numbers have faced the problem of credit-card fraud for years.

Now, many telemarketing companies use databases that will help eliminate this problem. One database, the Bin Number Directory of All Visa and MasterCard Issuing Banks, contacts the card-issuing bank and verifies names and addresses to determine whether a buyer is the cardholder.

Numerous databases such as the Visa and MasterCard Bin Number Directory are available to telemarketers. The Directory of All Mail Drop Addresses and Zip Codes allows marketers to see whether an order is being shipped to a mail drop location. The Directory of All Prison and Jail Addresses and Zip Codes database allows the marketer to see whether an order came from or is being sent to a prison or jail. These orders often involve stolen credit-card numbers.

## MISTAKE 482

**Not using interactive 800 and 900 response numbers to handle large volumes of calls.**

### How to Avoid It

Computer-assisted voice response (IVR) technology (a marriage of the telephone, PCs, and databases) has become an important component in many 800- and pay-per-call 900-number telemarketing programs used in conjunction with other forms of advertising such as TV, radio, direct mail or print especially those requiring large call-handling capacity.

For example, a well-executed TV commercial making a valuable offer tied to an 800 or 900 response number can generate many thousands of calls a minute, every minute, for the first 10 or 15 minutes after the commercial runs. Marketers want to be assured they are logging every call and getting all the information they can from the caller.

When a customer responds to an advertised offer by calling an 800 or 900 number, the IVR system they connect with becomes a direct link between the advertiser and that customer, so it is essential that the caller is treated politely and efficiently.

Most IVR systems answer choices made by callers using a touch-tone telephone keypad. They can run 24 hours a day, seven days a week, offering callers greater convenience. And they can be designed to digitally record spoken information such as a caller's name and address or route the call for the most effective order processing. If necessary, the system can connect the caller to a live operator.

The interactive voice information system automatically gathers statistics about each caller (consumer demographics, preferences, etc.), which are reported to the marketer in print-outs and used later for targeted direct response campaigns.

## MISTAKE 483

**Not using interactive 900 response numbers to cut marketing costs and increase profits.**

## MISTAKE 484

**Not recognizing the many benefits of using interactive 900 numbers.**

### HOW TO AVOID THEM

Interactive 900 marketing campaigns can not only be a way to self-liquidate advertising and other costs, they can actually be profitable.

Since either the person responding to the advertised offer pays for the 900 call, or the call is sponsored by some noncompeting company, it is possible, if priced properly, to self-liquidate the promotional costs and even make a profit *before* the customer buys the product or service. At worst, a portion of the advertising expenses can be recouped.

Some 900 IVR applications, for example, provide caller-paid or sponsor-paid live or recorded one-way messages, two-way conversations, and electronic counting for opinion polls. Other benefits in using interactive 900-response numbers include:

▮ Interactive 900 campaigns used as a source for gathering detailed databases and qualified leads enable marketers to realize savings because the cost of gathering the information can be self-liquidating.

▮ There's the immeasurable benefit derived from the fact that interactive 900 campaigns enhance customer relationships. Respondents have the opportunity to express their opinions, while marketers can carry on previously unaffordable "loyalty and brand-building" dialogues with large numbers of targeted individuals at an affordable cost.

▮ 900 campaigns give prospects the opportunity to respond immediately on impulse.

▮ 900 campaigns encourage shorter customer reaction time because customers know they are paying for the time.

▮ 900 campaigns are a vehicle for sales promotions. Innovative marketers have created new and exciting "tele-techniques" to enhance direct marketing campaigns—promotions such as games, contests, sweepstakes, coupon dissemination, product sampling, and fund raising.

▮ Using interactive 900 for couponing, cash refunds, and product sampling, marketers are able to measure the results of campaigns more accurately because they find out immediately who responded to a particular offer.

They also find that running contests, games, and sweepstakes on the telephone delivers interactive "instant win" excitement that is not possible through other forms of media.

A cosmetics manufacturer we know of ran a 900-number direct response beauty-care sweepstakes promotion that targeted women 18 to 49 years of age. The company advertised the sweepstakes to 52 million households by using a color insert in hundreds of newspapers throughout the United States.

A 900 response number was included in the insert. Readers called the number and gave the 4-digit code on their insert to find out if they were "instant winners" in the $2 million sweepstakes. The self-liquidating sweepstakes not only generated a database of phone-responsive names and demographic information, it also provided a short phone commercial for its products. And by donating a portion of the revenue from the 900 calls to a charity, the cosmetics firm created a "corporate/community" tie-in for building brand loyalty.

Television and radio stations often use interactive 900 numbers for instant polls on current situations in the news. Television networks use interactive 900 numbers to provide viewers with the opportunity to answer questions, or choose their favorite football plays and players, as well as voice their opinions about their favorite programs.

With a single 900 telephone call, respondents to an ad can hear variable messages or upsells based on their locations, demographics, and buying histories. They can be immediately connected to the nearest dealer selling a product. They can receive faxes-on-demand with coupons, contest details, product information and other ad-enhancing information, all within minutes, all at self-liquidating costs.

Fax-on-demand (an offshoot of IVR) has become an increasingly critical marketing tool as customers insist on instant access to information. Using their telephone keypads, callers instruct an IVR system to fax documents to them immediately, instead of having to make a call and then wait a long time to get the information through the mail, usually forgetting why they wanted it in the first place. Depending on the system, customers can call from either their phones or from fax machines.

Other trends that seem to be getting more popular as IVR technology expands include offering a 900 number for pay-as-you-need service in place of service contracts and segmenting markets by need and willingness to pay for convenience or customized treatment.

## TWO MISTAKES MADE WHEN GETTING PERSONAL WITH DIRECT RESPONSE

With database marketing performing as a "neighborhood store," marketers are pinpointing new and potentially loyal customers through what they euphemistically call tangible relationship marketing and interactive real-time data generation—also known as direct response marketing.

## MISTAKE 485

**Believing customers don't expect personal service.**

## MISTAKE 486

**Not using customer information to get to know and sell customers more effectively.**

### How to Avoid Them

There was a time, not too long ago, when many neighborhood store-owners knew their customers by name and always managed to save the best apples or the last magazine just for them.

Customers went out of their way to shop at those stores and even recommended them to friends and relatives. Why? Because by treating their customers as individuals, finding out what their specific needs were, and satisfying those needs, the storeowners created a personal rapport with the customers, a concept that sometimes gets forgotten in our hi-tech world of mass marketing.

But things seem to have come full circle. Today, customers expect and even demand this personal kind of service from the companies they deal with, no matter if those companies serve a dozen or a million customers.

Progressive companies have learned that the better they know their customers, the better they can run their business; that in this, the age of information, the data gathered from 800 and 900 calls makes it easier than ever to keep track of and stay in touch with customers on a give-them-what-they-want basis. And that without some form of personal service they will not keep their current customers or attract new business.

Enter direct-response marketing—a form of marketing based on the idea that no matter what you are selling, people respond best when they are treated as individuals and offered products they want or need.

Direct-response marketing can be placed as a communications and marketing tool somewhere between image-building media advertising (print, broadcast, and direct mail), and sales promotion, which usually offers dollars off but says nothing about quality or filling customer needs. It attempts to discover and understand the desires of customers and prospects through the use of a continually updated database and then create personally targeted communications programs to meet their individual needs. Sometimes referred to as personal marketing, this concept has been the inspiration behind the rapid growth of the multibillion-dollar-per-year direct response industry.

The most often used means of getting direct response through direct marketing on a mass basis are via direct mailings, television, print, and the telephone (telemarketing). With the proper blending of creative advertising and the advanced technology available to reach your customers through these media, direct response marketing can be a very powerful, cost-efficient, and successful means of selling your prospects products and services and keeping them as loyal, long-term customers.

Through direct-response marketing, it is possible to build a database for every prospect and customer that will tell you among other things:

■ Who all your customers are by name, address, and occupation.

■ Which of your products or services they like best and why.

■ Which cities and area codes they are calling from.

■ How many times they tried to reach you.

■ How many total callers there were, hour by hour, and how many callers were lost.

■ Which days of the week had the heaviest number of calls.

■ The average duration of each call.

■ Which advertising campaigns worked best.

■ The best time to get back to a caller.

Personalized relationships between businesses and their customers will grow with the advancement of interactive media. Traditional mass-marketing media have consisted of one-way communication—monologues presented to consumers through print, audio, and visual media. Interactive marketing allows the exchange of ideas between the marketer and the consumer, providing real-time feedback about consumers' choices and reactions. The key to the success of interactive marketing is empowerment—of the marketer and especially of the consumer. People will be able to respond and interact to whatever messages they want to see, whenever they want to see them. In a world of 500 or more channel choices, for instance, in which people hold a remote in their hand and will zap anything that is boring or irrelevant, the trick is making sure your message grabs them—with information, need, and entertainment. Once a consumer responds directly to your printed, broadcast, or telephoned offer, you the marketer, will be empowered to set up a dialogue, learn about, answer questions, and convince the caller to buy with maximum efficiency.

## EIGHT MISTAKES IN MAKING COMPANY VIDEOS AND PRODUCT INFOMERCIALS

As competition gets more intense and the cost of making sales continues to rise, more businesses are showcasing themselves on company videos and infomercials.

### MISTAKE 487

**Not considering a company video as a marketing tool.**

#### HOW TO AVOID IT

Company videos can add a whole new dimension to a company's overall marketing plan as well as extend its sales reach. For example, a video:

- Can be used in sales presentations in offices, homes, and at seminars.

- Can be used as an orientation/training vehicle for new employees.

- Can be mailed to prospects you can't call on in person or sell effectively over the phone.

- Is more likely to be watched and listened to than commercials, more likely to get attention than mailers and brochures.

### MISTAKE 488

**Believing a company video is more expensive and less effective than other promotional media.**

#### HOW TO AVOID IT

With the video equipment available today, companies can produce their own relatively inexpensive and highly effective video productions, or they can use the services of video production companies that will handle the entire project from writing, shooting, editing, and duplicating for about the cost of creating and producing a full-color brochure.

A quality ten-minute video, for example, can usually be produced for between $1,000 to $1,500 per minute. More sophisticated productions using special effects and lighting; fancy camera movement; professional actors; studio facilities; rented locations, scenery, and equipment (such as a helicopter for aerial shots); and music can run in the neighborhood of $3,000 to $6,000 or more a minute. The more sophisticated the production, the more time it will take to shoot and edit, the more it will cost. Some production companies work on a flat per-day rate, charging for the number of days it takes to complete the project plus out-of-pocket costs.

Sophisticated extras are nice to look at but aren't always necessary. Viewers watching company tapes are not expecting to see a spectacular Hollywood production. Sticking to a straightforward presentation will help keep costs down while showcasing the company in a businesslike manner.

When the tape is completed, duplicate cassettes can be purchased for as little as $1 to $2 apiece, depending on quantities ordered.

One way to produce a lower-cost company video is to shoot your visuals as slides and then transfer those pictures to videotape adding graphics, titles, effects, and music.

## MISTAKE 489

**Using a company video strictly for image building rather than to get your most important company messages seen and heard.**

### How to Avoid It

As we have said, company videos can add a new dimension to a company's overall marketing plan as well as extend its sales reach. Your company, for example, may be introducing a new product, expanding customer services, building, or changing its image. Using a video strictly for image purposes is okay if you have the budget to throw away. Such projects are usually inspired by top-level egos and are not as effective as showcasing your image in a brochure. Budget permitting, an ideal company video should feature a primary message aimed at a particular audience. It is common today, however, to find company videos featuring multiple messages that appeal to a variety of audiences. It is possible, for instance, to produce a video that will serve as an image builder when shown to financial institutions, a sales tool when shown to reps and distributors, and an orientation or training tool when shown to employees. If you can get across two or three messages without cluttering up or confusing the presentation, the more you will get for your production money. A real estate developer might design a video targeting both brokers and individual home buyers. A manufacturer of medical products might aim its video at physicians by showing how patients should be treated with a particular product, and at the same time target pharmacists by explaining side effects or problems that might occur from use of the product.

Getting the right message across in the most efficient and effective way starts with the script. Aside from providing a guide for shooting the visuals, a good script should:

- Tell viewers about your company history, location, expertise of the staff, and its current and past products or services.

- Detail the markets your company serves and the needs your products or services fill.

- Describe and show the features and benefits of the products or services featured.

- Show viewers how they can get the product or service.

Some Do's and Don'ts:

Do begin with a written set of objectives that the video needs to achieve. Keep every scene in line with those objectives.

Do visualize, plan, and stage each scene to allow for camera placement, lighting, noise reduction, amount of time a product is on screen.

Do get to the heart of even the most complex topic.

Don't use jargon, highly technical language, or detailed product specifications.

Do write the narration the way people talk.

Don't assume everyone knows what you're talking about.

Do keep the script length to ten minutes or less. The longer the video, the more likely your audience will lose interest.

Do try to be interesting and entertaining.

Do conclude with a reminder of who you are, what you have that will be of benefit to the viewer, and how they can buy the product or service or reach you for information.

Do rehearse each scene a number of times before shooting.

Do make sure you have the right to use music, effects, and graphics.

Do make sure you have signed consent and release forms from all persons appearing in the video.

## MISTAKE 490

**Not recognizing the infomercial as an effective direct response and educational image-building vehicle for expanding the customer base.**

### How to Avoid It

What started out as a showcase for entrepreneurial hawkers of kitchen gadgets, exercise tapes, and beauty aids, the infomercial (also known as long-form, program-length, and high-content commercials) has become an effective marketing vehicle for building company image, driving retail sales, generating leads, and selling products over the phone or through the mail. For many companies, the infomercial has replaced more traditional direct-response tactics.

A major computer software company generated so many calls with its 30-minute infomercial, it had to employ a second telemarketing company and reprint fulfillment material three times to keep up with the volume of incoming viewer calls.

A well-known exercise guru gets an average of 12,000 telephone orders every time his exercise tapes or diet programs are offered, and they can be offered as many as four or five times a day on various cable networks, every day of the week.

Infomercials, which are usually 28- or 58-minute commercial shows presented in an entertaining and informative way, give marketers the opportunity to stand apart from the competition. Because there is more time to give more information and assistance to potential customers, more value is added to the products or services being sold.

Infomercials are also a tool for expanding a potential customer base by targeting consumers who might not be exposed to your promotional efforts in other media. An investment company, for example, would put most of its promotional budget into financial newspapers, magazines, and direct mail. But exposing the same message on an infomercial would open a whole new potential market of consumers who might not read those kinds of publications or be on a targeted mailing list.

Some other reasons for the strong interest in the infomercial as a marketing tool are:

∎ Infomercials are highly educational.

∎ Infomercials can deliver multiple messages in a single viewing.

∎ Infomercials have the ability to deliver a compelling message and even change consumer attitudes toward a product or service.

∎ Because you have more time to explain attractions and benefits the products offer, messages delivered through infomercials have more impact and are retained in surprising detail.

∎ The results of infomercials are measurable, sometimes immediately.

∎ Infomercials can result in immediate leads and sales, thereby making the advertising a revenue source rather than a cost.

∎ Infomercials can help build strong databases for future sales.

∎ Infomercials can help build loyalty and long-term relationships with potential customers.

∎ Use of infomercials presents opportunities for "partnering" with noncompetitive companies in order to strengthen credibility and lower production costs.

## MISTAKE 491

**Losing viewers because the format is too straightforward and not entertaining or interesting enough.**

## MISTAKE 492

**Not using the right incentives to get viewers to respond.**

### HOW TO AVOID THEM

Offer it and they will call. This was the case when infomercials first started with hard-sell copy focusing exclusively on features and benefits and were showcased in formats that included talk shows, lectures, studio demonstrations, and documercials.

Marketers, however, have found that infomercials can do a lot more than produce immediate phone orders and leads, and today they are creating long-form infomercials that are entertaining, informative, fascinating to watch, and effective quality productions— infomercials that can stop the channel surfers and capture their interest and stand out from ordinary formats.

Long-form commercials and media buys are now prominent components in yearly ad campaigns and budgets, and dramatically different formats now include fiction-based concepts such as variety entertainment shows, dramatic storymercials, news and sportscasts, sitcoms, and more. Hard-sell tactics are giving way to soft-sell. Image building is becoming as important as retailing, emotion and fantasy as important as reality, delayed response as important as immediate response.

Marketers are also finding that the right incentive is critical to getting viewers to pick up the phone. Many advertisers offer free gifts and samples. Some use techniques such as breaking away from a show three different times within the 30 minutes for calls to action. Still others use celebrities to generate interest. They are also buying high-visibility time periods such as weekend afternoons leading out of sports on network affiliates and weekday afternoons to get their message to the right demographics, instead of the usual late late nighttime periods.

## MISTAKE 493

**Not complying with rules regulating infomercials.**

### How to Avoid It

Just as in the case of producing regular short-length commercials or company videos, it is important to get model, music, and other necessary releases and be aware of any rules and regulations that might apply to your product or service or claims you may make about them. For instance, if you are showing a product being used or endorsed by a "doctor" or "hospital" and you are not using real doctors, it is necessary to put a disclaimer on screen advising viewers that what they are seeing is a dramatization. Investment offers are regulated by the SEC and other government agencies and require certain disclaimers.

## MISTAKE 494

**Dating the production and limiting its run.**

## How to Avoid It

Never "date" your infomercial with time frames or references to current events. You always want your message and image to look fresh and current. Dating a production limits its use and makes even an inexpensive infomercial more costly. One large insurance company I know of spent over $1 million producing a half-hour infomercial featuring a dozen famous comedians celebrating the eighty-eighth birthday of one of their own. Not only would it have been safer investing that kind of money in someone much younger, if the producers and company marketing experts had looked ahead, they might have realized that in 12 months when the world was informed that the comedian was 89 the infomercial would be out of date and its effectiveness would be significantly diminished.

# Chapter 19

## COMMUNICATING THROUGH DIRECT MAIL

$O$f all the ways a business can communicate with its prospects and customers (as well as its vendors and employees), one of the most personal and direct, outside of a face-to-face meeting, is through the written word in a direct-mail piece.

Business direct mail can be sent through the U.S. Post Office or other private delivery services—or more likely in today's electronic world, through computer and fax phone modem download or on diskettes and CD-ROMs as digital mailers—and can include myriad written material such as:

- Advertising flyers, catalogs, sales letters, cover letters, handwritten and business note cards.

- Customer invoices, statements, and statement stuffers.

- Product documentation including instruction and demonstration booklets.

- Legal notices.

- Surveys.

- Interoffice employee memos.

- Vendor orders and contracts.

While verbal communication may be quicker and as personal as direct mail (and allow you to observe body language), it is not always possible or the best method of communication. You may not, for example, be able to reach a customer or prospect by phone or in person. Or, you may need to send additional information after concluding a phone or person-to-person deal. Or, you may want to create a paper trail that can help track a service transaction that has spread out over a long period of time. Even when there's no pressing need, a direct written communication after a conversation can be the best way to confirm facts and details and, of course, to say thanks for the order.

Direct mail as a selling tool is similar to telemarketing except it uses the written word instead of the spoken word. Because it does not have time and space limitations, direct mail allows a business to explain the benefits of its products or services in greater detail. It is a form of marketing that pinpoints your prospects and provides measurable results, so you can not only see what works best for your company, you can also account for every dollar spent and know when to stop spending marketing dollars on people who are not buying. And by feeding the information gathered from various mailings into a database, companies get to know who and where their prospects and customers are and how often, what, and why they buy.

---

## ELEVEN MISTAKES IN COMMUNICATING EFFECTIVELY AND INEXPENSIVELY THROUGH DIRECT MAIL

---

It sometimes takes more than one or two impressions to make a sale and build a relationship with customers, but because it isn't always possible to make those impressions in person or on the phone, many companies turn to direct mail as a quick, effective, and inexpensive alternative.

## MISTAKE 495

**Not targeting the most likely prospects.**

### How to Avoid It

Many direct-marketing professionals will tell you that the single most important factor in creating a successful direct-mail program is getting your message to the right person.

Once you know why you are writing, you can consider who will be receiving your correspondence. What you know about those you want to reach will help you isolate them and set the tone and language of your message. If you are selling baby products, for example, you wouldn't want to send your mailing to people 50+. If your target is a disgruntled customer, sending her an announcement of a new product or a special sale may be wasted effort and dollars. On the other hand, if your company is introducing a new product, you may want to cross-sell to existing customers as well as to the customers of competitors.

## MISTAKE 496

**Not understanding or using mailing lists to best serve your needs.**

### How to Avoid It

An essential element for effective direct mail is the mailing list. Whether it comes from your own database, customer referrals, or from a list service, there are three things you should always keep in mind:

1. The demographics of the list should include as many characteristics as possible for the segment you are focusing on.

2. No list is absolutely perfect.

3. The key to an effective list is to continually "clean" it.

The best mailing list any company can have is one they have developed to fulfill their own marketing needs. It should include the following characteristics to help isolate the ideal prospects:

- Demographic—providing statistical information with reference to size, density, distribution, and vitals (age, income, home ownership, etc.) of prospects.

- Psychographic—providing information on lifestyle, interests, personal profile, buying habits, product likes and dislikes, vocation/avocation, and hobbies.

- Geographic—providing information on geographic elements such as roads, counties, cities/towns, zip codes, and so forth.

Most mailing lists available from list services and other sources are generated from public and proprietary record sources such as motor vehicle licenses and registrations, telephone directories, census tract, real estate tax files, consumer, trade and professional magazine subscribers, professional and occupational licenses, Yellow Pages, business and association directories, surveys, mail orders, question-naires, warranty cards, credit card holders, phone and written inquiries, and any other sources, wherever they can be found.

By considering the common characteristics of your current best customers, you will have a good idea of the kinds of prospects you want to reach. A good list company can probably provide you with thousands of names of people or companies who meet most of your criteria. You can be highly specific and selective in creating an ideal prospect and then letting the list company find people who meet most of the criteria. In general, mailing lists fall into four basic cate-gories:

1.  Occupant—resident by address only. You are able to select cities, states, neighborhoods, routes, development areas, zip codes, sin-gle or multifamily dwellings.

2.  Resident by name—head of household. You can select by age, gender, household income, homeowner or renter, assessed valu-ation of home, date of home purchase, year home built, date of mortgage transaction, permanent or seasonal resident, married with children, number and ages of children, year and make and type of vehicle, lifestyle (golfer, surfer, musician).

3.  Business/professional—you can select by type of business (SIC code), profession by specialty, company size by number of employees or sales volume, seminar or trade show attendees, and zip codes, among others.

4.  Response—this list includes those who have shown interest in or previously initiated contact for a similar product or service. In this category, selection requires research.

List houses have databases with millions of names of individu-als and companies in every category imaginable, usually with enough in-depth detail to extract just the names you need and get your mes-sage to the person who actually decides whether to buy your product or service. Furthermore, these list companies update their databases monthly so that all the information is current and offers the maxi-mum in effectiveness.

Of course, such targeted lists cost more per additional criterion than standard lists, but they often pay for themselves by reducing the randomness of selection and increasing the efficiency of the mailing because you can tailor your message to meet the probable needs of these people.

If you are too narrow in your focus, the list company will let you know that they cannot supply the quantity of names you requested and will help you modify your criteria.

## MISTAKE 497

**Not using the right direct-mail piece to get your message across.**

## MISTAKE 498

**Assuming the more expensive or elaborate the direct-mail piece, the more effective it will be.**

### How to Avoid Them

Your next job will be to design and produce a mailing piece that serves a specific purpose or most likely appeals to the particular reason a customer wants to buy the product or service you are marketing. Such pieces usually include a mail-back card or a toll-free phone number for direct and/or immediate response.

In addition to sales letters, brochures, catalogs, and flyers, which can be costly to produce and mail, there are many inexpensive ways to keep in touch with prospects and customers through direct mail, including:

- Thank you notes for orders.
- Thank you notes for referrals.
- Thank you notes for continued and valued business.
- Short notes confirming meetings or phone conversations.
- FYI notes about something of interest to your prospect.
- A birthday or anniversary card.
- A "Congratulations, I read about you in the newspaper" note.
- A service reminder.
- A private or special sale or offer.
- A company newsletter.
- A notice of an upcoming appointment or a meeting or seminar that might be of interest to a prospect or customer.
- A reminder of a pending order or reorder.

Sometimes the piece you want to send is already produced, such as an article that pertains to something of interest to your target. All that remains for you to do is photocopy it, put a Post-it™ note or your business card on it, and send it.

Most of the pieces mentioned above are extremely cost effective communication tools that are remembered, build goodwill and loyalty, and make the customer or prospect feel good.

## MISTAKE 499

**Expecting too big a response.**

### How to Avoid It

Discuss direct mail with people who have never used it and the first question they usually ask is, "What percent response will I get?" The answer is, nobody knows exactly. Most companies we spoke with reported a response rate of 2 to 3 percent on an average direct-mail piece. Experts can take an educated guess based on similar experiences they had on previous mailings, but every mailing is different and depends on a multitude of factors such as:

■ Is the direct-mail piece going to prospects or current customers? Studies show direct mail is almost always more effective when sent to current customers, mainly because the recipient knows who it is coming from and is less likely to throw it away with other junk mail—unopened!

■ Does the mailer have a headline that grabs the reader? It should appeal to the recipients' interests or particular needs. If it doesn't, chances are they won't read beyond the headline.

■ Is the direct-mail piece the bearer of good news or bad news? Believe it or not, studies conducted by Stanford University show bad news is more likely to get attention because a person's mental automatic-processing system responds to negative stimuli better than it does to positive stimuli, possibly as a natural protection from harm.

■ Is the format of the mailer deviating from traditional formats? A well-received mailer is usually one that looks professional, is fresh and engaging in its approach, gets attention, and is easy to read.

■ Is the copy approach low key or high pressure? Like most other kinds of advertising, direct mail must firmly ask for the order—by toll-free phone or postage-paid reply card—and be urgent about it.

■ Is the message impersonal or personal in approach? As we discussed earlier in the direct-response section, the more personal the approach, the more effective the results. With the vast information available from databases, details such as names, past transactions, and other information can be easily inserted into the copy for maximum personalization.

## MISTAKE 500

**Not testing a large mailing before sending out the entire run.**

### How to Avoid It

Many companies rely on testing to more accurately estimate budgets and effectiveness. By testing, say, 10 percent of your mailing list, you can get an idea of how effective the message is and how good the list is. The greater the number used in the test and the more test mailings that are conducted, the more accurate you can be in predicting the results. Formal list testing makes more sense for large regional or national mailings than it does for small, local mailings.

## MISTAKE 501

**Estimating response instead of measuring return on investment.**

### How to Avoid It

If you understand your market and know the viability of your product or service, you can be more realistic in your expectation of responses. Measuring the return on investment is more important than calculating and predicting response rates that represent only an estimating tool to figure projected activity.

Each mailing you do will provide answers to more questions:

■ Did the mailing pay for itself or make a profit?

■ Will you be able to enlarge your customer base and create repeat sales?

■ Can you make the message stronger?

■ Can you target the list better?

## MISTAKE 502

**Discarding or not following up on "no" responses.**

## How to Avoid It

While "no" responses and undelivered returned mail can be helpful in "cleaning" mailing lists, it is important to try and contact nonresponders at least one or two more times before taking them off your list. Sending out a follow-up mailer or calling the prospect or customer can pay off. Unlike a cold call, which many people consider an invasive tactic, a follow-up contact is reminding the recipient of a unique offer they are already aware of and may not have had the time to take action on.

## MISTAKE 503

Not using U.S. Postal Service (USPS) endorsements to fill a particular need, such as cleaning your list.

## MISTAKE 504

Not understanding the implications of using certain endorsements.

## How to Avoid Them

Endorsements printed on mail pieces by the mailer are directives to the Postal System ordering a variance in handling services. They are the "exception to the rules" that provide a service twist to suit an unusual need. Though most come at an additional cost, that cost is often far less than the alternative.

Endorsements are regulated by the post office as to position, type size, and terminology, as well as other factors such as color of paper and reversing of copy.

The most common circumstance encouraging the use of an endorsement is in "cleaning" a list via third-class bulk-rate mailing. Standard USPS handling of bulk-rate mail is to dispose of any pieces that are undeliverable as addressed. If you want to keep your list current, use the endorsement "Address Correction Requested." Undeliverable mail pieces will be returned with an address correction if the addressee's change-of-address forwarding order is still active (one year) or with the reason for nondelivery.

Each mail classification has its own set of endorsements, rules and regulations. Information is available at any post office or from your list house. First- and third-class comprise the majority of pieces handled by the Postal Service and include these typically used endorsements:

### FIRST CLASS

ADDRESS CORRECTION REQUESTED

DO NOT FORWARD

FORWARDING AND ADDRESS CORRECTION REQUESTED

### THIRD CLASS

ADDRESS CORRECTION REQUESTED

DO NOT FORWARD

FORWARDING AND RETURN POSTAGE GUARANTEED

FORWARDING AND RETURN POSTAGE GUARANTEED, ADDRESS CORRECTION REQUESTED

DO NOT FORWARD, ADDRESS CORRECTION REQUESTED, RETURN POSTAGE GUARANTEED

Though the choices appear to be self-explanatory, be sure you understand the implications of using each endorsement.

▪ Use "RETURN POSTAGE GUARANTEED" only when the mail piece has greater value than the cost to have it returned.

▪ Use "ADDRESS CORRECTION REQUESTED" only when mailing to your own updated private list and never to a commercial list.

▪ Use "OR CURRENT RESIDENT" or "OR CURRENT BUSINESS" to increase deliverability on the next line after the name.

▪ Use a title instead of a name when mailing to a business list, unless you are certain the person you are mailing to is still there.

---

## MISTAKE 505

**Relying only on the USPS and not using alternate delivery methods.**

### How to Avoid It

A growing number of companies are now providing private mail delivery service. Magazine publishers and large mail-order catalog marketers have used alternate delivery and have found it produces higher response rates and no mailbox clutter.

Many newspapers already have private delivery systems in place. By using the databases they've developed in their markets, dailies are combining with fledgling delivery services to target home deliveries of magazines, catalogs, samples and a variety of ride-along ads. Alternate delivery gives newspapers a way to use their often extensive databases to fend off saturation mailers and other direct marketers, which have been taking away an increasing amount of advertising from newspapers.

The papers also make money by selling additional advertisements to go in the home delivery package. This includes very targeted ride-along ad pieces. A newspaper can, for instance, group magazines delivered by the segments they want to focus on. A sporting goods company could advertise only to households that receive sports-oriented publications.

The products most often used in private delivery are magazines, catalogs, and third-class letter mail. However, companies selling pet food, video cassettes, sunglasses, and record albums are among the many using the private service and bypassing USPS.

## TWENTY-TWO MISTAKES IN CREATING DIRECT MAIL THEY WON'T FORGET

A blank piece of paper or an empty computer screen can be terrifying to anyone who communicates in print. Mediocre and bad writers will fill the space with blank thoughts, stiff, boring verbiage, clichés, and jargon. Good and great writers fill the blank space with words that sizzle with clarity, impact, and power that gets under a prospect's skin and makes him itch to buy.

It doesn't matter if you are writing a memo to an associate, reports to a superior, sales letters to customers, or the next *War and Peace*—your writing reflects your ability and confidence and affects the respect you get.

As with other forms of communication, there are elements of style and substance that should be combined whenever written communication is used. While some, such as bills and order forms, are standardized and less personal, in business the communication of your ideas is only as good as your ability to express them.

## MISTAKE 506

**Letting your fear or dislike of writing prevent you from communicating effectively in a direct-mail piece.**

## MISTAKE 507

**Focusing the direct-mail piece on the writer's needs instead of on the reader's needs.**

### How to Avoid Them

Have you ever wondered how good writers get most of the important information about a product or service into the first paragraph of copy? Or how some people can write a headline that would stop readers dead in their tracks? Or how someone could condense pages and pages of descriptive verbiage into 50 words of elegant, clever, flowing copy?

Everyone in business would like to write impressive direct-mail pieces, sales letters, memos, and reports, but most fear writing because they don't know what constitutes good business writing and subsequently believe that their self-respect and self-esteem are on the line with each piece they write.

If your background is not in the creative end, you will need to know something about direct-mail writing and how it fits in with other business communication.

First, every direct-mail piece should be designed to focus on the specific needs of the recipient. Therefore your writing must come across as reader-oriented, not writer-oriented.

There are various kinds of writing approaches that adapt themselves to accomplishing this.

1. Straight-line copy—in this approach, the body text begins immediately to develop the headline and/or illustration idea in direct selling of the product, using its sales points in the order of their importance and tying them in to the reader's needs by using "ownership" words and the reader's name throughout.

2. Narrative copy, of which there are two kinds—the establishment of a story or specific situation that by its nature will logically lead into a discussion of a product's selling points, or the so-called "institutional" type of writing, in which the copy sells an idea, organization, service, or product instead of presenting the selling features.

3. Dialogue and monologue copy—in which the characters illustrated in your direct-mail piece do the selling in their own words (testimonials, pseudo-testimonials, comic strip, and continuity panel).

4. Picture and caption copy—in which the company's story is told by a series of illustrations or photographs and captions rather than by use of a copy block alone.

5. Gimmick copy—unclassified effects, in which the selling power depends upon such things as humor, poetry, foreign words, great exaggeration, gags, and other trick devices.

While company memos and reports, editorial, technical, publicity, and other kinds of writing may have a variety of purposes, the main purposes of a direct-mail piece is to provide information and persuade the reader to buy.

There is a logical order to persuasive writing that carries the reader to the point of favorable action. Various authorities on the art of persuasion have advanced numerous formulas for this process, but they are all fundamentally variations on a relatively simple theory often used by advertising copywriters—AIDA.

The AIDA theory suggests that in order to persuade, an advertisement must first attract *Attention,* then create *Interest,* next stimulate *Desire,* and finally get *Action.*

To persuade people to buy, it is essential first to grab their attention. Getting attention can start even before the recipient opens the envelope. Many companies use attention-grabbing copy on the address panel of the envelope such as "Contains important information concerning your federal taxes," or "Time dated material enclosed." Techniques that can be used to get attention include: news, curiosity, conflict, humor, analogy, history, and shock.

A word of caution about attention-getting devices. Attention is a means of attracting readers to read the whole message. Therefore, these devices should be related to the rest of the information in the piece. The reader whose attention is attracted by a headline, only to find that it has little or no relation to the rest of the mailer, is apt to be resentful. Using an illustration of a scantily clad girl in an advertisement for office furniture will disappoint the reader, who may lose interest in the copy or think it is in bad taste, and that becomes a negative reflection on the advertiser.

Because few persons read direct-mail advertisements in their entirety, the attention-getting devices should try to include as many of the other AIDA factors as possible. If a headline, in addition to gaining attention, can also promise some benefit to the consumer and identify the advertiser, it is likely that more people seeing the advertisement will get the message.

Ideally, the attention-getting devices should lead the reader to the body copy and hold their interest. There is no better way of stimulating interest than by appealing to the reader's self-interest. All too often, the writer writes in terms of the company rather than in those of the consumer. The approach needed is what is referred to as the "you" attitude. Consumers are not necessarily interested in how wonderful the company is; they want to know what the product will do for them. Some appeals to readers' emotions that are effective in sustaining interest are:

- Appeals to basic needs—food, drink, sleep, physical health and comfort, and so on.

- Appeals to emotion, feelings, and attitude.

- Appeals to social motives.

Having stimulated interest, the writer's next task is to stimulate the reader's desire for the product. The easiest way to stimulate desire is to show that the product will benefit the reader, and prove it. Again, the emphasis should be on consumer self-interest. Claims may be met with skepticism, so it is necessary to convince the reader that the claims are valid. Not only should they be substantiated, but they must be believable.

No direct-mail advertisement is complete unless it "asks for the order," some kind of action on the part of those experiencing the advertisement. This may be stated directly: "Call right now, toll free." In some cases the call to action is implied in the copy without being explicitly stated. It can be urgent: "This is a limited time sale, get here early!" The copy can ask readers to respond to an 800 telephone number or mail in a coupon. It can suggest they tell or bring a friend.

Good writers never assume they are typical consumers, for by the nature of their role, theirs is a very biased and distorted point of view.

---

## MISTAKE 508

**Writing too lengthy a direct-mail piece.**

### How to Avoid It

There is little question that you must capture and hold your target audience, but the longer that audience has to be held, the more likely you are going to lose it. Copy should be as long as is necessary to tell your story but without unnecessary verbiage.

## MISTAKE 509

**Not using a headline to grab and convince recipients to read further.**

### How to Avoid It

The importance of the few words that make up the headline or opening statement cannot be overestimated. Upon them often falls the task of capturing the attention of the reader and providing the stimulation for the reader to learn more. The gist of the appeal is usually contained in those four or five words, and the effectiveness of the entire direct-mail piece may depend on how well those words are chosen.

There are several types of headlines, including:

▮ The news headline—tells readers something they want to know about the product. Wanting to keep up with the latest developments in any field is a common human trait. The news headline plays upon this desire by telling the reader what is new about the product advertised. Such news should be of real interest to the audience, "Why this house withstood the hurricane and the house next door didn't!"

▮ The advice-and-promise headline—advises the reader to use the product and promises gratifying results if they do. It is essential, of course, that the product fulfill the promise.

▮ The self-interest or "what's in it for me" headline—shows how the product will benefit the user: " Now get 150 channels with a satellite dish that's 1/20th the size and 1/3rd the cost of other dishes."

▮ The curiosity headline—deliberately conceals what the advertisement is all about. The object is to get the audience to want to know more, "Do you race your car engine just before turning it off?" However, if the audience is not challenged to read the copy that follows, it is likely that the advertisement will be completely wasted, for the headline does no selling. Curiosity headlines can be divided into two categories: provocative and dramatic story. Provocative headlines challenge the reader to read on. An example is: "Read how you can send your child through four years of college for only $5,000." The dramatic-story headline appeals to the universal interest in a good story. For example, "Few things in life work better than XYZ."

▮ The selective headline—singles out a particular reader. Such headlines may select the reader through the nature of the subject discussed or by addressing the particular audience. Examples of those headlines selecting an audience because of the nature of the subject include, "Feet Hurt, Burn?" "Now, a better medical plan for people over 55 that promises never to raise premiums!"

Direct-mail specialists disagree as to how long the ideal headline should be. To be sure, a short headline can be grasped more quickly. However, brevity can sacrifice effective statement of an idea. Subheads are additional display lines that provide the transition between the headline and the body copy. They usually amplify the main headline, and because they are generally set in smaller type, they may be considerably longer. The same kind of care must be taken in writing subheads as in writing the headline. The importance of the headline cannot be overstated. If the headline does not do the job it should, the advertisement may be a total waste because the attention and interest of the reader will be lost.

## MISTAKE 510

**Not using clear, easy-to-read-and-understand copy to inform and persuade.**

## MISTAKE 511

**Using dull, repetitive, and uninspired words instead of colorful, lively, convincing words and phrases.**

### How to Avoid Them

Using crisp, clear, vibrant, and colorful wording throughout the piece not only captures attention and holds readers, it also motivates them to buy. Phrases such as:

▮ "Wonderfully practical" instead of "Quite good."

▮ "Dynamic results" instead of "It really works."

▮ "An amazing phenomenon you won't want your family to miss" instead of "An interesting event for the whole family."

Keep in mind that words, sentences, paragraphs, whole compositions—even punctuation marks—have concrete values in real dollars and cents. Take the use of percentages instead of dollar savings in a sale mailer, for example. The recipient will understand "Was $50. Now only $25" better than "Save 50%." Any mistake in the proper selection of words in any kind of advertising can result in severe penalties.

## MISTAKE 512

**Losing readers because the mailer has no visual impact.**

### How to Avoid It

The most brilliantly composed sales letter or direct-mail advertising piece loses its appeal if it doesn't look appealing on the typed or printed page. If spacing, typeface, underlining, or use of bullets is not consistent, for example, it can confuse the reader and make the mailer less effective.

Today's computer programs for word processing and desktop publishing—along with incredible printers—make it easy to produce direct-mail pieces that look sharp and professional.

## MISTAKE 513

**Sending out a direct-mail piece without proofreading for spelling and grammatical errors.**

### How to Avoid It

Never send out anything in writing until it has been proofread for spelling, grammar, and punctuation by you at least two or three times, and by two or three others who can spot mistakes you may have made. Sending out mailers with obvious mistakes makes you and your company look unprofessional, uneducated, sloppy, and unconcerned—and can have an immediate negative effect on readers, including people who could make or break your career.

## MISTAKE 514

**Underutilizing direct mail as a marketing tool.**

## MISTAKE 515

**Believing direct mail must be sent out in large numbers to be effective.**

## MISTAKE 516

**Believing that positive results from direct mail cannot be seen immediately.**

### How to Avoid Them

Many companies are under the impression that selling by mail means sending out huge numbers of expensive brochures, fliers, sales letters, or catalogs. So, to avoid laying out large sums of money for mailers that might well miss the mark, they turn to other methods of reaching prospects and customers, such as telemarketing and print advertising. But the fact is, with markets splintering into smaller segments, each seeking its own customized treatment, mass mailings and other forms of advertising don't make as much economic sense as they once did.

Segmented mailings, on the other hand, give you the power to address each prospect on a one-on-one basis. They can generate immediate responses via postage-paid business-reply cards or 800 toll-free numbers, and they open up opportunities for setting up sales appointments.

Segmented mailings are as effective in business-to-business selling as they are in retail selling. One residential development company we know of sent a mailing to its 8,000-name list of home buyers to announce a referral program that was unique. The mailing offered membership in a special club within the community to anyone who brought in a friend or relative to look at the developer's models. If the friend or relative bought, a sizable donation would be made—in the name of the person who referred the buyer—to their favorite charity. The development now gets nearly 70 percent of its new buyers from referrals.

## MISTAKE 517

**Neglecting to use your list of current customers as a source for additional business.**

### How to Avoid It

Without a doubt, direct mail is more effective with current customers than it is with prospective customers. It is estimated (by many of the direct mail specialists we spoke to) that 48 percent of Americans throw away mail they receive from unknown senders without ever opening it, while those who earn $50,000+ per year throw away an average of 60 percent, and college graduates and influential business-people throw away 70 percent of their mail unopened.

## MISTAKE 518

**Designing direct mail pieces that don't include a letter as part of the offer.**

### How to Avoid It

All too often, companies send out expensive, detailed brochures, fly-ers, and catalogs that feature beautiful pictures and product informa-tion and reminders throughout on how easy it is to order—but no let-ter that personalizes and explains the offer and ties all the elements of the mailing piece together.

According to information gathered from direct-mail users we contacted, in a typical direct-mail package:

■ A letter can account for nearly 75 percent of all possible orders.

■ Brochures alone account for about 25 percent of all possible orders.

■ Order forms account for approximately 10 percent of possible orders.

## MISTAKE 519

**Failing to personalize your direct-mail package with respect to both the sender and the receiver.**

### How to Avoid It

Direct mail is a personal, one-on-one medium and should appear to the reader to have been written just for him. To accomplish this, the writer must focus on the reader's needs and whenever possible (such as when sending sales letters), sprinkle the reader's name as well as "ownership" words throughout the writing. Include as much data-base information about the recipient as you can; it is equally as important to convey a personal message from you to the recipient, signing your name and even showing your picture.

## MISTAKE 520

**Not using visual devices that emphasize key points.**

## How to Avoid It

Visual devices such as underlined, colorized, or circled words or phrases can add urgency and draw attention to key points in your mailer or letter. So can testimonials (with or without pictures) from current customers. Subheads are effective in encouraging recipients to read further. A postscript (P.S.) can be a great attention-getter, too. People find it hard to resist reading the P.S. at the end of a letter, so why not use it to your advantage by stating a vital point you definitely want your reader to notice.

One "visual" that can work against you is when the inside copy of a foldover mailer is upside down. This happens when the sender puts the address on one side and an offer on the back that they assume the reader will see first before opening the mailer. Good luck! Most people open the fold of a mailer from the side with their address, which puts the message inside upside down.

## MISTAKE 521

**Not using legible colors in your mailer.**

## How to Avoid It

Recently, I received three pieces of mail that were perfect examples of how *not* to use color.

One was a flyer with all the copy printed in pale yellow on a white background. It was nearly impossible to read.

The second was an invitation printed with raised, dark-black varnished (shiny) type on a black card. It was very different, but I nearly missed the wedding.

The third was a one-color brochure advertising a seminar. It had lots of pictures of speakers and a photo of food on the buffet table. The entire piece was printed in a teal (bluish-green) color. Needless to say, the people looked ghoulish, and the food didn't look too appetizing either. For practically the same amount of money, using a printing company with a two-color press, all the photos and some of the copy could have been printed in black and the headlines, subheads, and other copy that needed to be emphasized could have been in teal.

Another color mistake many marketers make is printing color on color or using benday (shaded) screens in back of copy. This may be nice for contrast purposes, but not for reading purposes.

When you have a choice, don't use reverse (white) printing. Though it attracts attention, unless the typeface is simple, bold, and without fancy details, and unless the printing is large enough and on a dark enough background, reverse letters can be difficult to read. Sometimes you see travel brochures with reverse copy in a light blue sky. If the background is light gray, blue, or yellow, use a solid dark color rather than reverse.

## MISTAKE 522

**Not using "compelling" or "power" words to describe your offer.**

### How to Avoid It

The words you use in your mailer can make or break its effectiveness. The most compelling words in any mailer are *free* or *extra offer* (such as an introductory discount). Offering a free trial, a free gift, or a free sample encourages responses.

Other "compelling" words and phrases that are proven winners are: *New, Announcing, Introducing, Grand Opening, Fast, Easy, Quick, No Obligation, Money-Back, Guaranteed, Breakthrough, Revolutionary, Unique, Quality, Valuable, Exclusive, Limited Time, You Must Act Now, Here's How Easy It Is to Order.*

Some "power" words that are distinctive and descriptive are: *Alive, Alluring, Bold, Brave, Beguiling, Boundless, Breathtaking, Celebrated, Charismatic, Daring, Dashing, Definitive, Distinguished, Dramatic, Dynamic, Dreamy, Elite, Enriched, Exceptional, Exhilarating, Expressive, Flattering, Fascinating, Glorious, Gracious, Gadabout, Heavenly, Heady, Haunting, Hip, Hot, Jazzy, Idyllic, Illustrious, Immaculate, Impeccable, Imaginative, Inspiring, Inventive, Irresistible, Joyous, Knockout, Kicky, Keen, Kinky, Landmark, Lasting, Legendary, Lively, Logical, Notable, Opulent, Outrageous, Panache, Passionate, Peerless, Persuasive, Picturesque, Poetic, Poised, Practical, Praiseworthy, Precise, Premium, Prestigious, Pristine, Pure, Purposeful, Peppy, Priceless, Provocative, Qualified, Quintessential, Razzle-dazzle, Radiant, Refined, Resplendent, Responsive, Romantic, Regal, Satisfying, Scintillating, Sensational, Sensuous, Sophisticated, Sleek, Solid, Splendid, Tailored, Timeless, Turbocharged, Tantalizing, Uncommon, Unconventional, Understated, Unmistakable, Unparalleled, Vivid, Vibrant, Visionary, Voluptuous, Wonderful, Zesty, Zippy, Zingy.*

Don't go overboard with superlatives. They are likely to generate skepticism. If you claim your offering is best, fastest, or least expensive, be prepared to back it up.

## MISTAKE 523

**Using multiple messages and rambling language that seem never to get to the point.**

### How to Avoid It

Most recipients of direct mail will scan the contents rather than read every word, so don't clutter up the piece with too many messages. Keep it simple, uncomplicated, easy to read and to understand. Write as if you are talking to the prospect. Use contractions such as "We're" and "They're," and connecter words to start sentences such as "And" and "But." It's the way people really talk.

## MISTAKE 524

**Not anticipating the recipient's questions.**

### How to Avoid It

Successful mailers anticipate questions—and answer them. For example, if your mailer is for a men's clothing sale, specify what kinds of clothing (suits, shirts, sports coats, slacks, accessories), how much the savings are (regular price and sale price), how long the sale will last, and any restrictions (minimum charge for alterations that are normally free).

## MISTAKE 525

**Not giving a reason for the mailing.**

### How to Avoid It

Successful mailers also give a reason for the mailing, which gives credibility to the promotion. Using a headline such as "Everything Must Be Sold" does not say why as much as "Going out of Business—Everything Must Be Sold by October 10th!"

## MISTAKE 526

**Not giving ordering and payment choices.**

## How to Avoid It

You would be surprised how many mailers go out that give the recipient only one way to order and never mention payment choices. The more choices a prospect has, the more likely she is to buy. Choices can include ordering by reply card, in person, by phone, or by fax. Payment choices can include charge, credit card, cash, check, layaway. Don't be bashful about giving precise instructions and making it easy to follow them, such as "Call our 24-hour toll-free number and order now—operators are standing by."

## MISTAKE 527

**Using literal translations when sending a mailing out in languages other than English.**

## How to Avoid It

Taking a well-written, effective English-language idea and making it just as effective in another language is not always as easy as it may seem. Most marketers will simply take the idea to a translation service that in most cases will translate literally. Instead, it is important to find a translator who understands the idioms, expressions, nuances, dialects, and double meanings of the language you will be using.

The fact is, according to a brochure "The Trans-Creator," published by Ghost Writers, creative writing consultants and language specialists in Miami, even "Among English-speaking countries like England, America and Australia, the language is 'separated by a common tongue.' The same is true of Spanish speaking countries. The language of Cuba, Spain, Mexico, Puerto Rico and many South American nations is Spanish. But each has its own regional colloquialisms."

I will never forget an experience I had when an advertising client asked my ad agency to produce an elaborate brochure for his very expensive apartments—in English and four other languages. We were able to find professional copywriters to do the Italian, Spanish, and French translations, but had to use a translation service for the German version.

A few weeks later, the developer of the building sent a sales team to Germany to make a presentation to an investment banking group. As they went through the features of the apartments listed in the brochure, they got to the description of entering the "overwhelming and exhilarating living room with its scintillating appointments and breathtaking views." What sounded wonderful in English translated literally in German to "When you enter the living room you will have an orgasm." The group of stodgy German bankers didn't think it was funny. Needless to say, it took a lot of explaining to make that sale.

"The point is," says Don Rincones, founder and president of Ghost Writers, "literal translations are just that. And when you entrust your precious mailer copy to a professional translator, or to a secretary or friend who speaks or is familiar with the particular language you are interested in, all they will do is exchange words, not communicate feelings, emotions or ideas. Words or colloquial phrases can mean one thing in English and something very different in another language." And mistakes in cultural interpretation can result in recipients who are confused, amused, turned off, or even insulted. Rincones suggests, "Find someone who can translate your intent, not just your words."

## FOUR COMMON MISTAKES IN USING DIGITAL MAILERS

Sometimes called "digital mailers" or "digital brochures," CD-ROMs and diskettes have become popular new media for communicating sophisticated electronic marketing, sales, promotional, and advertising messages. By utilizing computer technology, including such attributes as random access, interactivity, sound, and motion, these innovative, high-tech marketing tools go beyond the impact of traditional print communication and provide more information in a more useful and appealing format.

## MISTAKE 528

**Assuming what works creatively and persuasively on paper will also work in the digital medium.**

### HOW TO AVOID IT

Simply scanning a brochure or other printed material into a computer, rearranging the elements, adding music, voice, and motion is not enough for creating an effective digital brochure. Producing mailers in the digital format is more like producing commercials for the television format. Consideration should be given to visuals, lighting, motion, special visual effects, sound, and how they all relate to and tie-in with the content and purpose of the finished piece.

There are various types of digital mailers, including:

▮ Information mailers—electronic slide presentations on disk that typically use simple text and images and run like a commercial. Some incorporate basic branching, which is analogous to turning the pages of a printed brochure.

▮ Multimedia mailers—employ sound, animation, text, graphics, even video, and have a greater degree of interactivity.

▮ Marketing mailers—similar to information mailers with some multimedia elements. Can incorporate programming that provides interactivity such as rate calculations, customer profiling, custom product recommendations, and other functions.

▮ Sales mailers—are more sophisticated CD-ROMs with greater storage capacity. They often incorporate an in-depth database with pricing information, product specifications, electronic ordering, and other functions that assist the sales process.

▮ Network solutions—are fully integrated sales presentation solutions that link to networks for updates. They function as sophisticated electronic catalog sales facilitators and sometimes as integrated interactive training systems. They are not suited for large mailings because hard drive downloading is required.

## MISTAKE 529

**Overlooking content as a criteria for using digital mailers.**

### How to Avoid It

If the message (and visuals) to be conveyed is relatively short, there is little if any justification for the time and expense of making a digital production. But when there is lengthy, complex, or conceptually difficult information, one of the more effective ways of presenting it is in a disk-based format.

Recent studies show that viewers of diskettes and CD-ROMs spend an average of 20 to 25 minutes watching presentations. The more interesting and entertaining the presentation, the longer the recipient will be willing to watch. Therefore, if the content is basically something simple like "We make a better gizmo," a 20-minute digital production would be obvious overkill. However, if you are introducing a product or service that needs in-depth explanation or demonstration, digital delivery gives you the extra time and multimedia elements you need to present your story in greater detail.

## MISTAKE 530

**Rushing to produce a digital presentation without knowing the playback capabilities of the target audience.**

### How to Avoid It

With all the new (and noncompatible) technology emerging so quickly, it is essential to know the playback capabilities of your target audience *before* you invest in a costly digital production. Creating a mailer that few recipients will be able to view will result in wasted effort and dollars. There is also the possibility that recipients will not have the necessary computer technology to play back a multimedia presentation properly, which could create a negative impression of the product or service being promoted.

To avoid wasted mailings, and to be sure your target audience will be able to play back your digital mailer, send an inexpensive printed direct-response mailing to your prospects in advance of producing the presentation. Announce the availability of the presentation and clearly explain the system requirements to view it properly. Ask those with proper equipment who are interested in receiving it to respond by mail or phone. You might ask all who receive the advance mailer to specify what technology they have so you can decide on the format that will best serve the majority of prospects.

Of course, you could always create a presentation to run on the lowest-denominator equipment and hope for the best.

## MISTAKE 531

**Producing a digital presentation without relating its goals to your overall sales and marketing strategy.**

### How to Avoid It

Producing a technically distinctive digital mailer just to be impressive or because "it's the thing that everyone's doing" may not benefit your overall sales and marketing goals.

You must first determine what you expect a digital mailer to accomplish in relation to those goals. Will the mailer provide complex product information or in-depth instruction? Will it generate sales or leads? Is it designed just to create awareness? Does it tie in with other promotional, marketing, and sales objectives? If the mailer is strictly for demonstration purposes, for instance, a simple animated presentation may be all that is needed. If conveying a high-tech image is the objective, you will want a more elaborate presentation.

The digital mailer should not be an isolated promotion. Once you decide on the purpose of the presentation, you must determine if and how it will relate to all your other sales and marketing efforts.

∎ Can the elements created for this digital presentation be reused and updated easily?

∎ Can they be interrelated with your present advertising, public relations, online services, or training programs?

If your marketing objective is very narrow, digital mailers may not be the ideal medium to use. If the various attributes of a digital presentation fit multiple sales and marketing goals, however, you will find this medium highly adaptable, excitingly different, and probably very effective in reaching those goals.

# Chapter 20

# SPEECHES, SALES PRESENTATIONS, SHOWS, AND SHOWROOMS

According to national surveys conducted by R. H. Bruskin Associates on what people fear most, the fear of death, sickness, plane crashes, heights, lack of money, loneliness, spiders, snakes, and deep water all came in far behind the fear of speaking or presenting before an audience.

While many successful businesspeople have no trouble communicating their ideas in writing, visually, on the telephone, even on video tape, they become terrified at the thought of making a speech or a presentation, whether it is to a handful or a hallfull of people.

## TWO MISTAKES IN COPING WITH STAGE FRIGHT, PLATFORM JITTERS, AND BUTTERFLIES

Stage fright, platform jitters, butterflies, pounding heart, tightening throat that seems to cut off your voice, loss of confidence—most speakers and presenters get them, whether they are veterans of public speaking or first-timers. And many people can never get rid of them. I know some top entertainers who, after 40 and 50 years of appearing in front of huge audiences, still tremble at the thought of walking onstage and performing.

### MISTAKE 532

Not understanding what may be causing the problem.

## How to Avoid It

Typically, people are fearful of making presentations for a number of reasons, including:

∎ Fear of failure—of not living up to your own, and the audience's, expectations.

∎ Lack of confidence—especially when speaking about or presenting a topic that is new or unfamiliar to you.

∎ Inadequate preparation—winging it when you don't have the time to thoroughly prepare for it.

∎ Poor self-image—feeling that you don't look or sound good.

∎ The "fight or flight" body response syndrome—a form of physiological stress that can be traced back to our Neanderthal ancestors.

## MISTAKE 533

**Not trying to control and manage your fear.**

## How to Avoid It

Whether the reasons are real or imaginary, the fear is definitely there. Now it must be managed and overcome so it won't cause your audience to be distracted or lose respect for your credibility or competency. Here are seven steps you can take:

1. *Focus* on positive thoughts and push the negative stressful thoughts out of your head. Look ahead to the end result you want and work backwards to achieve it. Believe that the audience really wants you to succeed and that they envy you for being able to stand up and talk in front of strangers. Visualize them giving you a standing ovation and calling you for weeks afterward to tell you how great you were.

2. *Be confident.* Confidence comes from knowing what works—and from experience. Experience is solidified in three ways: knowing your material cold; knowing yourself and how you come across; and having a clear, focused point of view. To help you achieve confidence:

   A. Volunteer to make a presentation whenever the situation arises or make your own opportunities. Find out when the next meeting, convention, presentation is coming up and play a part in it.

B. Practice in front of people—family, friends, coworkers.

C. Stand up in your own meetings, deliver reports and updates.

D. Don't panic when you feel nervous; it's normal. Just increase your interest in giving your audience the best of your experience and knowledge.

3. *Prepare.* Working backwards from the date of the event, set deadlines for completing the preparatory tasks required. Allow time for research, writing, and practicing your talk. Set aside time for rehearsals and for trying out audiovisual equipment. Analyze the group you'll be talking to. Determine what information and how detailed an explanation of it your audience will need. Talk to key audience members to reassure yourself about the suitability of your comments. Be organized, clear, and concise in terms of the content of your presentation.

4. *Practice.* You may have heard this timeworn joke before, "How do you get to Carnegie Hall?" Answer: "Practice, practice, practice." While practice doesn't always make perfect, it does make for a better presentation. Practicing the way you'll actually deliver your presentation—out loud, standing up, in the actual room, with the actual equipment and visuals, going through the movements and gestures you'll be making, saying the words you'll be using, pretending there's an audience—is the way professionals make it look so easy and natural.

5. *Polish your delivery.* Make your presentation dynamic and interesting. Look and sound competent, credible, convincing, and comfortable. Use short sentences and simple words that allow you to breathe naturally while speaking. Avoid technical terms. Translate complex ideas into everyday language. Inject anecdotes and humor, especially as part of the introduction or conclusion. But don't tell jokes if you're not comfortable doing so. Take out any language that could be interpreted as being in bad taste.

6. *Psych up.* Just as athletes warm up, actors get into their characters, and musicians tune up, presenters should too. Before going on, give your vocal cords a little workout by reciting some of your dialogue. Stretch your arms and legs and roll your head from side to side to relieve any neck or muscle tension. Take deep breaths. Some people eat chocolate before a presentation because it produces natural endorphins in the body that can relieve stress. You might try closing your eyes and imagining yourself in a warm bathtub. Visualize the water swirling down

the drain taking all your anxiety with it. Once you step onto the platform, look at the audience and tell yourself how great you're going to be. If you feel anxiety before you begin talking, imagine that the fear is a closed rosebud. Picture the petals spreading and the anxiety dissipating as the rose opens to full bloom. Then smile at your audience, start talking and have fun.

7. *Remember*—it doesn't matter how you feel while making your presentation. What matters is what the audience sees and hears. So while the techniques mentioned here probably won't cure your fear, they will help you manage and overcome it so you look and sound terrific to your audience.

## SEVENTEEN MISTAKES IN MAKING A SALES PRESENTATION

Most businesses have the need for a steady, ongoing supply of new customers. Unless your business has a storefront, new customers will seldom walk through the door. One effective way of getting new business is to present your company credentials to qualified prospects via person-to-person communication or, as they say in the business world, make a sales pitch. Every presentation starts with people—the personalities of those who represent your company, the feelings of mutual respect and trust they generate, and the way they relate to the people they are presenting to. Today, more than ever, personal communication is high on the requirement list for success in business. Let's look at the most common mistakes made by individuals in the course of making a pitch, whether it is to another individual or to a group.

## MISTAKE 534

**Not finding out as much as you can about your audience.**

### How to Avoid It

You are probably making the presentation because you know something about the subject of the presentation. Still, it helps to find out about your audience first:

▌ Whom are you preparing your presentation for?

∎ How old are they?

∎ What is the gender distribution?

∎ What is the educational level?

∎ Why are they there?

∎ What are they interested in?

∎ What's the size of the audience? If you prepare for an audience of 30 and 300 attend, you may not have enough handouts and your visuals may be too small to see.

∎ How much do they already know about your subject?

∎ What is the attitude of the audience toward you and the subject matter?

∎ Do they support your beliefs? Or are they uninformed, apathetic, hostile?

The better you know your audience, the more opportunity you have of tailoring your presentation to them. Chances are, you already know something about them because:

∎ Based on the topic of your presentation, most of the people will probably come from similar backgrounds: business, industry, education, and the like.

∎ They have come to hear what you have to say, so you share their interests and concerns.

∎ They have come to get your help in improving their businesses or their lives in some way—to sell more, produce faster, cut costs, be more creative, manage better. In short, to be more effective at what they do.

Before you can put together a good presentation, you must look at your material from the point of view of those you will be talking to. They will be asking:

∎ What is this person talking about?

∎ Why should I care?

∎ What will it do for me?

∎ How can I be sure it will work?

## MISTAKE 535

**Not planning what you'll say and show.**

### How to Avoid It

Here is where you must do your homework.

The more you sweat in advance, the less you'll have to sweat on stage. Collect your data. Even though you may be the expert on the subject, you may not have all the information you need. Putting down what you know on paper will help you identify where the holes in the information are and where you need to research. Research your topic thoroughly. Check the library for facts, quotes, books, and timely magazine and newspaper articles you may refer to. Get in touch with other experts in your field. Get their opinions to help round out your material.

Now start organizing and writing. Outline the main points. Gather supporting information. Design an imaginative, energetic introduction that will catch the audience's attention and arouse their interest. This is important because an audience makes up its mind quickly, and once its mood is set, it is difficult to change. Make sure your introduction previews the subject. In the main body, establish what's in it for them and establish yourself as a credible source. Try to be entertaining, instructive, persuasive, and inspiring. The close is where you should "ask for the order." An ending should incorporate a sentence or two that sounds like an ending—a short summary of the main points of the presentation or the repeat of a phrase that most embodies what you hoped to convey. Plan the audio and visual aids you will use and where and how you will use them.

## MISTAKE 536

**Inhibiting your physical energy.**

### How to Avoid It

The secret to relaxing in front of groups is to be as comfortable and natural as you are when you are conversing. Use your natural gestures. Your hands can emphasize and clarify points.

## MISTAKE 537

**Not sounding spontaneous.**

## How to Avoid It

The best presenters are those who make their words sound spontaneous, even if memorized (which is not the best of ideas). It's best to practice a presentation point by point, not word for word. Careful preparation and a good deal of rehearsal will make it all come together smoothly and easily. Pace yourself to a conversational tempo.

Make sure your posture is right. Good posture is essential for breathing, gesturing, and the nonverbal message of confidence you'll be communicating. Stand with your weight evenly distributed. If you're seated, sit up and forward in your chair. Relax your voice. Nervousness constricts the vocal muscles. Speak slowly, distinctly, and resonantly; talking in an artificially fast, high-pitched manner will reveal your nervousness. If your normal speaking voice is soft, don't hesitate to use a microphone. Avoid "ums" and "ahs" by pausing occasionally.

## MISTAKE 538

**Making a poor first impression.**

## How to Avoid It

Tape your presentation on a cassette and listen to yourself. Do you talk more slowly than you thought? Do you talk in one tone? Monitor how you speak when you are in a comfortable conversation and use those elements in your presentations.

## MISTAKE 539

**Staying frozen in one spot.**

## How to Avoid It

Move when you talk. There is nothing as boring as an inanimate presenter. Keep your legs relaxed and flexible. Moving helps release nervous energy. If there's a lectern, try to move away from it to break down the barrier between you and the audience.

## MISTAKE 540

**Not making eye contact with the audience.**

## How to Avoid It

Maintain steady eye communication with individuals in the audience. Pick out a few people, ask their names, and direct questions to them from time to time.

## MISTAKE 541

**Being dull, dry, and boring.**

## How to Avoid It

Use your sense of humor. Treat your subject seriously; take yourself lightly. Don't break your stride waiting for laughs.

## MISTAKE 542

**Not checking your grammar.**

## How to Avoid It

Consult a dictionary for proper meanings and pronunciations. Your audience won't know if you're a bad speller, but they will know if you use or pronounce a word improperly.

## MISTAKE 543

**Not dressing comfortably.**

## How to Avoid It

Tight, new shoes, for example, could cause unnecessary anxiety and distraction if they are pinching your feet.

## MISTAKE 544

**Making things more complicated than they are.**

## How to Avoid It

Here are five surefire ways to avoid this:

1. Stay focused on your point of view.

2. Keep each subject short, making your point and moving on. According to the Northwestern School of Speech, the attention span of an audience is approximately nine seconds.

3. Use audio and visual aids (such as video tapes, flip charts, or slides) only if they enhance your presentation, and keep them simple.

4. Repeat your key points—most people won't remember more than two or three—emphasize those and toss out distracting side issues. Don't assume everyone is listening attentively.

5. Stay within the time expectation of your audience.

## MISTAKE 545

**Lack of preparation.**

## MISTAKE 546

**Misjudging your time.**

### HOW TO AVOID THEM

Great speakers are not born that way, so plan to prepare, but do it right. Good preparation compensates for lack of talent and gives you confidence. People respond to, and remember most, how we say something. So you must prepare yourself along with your message.

Content alone will not carry you. Here are nine steps to take:

1. Don't delay—begin the thinking process well in advance of your next pitch.

2. Prepare yourself to speak. Start polishing your skills by volunteering at community and business groups, taking a seminar, joining a club or association.

3. Jot down notes, clip magazine and newspaper articles, keep track of current ideas that relate to your subject and make you look as if you're up on the latest trends.

4. Organize the salient points (not the full text) of your presentation and jot them down on 3 x 5 inch reference cards (using bulleted words or pictures) that you can refer to once you begin addressing your audience. Don't try to memorize your entire

speech word for word and don't expect to read it verbatim from sheets of paper. Make sure you integrate any visual aids you will be using.

5. Rehearse, rehearse, rehearse. Do it in front of others, on audio tape, on video tape. Get feedback. Rehearse three, four, even five times. You want to appear spontaneous and organized, not memorized. If possible, rehearse in the room you'll actually use. You'll be more comfortable when you do the real presentation.

6. Time your presentation. People in your audience have other things to do, and throwing them off schedule can lose you points. Staying within a reasonable time limit is both considerate and businesslike. Remember that your actual presentation time will run about 20 percent longer than your rehearsal time, so consider that fact when setting your time limit.

7. Psych yourself up well ahead of making the presentation. Keep thinking of yourself in action as the world's greatest expert on the material you are presenting, having a good time, giving people useful, interesting information. You'll end up looking and sounding the part.

8. Find out all you can about the group you will be speaking to ahead of time. Then tailor your ideas, humor, and examples to meet those interests.

9. Keep changing the pace of your presentation. Pacing can be the key to a more effective presentation, and if nothing else, it shows your creativity. Varying the visual media (for example, alternating use of an overhead projector and a large-screen video) and having male and female staffers take turns delivering materials can add punch and enthusiasm and make your audience members feel that you're excited about getting their business.

## MISTAKE 547

**Neglecting the importance of visuals.**

### How to Avoid It

If you want to communicate a fully dimensional message, the old adage "a picture is worth a thousand words" applies. Just be sure they are the right pictures for maximum memorability and effectiveness. Here are five things you can do:

1. Develop graphs, picture symbols, size comparisons, diagrams, and key words to emphasize your ideas.

2. Choose the right visual medium. Flip charts are okay for small groups and can be self-drawn. Be sure they are large and bold enough to be read in the back of the room. Overhead projectors can be used with large or small groups, and a big advantage they have over slide projectors is that you can keep the room lights on. Slides and/or big-screen video are best for formal, structured presentations in which visual professionalism is important.

3. Make *yourself* a visual aid. Use your face, arms, hands, and fingers to illustrate your points.

4. Use action verbs, color words, taste, sound, touch, and emotional-feeling words to stimulate pictures.

5. Use physical demos, examples, samples, or physical analogies to extend and embody your message.

## MISTAKE 548

**Neglecting to use current technology to improve your presenting abilities.**

### How to Avoid It

In this age of interactivity and video teleconferencing, all businesspersons have the opportunity to see and hear themselves as others do. There's no reason to lack confidence or feel ineffective as a speaker. Here are three simple steps to take:

1. Record your presentations, conversations, and phone calls on audio and video tape as often as you can. Listen to and watch yourself in everyday situations. Get feedback from family, friends, and associates.

2. Record as many video tapes as you can of your favorite entertainers, newscasters, politicians, and speakers. You might want to include people who are not your favorites, too.

3. Start a library of these tapes. As you play back and study them, make lists of positives—the words, gestures, facial expressions, posture, movement, and other points that you have that you can improve on—as well as others that capture your interest and that you feel you can emulate. Notice their hands. How they

register key points. Listen to the range of their voices. Pay particular attention to the length of their sentences. How they close. Make a similar list of the negatives you spot. Be sensitive to the mistakes you see and work on correcting or avoiding them.

## MISTAKE 549

**Using copyrighted materials without permission.**

## MISTAKE 550

**Negotiating for the use of copyrighted properties yourself.**

### How to Avoid Them

Well, it's over. You've just made the greatest multimedia computer presentation of all time. Your audience loved the special effects in your E.T. video clip. The Nat King Cole version of "When I Fall In Love," was exactly the right music to open and close with. Your animated Charlie Chaplin doing his funny walk around the screen helped emphasize all the important points you wanted to make, and using the Porky Pig cartoon ending, "Ttthat's all ffffolk's!" was perfect. The audience was charmed by your ingenuity and wit, dazzled by the electrifying technology. It was the presentation to end all presentations, a day you'll never forget. You thought you'd never get off cloud nine—until the next morning when you found out you were being sued by the estates of two departed performers and a couple of giant corporations.

The first mistake you made is a very common mistake thousands of people make—using copyrighted properties of composers, authors, and artists without first getting permission. It makes no difference that you were not deriving monetary benefits from someone else's creative efforts and were using the music and visuals only to jazz up your sales presentation. Here are some suggestions if you intend to use existing copyrighted properties:

▮ Find out if it's necessary to obtain permission. If the copyright on a particular property has expired, it enters the public domain and can be used without permission or restriction.

▮ If a copyrighted property is not in the public domain, you will have to find the owners of the property and get their permission. If a popular song is involved, for example, you will have to identify the music publisher (usually mentioned in album liner notes or on sheet music) and then contact either Broadcast Music, Inc. (BMI) or the American Society of Composers, Authors & Publishers (ASCAP), for help in identifying and contacting copyright holders. To secure permission to use published photos or artwork, you will have to track down the original source of the material. Start by contacting the publication you saw it in. If they don't own the rights, they can tell you where they obtained permission for use. Current news photos, for instance, may have been licensed from a news service such as the Associated Press. Graphic art may belong to the artist that created it or to the publication in which you saw it. Sometimes the name of the copyright holder appears next to the image in small print.

- You may have to pay a fee, per-unit royalty, or some other compensation depending on how you are using the material, how many people will see it, and how you are benefiting from it.

- Additional releases may be needed if you are using the likeness (including caricatures and animated versions) of celebrities or private individuals, dead or alive. You may also need a release for photographs that show personal property, such as a private home. Though you might think that reproducing a centuries-old piece of fine art is okay because it must be in the public domain, you will probably have to get permission from the museum or other entity that owns and displays it. Obtaining film and TV rights can be both complicated and expensive. You will have to negotiate with the studio or network that owns the property and with all the performers, writers, directors, guilds, and trade unions involved in the sequence you want to use.

- If you have any doubts about whether something is copyrighted, don't use it.

The alternatives to using copyrighted properties include:

- Purchasing royalty-free "clip media," collections of photos, music, and video clips that can be incorporated into a presentation or multimedia production without additional payment or permission. These materials are available on CD-ROM as well as from news archives and stock photo, illustration, and film services.

▌ Create your own graphics, animation, and special effects. Take your own photos or have them taken by a professional for a flat, one-time fee. Make sure you get releases from all persons who appear in the photos.

If you will use very well known copyrighted properties, or any copyrighted properties on a regular basis, or you want to incorporate them into a major presentation or promotional effort, you would be wise to hire an attorney who specializes in copyright and contract law or a rights-clearance service, rather than handle it yourself.

A rights-clearance service can locate copyright holders and negotiate prices on your behalf. For a relatively small fee, the U.S. Copyright Office or the Library of Congress in Washington, D.C., can also identify the owners of copyrighted properties and advise you if a property is in the public domain.

One quick story about copyrights that might provide another interesting alternative.

A publisher planning to run two million copies of a book about Franklin D. Roosevelt, contacted various sources to obtain photographs of Roosevelt and others that were needed in the book. The cost was prohibitive. Even more prohibitive was the penalty set by copyright law for using those pictures without permission: about one dollar per copy.

Instead, a creative executive at the publishing company came up with a unique idea. He ran small ads in nationally distributed newspapers and magazines announcing: "Major company publishing two million copies of revealing new Franklin D. Roosevelt book. Great publicity opportunity for anyone with pictures of Roosevelt and others taken during his last term as President. What will you pay us to use your photos and get acknowledgment in the book?"

At least one reply came back: "Thanks for the opportunity. I have twelve great pictures but can't pay you more than $200 total. If that's agreeable, we've got a deal."

---

## THREE MISTAKES IN GETTING YOUR AUDIENCE TO ABSORB YOUR MESSAGE

---

While young minds are like sponges, absorbing information in all shapes and forms, adult minds are often cluttered with thoughts of mortgage payments, overdue business proposals, a slump in sales. When adults walk into a presentation room, they already have countless demands on their time and attention, which can make it difficult for them to absorb the new information you will present.

## MISTAKE 551

**Not considering or understanding what it takes for the adult mind to absorb and retain information.**

## MISTAKE 552

**Underestimating the audience's motivation for attending the presentation and their desire to learn.**

### How to Avoid Them

While today's generation of business audiences is without a doubt the most highly educated, most presentations fail to challenge them or hold their interest. Based on new studies by educators, management consultants, and psychologists, many companies now orchestrate their presentations with a nod to the principles of adult learning.

After asking a number of sales management consultants and companies that frequently make sales presentations what they thought it takes for an adult business audience to absorb and retain information from a presentation, we came up with six points to consider:

1. Adults value information that relates to their experiences.

2. They have diverse learning styles; what works for one may not work for another.

3. They respond best to solution-based information that is presented in an interesting way and can be directly applied to their lives.

4. They need to be active participants in the learning process rather than passive recipients of data.

5. They learn through interaction with other adults.

6. They want feedback.

One company we interviewed told us they sometimes interview attendees before a presentation to discuss in detail what they expect to come away with. They also try to research the purchasing history and business needs of each attendee to get a baseline understanding of who's coming and how they can make sure the presentation meets the audience's needs. They often kick off their presentations with an attention-getter, such as a mind game. Then, to keep the audience's interest, the presenter uses a number of educational tools—quizzes, games, videos—to provide valuable information and involve the audience in the process. They have also found that well-timed breaks allow audience members to digest new facts between sessions.

## MISTAKE 553

**Introducing new ideas in your finish.**

### How to Avoid It

Introducing new ideas at the close of your presentation is like a lawyer bringing up new evidence in his closing argument. It's too late to do any good and will only confuse your audience.

## SEVENTEEN MISTAKES IN USING HIGH- AND LOW-TECH VISUAL AIDS

The worst visual aid is no visual aid.

You don't have to be an artist to use images that can add impact to your presentation, not when there are so many devices and techniques to use. Today's offerings range from discussion blackboards to computerized electronic extravaganzas. The questions are: What's best for you? What's best for your audience? What will suit your purpose best?

Creativity, though, is the secret element in every audio-visual presentation that's exciting. Slide presentations, in particular, need all the creativity they can get: good photography, a great music track, strong narration, and superior sound effects as well. When you mix these elements successfully, you come up with a slide presentation filled with pizzazz.

On the low-tech end, slides are best for formal, structured presentations in which full visual professionalism is important.

## MISTAKE 554

**Making multiple points on a single slide.**

## How to Avoid It

Make one point per slide. If you put ten points on a slide, your audience is going to jump ahead of you. Slides enable you to focus the attention of your audience on a single thought or idea.

Please, never use more than ten words per slide. Slides should be regarded as billboards. They are not pages in a text. Make your words as big as your ideas. With ten words or less per slide, you can give your words some size. They'll be easier to read and they'll look important.

Slides should trigger your thoughts. They are not substitutes for scripts. Too many presenters dutifully read slides as they appear, slide after slide after slide.

## MISTAKE 555

**Not varying the look and content of your slides.**

## How to Avoid It

Don't make every slide look like every other slide. Surprise your audience. Vary the content: words, charts, simple graphs, cartoons, photographs. Don't always do the expected.

Slides are a visual medium. If you use pictures to pick up your slides, don't assume you have to label or title everything you show. If you're showing a spreadsheet, use a horizontal slide. If you're showing a tall building, use a vertical slide.

## MISTAKE 556

**Cluttering a slide with statistics.**

## How to Avoid It

Lots of statistics on a slide are a surefire turnoff. Most charts and graphs can be simplified. Long rows of figures and statistically overpowering graphs, for instance, will cause most audiences to lose interest. Give every slide a focal point. The bigger the message looks, the better the response. Use color functionally, for emphasis, not ornamentation. Color for color's sake is an extravagance.

## MISTAKE 557

**Changing slides too fast—or too slowly.**

## How to Avoid It

Operate the slides at a pace that gives you the absolute freedom to say exactly what you want to say about each slide, then move on to the next one.

Don't leave a slide on screen after you have discussed it. Never have a subject on the screen that doesn't correspond to what you are saying. It splits attention in two.

## MISTAKE 558

**Not checking slides for their order and proper placement in the projector.**

## How to Avoid It

Know what's coming up next. Don't stand there with egg on your face when slides suddenly appear upside down, backwards—or both. Rehearse with everything exactly as it will be. Say every word. Make every move. Don't leave anything to chance. This is the most important—and most often violated—principle of persuasive presentation.

## MISTAKE 559

**Adding commentary that does not appear on the slide you are showing.**

## How to Avoid It

If you read the words on the slide, read them word for word. Don't rephrase the wording. Don't inject new thoughts. Read the slide exactly as it appears. After you have read the slide, you can add commentary of your own.

Another often used low-tech visual aid is the flip chart.

## MISTAKE 560

**Not making cards large enough to be read in the back of the room.**

## MISTAKE 561

**Not allowing more time for flip cards than you might for slides.**

---

## MISTAKE 562

**Not disposing of flip cards in a nondistracting way.**

---

## MISTAKE 563

**Using your finger instead of a pointer.**

### How to Avoid Them

Flip charts work for small groups and can be self-drawn. Make them bold enough to be read in the back of the room. Here are seven other fundamentals to keep in mind:

1.  The lights will be on. Plan for more comments from your audience. Cards stimulate conversation. So allow for more time to show cards and charts than you would for slides.

2.  Be simple, telegraphic. Generally, the same design rudiments that create good slides also produce good cards and charts. One thought or idea per card. Make sure your cards are large enough for everyone to read easily. Use the cards as thought joggers for yourself. Don't just stand there and read. Vary your cards. Surprises are spice—and hold attention. Use color, but sparingly.

3.  Cards are bulky. Plan to get rid of them gracefully. There's nothing more amateurish than a presenter who presents a splendid posterior view every time he or she bends over to put away a card or a chart. The secret: Don't bend over. Dispose of cards by placing them behind the cards you have yet to show (if you are using an easel). Or, place them on a nearby rack or stand at the same level as your other boards.

4.  Arrange your lighting. Make sure your cards are positioned in a pool of light. This is a touch of theater that can make a significant difference in the "atmosphere" surrounding your presentation.

5.  Consider using a pointer. A pointer has two distinct advantages. It makes you look professional, and it enables you to "get involved" without your cards getting in the way.

6.  Write notes to yourself on the cards if your memory needs help. Keep them on the side from which you are operating.

7. An advantage of cards is that they can be placed around a room to reprise a thought sequence you want to register—or they can demonstrate a variety of ways to execute an idea. Example: The potential of an advertising campaign idea can be vividly demonstrated by putting a lot of headlines on separate cards and surrounding your audience with them.

Now let's look at today's high-tech methods of making a presentation.

As you read these words, businesspeople throughout the nation are preparing presentations in their offices and homes, on airplanes, in hotel rooms, even in the back seats of taxicabs. They're generating snappy bullet charts, graphs and diagrams, electronic screen-shows, handouts, and speaker notes—all from a single file on their laptop computers, just minutes before they present them to an audience.

Today's presenters are bypassing the tried-and-true flip charts, overhead transparencies, and 35mm slides, and instead are creating visuals on faster, lighter-weight, more powerful computers with easy-to-use software that incorporates special effects, sound, photography, and animation for a more electrifying presentation that not only can save them time and money, but can also be projected directly from their computers to nearly any size audience.

But while all this up-to-the-minute technology offers versatility, quick updating, low cost, and dynamic impact, it does not guarantee that the presentations produced will be successful. It is still the presenter who must make the message memorable and secure the sale. It is still the presenter who must know how to harness and tame the technology to fit the unique requirements of each presentation.

## MISTAKE 564

**Getting so enamored with the technology you forget the reason for the presentation.**

## MISTAKE 565

**Letting the medium get in the way of the message.**

## MISTAKE 566

**Using a presenter without the professional and technical skills needed for a high-tech electronic presentation.**

## How to Avoid Them

High-tech multimedia presentations are exciting, colorful, entertaining, sometimes interactive—and often complete failures! There are two major reasons:

1. Too many presenters get caught up in the marvelous applications of the technology and find that it overpowers their message.

2. Many speakers are unable to communicate effectively enough to meet the sophistication of the technology.

While hours may be spent creating informative content and exciting visual support, the presentation's success ultimately depends on competent communication skills. An ineffective presenter making a polished, high-tech presentation will result in a confused and possibly critical audience.

The creation of a successful high-tech presentation involves many elements starting with:

▮ Who is your audience?

▮ What are their needs?

▮ What points do you want to make?

▮ What are your goals?

Once you've determined the answers to these questions, you can create the outline for your presentation.

Keep in mind that the bigger the electronic extravaganza, the smaller the presenter becomes. When the razzle-dazzle is over, someone has to make the audience believe in, understand, and buy what has been presented. So to avoid having the message run a poor second to the technology, make sure:

▮ The presenter is the prime medium.

▮ The message gets across loud and clear. Your power to project the message, to interact warmly and intelligently with the audience, and to modify the program, should it need instant modification, cannot be duplicated by any kind of electronics. The audience may forget every word you say and every picture you show, but they will remember the image they have of you.

▮ The visual aids don't substitute or overpower the presenter but rather support and enhance the quality of the presentation.

When put together properly, the technical, tactical, and persuasive advantages of a high-tech sales presentation are powerful and compelling.

▮ It's a sales, educational, and training tool all in one.

▮ It makes you look credible and professional.

▮ It sets you apart from the competition.

▮ Working with the leading edge of technology makes you look like a leader.

▮ It's more fascinating to a prospect than a low-tech presentation.

▮ When planned properly, the presentation will anticipate and answer the audience's questions. By anticipating problems in advance, the presentation can be programmed to overcome negative reactions from the audience during the presentation.

▮ Using interactive features available in presentation software packages, it can be used to ask closing questions and have the audience interactively answer with information that confirms the sale.

## MISTAKE 567

**Overestimating the audience's knowledge and underestimating their intelligence.**

### How to Avoid It

Earlier in this chapter we emphasized the importance of knowing your audience. When you do, you can develop an expansion and contraction sequence in presenting your content. By breaking the presentation down to segments, you can intersperse some basics that won't alienate the people in your audience who have little or no knowledge of your subject with in-depth points that will keep the interest of more knowledgeable audience members. Then continue this expansion and contraction throughout.

## MISTAKE 568

**Making the presentation too detailed.**

## How to Avoid It

Never talk over the heads of your audience. A very detailed presentation may go over well with scientists, engineers, and other technical professionals, but a too detailed program will make the audience feel uncomfortable, annoyed, and frustrated if they are unable to understand the content or technical language.

Present the general idea before the details. If you're describing characteristics, help your audience by zeroing in on the specifics. How big is too big? What do you mean by not enough time? Decide how much detail your audience needs to know.

People remember information better if is closely associated with something familiar, is sequential, or contrasts with something they know. By using metaphors, similes, and analogies, you can enliven dull data and help the audience discover they know more than they thought they did.

If you must use jargon or detailed terminology, make sure the audience understands the terms you are using. Repeat them often so they will remember them better. You may even want to include a glossary in your handouts.

## MISTAKE 569

**Not being confident or flexible enough to adapt to stressful circumstances.**

## How to Avoid It

Unexpected or stressful circumstances can occur in any presentation. If you haven't mastered your material and the technical equipment you will be using, it will be difficult to adapt to these circumstances. Coordinating your computer with your thinking and with the audience interaction while trying to concentrate on your presentation style is a little like chewing gum, walking, talking, dancing, and singing all at the same time. If that's more than you can handle, you may need an assistant to run the computer while you make your pitch. Rehearsing over and over, especially with unfamiliar equipment, will give you the confidence and flexibility that allows you to make creative choices while communicating your message. Don't rent the equipment the day before the presentation; you may not have enough time to become familiar with it. An extra day of rental charges will seem very small compared to blowing your opportunity at the presentation.

# MISTAKE 570

**Not taking advantage of multimedia software and hardware to make your message clearer.**

## How to Avoid It

There is no doubt that audio-visuals can be especially helpful when presenting nontechnical audiences with technical subjects. Illustrations convey complex ideas in a more simple way.

Special effects, sound, and animation, for example, enhance introductions and reinforce major points. Animation and special effects can be used to make bars or other objects grow naturally—sweeping up for increases, down for decreases. Used on a pie chart, animation can emphasize a slice by moving it away from the other slices. In any chart describing a complex process, animation can clarify the information by "building" the process. If it's a flow chart, for instance, have the steps and processes build one at a time. Bring bullets in one at a time from left to right, the same way the eye is accustomed to reading. Use color to emphasize your points. Make the current point you're talking about a bright color while making the previous point a muted but visible color. Don't make too many transitions as they tend to interrupt the flow of information.

Use audio to enhance your information and make it thought-provoking. A voice-over narration of a point is compelling. It provides an objective level of veracity, rather than the presenter's point of view. Don't use silly, meaningless sound effects. Video can be used to illustrate a process. Add a talking testimonial, such as a person appearing and reinforcing a point with a quote. Be aware of the limitations of your system as you develop your presentation. Audio and digital files require a lot of storage and RAM for proper sync and speed.

Set up the presentation so you need only a mouse click to advance or reverse a slide. Sitting at a keyboard becomes a barrier between you and the audience.

Electronic presentations can be tricky, so learn how to walk before you run. Start with simple slide presentations and gradually work up to more complicated shows. Don't try to use all the features available to you at once. You may get so bogged down in technology you'll go back to flip charts.

Make yourself a checklist of things to bring with you to the presentation, such as backup software and disks, extension cords, computer cables, handout literature, pointer, remote control, sound unit and amplifier—and your speaker's notes.

In case of equipment failure:

∎ Don't panic.

∎ Don't apologize.

∎ Take a break.

∎ Be prepared with and use backups.

Here are a few tips that will ensure your presentation materials get to the destination on time:

∎ Begin packing a week or two before the presentation.

∎ Use strong "banker's boxes," available at most stationary stores.

∎ Use the strongest packing tape you can find. It's better to use too much than too little.

∎ Itemize everything you pack and note on a separate sheet which box you packed it in. Number each box with a black marker.

∎ Prepare shipping labels in advance. Send everything to one point of contact. Make sure all the pertinent information is on the label.

∎ Add one day to the shipper's guaranteed delivery date.

∎ On your inventory, note the date each box was sent and the method of shipment used. Keep copies of all shipping bills together and keep them with you. Don't ship them with everything else.

∎ Heavy boxes should be identified so workers can avoid injury when lifting them. Fragile items should also be identified.

∎ Make sure that others sending materials to your presentation follow your procedures.

∎ Be prepared for the inevitable foul-up. No matter how careful you are in packing, labeling, and making arrangements, once your materials are picked up, you have lost control.

---
# A COMMON MISTAKE IN USING
# QUESTION-AND-ANSWER SESSIONS
---

## MISTAKE 571

**Refusing to have a Q & A session.**

### How to Avoid It

Often presenters get to the end of their program, rush off the plat-form, and refuse to take any questions. Unless your presentation thoroughly covered every possible question or objection that could be asked, you may miss a big opportunity to advance your message further and to clarify any points that are not fully understood.

While there is little doubt that a question-and-answer session is a valuable asset to any presentation, as a presenter you must decide the best time to take questions. There are two schools of thought on whether it is better to have the Q & A sessions during or after a pre-sentation.

Taking them anytime during the presentation makes you seem:

∎ Flexible, responsive, and confident.

∎ Increases the likelihood of audience participation and under-standing of your topic.

However, questions can get out of control, cause loss of focus, and get you off on tangents. You may also run out of time before reaching the end.

Taking questions at the end may:

∎ Detract from your close.

∎ Bore most of the audience.

∎ Make you seem less flexible and lose whatever enthusiasm you may have built to that point. This will decrease the number of questions and audience participation.

If the questions get hostile and you can't handle it, that will be the last thing the audience remembers.

Here are some Don'ts and Do's to consider whatever way you decide to go:

DON'T bluff or lie.

DON'T browbeat a questioner, even if it's warranted.

DON'T extract humor at the expense of a questioner.

DON'T call on someone else to answer a question unless they are part of the presentation. If they are not, and you need them to give an answer, give them warning.

DON'T use expressions such as, "Frankly," or "To be honest with you." People will wonder what you've been up till then.

DON'T be opinionated or patronizing.

DON'T compliment one questioner for asking a good question unless you intend to compliment all questioners. Otherwise, those who were not complimented will think their questions were not appropriate.

DON'T use one person's name unless you do it with everyone.

DON'T let a questioner take control.

DO encourage questions with positive phrasing and body language.

DO invite questions with a raised hand.

DO let the audience know early when the Q & As will occur.

DO try to anticipate and be ready for any questions that might be asked.

DO admit if you don't know the answer.

DO show an appropriate visual, if you can, when answering a question.

DO take questions from all parts of the room.

DO treat every question as legitimate and well intentioned, even if it's not.

DO let all questioners finish their question even if they interrupted you.

DO listen carefully and repeat or rephrase a question before you answer. When repeating, look at the questioner; when answering, look at the audience.

Do set a time limit if you start getting hostile questions.

Do let hostile questioners vent their anger, then refute or problem-solve.

Do respect questioners; don't be defensive.

Do answer briefly.

Do be positive when you answer.

Do end the Q & As with a closing statement.

---

## THREE MISTAKES IN SHOWROOM, EXPO, AND GROUP SELLING

---

Not every company can afford selling its products or services through mass media and marketing channels. There are, however, other less expensive means of getting multiple sales with sales tools such as the company showroom, business fairs and expositions, and group selling.

## MISTAKE 572

**Overlooking the company showroom.**

### How to Avoid It

Any business that can't afford mass marketing and believes that the only way to sell its products or services is in-store, one-on-one, or through salespeople on the road is overlooking the benefits of showroom selling. For one thing, showing a product in a store is not always the most effective way to show it. Often there is little room for display, and if the store clerks are busy, they may not be available to answer the questions of prospective customers. Outside salespeople are also at a disadvantage because they cannot always carry the full line of actual samples with them, and they cannot always show them under the best lighted and comfortable conditions.

Consider these benefits to showroom selling:

▌ Customers get to see the entire line.

▌ The showroom is designed to present your product in the best light: tasteful decor, handsome fixtures, flattering lighting, creative displays.

■ Buyers are in a more relaxed, leisurely atmosphere without distractions, and are more likely to be in a buying mood.

■ Buyers get the personal attention of company executives.

■ Company executives get closer to the buyer's needs and problems.

■ There is more time for selling.

## MISTAKE 573

**Not using business fairs, trade exhibitions, or conventions as sales tools.**

### How to Avoid It

I'll never forget the first business show I went to. One of my marketing clients had discovered a better way of catching, maintaining, and shipping rare, expensive tropical fish. At the time, pet stores were experiencing mass refunds because other suppliers' fish were not living much longer than a few weeks after customers bought them. Using the client's methods, most of our fish would live out their normal lives. My job was to introduce and market the client's services to the pet industry on a national level, and on a small budget.

I decided to announce our unique story at the annual convention of pet store owners, which was being held at the Superdome in New Orleans. We set up a small but attractively designed booth with large tanks of rare tropical fish and graphics with bulleted copy pointing out the benefits of buying tropical fish from us.

To ensure getting our share of the seven thousand or more qualified target prospects who attended the show each day, we used models, costumed as beautiful mermaids, to attract attendees. We also had a fishbowl drawing for a valuable prize and gave out unusual ad specialties.

By the end of the three-day exhibition:

■ The client had written up nearly $2.5 million in orders.

■ We had leads that eventually resulted in an additional $1.5 million in sales.

■ The client was established as a credible new source for healthy rare tropical fish.

The costs to accomplish this, including exhibition fee, booth design and construction, shipping, travel expenses for five people, grand prize, ad specialties, and so on, was under $30,000.

Aside from becoming a hero with the client, I learned some pointers about working a show.

■ Before you design your booth and marketing strategy for a show, visit other shows to see, among other things, which types of exhibits attract prospects best and why, how exhibitors handle prospects who visit their booth, and how they manage their personnel working the booth.

■ Find out everything you need to know about your show and especially any exhibitor restrictions. Music or sound amplifiers may not be allowed, for example.

■ The best exhibits are not always the largest, most elaborate, and expensive ones. When designing your exhibit try to be "stand-out different," informative with your visuals, entertaining if possible, accommodating and comfortable for prospects, and efficient in handling traffic.

■ Never leave ad specialties on display for anyone to take; have those attending your booth hand them out personally.

■ Assign booth responsibilities if more than one person is attending from your company.

■ Be sure your booth is attended all the time.

■ Give prospects immediate attention.

■ Have lead sheets, order forms, and collateral advertising material handy. Make sure you have enough of everything including business cards, pens, computers, staplers, and so on.

■ Make your booth a comfortable, inviting place to conduct business. Offering refreshments helps.

■ Read badges quickly. Stay alert for prospects you have selected or customers you have not dealt with before.

■ Try to qualify prospects quickly by establishing rapport, determining their needs, establishing interest, and concluding with an order or a future appointment.

■ Your exhibit is not the only place to make contacts. The aisles, eating areas, other exhibits, elevators, your hotel—have your business cards with you when you go to the bathroom—you never know.

- If you can't get the order at the show, get an appointment.

- There's nothing wrong with selling other exhibitors. If you do, be courteous and never interrupt their presentation or conversation. Let them know you are an exhibitor, too. Don't take up too much of their time.

## MISTAKE 574

**Attempting to sell groups the same way you sell one-on-one.**

### How to Avoid It

When you're selling one-on-one, you must please the prospect to get the sale. The same is true if you're selling groups of 50 or 500—only you must please *everyone.* We have heard accounts of companies that sold 99 percent of the group they were presenting to and *didn't* make the sale.

If you're presenting to two or more decision makers, here are some tips:

- Dress conservatively. Your clothes should not distract your audience. You want them to concentrate on what you're selling, not on what you're wearing.

- Be on time. Try to be early, if possible, and introduce yourself to whomever is there. Try to isolate those who seem most enthusiastic.

- As in any presentation, find out as much about the group as you can in advance.

- Try to remember names. People love to be recognized by name. If the group is large, use name badges.

- Play to the "power person" of the group who appears to have the group's attention.

- Confront any problem members of the group early and head-on. Try to anticipate concerns and questions and be prepared with concrete answers.

- Encourage interaction by asking for questions from the group. Go over any concerns one by one.

- Be prepared with solid, proven facts for those analytical members of the group.

▌ Distribute informative sales literature that will back up your claims and support your integrity and your company's ability to deliver quality and service.

▌ Being humorous can win over a group and create a favorable buying mood. Just be sure your humor is not offensive, degrading, or in bad taste.

## Chapter 21

# Negotiating Successfully

$F$ace it. Life is one negotiation after another—with an irritable spouse, an ornery superior, a rigid supplier, a demanding customer, an IRS agent who thinks he's Attila the Hun, a kid who won't eat the broccoli—and in the workplace, the smartest don't always finish first. More often, it's the best negotiators.

Many of the skilled dealmakers we researched agreed that successful negotiators:

- See conflict as an opportunity for understanding and growth.

- Believe compromise is more effective than victory.

- Are patient and sensitive to the needs of others.

- Don't get overly upset when attacked personally.

- Know how and when to ask smart questions and use that information to control the direction the negotiation takes.

- Are unshakably committed to a win-win solution.

    And that successful negotiation:

- Is not beating the other side as much as it is compromising on an agreement that benefits all involved. In other words, both sides have to believe they are winners.

## NINE COMMON MISTAKES IN NEGOTIATING WIN-WIN DEALS

Three possible outcomes can result from the negotiating effort: lose-lose, win-lose or win-win situations.

In a lose-lose situation, both parties usually end up worse off than before the negotiation started.

In a win-lose scenario, obviously one side wins and the other loses—which you might think is okay—as long as you are the one who wins.

In a win-win solution, the best possible solution in any negotiation, every party in the negotiating process gets something it needs. It may not be all it wants, and everyone may not be completely satisfied with the solution, but because no one is left empty-handed, and everyone will gain something from it, all are willing to work together to make the solution a success.

### MISTAKE 575

**Not seeing the other side's point of view.**

### MISTAKE 576

**Not separating needs from wants.**

#### How to Avoid Them

The critical element in negotiating a win-win solution is for both sides to focus on each other's needs—to put themselves in the shoes of the person they're negotiating with and see the other's point of view.

### MISTAKE 577

**Not considering what you're willing to give up to get an agreement.**

#### How to Avoid It

Negotiating a win-win solution means knowing in advance of negotiating how much you can afford to give up to get what you want and how much you will settle for if you can't get all you want.

## MISTAKE 578

**Not knowing much about the people you're negotiating with.**

### How to Avoid It

Take time to get to know whom you're dealing with. Have breakfast or dinner with them before the meeting. Explain that you don't want to discuss the issues for negotiation, you just want to get to know them better and meeting beforehand might help establish a climate for easier communication. Learn what you can about their position and identify the common interests necessary for creating a solution that benefits both sides.

## MISTAKE 579

**Treating the other side as "the enemy."**

## MISTAKE 580

**Losing your cool before closing the deal.**

### How to Avoid Them

If for some reason the negotiation becomes heated or delicate, don't resort to intimidating behavior, don't lose your patience or your temper, never issue an ultimatum or raise your voice. You'll undermine whatever strength your argument has, you'll be seen as uncooperative, loud, and desperate, and the best you will be able to accomplish will be a win-lose solution.

## MISTAKE 581

**Not clearly explaining the reasons that justify your position or not anticipating the other side's reaction.**

### How to Avoid It

Present your side, but do it in terms that support the definition of the issue you and the other party have already agreed on. Show how your solution benefits the needs of both parties. Listen to the other party's response. Identify its needs and decide if you are able to provide it. Then repeat what you believe you heard and represent your position from the other side's point of view. If you didn't understand the other side's response, ask questions to clarify the matter.

## MISTAKE 582

**Not paying attention to inflections, nuances, body language, and what isn't being said by the other side.**

### HOW TO AVOID IT

Observe the other person. Does he or she repeat certain points or introduce issues not covered in the definition of the problem? Knowing why these issues are important can help you negotiate more effectively. Do the other person's eyes, expression, or body language telegraph a different message from what you are hearing? Does the person seem relaxed or uncomfortable? Do hand gestures indicate happiness, anger, or indifference? Knowing what's really at issue for the other side provides you with bargaining power that will help you later.

## MISTAKE 583

**Failure to recognize that without give and take there is less likelihood that the negotiation will be successful.**

### HOW TO AVOID IT

Though they always try to get what they want, skilled negotiators also know what, when, and how much to give—as well as what, when, and how much to expect in return. The smart ones give from what you want, and hold out for what you need. If you are not willing to give and take, you'll end up with a lose-lose outcome.

## TWENTY-THREE MISTAKES THAT CAUSE NEGOTIATION BREAKDOWN

## MISTAKE 584

**Not establishing the proper mind-set.**

### HOW TO AVOID IT

Every skilled negotiator lives by these rules:

- Everything is negotiable.

- Take nothing for granted.

- Ask for as much as you can.

- Be willing to give in order to get.

- Consider the other party's point of view.

- Explore every option that may be open.

- Look for a solution that is mutually beneficial.

## MISTAKE 585

**Underestimating your own power.**

### How to Avoid It

It's been said there are three key elements in every negotiation: power, time, and information. And the more you have of each, the better positioned you are.

Most people think having power is having the ability to provide financial rewards or inflict some kind of penalty—or when the other side has no other choice or has made such an investment that they can't fold their cards and walk away. But if negotiators are committed to their beliefs, are well prepared with information, have bargaining skills, and are willing to work hard, take risks, and stick to whatever limits they set for themselves, they have the power to be successful.

## MISTAKE 586

**Letting the other side intimidate you or vice versa.**

### How to Avoid It

When negotiating, you must disregard all your preconceived attitudes about the superficial status of those you are dealing with, as well as any principles or regulations that may be outdated or irrelevant. If you allow the other side to invalidate your position, research, or reasons and berate you personally—they will. By the same token, you should never belittle or offend the other party.

## MISTAKE 587

**Assuming each party knows what the other wants.**

### How to Avoid It

It is much safer not to assume anything and instead discover, through questioning, what everyone actually wants. Negotiating with unsubstantiated assumptions can be disastrous.

## MISTAKE 588

**Not realizing that two people can perceive the same situation very differently.**

## MISTAKE 589

**Not understanding the other person's limits.**

### How to Avoid Them

Each side sees every element of the negotiation from its point of view. Don't assume the other party has the same values you do or that it will be reasonable in its demands. Find out all you can about the person or persons you're dealing with. Ask questions. Repeat their statements as you understand them. Differences in perception can lead to hostility and a breakdown in the negotiating process.

## MISTAKE 590

**Leaving yourself or the other side no out.**

## MISTAKE 591

**Not trying to save face for both parties.**

### How to Avoid Them

Avoid issuing ultimatums or taking public positions with no escape route. Hard ultimatums such as "Take it or leave it!" or "It's this way or I'm walking!" are self-defeating. Soft ultimatums such as "I understand your position and think it's valid, but this is all I've got. Help me out" is more likely to get a favorable response. Always make it easy for people to change their minds. Without acting defensive, leave the other side an alternative—a choice of options—but make sure the option you want them to take is superior.

## MISTAKE 592

**Not knowing when to keep quiet.**

### How to Avoid It

Talking too much can always get you in trouble. Successful negotiators recommend that you should not try to outtalk your opponent. Besides, if you keep your mouth closed you can't give anything away.

## MISTAKE 593

**Giving something for nothing.**

## MISTAKE 594

**Not using compromise as a psychological edge.**

### How to Avoid Them

It's okay to give up something you want, but only to get something you need. And as we said before, know how much you can afford to lose—without great sacrifice. But when you do give up something you consider nonsignificant, create the impression that it's a major compromise on your part. When negotiators win a major concession by giving up something minimal, they give themselves a great psychological boost.

## MISTAKE 595

**Not setting a deadline.**

### How to Avoid It

Setting definite but reasonable time limits gives you an advantage when negotiating. The more time invested, the more the other party has at stake. If the other side sets a deadline, don't be shy to request another meeting to continue the negotiation.

## MISTAKE 596

**Not acting assertively.**

### How to Avoid It

Stand up for what you believe in, but be open to what the other party believes in, too. Successful negotiators have one thing in common: They communicate their confidence. A confident negotiating style goes a long way toward giving you the psychological advantage you need to win. If you seem convinced that what you're asking for is the best choice, others will be too.

## MISTAKE 597

**Not having patience.**

### How to Avoid It

If you can't master this personality trait, don't enter into any negotiation. When it comes to successful negotiation, patience is truly a virtue. A negotiator who is anxious and impatient for a quick outcome can seriously hamper the chances for getting the best deal. Skilled negotiators are able to take a long-term view. Even when they have a need for a quick agreement, they will give a clear impression that they have all the time in the world. Your time deadlines and other pressures should not be made known to the other person.

## MISTAKE 598

**Negotiating alone when you're part of a team.**

### How to Avoid It

When you are negotiating on behalf of your company, unless you are completely knowledgeable about what you are negotiating for, you will have the least leverage. For example, you may be the manager of a division and have the most authority to negotiate with one of the division's suppliers. But if you are not well informed about past experiences with this supplier, if you don't have information about competitive suppliers or the requirements your company has regarding suppliers, you should call in your colleagues or other experts to help.

## MISTAKE 599

**Not evaluating your negotiating performance.**

### How to Avoid It

Which of your goals did you achieve? Did you have to give away more than you expected? What tactics worked best for you, and which ones didn't work? Evaluating your performance will help you prepare for your next encounter.

## MISTAKE 600

**Not keeping track of issues requiring in-depth discussion.**

### How to Avoid It

Negotiations can sometimes get complicated and confusing. Customers, for instance, often get frustrated by an apparent lack of progress and go back on agreements already made or raise new issues at the last moment. One good way to avoid this kind of problem is to summarize what has already been accomplished and outline what still needs to be discussed. Brief but frequent recaps help maintain momentum, and they reassure the other party that you're listening to their arguments.

## MISTAKE 601

**Belaboring one point when there are many others to work out.**

### How to Avoid It

Some negotiators will repeat a single point and inundate the other party with logic and constant explanations until the other party feels badgered and put down. This accomplishes little and wastes a lot of time.

## MISTAKE 602

**Giving in to emotional blackmail.**

### How to Avoid It

Negotiators sometimes use emotion—usually anger—to rattle the opposition into making concessions they wouldn't otherwise make.

Some use anger as a premeditated tactic. Others really do get angry. It doesn't matter whether the emotion is genuine or counterfeit, what matters is how you react. Here are some defensive techniques you can use:

∎ Withdraw. Ask for a break or reschedule the meeting. A change in time and place can change the atmosphere.

∎ Listen quietly while the other side vents its anger. Maintain eye contact and a neutral expression, but do not reinforce the other party's behavior. When the tirade is done, suggest an alternative solution.

∎ React openly and strongly to the other party's anger. Tell the others you find it unproductive and suggest focusing on specific, nonemotional issues. Sidestep the other side's attack and convince it that a common effort at problem solving will be more productive and profitable. If you don't allow your opponents to land a punch, chances are they'll stop throwing them.

## MISTAKE 603

**Offering a proposal in the form of a range.**

### How to Avoid It

This kind of proposal signals that you aren't firm in your position. Make your position specific. Be prepared to concede, but don't broadcast your willingness to do so. If the other party offers a range, it is fair to assume that your opponent's minimum is your maximum.

## MISTAKE 604

**Not putting the details of your proposal in writing.**

### How to Avoid It

Referring to something in writing has more impact than does the same information delivered orally. Once you have decided on the position you will take, put the details in writing and keep them handy. Once written backup has been introduced into a discussion, it is unlikely to be modified by an opponent with mere oral weaponry. Good negotiators go into every negotiation with a written agenda. Even if it's handwritten, such a document can be a powerful tool. It forces the other party to go along with your format, starting with item one. But don't assume that just because a point is presented in writing that it is nonnegotiable.

## MISTAKE 605

**Accepting a verbal rather than a written final agreement.**

### How to Avoid It

Any successful negotiator will tell you, "Beware of verbal agreements." A written agreement eliminates misunderstandings and minimizes future conflicts. It gives you some degree of assurance that the other party will not back out of or not live up to something agreed on verbally. The agreement does not have to be formal or contractual in format, nor does it have to be signed by both parties (even though that would be best). It could be something as simple as a memo spelling out who, what, when, where, and how much. Courtesy copies of written agreements should be sent to colleagues, superiors, or anyone else who may be affected by the outcome of the negotiation.

## MISTAKE 606

**Not congratulating the other side at the conclusion of the negotiation.**

### How to Avoid It

At the conclusion of each negotiation, you should always congratulate the other party for:

▌ Getting the better end of the deal.

▌ Doing a great job of negotiating.

    Or

▌ Getting you to compromise more than you planned.

Even though your congratulations may not be sincere or truthful, you may have to negotiate with this person sometime again and you want the person to leave feeling good about you. It will help make your next encounter go more smoothly.

Giving a compliment also helps the other party feel good about the outcome of the negotiation—that the other party made a wise choice.

Compliments will undoubtedly come your way, too. When they do, just say thank you and move on. Telling other persons who compliment you that you could have been better will make them feel that they misjudged your strength and possibly could have made a better deal for themselves.

## NINETEEN MISTAKES IN NEGOTIATING ON THE PHONE

Although it is better to negotiate face to face, there are occasions when you will deliberately want to negotiate on the phone. It may be the only way of reaching a hard-to-talk-to person. Or you may want to make a quick and easy deal and don't have the time to meet face to face. Whatever the reason, if you have to use the phone to negotiate, be sure that you, not the one you're negotiating with, is the better prepared; and always keep in mind that some of the biggest and most costly mistakes have been made during telephone negotiating. Here are the most common mistakes and ways to avoid them.

### MISTAKE 607

**Not having enough information to negotiate.**

### MISTAKE 608

**Negotiating without having a prepared position or fully understanding the issue.**

### How to Avoid Them

The caller has the advantage of surprise; the person being called is likely to be disorganized, so it's always best that *you* initiate the call. If you are called by surprise, listen to the story, then call back after you've had time to think about the issues, do some field work, and establish the position you want to take. If there are points that are not clear, make a list and go over those items thoroughly so both parties are in complete accord. Remember that it is more likely that either party will misunderstand something said on the phone than in person-to-person talks.

## MISTAKE 609

**Rushing to a quick decision because phone charges are mounting.**

### How to Avoid It

Calls can be costly and cause pressure to rush negotiations. Though telephone negotiations actually can help reduce business costs, a bad decision made under pressure can be much more expensive than the cost of a phone call. A great deal of pressure can be avoided by following these five steps:

1. Rehearse the phone conversation before you make the call.

2. Have a list of items to be discussed, a list of questions you want to ask, and objections you may have.

3. Keep it short. Don't ramble.

4. Set yourself a time limit and keep to it.

5. If you feel yourself being pressured to make a fast decision, prepare an excuse for discontinuing the conversation.

## MISTAKE 610

**Not calling back promptly when you discover a misunderstanding or computation error.**

### How to Avoid It

Everyone makes mistakes. Don't be afraid to point out an error you or the other party made or admit you don't understand an issue. Often, misunderstandings occur because we avoid asking questions that:

▮ Reveal our ignorance.

▮ Show that we haven't been paying attention.

▮ May embarrass the other party.

Any error in fact, judgment, or statistics that affects the final agreement should be discussed promptly. Unless you're 100 percent sure about all issues, suspend the negotiation until those matters are resolved.

## MISTAKE 611

**Not having courage to call back after finalizing a deal you don't like.**

### How to Avoid It

The mistakes made at the end of a negotiation, when tensions and concessions are at their peak, often are not recognized until after the deal and the call are concluded. Admitting you made a mistake and want out of a deal takes courage. Don't feel this will be interpreted as a sign of weakness or distrust. A bad deal costs more than bad feelings. Take these three steps:

1. Call back immediately and tactfully but strongly announce your decision and reasons why.

2. If the other party has not gone to any expense as a result of the agreement, there should not be any objection to voiding the deal. If there were expenses, try to minimize the loss and offer to pick up the costs. There should be no objection to canceling the agreement if the other party is ethical and wants your future business.

3. Always leave yourself a way out of an agreement such as either party may cancel before the first order is shipped or either party may cancel with 30 days' notice.

## MISTAKE 612

**Not having a calculator or checklist of things to discuss at hand.**

### How to Avoid It

The person who is best prepared has the advantage in any negotiation. Three steps to take:

1. Have your notes, files, and calculator on your desk. If your secretary is involved, be sure she is close by.

2. Make a checklist to avoid omissions.

3. Lay out your work papers on a roomy table.

## MISTAKE 613

**Not giving yourself enough thinking time on important issues.**

### How to Avoid It

Don't get into a phone negotiation without first building a "thinking buffer" to keep yourself from being pressured into a decision. Here are nine suggestions that work well, whether you are dealing with a customer, a vendor, the IRS, or your spouse:

1. Arrange to get an important, unexpected surprise visitor or phone call at some crucial point.
2. Plead ignorance. Ask for time to learn more about the facts.
3. Have your expert unavailable.
4. Introduce a third party—a lawyer, your boss, a translator.
5. Ask for demands or offers in writing.
6. Change the terms of the deal.
7. Load the other party down with statistics to check out.
8. Don't have the backup material available.
9. If all else fails, get hungry or thirsty or say nature is calling and you'll have to get back to the other party.

## MISTAKE 614

**Not being assertive and initiating the call.**

### How to Avoid It

As we said earlier, the caller has the advantage of surprise while the person being called is likely to be caught off guard and disorganized. If you expect to negotiate by phone, be aggressive, prepare your position, call first, and push for a quick decision.

## MISTAKE 615

**Giving in to pressure to close the deal before you are ready.**

## How to Avoid It

There are times when it is better to deal on the phone than face to face, especially if the other party is overbearing and pressuring you to close. On the telephone it's easier to disagree, act tough, hold back on important facts, cut off a discussion, and interrupt, if need be. When you're negotiating on the phone, status differences are minimized, and it's easier to listen and let the other party do most of the talking.

## MISTAKE 616

**Not listening hard. Letting your mind drift.**

## How to Avoid It

Four quick tips:

1. Find a quiet, private area without distractions to conduct your phone negotiation.

2. Make notes on important points.

3. Take or make negotiating calls early in the day when you are more alert.

4. After the conversation, ask the other party to put its proposal in writing.

## MISTAKE 617

**Allowing interruptions on your end.**

## How to Avoid It

Ask your secretary to hold all your calls and visitors. Assign someone to handle any problems that may arise while you are on the phone. Let employees know that when your door is closed or you are on the phone, you are not to be disturbed unless it's an emergency.

## MISTAKE 618

**Talking too much.**

## How to Avoid It

Many people have longer conversations on the phone than they would speaking person to person. When you're negotiating, talking too much can be a critical mistake. The less you talk, the more the other party will. If you find yourself giving out more information than intended, remember these four tips:

1. Establish your point of view as soon as you get on the phone. Stay focused on it.

2. Keep it short. Make your point and get on with it.

3. Establish a time limit and stick to it. Say something like, "I have a meeting in ten minutes, if we don't conclude by then, when will it be convenient for me to call you back?"

4. Cut the conversation short and call back after you've organized your thoughts.

## MISTAKE 619

**Not asking for proof of statements made in conversation.**

## How to Avoid It

If you have doubts about any claims or statements made during a phone negotiation, ask the other party to send a quick fax that you can check out while you continue to talk or have the other party put the verification in the mail. Reserve any final decisions until all the facts are verified.

## MISTAKE 620

**Not anticipating surprises.**

## MISTAKE 621

**Responding to a surprise without being prepared.**

## How to Avoid Them

There are negotiators who feel that surprise is a good way to keep the pressure on. Actually, it becomes a communications block. This is not to say that a negotiator should reveal surprises before the negotiation. Surprise is an important negotiation tactic. But before you can defend yourself against surprise, you must first recognize the kinds of surprises you're likely to encounter, such as:

- *Issue surprises* such as new demands, backing away from concessions, position changes, risk changes.

- *Time surprises* such as deadlines, short and long sessions, lost weekends.

- *Move surprises* such as hang-ups, recesses, delays, smokescreens, emotional outbursts, frequent interruptions, displays of power.

- *Information surprises* such as special rules, new source of information, tough questions, peculiar answers.

- *Ego surprises* such as bursts of abuse, anger, distrust, one-upmanship, attacks on intelligence and integrity, disbelief.

- *Expert surprises* such as the introduction of specialists or consultants.

- *Authority surprises* and lack-of-authority surprises.

- *People surprises* such as changes in buyers, sellers, team members, status differences, the appearance of the boss, bad guys-good guys, nobody calling for the other side or calling late.

The best thing to do when surprised by a turn of events is to give yourself time to think. Listen, say as little as you can, and take a break. Don't respond to something new until you are prepared.

## MISTAKE 622

**Not taking notes and filing them quickly.**

### How to Avoid It

Four tips to remember:

1. Tell the other party you will be taking notes during the conversation.

2. Ask them to speak clearly.

3. If the other party doesn't mind, have a secretary take notes on another extension. Aside from freeing you to concentrate on

negotiating, a third party becomes a witness to the transaction. You may even want to tape-record the conversation (with the other party's permission).

4. When the conversation is ended, go over your notes, organize them, and make memo copies for files and distribution.

## MISTAKE 623

**Not confirming agreements promptly in your own words.**

### HOW TO AVOID IT

As soon as you have agreed on a deal, have the arrangements typed up and faxed, mailed or overnighted to the other party as soon as possible. Follow up with a phone call to make sure the agreement, as you understand it, was received and accepted.

## MISTAKE 624

**Not having a ready excuse to break off the conversation, should you need to.**

### HOW TO AVOID IT

If you are not prepared to continue negotiating, it is wise to have an excuse ready for time-outs. Five good excuses are:

1. You need time to study the issues.

2. You have to run it by an associate.

3. You want to arrange a summit meeting or a conference call.

4. You have to check regulations, consult experts, review options.

5. Change the bargaining emphasis from a competitive mode to a cooperative problem-solving mode. Get engineers involved with engineers, lawyers and accountants with lawyers and accountants, bosses with bosses.

## MISTAKE 625

**Complicating the simple.**

## How to Avoid It

Often, telephone negotiations, especially involved ones, fail because too much information is being communicated back and forth without the benefit of seeing what the other party is talking about. Steps to take:

- Don't drone on . . . and on with facts, figures, descriptions, and the like. Be brief in making your point and moving on to the next item of discussion.

- If you're giving an example, keep it simple and make sure it relates to the point you're making.

- If your negotiation involves complicated information, lots of facts, photos, demonstrations, or graphics that are on paper, fax them to the other party so both of you can be looking at the same things while talking.

- Work from note concepts—the fewest number of words or pictures that will trigger an idea you can talk about for a minute or so.

- Make a list of the items you want to talk about. If you have too many, don't try to cram it all into one phone conversation.

- Repeat your key points at least twice, in different ways if possible.

*Part*

# 3

# THE MOST COMMON MISTAKES BUSINESSES MAKE COMMUNICATING WITH VENDORS, PROFESSIONALS, GOVERNMENT AGENCIES, AND UNIONS

# Chapter 22

# COMMUNICATING WITH VENDORS, PROFESSIONALS, AND CONSULTANTS

Every business must rely on its suppliers, accountants, bankers, lawyers, and consultants for things it can't, or shouldn't, do itself. Being selective about whom you engage for goods or services and for expert advice—and how—can maximize your peace of mind, as well as save you time, money, and unnecessary grief.

## THIRTEEN MISTAKES IN DEALING WITH VENDORS

### MISTAKE 626

**Not making your suppliers part of your team.**

#### HOW TO AVOID IT

Teamwork among various businesses within an industry can improve the image of that industry as well as increase customer awareness of the products or services the industry provides. Everybody wins. That's especially true when companies and their vendors cooperate.

Companies and their suppliers don't have to look far to find common interests. First of all, your suppliers are in business for the same reason you are: to make money. When they do things right, it helps your business. When they make mistakes, it can hurt your business reputation and cost you time and money to correct. Suppliers can also provide a valuable service to your business, trade credit, which will be discussed later in this chapter.

## MISTAKE 627

**Selecting a supplier solely on recommendation or price.**

## MISTAKE 628

**Not setting standards for selecting your vendors.**

## MISTAKE 629

**Not involving all departments of your business in setting vendor standards.**

### How to Avoid Them

In shopping for vendors, it is important to network with business peers and to ask chambers of commerce and trade organizations for referrals. But first it is important to set the standards for what you expect from your suppliers. After all, your reputation is riding on their service.

In order to make sure the standards you establish benefit your entire company, it is essential that you involve all your departments—sales, sales support, operations, purchasing, production, accounting, even the warehouse—in setting those standards. You'll want to know among other things:

- How long have the firms been in business?

- Do the suppliers offer top-quality products or excellent service at perceived value?

- Are the firms fully staffed?

- Can the vendors be reached after hours?

- How responsive are they?

- How do they handle agreements and contracts?

- What is their payment schedule?

- Do they give volume rebates or discounts?

- Are they willing to accept long-term purchase agreements that would be financially beneficial to your company?

- Are they are willing to extend you credit?

- What is their policy on cancellations?

▌ Who will be the contact to handle your company's needs? Is there a backup contact? Is the contact available to attend meetings if the occasion arises?

▌ Which of your competitors do they supply?

▌ Have these vendors ever dealt with anyone now in your employ?

▌ Do the suppliers provide training in using their goods or services?

▌ Do they offer in-stock product availability and immediate delivery?

▌ Do they ship and deliver on time?

▌ Have you heard of problems concerning incorrect billing or products arriving damaged?

## MISTAKE 630

**Not having other vendors as a point of reference to be sure you're getting the best prices, selection, and service.**

### How to Avoid It

Once you have determined what you need and expect from your vendors, call in at least three in each category for interviews. Discuss your standards with them. Raising the question of standards will get the vendors thinking about future performance, not just past.

By the time you've talked to the candidates, you'll have an idea of whom you find compatible. And you'll have learned a great deal about the services available.

Be honest about your company's size and ability to pay. Beware of low-balling.

After you've made a decision:

▌ Let the companies you've selected know as soon as possible.

▌ Don't use too many suppliers in any one category. Purchase your goods and supplies from the fewest number of vendors supplying the maximum number of products at the lowest possible total "ownership cost" (the price of a product with quality and service factored in). Successful companies usually have a prime vendor and two backups as points of reference to make sure they're getting the best prices and service—not to mention keeping vendor number one on its toes.

■ Be certain that all team members of your company are satisfied and committed to retaining the business vendors that are helping you build your business.

■ Don't use a vendor only because of low price. Low price does not justify poor quality and inadequate service, which in the long run can substantially increase the low price you thought you paid.

## MISTAKE 631

**Complaining to vendors about something on nearly every order.**

## MISTAKE 632

**Constantly putting suppliers in highly competitive bidding situations.**

## MISTAKE 633

**Trying to get suppliers to shave prices after you've already agreed on those prices.**

## MISTAKE 634

**Failing to pay your bills when due even though goods or services were delivered when promised and in good condition.**

## MISTAKE 635

**Expecting to command the same kind of attention and pricing from suppliers that your larger competitors are getting.**

### How to Avoid Them

Good, reliable suppliers are valuable assets to any business. They can "bail you out" when your own customers make difficult requests and demands upon your company. They can advance inventory and extend your deadlines for payment. And because they are in business to make money, most will continue to serve you only so long as your business is profitable to them. If you go to the mat with them on every order they ship, squeeze them on every price they quote, force them into unreasonable bidding wars with their competitors, and if, by purposely paying your bills late, you take advantage of them by letting them unwillingly finance you, this can destroy your relationship and the vendor's ability to meet contractual obligations and support its products. Don't be surprised if they decline to do business with you, and worse, spread the word to other vendors.

As an executive in a competitive business, you should always look for the best deal you can get from those that want to supply you. But remember that vendors are human, and they, like you, want to be successful. If they cannot make a fair profit by doing business with you, they will sever the relationship, just as you would do under similar circumstances.

And just as you, as a businessperson, would treat your biggest and best customers specially, you must expect that your vendors will do the same. While you may not be their biggest customer receiving volume prices, developing rapport and a good working relationship with your suppliers will pay off in the long run as these suppliers help you meet your obligations to your customers. No business arrangement that is worthwhile can continue for long unless something of value is rendered and received by all those involved. This is the basis for every continuing relationship you will have in business, including those with your vendors.

---

## MISTAKE 636

**Not training and helping your suppliers understand your special needs and problems so they can help you.**

### HOW TO AVOID IT

Getting more out of your purchases increases your bottom line. Your vendors are more than likely to be willing and able to help you do this. After all, growth in your company means growth in their company. But they can't help you unless they understand your business and goals and feel that they are part of your team.

Just as you would orient your own employees to your company and their department, it is important to do the same with your vendors by training and helping your suppliers to understand:

∎ How their goods and services relate to your needs.

∎ The functions of the department they are supplying.

∎ How that department relates to other departments.

∎ The kinds of work performed by department employees.

∎ The importance of the department's work to the goals of the company.

Introduce vendors to workers with whom they might interact. Ask for their questions and be as informative as possible with your answers. Treat your suppliers as partners, not servants.

## MISTAKE 637

**Not encouraging improvement in supplier quality in your efforts to improve *your* quality.**

### How to Avoid It

Getting your company's quality up to the standards you have set and keeping it there is an important and sometimes complex task. Supplier quality plays a key role in the effort. Your list of priorities for improving supplier quality should include:

- Making quality a top criterion for source selection.

- Improving the skills of your source selectors.

- Improving the skills of supplier quality inspectors.

- Designing purchased components for better manufacturability.

## MISTAKE 638

**Not recognizing and rewarding your vendors as you would your employees.**

### How to Avoid It

In Chapter 3, Mistakes 73, 74, and 75, we discussed rewarding employees as a way of saying "Thank you for doing your best, we appreciate your efforts." Some companies we contacted do the same with their best vendors.

While giving suppliers your business is, in itself, a powerful incentive for them to provide the best quality, prices, and service, recognition and reward can be even more powerful. It often costs little or nothing, and almost everyone responds to them. Most people (including vendors) will try harder when the payoff is feeling appreciated and important. They will feel that they are an important part of your team helping to satisfy specific needs and problems of your customers.

So how do you reward suppliers? Use your imagination and you'll come up with dozens of ideas to fit the companies you work with. Here are some of the more popular rewards our research uncovered:

- Monetary incentives based upon incremental business they help generate for their category as well as their own brands.

- Quality Vendor of the Year plaques, certificates, citations, and trophies for best service, quality goods, most dependable delivery, or whatever you designate as most important.

- Preferred Vendor programs that give the vendor the opportunity to work directly with various departments and become part of the company team.

- Inviting vendors to company functions: picnics, conventions, and open houses, for example.

- Giving vendors the opportunity to learn what your customers want, as well as the opportunity to arrange for your customers to become pilot sites for testing new products.

- Public praise for a job well done, such as a write-up in the company or local newspaper.

- Special praise or a congratulatory letter from top management.

- A vendor's "Hall of Fame" with names and photographs displayed where employees and visitors can see it.

## SIX COMMON MISTAKES IN OBTAINING VENDOR CREDIT

## MISTAKE 639

**Inflating financial statements to bridge reference gaps.**

### HOW TO AVOID IT

When applying for vendor credit, never present grossly inflated financial statements to compensate for lack of financing and references. Aside from the fact that this practice is illegal and a felony, it's also easily detected by a competent credit manager. If your honest financial statement and references are not enough for a credit line, ask your suppliers to put you on a COD basis for a specified period of time with the understanding that if both parties are satisfied at the end of the COD period, the supplier will issue you a line of credit.

Most suppliers know that if you are underfinanced, it won't be long before you have problems with COD.

## .   MISTAKE 640

**Not taking steps to correct inaccurate credit reports.**

### How to Avoid It

If you are denied credit because of mistakes on your credit report, there are a number of things you can do to correct the situation. First, ask the credit reporting agency the vendor uses for a copy of the report. Federal law mandates you have the right to have it, free, if you've been denied credit.

If you believe there is something inaccurate about the report, circle it and send it back to the agency. Include any backup material, such as a canceled check or receipt, that substantiates your claim.

The credit reporting agency will then verify if the negative information is in error. If, when the reporting agency gets back to you, it maintains the negative information is correct, you can:

▪ Write a retort of 100 words or less and send it back to the reporting agency. Anyone who requests your credit history will get the inaccurate report, along with your retort.

▪ Contact the party that supplied the negative information and try to convince it that it has made an error. If you do, have it send amended information to the credit reporting agency.

If, after receiving the amended information the agency refuses to make the report accurate, demand in writing that it be fixed. If it still refuses to do so, contact the Federal Trade Commission (FTC) in Washington, D.C.

## MISTAKE 641

**Not requesting copies of your credit report on a regular basis.**

### How to Avoid It

It is important to get copies of your credit reports on a regular basis so you can catch and correct errors before it's too late. There are a number of credit reporting agencies; names of the major ones are available from the FTC or your local bank or chamber of commerce.

## MISTAKE 642

**Abusing vendors and losing a source of trade credit.**

### How to Avoid It

For many businesses, the readiest sources of capital are extended terms from vendors (trade credit) and accelerated payments from customers.

Getting suppliers to advance inventory for long periods of time or extend credit in the form of delayed payments, for example, are backhanded forms of financing and much easier for many businesses to get than obtaining bank loans.

CPAs and lawyers we researched told us that many of their clients found trade financing easiest to get when they, the borrowers, were willing to make concessions to their vendors, such as paying higher unit prices in exchange for delayed payments or promising never to buy less than a fixed percentage of their usual volume.

Smart vendors know that as their customers' businesses grow, their business opportunities with those customers also grow, so it is in their best interest to work with good customers by offering deals.

Vendor credit can be a great source of inexpensive capital for any business. Making your vendors part of your team effort, keeping them informed of your growth, giving them an interest in that success, and not abusing your relationship with them can pay off big in the form of "life-saving" credit should you need it.

## MISTAKE 643

**Not checking the vendor's financial condition.**

## MISTAKE 644

**Not having backup vendors that can step in quickly if your prime vendor fails.**

### How to Avoid Them

It's difficult enough to spot signs of financial trouble in your own company. But the astute businessperson must also be able to detect danger signals among customers and suppliers. A supplier suffering financial difficulties can jeopardize the well-being of your business. Should a vendor fold, for instance, you could lose weeks of production or become short of inventory while looking for a replacement vendor. You could also lose advance payments or deposits you made on orders that have not been delivered. And because underpricing is often the cause of vendor failure, your new suppliers may well charge more than their predecessors.

Just as with any business, your vendor's top management may try to keep its problems quiet. However, your own employees may pick up valuable information from lower-level vendor employees or from competing suppliers, especially if you put them on the alert.

Here are seven warning signs that a vendor may be in financial trouble:

1. Trying to collect monies early or in advance of shipment.

2. Suddenly offering discounts for immediate payment. Even a small discount such as 5 percent on a net 30 bill, translates into an annual interest rate of about 60 percent for what is essentially a 30-day loan. This is surely a warning signal that the vendor may have financial difficulties.

3. Offering a discount if you'll accept a shipment COD.

4. Sending orders earlier than the specified shipping date, hoping that by getting it early, you'll pay for it early.

5. Chaotic warehouse conditions or large amounts of return shipments on the loading dock.

6. Vendor employees who are hostile, depressed, sarcastic, seeking other employment.

7. Departure of key vendor employees, such as middle managers. They're likely to jump ship before the top brass because they have no stake in the company and want to protect their futures.

Having backup vendors that can step in on short notice is a good precautionary measure.

## ELEVEN COMMON MISTAKES IN PURCHASING GOODS, SERVICES, AND SUPPLIES

The mistakes your company may make in the area of purchasing can mean the difference between profits and losses.

## MISTAKE 645

**Treating purchasing as a necessary evil rather than as a source of profits or a way of reducing costs.**

## MISTAKE 646

**Not comparing vendor prices.**

### How to Avoid Them

Many companies tend to overlook or totally ignore their purchasing operation, or even worse, take the word of vendors on prices. This can result in overpaying dearly for goods and services. Purchasing should be treated as a source of profits and as a task that requires a great amount of skill, including getting comparative prices.

## MISTAKE 647

**Letting employees buy what they need instead of purchasing through a qualified person or department.**

### How to Avoid It

We were surprised to find that many companies allowed employees to order whatever supplies or materials they needed themselves. But because they are not qualified purchasers or negotiators and do not have the time to bargain, their employers end up paying the price, often dealing with many more suppliers than is necessary.

Purchasing responsibilities should rest with one person or one department. Otherwise, keeping track of what has been ordered and what should be ordered becomes difficult. By centralizing purchasing, you have better assurance that purchases are made from qualified suppliers with whom you have better leverage. Continually reviewing your purchasing-and-receiving practices is a necessary step toward reducing costs and increasing profits.

## MISTAKE 648

**Allowing anyone to receive and sign for delivered goods and supplies.**

## MISTAKE 649

**Signing for goods without checking the purchase order or with the person who placed the order.**

### HOW TO AVOID THEM

Another bad habit that many businesses practice is letting anyone sign for delivered goods. Once the receipt is signed, it's less likely inaccurate counts will be reported, which means bills that should be adjusted won't be.

One person or department should be responsible for receiving goods and signing for them. It is important, however, that whoever receives the goods should check the shipment (for quantities, damage, description) against the purchase order or with the person who does the purchasing *before* signing for the delivery. Only then can you be sure you are getting what you ordered.

## MISTAKE 650

**Mixing vendor business with pleasure.**

## MISTAKE 651

**Accepting gifts and favors from vendors.**

### HOW TO AVOID THEM

Becoming buddies with suppliers can work for you, but mostly against you. Like an office romance, it may start off on a happy note, but eventually getting personal with suppliers can lead to your "overlooking" shortages, overcharges, broken promises, damaged merchandise, excuses for late delivery, and so on.

No matter how large or small a business may be, the person who does the purchasing is fair game for every vendor who wants the business. In Chapter 10, Confronting Employee Theft, we pointed out how gifts, favors, even kickbacks are common inducements vendors use to get business, and they are not always easy to detect.

The situation can become especially dangerous if the purchasing person is socially friendly with the vendor and accepting expensive dinners, tickets to sporting events, and the like. Because vendor favors and gifts are factored into their prices, you can't be getting the best deal possible. Steps to take:

- Have backup vendors to keep prices in line.

- Periodically review your relationship with vendors and interview new vendors.

- Keep an eye out for employees who become very "chummy" with suppliers.

- Go over all vendor bills carefully. Sometimes you may pick up a clue that someone in purchasing is on the take.

## MISTAKE 652

**Not using sales flow information to make purchasing more effective.**

### How to Avoid It

Sales flow reports will point out those periods when customer purchases are the highest. By identifying those periods in advance, you will be able to purchase goods and services more efficiently. This can also be helpful in keeping inventory down and improving the efficient use of labor, both of which will help your bottom line.

## MISTAKE 653

**Not teaming up with other purchasers to get better prices by buying in bulk.**

### How to Avoid It

Buying in bulk can often translate to major savings. We talked with a number of companies that joined purchasing groups to get better deals from suppliers.

You should talk to your suppliers to see what kind of price difference there would be if you were buying two or three times your present quantity. Also talk to a couple of your competitors to see if they are interested in co-op purchasing to lower the cost of goods.

## MISTAKE 654

**Not investigating outsourcing your purchasing for possible savings.**

## How to Avoid It

If your company is a large purchaser of goods and services, you might want to look into the possibility of substantial savings (5 to 35 percent) by working with outside purchasing specialists—companies that assume control of all or part of your purchasing chores. These services buy in large volume from a global database of thousands of vendors who meet the quality, pricing, and servicing qualifications of each client. They negotiate contracts and provide extensive reports that verify savings.

Outside purchasing services work with their clients in many ways. The two most common arrangements are:

1. Negotiating vendor agreements for specific supplies and earning a percentage of the savings (usually 30 to 50 percent).

2. Taking over the purchasing completely, absorbing some of the client's staff, getting a fee based on the total annual purchasing volume plus a smaller percentage of the savings.

Though outsourcing is relatively new in the area of purchasing, some companies are finding that for them it is by far the most efficient way of purchasing.

## MISTAKE 655

**Keeping slow-moving goods in inventory.**

## How to Avoid It

One of the biggest expenses a business has is the cost and maintenance of goods (inventory). For every $100 in inventory, it's costing approximately $20 to $25 to keep it.

Back in the nineteenth century an Italian economist named Pareto developed the 80–20 formula now referred to as Pareto's Law.

Applied to purchasing practices, the bottom line of the formula is this: 20 percent of your inventory accounts for 80 percent of your sales. If you know which 20 percent of your inventory is moving, you can substantially decrease the other 80 percent and realize sizable savings.

## TEN BIGGEST MISTAKES IN DEALING
## WITH ACCOUNTANTS

An accountant may well be the most important outside professional a businessperson engages. While the services and advice of an attorney may be vital in times of trouble or from time to time on specific situations, the accountant's continuing role has greater impact on the success or failure of a business.

It is foolhardy to attempt to operate a business without retaining the services of a skilled financial professional who is well versed in your line of work. Therein lies your task: finding the right accountant at a price you can and are willing to pay.

## MISTAKE 656

**Using an accountant who doesn't fully understand your business.**

### How to Avoid It

Price is only one of the important considerations in choosing an accountant. While some may be happy to take your account on at a reasonable price just to expand their practice, they may have little or no practical experience with your kind of business. The best accountant for your business is obviously one with a knowledge of your business, its procedures, its needs and its goals.

Here are some characteristics to consider when choosing an accountant:

■ A confidant who will make sure you play by the rules, even when doing so costs you money.

■ Trust and rapport are essential. You should be able to talk to your accountant on a confidential basis, revealing things about your business that you might not reveal to others. You must feel that you can trust your accountant with all the financial details of your business, and you must have confidence that this information will go no further. And, you must be willing to accept and follow the accountant's direction and advice.

■ A technician who will keep you in compliance with the many rules and regulations that affect your business, including Labor Department regulations on hiring, employee relations and discrimination, and rules on retirement and other employee benefits.

■ A tactician who understands how you run your business and can help you plan business strategy and manage income and expenses.

■ A financial professional who is respected by lenders and creditors. If bankers and creditors believe what your accountant says about your company, you can benefit greatly.

■ A tax planner and return preparer who is adept at keeping your taxes low and the IRS off your back.

## MISTAKE 657

**Settling for other than a certified public accountant (CPA).**

### How to Avoid It

CPAs are required to meet certain proficiency levels in order to be licensed by the state in which they practice. They must also subscribe to certain standards of ethical behavior concerning their relationship with clients and other CPAs. While this is no guarantee that the CPA will do a good job for you, it does reduce the chances of your getting an accountant who could foul up your books and records and misadvise you on business matters.

Some important questions to ask before you make a decision to retain:

■ How long have they been practicing accountants?

■ How much experience do they have in your field?

■ Are they public accountants or certified public accountants?

■ What professional organizations do they belong to?

■ Are they solo practitioners, or are they members of a firm that can provide additional support?

■ How often do you need to meet with them?

■ What additional services can they provide if necessary?

∎ What is their retainer fee?

∎ What are their charges for services not covered by the retainer?

∎ Do they have other clients in comparable businesses, and are they willing to have you call some for references?

## MISTAKE 658

**Using an accountant solely as a provider of financial and tax information and not as a business adviser, too.**

### How to Avoid It

Many business executives call on their accountants strictly for tax matters and other services such as providing financial statements, organizing the statistical data concerning your business, and keeping you in compliance with myriad legal requirements and shifting interpretations of regulations—and neglect using them as business advisers and facilitators.

A good accountant can also:

∎ Make introductions to financing sources.

∎ Help negotiate financing rates and terms.

∎ Advise on financing structure and overall financial strategy with regard to purchasing, capital investments, and similar activities.

∎ Prepare business plans, projections, and forecasts.

∎ Analyze your current financing and make recommendations for improving it.

∎ Provide answers to financial questions.

∎ Interpret financial data and help improve communications during negotiations.

∎ Assist you in charting future actions.

∎ Advise on government regulations concerning employee hiring, firing, and discrimination.

∎ Advise and implement retirement and profit-sharing plans.

## MISTAKE 659

**Using an accountant who does not keep pace with your company's needs.**

### How to Avoid It

A good accounting firm for your company is one that keeps up with your needs in areas such as data processing, cost control, capital investments, and tax planning. If this is not the case with your accountant, it's time to shop around for a firm that can adequately handle your needs.

## MISTAKE 660

**Engaging an accounting firm with expertise in your field but settling for an unqualified individual to service you.**

## MISTAKE 661

**Not conducting an in-person interview with the accountant who would handle your account.**

### How to Avoid Them

There is nothing more frustrating than asking your accountant an important question and then having to wait while he consults with an expert back at his office.

Only with an in-person interview can you get a sense of intangibles you should be aware of, such as personalities. Will you feel comfortable with this person discussing your most intimate financial details? Does this person consider your account equal to all others or of insignificant value?

## MISTAKE 662

**Not involving key managers in the final decision-making process.**

### How to Avoid It

It makes good business sense to involve all key managers who would be dealing with the accountant to be part of the decision-making process. Their input can be important, especially if they have had experience with accountants before or if their job requires closer, more frequent contact than do other managers. Everybody should feel compatible with the firm or person finally chosen.

## MISTAKE 663

**Not having a clear understanding about fees charged and services to be provided.**

### How to Avoid It

Fees for accounting services, like those of other professionals, vary widely. A small firm might charge less for its time than larger firms, but fees are often determined by services performed and expertise required. Bring up the matter of fees and services to be provided at the outset of your relationship with your accountant and review them at least once a year. You might want to request written estimates from each prospective firm you are considering about the kinds of services it would provide and the anticipated cost. There may be certain services that are included in an estimated fee that are not necessary, and adjustments should be made.

## MISTAKE 664

**Not feeling comfortable enough in your relationship to question certain charges.**

### How to Avoid It

Be sure to go over all invoices submitted, and don't hesitate to question charges you don't understand.

## MISTAKE 665

**Signing tax, corporate, and other forms prepared by your accountant without fully understanding what they are.**

### How to Avoid It

Don't be embarrassed to ask your accountant to explain "confusing" forms and other material she prepares for your company. Often, accountants will prepare a tax form, for example, stick it in front of you for your signature, tell you how much to send in with it and when to mail it, and then dash off to another appointment. You owe it to yourself to know what you're signing, and why.

## TEN COMMON MISTAKES IN OBTAINING
## LEGAL COUNSEL

In today's fast-paced, highly competitive, and often, "I'll see you in court" workplace, the need for legal counsel can arise at any time.

A business may use the services of attorneys for a number of reasons including:

I To recommend and establish the structure of a new business.

I To draw up and file partnership and limited partnership agreements and file incorporation papers.

I To provide advice and other services for a variety of liability and contractual matters.

I To provide advice and draw up lease or purchase agreements.

I To provide advice and draw up employment contracts.

I To provide representation in labor disputes.

I To provide advice and draw up filings in trademark, copyright, and patent situations.

Many of the mistakes we covered in dealing with accountants also apply to dealing with any professional. Here are some common mistakes and solutions that pertain to lawyers.

### MISTAKE 666

**Not knowing whether to hire in-house general counsel or retain an outside firm.**

#### How to Avoid It

We questioned dozens of business owners and managers throughout the country and most had these recommendations:

I Determine if legal issues come up regularly.

I Decide if it's more cost-effective to retain an outside firm or hire your own in-house attorney.

I If you decide to hire in-house counsel, determine your company's specific needs—security work, dealing with regulatory agencies or unions, product or service liability, government contracting, to name a few—and employ those with appropriate expertise.

■ If you hire in-house counsel and a situation arises that requires skills your counsel doesn't have, let your counsel be responsible for hiring the right outside attorney.

■ If you choose to go with an outside law firm, look at the qualifications of the individual who will be representing your company.

## MISTAKE 667

**Retaining or hiring qualified counsel with whom you have no rapport.**

### How to Avoid It

The most important criteria in choosing counsel, according to the companies we interviewed, is their ability to handle your firm's particular needs and their ability to relate to you and your business.

## MISTAKE 668

**Using general in-house counsel for all your legal needs including those that require highly specialized experience.**

## MISTAKE 669

**Retaining a big-name firm without determining the expertise of the individual you will deal with.**

## MISTAKE 670

**Not asking law firms and lawyers for formal resumes.**

### How to Avoid Them

Once you have narrowed down your list of legal candidates:

■ Interview each of the candidates.

■ Ask lawyers and law firms for formal resumes.

■ Determine and evaluate the track record of each person or firm you are considering. That means getting to the bottom line of cases won and lost.

## MISTAKE 671

**Interviewing prospective outside lawyers in your office instead of theirs.**

### How to Avoid It

Always try to conduct the interviews at the office of the lawyer or firm, and get there early. This gives you the opportunity to observe the lawyer's offices and staff, as well as other clients dealing with the firm. An honest attorney will tell you if what you are asking of him is far afield from his experience.

Here are some typical questions to ask of candidates:

■ Have you had experience with this specific situation before? How often? What was involved? What was the result?

■ If I hire you, do I get you or some associate? If another person is doing the basics, how experienced is that person with my problem? How will it affect the fee or relationship with you?

■ Will you provide copies of all documents and correspondence received or written in this case?

■ Will you keep us informed about all developments relating to this case?

■ Do you keep up with changing laws? How much time do you spend participating in continuing education?

■ Will you give me the names of some current or former clients who would tell me about you?

## MISTAKE 672

**Hiring a busy attorney who cannot give you the time you need.**

### How to Avoid It

Great attorneys you can't reach are like having no attorney at all. Unless they have the time and willingness to meet with you in person or on the phone—when you need them—they can't be of much help to you, no matter how nice, competent or qualified they are.

## MISTAKE 673

**Not setting deadlines and guidelines when working with lawyers.**

## MISTAKE 674

**Losing control of your legal dealings.**

### How to Avoid Them

Outside attorneys often will do anything to "keep the meter running," while in-house lawyers often think they have to spend time in order to justify their jobs. In either case, *you* usually end up paying for the nit-picking details they use to delay matters. Here are some tips that will help save time and keep you in control of the situation:

▮ If you're the plaintiff in a matter, try to hire the attorney you want on a contingency basis. Under this arrangement, the attorneys' fees are based on a percentage of the amount that is recovered for you. If nothing is recovered, it costs you nothing. The advantage to you is that the lawyer is highly motivated to work quickly for a successful result.

▮ If you're the defendant in a matter, encourage the lawyer to settle the matter, if that decision is appropriate. The advantage to your lawyer is that settling a case is more profitable than going to trial. A lawyer can settle 20 cases in the time it takes to try one. If you're not working with that lawyer on a contingency basis, settling early can save you a lot of expenses down the line.

▮ Don't allow opposing lawyers to negotiate. You do the negotiating of the details, then let the lawyers handle the legal language.

▮ If opposing attorneys are hopelessly ensnared in a legalistic quarrel, you go directly to the other party. They must be as frustrated as you by the delay.

## MISTAKE 675

**Not obtaining, in advance, an estimate of the time and charges that will be involved in handling a matter.**

## How to Avoid It

How many times have you heard about lawyers who speak to six or seven clients within an hour on the phone and bill each one $300 for that same hour? And all those calls were made on a cellular phone while the lawyer was at lunch with yet another client who would eventually be billed for the lunch and the time it took to eat it.

One way to avoid this scenario is to try and obtain from the lawyer, in advance, an estimate of the time and charges involved in doing the job, even if it's a ball-park figure. Then try and negotiate a reasonable flat fee plus verified out-of-pocket expenses. If the attorney agrees to this, put it all in writing. Be sure to include a provision that the attorney must check with you *before* making any sizable expenditures.

If a flat fee is out of the question, request weekly time charges and weekly bills. Not monthly, not when the job is finished, but weekly.

With weekly bills you won't have any surprises. You won't have to remember whether or not the lawyer really spoke to so and so for an hour a year ago. And if you think you're being overcharged, now is the time to change lawyers.

## THREE COMMON MISTAKES IN CHOOSING A BUSINESS BANK

While nearness to your business, convenient hours, and a wide range of services are important features to consider, selecting the right business bank for your company requires a hard look at your current and future needs and a willingness on the part of a bank to grow along with you.

## MISTAKE 676

**Overlooking banking services that could be cost-efficient for your business.**

### How to Avoid It

A bank's ability to handle your firm's payroll, for example, can save your business the cost of using in-house staff for that function. Your company may require more than just a commercial checking account. Your company may also need a bank that offers loan options, commercial account drive-in lanes, cash management services and direct deposit capability for your employees.

Your accountant and lawyer can provide excellent counseling on which banks will be best able to serve you.

## MISTAKE 677

**Not negotiating bank fees and charges.**

### How to Avoid It

Bank fees and charges are just as negotiable as the price you pay for a new car. Whether it's the amount of interest you're paying on a loan, the cost per check if your balance goes below a certain amount, charges for listing your deposits on your statements, or fees charged for stopping a check, there is room for negotiating charges or even eliminating many of them.

And you don't have to be a Fortune 500 company to get what you want. The fact is, banks compete actively for business, and in most cases they would rather lower or eliminate various fees and charges than lose your business to a competitor.

## MISTAKE 678

**Choosing a bank without considering the future banking needs of your business.**

### How to Avoid It

Select a bank that can provide for your firm as it expands and its needs become greater.

For instance, do you anticipate your borrowing needs to exceed the limits of the bank you're considering? If your business expands nationwide or internationally, will the bank be able to provide the same kinds of service?

Changing banks midstream can be inconvenient and expensive, so it is important to accurately assess your needs in advance of making a decision in this area.

## NINE COMMON MISTAKES IN HIRING
## A BUSINESS CONSULTANT

From time to time, companies need an expert and incisive outsider's view of their business. It may be because:

- A company needs technical knowledge to identify possible product modifications.

- A company needs help in troubleshooting special problems such as pricing and marketing strategies, or advice on foreign trade.

- Downsizing, reengineering, and rightsizing have reduced permanent staff, and uncertain economic times preclude adding full-time employees with expertise.

- A new company needs help in determining how best to enter a market and when.

- Management needs an efficiency or research study.

- A company needs an expert to audit management practices, analyze goals, and suggest methods to organize operations and staff.

- A company needs to devise ways to improve the quality of products and services and come up with fresh, creative, testworthy ideas to win larger market share.

- Upper management needs to be convinced that changes have to take place, but they will not listen to internal suggestions.

- A company is involved in a megadeal and needs a liaison between it and the other party.

When these and other needs occur, industry executives often choose to outsource professional consulting resources.

Consultants are human-resources gap fillers—utility players who are disposable, don't require severance packages, and aren't eligible for health-care benefits paid for by client companies.

Consultants can be found working for companies of all sizes and types, all over the world, selling expertise in about every field imaginable. They are used to teach, to gather information, to solve problems, and to bring in arms, legs, and brains during peak periods without increasing fixed costs. They can be independent firms, self-employed experts, university professors who consult part-time, or retired business executives.

The most important goal in choosing a consultant is to be sure you get the *right* one for you.

## MISTAKE 679

**Assuming you know what the problem is and directing a consultant to solve it.**

## MISTAKE 680

**Hiring a consultant to agree with you.**

### HOW TO AVOID THEM

Obviously, any company that has decided to hire a consultant wants to get the best possible advice for the lowest possible price. But before you can settle on the best consultant to fill your needs, you must first ascertain what those specific needs are.

One of the biggest mistakes some managers make is deciding what they *think* their problem is and then hiring someone to agree with them. Most consultants are happy to say what they think you want to hear, and you pay a tremendous amount for them to do so. Surprisingly, that's what many companies expect from consultants.

True consulting is when the consultant identifies the problem and then suggests ways to solve it. Look for a consulting firm that challenges the beliefs of your company and is skilled in what is to be evaluated. Just because you've done something a certain way successfully doesn't mean it's going to get you where you want to be in the future. Consultants should speak up on any topic, and their effectiveness should be judged by how many changes are suggested, not by how many things you are found doing right.

## MISTAKE 681

**Not hiring a consultant with expertise that fits your needs.**

### HOW TO AVOID IT

Companies sometimes hire consultants who are financial- or business-management experts and expect them to correct marketing problems or overcome technical production difficulties. The expertise of the consulting firm you engage must fit your specific needs.

The firm should have wide-ranging, practical experience in the field in which it is consulting. For instance, if you are hiring a consultant to analyze and improve your company's direct-mail strategy, ask if it has actually created and implemented direct-mail strategies. Without a background in performing the work, there will be huge voids in its knowledge about how systems operate and how processes really work.

## MISTAKE 682

**Choosing a consultant with limited practical experience.**

### How to Avoid It

Practical experience is not of much value to a company if it is limited to only one area of experience. Take the direct-mail example. A company may hire a consultant who has practical experience writing direct-mail pieces, but if that consultant has not had other types of experiences, those limitations may prevent that person from presenting all the options available.

In this case, the company should look for a consultant who can review your direct mail goals, marketing methods, response strategies, and media/list selections and tell you what's right, what's wrong, and how your direct-mail program compares to others. A savvy insider who knows what is and isn't working for others. Someone able to critique your ads, mailings, and reply-seeking offers and troubleshoot problems and uncover opportunities. Someone who asks penetrating questions and gives revealing answers with the widest possible view of the best way to handle the situation.

## MISTAKE 683

**Basing your decision to hire a consultant on price or home location.**

### How to Avoid It

Only if all else is equal should price and location be deciding factors in your selection of a consultant. Low bids for consulting services should always be examined carefully.

## MISTAKE 684

**Not checking references and past performance of the consultant hired.**

## How to Avoid It

Business consultants are not restrictively licensed like accountants or lawyers. Just about anyone can hang out a shingle and claim to be a consultant. Because of this, check references and past performance of such consulting firms to assure yourself of their competency and proven performance and that what the money is being spent on is what your company really wants and needs. Ask for copies of their reports. Ask to speak to some previous clients. If you're unsure about a company's experience in the market, get feedback from your peers, even your competitors.

## MISTAKE 685

**Hiring a consulting firm, paying the price, and ignoring the advice.**

## How to Avoid It

In these days of intense competition among consulting firms, those that show results win future business. If a company takes pains to select a competent consultant with feasible plans that can solve its problems, it would be sheer foolishness not to at least give the strategy a chance.

## MISTAKE 686

**Bringing in consultants only when business gets out of control.**

## MISTAKE 687

**Bringing in consultants for very short periods and expecting them to work miracles.**

## How to Avoid Them

Most companies wait and bring in consultants when something goes wrong with the business. These consultants usually end up looking like heroes because by that time the business is so messed up, any suggestion they make is positive. The sad and expensive part is that often all it takes to change what's wrong is to kick management out of their executive offices and into the ranks to ask the people who are doing the work what's wrong, and then change it. It would be a very inexpensive form of communication if it were only done that way—but most of the time, it isn't.

Smart companies, on the other hand, solicit the help of consultants to improve the things they do best—to help make the best even
better and to get the creative juices flowing.

Another thing smart companies do is allow their consultants to
spend time soaking up their corporate culture. They don't bring in
expensive talent for a day or two and expect all problems to be
solved. By getting to know the people who work in a company and
the customers and vendors that deal with the company, consultants
are better able to obtain an objective source of marketplace information that the company can't get by itself. Customers, for instance, are
more likely to give honest opinions about a company's product to
someone not affiliated with the product than they are to somebody
who is. Being able to barrage employees with questions you may not
have had the time or inclination to ask can also bring objectivity to
your day-to-day operations. If people on your staff get upset when a
consultant questions them, for example, you might want to find out
if they have anything to hide.

## SEVEN COMMON MISTAKES IN OBTAINING
## HEALTH INSURANCE

It's enough to make any company sick—buying health insurance for
its employees. With the insurance forest more densely populated
with choices than ever, and the costs spiraling upward at an alarming
rate, selecting and managing health insurance has become a major
financial nightmare for many businesses—a nightmare that comes
back to haunt you every 6 or 12 months when the renewal notice
shows up in the mail.

## MISTAKE 688

**Not accessing your needs before deciding on a plan.**

### How to Avoid It

Before embarking on an insurance safari, it's important to know what
class of insurance best fits the needs of your employees. Basically, you
have three options:

1. A traditional indemnity policy, or fee-for-service (FFS) plan that
   allows subscribers to choose their own physician. The insurance
   company reimburses a percentage of the "reasonable and cus-

tomary charges" (usually 80 percent); the subscribers pay the difference. The problem with these plans is that they often have the steepest premiums and deductibles and do not always pay for early preventative services.

2. A Preferred Provider Organization (PPO) provides subscribers with a network of primary-care doctors, specialists, and hospitals that have agreed to provide services for a set fee. Typically, the level of coinsurance is less for subscribers using PPO providers. If the subscribers use a non-PPO provider, the health coverage reverts to an indemnity policy with higher deductibles, coinsurance, and copayments.

3. A Health Maintenance Organization (HMO) provides subscribers with a list of participating physicians and hospitals who have negotiated with the insurance company to manage your health-care needs for a set price. The subscriber must choose a primary-care doctor from this list. If you need to see a specialist who's part of the plan, your primary care doctor has to arrange for it and sometimes get an okay from the home office. There are generally no out-of-pocket costs except for office visits, usually $5 per visit. Preventive health care is stressed and encouraged. The cost to the subscriber through HMO providers is typically less than the same services through FFS or PPO plans.

Once you've chosen the kind of health insurance you want, you have to figure out which plan offers the lowest deductibles and out-of-pocket expenses at the best price. Here are some points to consider:

■ Start with the doctors in the plan. How many are there? Are they conveniently located near your workplace? What about their qualifications? How many have certification from peers in their specialty? Will the doctor you want accept new patients through the plan? Just because they're listed in a pamphlet doesn't mean they'll take on new patients at this time.

■ Many of the questions you ask about doctors can be asked about hospitals, too. How many are included? Where are they? What specialties do they offer?

■ If you're considering an HMO, has it been reviewed by the National Commission for Quality Assurance to determine if it's worthy of accreditation? What happens if you get sick in a different state? What happens if you wind up in the emergency room of a hospital not covered by the plan? How flexible is the HMO in dealing with the unexpected?

■  What's the procedure if you have a complaint?

■  How long has the insurance company been providing this kind
of service? Is it financially stable? Can it survive if an epidemic
breaks out?

## MISTAKE 689

**Shopping for a health plan on your own instead of working
through a good agent, broker, or benefits consultant.**

### How to Avoid It

Most business executives don't have the time or expertise to shop the
vast number of health plans on their own. It's a decision that requires
the assistance of an experienced professional—a qualified agent or
broker.

Though the terms *agent* and *broker* are frequently used inter-
changeably, there is a difference. Agents work for one insurer, brokers
do business with many insurers. It costs you nothing to work through
an agent or a broker. Both get commissions from the insurer they
bring the business to, and the plans cost the same whether you buy
them through a broker or on your own. A good agent or broker can
be your best ally in making the right purchase, but with more than
one million licensed insurance brokers nationwide, how do you
know who's good and who isn't?

■  First, find out what kind of experience the person has. Ask for
references of business clients, and call them. Experience counts,
because you need someone who is available to answer your
questions and help you solve your problems *after* the commission has been paid.

■  Has the agent or broker you are considering taken continuing
education programs recently in order to remain up to date on
the changes that affect her work? Professional credentials are
good clues to a broker's commitment to employee benefits.

■  Is the broker a chartered financial consultant (ChFC), a chartered life underwriter (CLU), a registered health underwriter
(RHU), or a registered employee-benefits consultant (REBC)? All
of these designations require successful completion of an inten-
sive course of study and indicate a broker's investment in his
own professional education.

▎ Does the agent or broker belong to key associations that specialize in health care, such as the Association of Health Insurance Agents, the Society for Professional Benefits Administrators, or the National Association of Health Underwriters? These groups promote professional standards and education designed to hone a broker's skills.

Once you've selected the broker best for you, he will go about shopping the hundreds of insurance companies writing thousands of policies for the business market. Computerized database services make it possible for brokers to obtain detailed information on insurers and specific policies at the touch of a computer keyboard.

Most experienced brokers have already narrowed the field by doing business with insurers that meet their standards for financial stability and customer service.

Another source of objective health-care advice is from a benefits consultant. Such a firm doesn't sell health insurance, is not associated with or commissioned by any insurers, and won't give you a sales pitch.

For a flat fee, based on the number of employees in your plan, the firm will search its database of thousands of health plans to come up with what it considers the best three or four recommendations for your company. Recommendations are based on an insurer's financial stability, track record, customer service, and rating and renewal policies. Premium rates are used only as a starting point. If you don't have a broker, a benefits consultant will also help you find an experienced one from a preferred broker list.

## MISTAKE 690

**Buying a policy because of price instead of the insurer's rating philosophy.**

### How to Avoid It

While price is always a major part of any buying decision, the cheapest policy isn't necessarily the best one. You may start out with a low premium aimed at getting your business, then get a sizable rate increase when the renewal notice arrives.

To avoid this problem, find out what the insurer's rating philosophy is.

Does the insurer base your renewal increase on the experience of a pool of business groups within your geographic area, or on your own company's claims experience? Pooling helps stabilize increases by spreading risks among the companies in the group, while individual rating can lead to abnormally large increases.

## MISTAKE 691

**Not checking an insurer's financial condition.**

### How to Avoid It

Is the insurance company financially sound? After a series of recent health-insurance scandals, many health insurance companies found themselves on shaky ground and many others found themselves out of business, leaving tens of thousands of policy holders with hundreds of millions of dollars in unpaid health-care bills.

There are several rating services that provide information on the financial health of insurers. The services include A. M. Best, Moody's, Standard & Poor's, and Duff & Phelps, among others. The broker you select will have access to one or more of these rating services.

## MISTAKE 692

**Overlooking buying from an association.**

## MISTAKE 693

**Overlooking forming a purchasing alliance to bargain for lower premiums.**

### How to Avoid Them

Association plans are becoming more and more popular because they allow smaller firms to join a pool and use their collective leverage to get coverage for less than they would have to pay otherwise. For certain high-risk professions that are routinely denied coverage by commercial insurers, association plans offer a much-needed source of insurance.

There are two basic types of association plans:

1. Insured plans, which purchase coverage from a commercial insurance company.

2. Self-insured plans, which pay claims out of premiums collected from the members.

Insured plans have a good track record, largely because the insurance carrier behind the plan is subject to state insurance regulation. But before you buy an association plan, get the name of the plan's insurer and ask about financial stability, track record, and rate-renewal practices, just as you would if you were buying the policy on your own.

Also, be aware that some associations claim their health plans take advantage of group rates when rates, in fact, are based on individual company experience. As a result, you don't get the benefit of pooled experience, leaving your company vulnerable to large rate increases.

Many self-insured plans have also served their members well. But be on the lookout for those that have fallen though the regulatory cracks. Some fraudulent operators have collected millions in premiums from businesses but failed to pay claims.

Another method of purchasing lower cost health plans is through purchasing alliances. Many companies, large and small, form purchasing alliances to bargain with health insurers for lower premiums.

One small company we interviewed told us that over a six-month period they investigated such a purchasing alliance with other small companies in their general area. The group approached a number of insurers, who offered the proposed alliance savings on administrative and marketing costs. The insurers also indicated that they would use experience rating, which could mean lower premiums. Most important, some insurers agreed to share medical-underwriting data, the records of health-care use that determine whether a company is a good risk. Small companies usually can't get that data, so they negotiate in the dark.

After negotiations, the alliance selected an insurer that guaranteed no increase in premiums for the first 18 months and a cap on increases for two years after that.

## MISTAKE 694

**Not looking at the fine print.**

### How to Avoid It

Before signing an agreement, check the fine print of your policy. Often there are stipulations that you are not aware of that could cost you and your employees a lot of money. Here are some conditions to look for:

▌ What is *not* covered in the policy? Every policy comes with a list of exclusions. Read them over carefully. Among the medical services routinely excluded are birth-control pills, custodial care, hearing aids, private-duty nursing, well-baby care, and nursery charges.

▌ Does the policy cap employees' maximum out-of-pocket expenses? If, for example, an employee has an 80/20 plan with no maximum out-of-pocket limit and runs up a $150,000 hospital bill, the employee's share will come to $30,000 and possibly cause financial ruin.

▌ How does the policy set reimbursement rates? Does it pay 100 percent of the usual, customary, and reasonable (UCR) costs? Most policies establish a reimbursement schedule based on UCR costs. Some use other methods. Others simply stipulate reimbursement amounts. If costs exceed the allowable, fixed reimbursement levels determined by the insurance company—no matter how it was figured—your employees pay the difference. For example, if the UCR rate for a specific surgical procedure is $2,500 and the surgeon's fee is $5,000, the employee must pay the balance regardless of the maximum out-of-pocket limit. And none of that excess is applied toward the employee's deductible or coinsurance.

▌ Does the policy have a lifetime-benefits cap? Know your cap before you buy the plan. Many policies set a cap of $1 million, a level generally thought to be adequate. But some plans set lifetime caps at $500,000 or less. In a catastrophic case, an employee would be responsible for all bills after the insurer hits the cap.

▌ What is the intensive-care reimbursement limit? It is often calculated at three times the semiprivate daily room rate. But if that rate is $300 a day and the intensive-care charge is $2,000 a day, the employee has to come up with the $1,100 a day difference.

# Chapter 23

## DEALING WITH GOVERNMENT AGENCIES, UNIONS, AND GLOBAL SITUATIONS

### FIFTEEN MISTAKES IN HANDLING
### THE A TO Zs OF RFPs

Much of the goods and services purchased by government agencies (as well as many large corporations and consortiums) are procured through invitations to vendors known as requests for proposals (RFPs).

The RFP process was invented by government to determine and get the lowest bid on products, but because RFPs are lengthy and extremely complex and can take weeks, even months for vendors to prepare properly, it has become a way to procure products that are obsolete before they're installed—to get $900 toilet seats, $300 ashtrays, and $10 billion weapons systems that don't always work.

The most important justification for RFPs is that the process gives the appearance of fairness and legality in seeking goods and services from competing vendors, whether or not that is the true outcome. Thus, it prevents later trouble and charges against purchasing officials.

### MISTAKE 695

**Not responding to an RFP because you don't think it's worth the trouble.**

#### HOW TO AVOID IT

Doing business with government agencies can be a trying but rewarding experience for businesses of any size. More than a fifth of the hundreds of billions of dollars in federal government procurement spending each year goes directly to the coffers of small firms, according to the Small Business Administration. So is it worth the trouble for small and medium-sized companies to respond to an RFP? The answer is a resounding "Yes!" The fact is, a company can make more money in one government transaction than it could make in two or even three years of normal sales.

But first, you have to become a player in this market.

## MISTAKE 696

**Not getting your company plugged into the RFP marketplace.**

## MISTAKE 697

**Not responding to an RFP because you don't think your company is large enough to get the contract.**

### How to Avoid Them

In some fields, the very nature of your business will get you RFPs without any effort at all on your part to solicit them. Though my firm in Florida was far from the largest or most politically connected in the area, it was an established advertising and marketing company with a long history of success, which somehow got us on *the list*. Whenever any government agency had a contract that required such expertise, every company on that particular list was sent an RFP. I used to receive at least seven or eight a year from government organizations such as the Federal Deposit Insurance Corp., the Resolution Trust Corp., port authorities, tourist commissions, city, county, and regional planning commissions. These agencies were seeking proposals to provide advertising and marketing services for their various projects, which ranged from real estate developments and banks taken over by federal government agencies to tourist areas, commuter systems, and zoos.

But what if your company isn't on a list? How can you get in on the action?

The answer is networking. Establish a network of contacts and information sources so you can be alerted quickly when an attractive RFP is announced.

Start by identifying government agencies whose needs you feel your company can satisfy. Contact their purchasing officials and ask to be put on the bidders' lists. Once you are on a selected bidder list, you don't have to track down procurements; they come to you.

You can also list your firm and its capabilities with the Small Business Association's (SBA) Procurement Automated Source System (PASS), a database of nearly half a million small- to medium-sized vendors. PASS is used by hundreds of government agencies and large corporate contractors. To get on the database, contact your local SBA office. The SBA can also provide you with brochures that can help you better understand how RFPs work.

Watch the legal advertising sections of your local newspapers and the classified sections of your trade magazines for RFP announcements.

## MISTAKE 698

**Responding to an RFP without analyzing if it is worth pursuing or feasible to pursue.**

## MISTAKE 699

**Not assigning responsibility for analyzing RFPs to a person or team.**

### How to Avoid Them

When you receive an RFP you have a certain amount of time to respond, depending on the complexity of the procurement and the urgency of the buyer's need.

Before rushing off a response, experienced bidders suggest that you assign the responsibility of analyzing new RFPs to see if, in fact, you should pursue them. Using staff members from engineering, finance, production, and marketing, for example, you can decide whether your company can deliver the skills and resources called for in the RFP in the time allotted, and make a reasonable profit for the effort.

## MISTAKE 700

**Not clarifying requirements you don't understand.**

## MISTAKE 701

**Not knowing or finding out the criteria the buyer will use in choosing a bidder.**

### How to Avoid Them

Understanding the language, requirements, and specifications of a typical RFP is a task in itself. If you come across anything you don't understand, or if there is not enough detailed information on a particular subject, don't hesitate to ask for a full explanation *before* you send back your response. Misunderstanding even the slightest requirement or not being aware of certain restrictions or specifications could mean the difference between profit and loss.

If the RFP does not spell out the criteria that will be used in selecting the winning bidder, ask for a detailed list. It could be, for instance, that the buyer requires the bidding firm to be 51 percent minority-owned. Knowing that you can't meet such a requirement would save you the time and effort of responding to that particular RFP.

## MISTAKE 702

**Submitting a price without understanding the buyer's objectives.**

## MISTAKE 703

**Not addressing the strategy of your proposal to the needs of the buyer.**

### How to Avoid Them

Writing a winning RFP means more than just submitting a well thought out price proposal. You'll need to understand the buyer's business and technical needs and to identify the factors the buyer thinks are especially important in awarding a contract. Such factors might include:

■ Cost.

■ Technology.

■ Reliability.

■ Business location.

■ Servicing ability.

■ Financial stability.

■ Experience of staff.

You can usually identify the issues that are important to the buyer by going through the information asked for in various sections of the RFP. These sections include:

- Business information—requiring a description of your firm's credentials in terms of experience, staff, client roster, financial resources, and special skills or technologies. Relate your strengths to the buyer's basic needs, making it clear that your company's skills, products, and business practices can directly benefit the buyer's objectives.

- Technical/functional information—requires in detail your solution or offering. This is the part where you must demonstrate that you understand the strategic and operational problems that must be addressed. Government procurers are interested in tangibles such as savings in terms of time and money, return on investment, quality, reliability, and competitiveness. Dealing with these motivations is at least as important as having the best price, product, or solution. Be sure to back up each claim with substantive data.

- Pricing—your strategy here is most important, especially if it sets you apart from other bidders. In addition to price, which is often negotiable, make mention of important related features, such as your special technical skills, experience, and maintenance capabilities, your ability to guarantee results, extended warranties you offer, your ability to train their staff, your willingness to be available on weekends or holidays if needed, and your willingness to license the use of your proprietary technology.

Here are some additional questions that can assist you in obtaining the initial information that will help you differentiate your company from your competitors:

- Who is your contact?
- What is that person's function?
- Who does the contact report to?
- Who is the final decision maker?
- What is the budget cycle?
- Are there any inside buzzwords you should know and be using?
- What differences do the buyers want you to make? Improving results? Meeting their needs? Improving their bottom line?
- How do they do things now?
- How do they like what they have now?

▌ What can be improved from their point of view?

▌ What do they lack or need?

▌ Do they have a preference for how to make the changes they want?

▌ What previous plans were acceptable to them?

▌ What is the transition period? Is it feasible?

▌ How will your proposal be measured?

## MISTAKE 704

**Promising more than you can deliver.**

### How to Avoid It

When responding to an RFP, keep in mind that your proposal is a person-to-person communication, and the person reading your proposal is taking you at your word. Don't overstate your capabilities or promise more than you can deliver; it can only get you in deeper trouble down the line.

In preparing the proposal, include a short nondisclosure notice to protect proprietary sensitive information about your business, if applicable. Also, to be helpful to those evaluating your response, include a table of contents listing each RFP requirement and the page on which it is addressed.

## MISTAKE 705

**Not answering all the questions fully.**

### How to Avoid It

Be sure to answer every question in as much detail as possible, even if the question seems silly or similar to another one you've already answered. Never use phrases such as "see question 16," or "ditto" as answers.

## MISTAKE 706

**Interrupting the proposal's "flow" with supporting documents.**

## MISTAKE 707

**Using charts and graphics for visual effect rather than to support an important point.**

### How to Avoid Them

Place supporting documents and reference materials in appendices so as not to interrupt the persuasive flow of the proposal. Charts and other graphics should be part of the section of the proposal they relate to and should be used only if they support an important point. You can also emphasize important points with headings, subheads, bullets, and boldface type. Highlighters are available in many eye-catching colors and should be used to bring attention to significant information.

## MISTAKE 708

**Not checking the final proposal for accuracy.**

### How to Avoid It

As in any written communication, check your proposal carefully for accuracy. That not only means checking performance claims and price quotes, it also means checking spelling and grammar and making sure you are addressing the RFP to the right person or committee.

## MISTAKE 709

**Not considering hidden issues that might affect your proposal.**

### How to Avoid It

You thought you did all your homework and wrote a brilliant proposal. Your product or service is exactly what the RFP calls for, and your experience, dependability, and price quotes have got to be the best. While good looks and logic may carry the day, there are often many variables, hidden agendas, and political issues that could affect the final outcome.

While it is difficult to control or influence such variables, it is possible to anticipate certain roadblocks that might affect the acceptance of your proposal. Here is a checklist of key factors to research and consider:

■ What are the major issues and needs of the buyers?

■ Have they been "burned" before? What were the circumstances?

■ What pressures do they have from internal or external sources?

■ Does your contact or any of the decision makers have vested interests in competing products or services? Is a competing vendor a "pal" of the buyer?

■ If so, how can they be converted from indifference or resistance to support for the issues that advance your cause?

■ Whom can you count on as allies?

■ Are competitors making claims and low-ball bids you know they can't fulfill?

■ Are payoffs or incentives expected?

■ If your proposal is not accepted, is it possible to salvage some of the situation?

## ELEVEN COMMON MISTAKES IN DEALING WITH UNION ISSUES

"Union" historically has been a feared word and sometimes even a dirty word in some sectors of American corporate management. However, dealing with unions and union issues is a fact of daily life for many companies.

In our research for this section we had occasion to speak to some union officials and one of the questions we asked was what character traits they thought were essential in good management.

Over and over the majority spoke of trustworthiness and fairness. They want to deal with employers whose word can be trusted. And they want to be sure that their union members are treated fairly and justly by those who manage the workplace.

## MISTAKE 710

**Believing union organizing activities is a thing of the past.**

## How to Avoid It

Contrary to popular belief, union organizing and election activity in the private business sector is on the rise nationwide, and in recent years unions have had more success in organizing smaller businesses than larger ones. According to statistics released by various state chambers of commerce, unions have won slightly more than 20 percent of elections at companies with more than 500 employees, but have won better than 50 percent of elections at companies with 15 or fewer employees. The reason is thought to be that smaller companies do not have the resources to hire labor lawyers to thwart the organizing effort.

As companies feel pressure to cut costs and be more efficient, the pace of work for employees has become more intense. Those employees with less seniority, less education, and fewer skills are hit hardest by these pressures. They have the least bargaining power on their own, and fewer job alternatives. They are the people who feel as if they need protection, and the unions stand ready to provide it.

## MISTAKE 711

**Not recognizing the signs of union activity in the workplace.**

## MISTAKE 712

**Not ensuring the employees' rights to determine if they do or don't want union representation.**

## How to Avoid Them

The law requires that a union seeking to represent employees obtain written authorization from 30 percent of the work force it seeks to represent (many unions will try for 50 percent or more). Once the signatures are obtained, the union may file a petition with the National Labor Relations Board (NLRB) to seek an election to determine if the employees desire to be represented by a union.

It is important for employers to recognize the signs of union activity and to ensure that they do not violate their employees' rights to determine whether to remain nonunion or seek representation. One good indication of union activity would be a substantial increase in employee complaints about workplace conditions. Even after an employer addresses those issues, employees immediately begin to complain about other issues.

## MISTAKE 713

**Taking actions or making threats against employees considering union representation.**

## MISTAKE 714

**Trying to influence employees against unions with promises of benefits.**

## MISTAKE 715

**Questioning employees who have joined a union about their union activities.**

### How to Avoid Them

If an employer receives a union petition, the employer is legally prohibited from taking certain actions, including:

- Spying on employees to determine their inclination toward union representation.

- Threatening employees in order to keep them from voting for the union.

- Making promises of any benefits in an attempt to keep employees from joining a union or voting against a union. Benefits can include such items as promising extra privileges, more overtime work, pay increases, or changing working conditions that existed prior to the receipt of the union petition.

- Questioning or advising employees who have joined a union about their union activity, their opinions of the union, whether they support the union, or how they intend to vote on union issues.

If an employer does not abide by NLRB rules, the employer may be found guilty of unfair labor practices, and the NLRB can void an election that was lost by the union and order a rerun election.

## MISTAKE 716

**Not knowing your rights as an employer when dealing with unions.**

### How to Avoid It

While employers cannot threaten, make promises, or question employees about their union activities, there are certain actions an employer can take that will not be in violation of the law.

▮ An employer may advise the employees of its views and opinions about the union, as well as the history and character of the union and the union officials.

▮ An employer may inform its employees about the costs involved in joining a union, including dues and initiation fees.

▮ An employer may inform its employees that if a union and an employer cannot agree on terms or conditions of employment, the union has the right to call an economic strike. In many states, if a strike is called, employees who participate in the strike cannot collect unemployment compensation.

▮ An employer may advise its employees that they will not automatically obtain more wages or benefits simply because a union is voted in. Only if an employer agrees to such increases or changes will they become effective.

▮ An employer may inform its employees that even if the company loses a union election it is not required to automatically sign a contract with the union or agree to any benefits. An employer is required to bargain in good faith with the union only in an attempt to reach a collective bargaining agreement. If an impasse is reached, the employer, at that time, may implement its last offer to the union, even though it has not been accepted by the union.

## MISTAKE 717

**Not complying with union disciplinary procedure because it's too costly in productive time.**

## MISTAKE 718

Not complying with time-consuming union grievance procedures.

### How to Avoid Them

There are times when an employee's actions will require some kind of discipline. But going through all the steps called for in your union contract will cause a tremendous loss of productive time. Do you take matters in your own hands?

A union contract must be adhered to, and most unions insist on strict compliance. However, if you have a good relationship with union leaders, you may be able to compromise with minor variations in order to save time and trouble for all concerned.

But suppose the problem is trivial employee grievances. Must you go through the time-consuming grievance procedure called for in the union contract?

The answer is, most of the time, yes. But it depends on the aggressiveness of the union and your relationship with its officials. In some situations, the union pushes its members to report even the most insignificant matters to the union steward, who then makes the final determination about whether or not it should be filed as a grievance. In other situations, the employee and supervisor may try to work it out privately.

Most workers do not like the red tape and bad feelings that go along with typical grievance procedures. For this reason, and others, it's a good idea for managers in unionized companies to encourage workers to report things that bother them directly to supervisors so both employees and management can resolve problems without involving the union.

## MISTAKE 719

Breaking union work rules because they don't allow you to make changes that would increase productivity.

### How to Avoid It

If certain restraining work rules are written into your contract with the union, you must abide by them or try to change the contract.

Breaking the rules means breaking the contractual agreement and could mean legal and work-stoppage problems. Most likely, you will have to wait until the current contract expires and a new one is negotiated.

There are always some work rules that are not covered by the contract, but have been agreed upon by union and management as part of their ongoing relations. Such rules may be discussed with the shop steward or other union representative and, if all parties agree, may be put into use at once.

Many union contracts contain a "management prerogative" clause that gives management the right to decide on any matters not specifically prohibited by the contract. In such cases, changes in methods may be instituted unilaterally. But it is a good idea to sell the changes to the workers and the union before establishing them as part of the regular work procedure.

## MISTAKE 720

**Not motivating unionized employees to exceed minimum union performance standards.**

### How to Avoid It

Many managers of unionized companies feel that what *they* consider minimum productivity, the union will consider maximum for their members. As a result, they don't try to motivate employees to higher standards because they know they will get little or no cooperation from workers, and that being persistent will end up only with time-consuming grievances.

However, the survival of the company may depend on increased productivity. If this is the case, workers should be notified of the situation immediately and be given full details of the up and down sides and how they will be affected. Then management and union officials should try to reach an agreement on which work rules need to be changed to help the company—and its employees—through a difficult period.

Nobody, not the union, not the workers, and certainly not the management wants a company to fail or miss opportunities. If it does, everybody loses. So it is in the best interest of all involved to use whatever informal efforts they can to achieve increased production, even if it's only a temporary measure.

## TEN COMMON MISTAKES WHEN GOING FROM DOMESTIC TO INTERNATIONAL TRADE

No doubt about it, the marketing world is getting smaller, and communications technology is helping to shrink it even faster. While most of America's fastest-growing companies have found success conducting their business within the borders of this country, many now realize that by avoiding going global they are passing up big profits to be made in new markets larger than the United States, and the best they can hope for is to be an also-ran.

Today, companies are realizing that in order to meet or better the competition, counterbalance cyclical swings, compensate for customer turnover and shrinking orders, and continue building on previous success, they must overcome the "fear of the unknown," and commit to globalizing, by any or all of the following:

■ Exporting their goods or services.

■ Importing goods or services.

■ Licensing.

■ Joint ventures with foreign organizations.

■ International barter.

■ Setting up operations in foreign lands.

But when is the right time to engage in international trade?

Experts recommend waiting until your domestic business is large and stable enough to support the risks of international trade. They also suggest beginning with modest goals and small steps, dealing with nearby countries such as Mexico and Canada, where delivery and payment are more reliable than they are abroad.

### MISTAKE 721

**Assuming that international trade is no different than expanding in the United States.**

### MISTAKE 722

**Not assessing a product's or service's sales potential in foreign markets.**

## MISTAKE 723

**Assuming your product or service answers the same basic need in every country.**

### HOW TO AVOID THEM

For many companies, going global for new customers is more a necessity than a luxury. As their domestic market shrinks, they have nowhere else to turn but to foreign markets. In their haste to conquer new territory, they go into international trade believing that any product or service will be globally accepted simply by making it available on a global scale—never considering whether anybody out there wants it or not, never considering the ugly surprises and thorny obstacles that await them. They believe that if a company has the money and management determination for research and planning, the ability to adapt to new conditions, the wherewithal to find distribution and new customers, and the willingness to take the risk, it can put its product on the pipeline and point it at the world.

In many ways expanding into foreign markets is similar to expanding into new markets in the United States. You can, however, also pour most of that money down the drain if you don't first consider these and other factors:

- If your product or service is successful in domestic markets, chances are it will also be successful wherever similar needs and conditions exist internationally. However, your product or service may not be looked at in the same light wherever it's sold, even if it's technically identical wherever it's sold. Because of cultural differences, your product may be considered a necessity in one market, but marginal, even old-fashioned, in the market next door. You may be surprised to discover that your product conflicts with a country's political or moral "position." One quick way to find out if your product or service is marketable in another country is at the nearest office of the U.S. Department of Commerce (DoC). The International Trade Administration (ITA) and the United States and Foreign Commercial Service (US&FCS), both organizations related to the DoC, are also able to provide you with a multitude of services including an assessment of your product's export potential. They can even arrange introductions to foreign businesspeople, government personnel, and sources in whichever countries you plan to market.

## MISTAKE 724

**Trying to make an existing domestic product or service fit a new foreign market.**

### How to Avoid It

To participate in the global marketplace, your product or service must answer a basic consumer or business need in each market. It must also be a visible entity wherever it exists if you're going to achieve the economics of scale and profitability you're aiming for. Attempting to make existing products or services *fit* a market and running the risk of destroying some valuable long-term investments by trying to make them what they're not is not the way to expand internationally. It may be necessary to devise new versions of those products for that purpose. Some facts to consider:

▌ In foreign markets some products may have limited potential due to climate; environmental, social, and cultural factors; local availability of raw materials; and different forms of distribution, duties, quotas, licenses, and other regulations.

▌ You will have to create legally protectable product identities and package designs.

▌ Because distances will be greater, shipping, documentation, and insurance will be more complicated and costly.

▌ Pricing, financing, and payment terms will be different from country to country.

## MISTAKE 725

**Going into global marketing without the corporate financing, courage, and determination to persevere.**

### How to Avoid It

Your company must have the ability to persevere. Global marketing is a lot more than a matter of good intentions, and establishing your product or service in foreign markets is not an overnight process. One of the biggest obstacles U.S. businesses have in overseas trade (especially small- and medium-sized firms), once they have identified the product and targeted the market, is how they plan to pay for it. Only recently has the

DoC created financing options for smaller-sized companies. In addition to financing, your company will need the courage and determination of corporate willpower, a philosophical business conviction, and effective control of your corporate system. Once you have determined that your product is exportable, consider these four questions:

1. What do you expect to gain from international trade?

2. Are these goals consistent with overall company goals?

3. What demands will going global place on key company resources—management and personnel, production capacity, and finance—and can these demands be met?

4. Are the expected benefits worth the costs, or could the money be better spent developing new domestic business?

## MISTAKE 726

**Not seeking expert advice on pursuing international opportunities.**

## MISTAKE 727

**Not having a plan before entering a global marketing program.**

### How to Avoid Them

Once you have decided to get into international trading, your first step should be to seek advice and assistance to make up for your own lack of experience. Such advice is available at little or no cost and can help you avoid many problems and difficulties down the line.

As we said earlier, the best place to start is the DoC and its affiliated departments, ITA and US&FCS. These organizations maintain a network of international trade specialists in the United States and commercial officers in foreign cities to help American firms do business abroad. By contacting the nearest DoC district office, you can tap into all assistance programs available from ITA and all trade information gathered by U.S. embassies and consulates around the world. The DoC offers information about:

- Trade opportunities abroad.
- Foreign markets for U.S. products and services.

■ How to locate and evaluate overseas buyers and representatives.

■ Financial aid to overseas marketers.

■ International trade exhibitions.

■ Export documentation requirements.

■ Foreign economic statistics.

■ U.S. export licensing and foreign nation import requirements.

■ Export seminars and conferences.

In addition to the DoC, international trade advice is also available at District Export Councils (DEC), which provide advice from nearly 2,000 business and trade experts who volunteer to help U.S. firms develop solid international trade strategies. The DoC can put you in touch with these DECs, who run seminars and workshops arranged by their district offices. DEC members may also provide direct, personal counseling to internationally inexperienced companies suggesting marketing plans, trade contacts, and other ways to maximize your efforts in foreign markets.

The DoC also has available hundreds of trade specialists, expert in various areas of international business. These experts offer country counseling for any U.S. firm wishing to trade in a particular country. They inform you about the country's overall economy, trade policies, requirements for U.S. products and services, political situation, and other relevant factors.

Through an arrangement with the Federal Bar Association, international marketers can receive initial international legal assistance from qualified attorneys working through SBA field offices. The SBA also offers export training and counseling to U.S. firms going overseas.

Valuable international advice can also be obtained from international trade shows, trade publications, commercial banks with international departments, chambers of commerce and trade associations, and a number of private international trade consultants who can help select the right entry markets, help determine how best to enter a market and when, identify possible product modifications, and advise on pricing and marketing strategies.

But getting good advice is only the first step. Next you must (with the help of advisers if you don't have your own foreign experts) develop a definitive master plan to accomplish your objectives and overcome the problems that may arise.

## MISTAKE 728

**Not taking care in selecting foreign distributors.**

### How to Avoid It

One of the most critical decisions you make in each new market you enter will be choosing the *right* foreign distributor for that market. Because your company, its trademarks, and its reputation will more than likely be unknown in that market, and because of the difficulties involved in communicating and shipping internationally, the part played by your foreign distributor becomes much more crucial than that of your domestic distributor. Just as when using any professional service, you should be particularly interested in the distributor's experience, the qualifications of the personnel you will be working with, the distributor's facilities, and the management methods the distributor employs.

## MISTAKE 729

**Not offering foreign distributors the same promotional and marketing support you do your domestic distributors.**

### How to Avoid It

There is no reason why localized versions of your ad campaigns, discount promotions, sales incentive programs, special credit term plans, and warranty offers will not be as successful in foreign markets as they were in domestic markets.

## MISTAKE 730

**Not considering the services of an Export Management Company.**

### How to Avoid It

A mistake many smaller companies make getting into international trade is creating their own costly (and often inexperienced) export or international sales department. An alternative is to engage an appropriate Export Management Company (EMC).

An EMC can function as your "export department," selling your products in foreign markets along with other allied but noncompeti-

tive lines. Your regional DoC trade specialist can get you a list of recommended firms, or you may get recommendations at trade shows
overseas as well as in this country. To help in your selection of an
EMC, here are some services to look for:

- Expertise and successful results with your particular type of product or service and the references to back it up.

- Willingness and ability to warehouse your product, which would
  expedite sales.

- Willingness to take on all your product lines, not just the ones
  it thinks it can move.

- Market research facilities to help target your best-selling opportunities.

- Ability to locate, interview, and help you select distributors, representatives, or sales agents.

- Participation in trade shows and willingness to exhibit your
  products or services.

- Handling the nitty-gritty of making sure your product gets to
  where you ship it. This would include establishing a network of
  reliable freight forwarders who can guide your product through
  the mazes of paperwork and tariff regulations.

- Having financial contacts to assure for payment of goods shipped
  in U.S. currency, preferably accepting cash only, up front or with
  an irrevocable letter of credit through major banks.

- Willingness to handle all correspondence in the language of the
  country in which you are marketing.

- Knowledge of patent and trademark protection measures.

- Ability and willingness to provide cooperative shipping arrangements between several clients it represents and passing any savings on to the participants.

## THIRTEEN COMMON MISTAKES YOU CAN LEAVE
## HOME WITHOUT

When Americans travel to other countries, they take with them certain perceptions about the countries they are visiting and the people

they will do business with. More often than not, these perceptions are wrong. For example, all French people do not dislike Americans.

Unfortunately, such cultural stereotypes can distort and disrupt business dealings. Being well informed is the best asset a company going abroad can have to overcome the anomalies they will encounter.

## MISTAKE 731

**Assuming business protocol in foreign markets is the same as in the United States.**

### How to Avoid It

Every business pursuing international trading opportunities should expect to encounter a host of different business, social, political, technical, and cultural challenges.

One of the first lessons learned by the novice global marketer is that the way things are done in this country can be very different from the way they are done in other parts of the world. For instance, never tell a joke to a prospective customer in Japan or touch anyone in a Moslem country with the left hand, as that hand is considered unclean. Never cross your legs in the company of an Asian or a Middle Eastern counterpart to make yourself physically comfortable during a business discussion. Doing so will reveal the bottom of your foot and cause you to point with the toe, considered offensive in much of the Eastern Hemisphere. Latins accept and encourage people to stand close to and touch the lapel or shoulder of the one being addressed. Asians and Africans, however, are offended by such close quarters, and usually stand at least three feet away from the person with whom they are conversing. But in the Middle East, backing away in the midst of a conversation is considered rude.

## MISTAKE 732

**Failing to consider the effect of language as a cultural challenge.**

### How to Avoid It

Language is the first and most conspicuous barrier preventing clear communications between people of different countries.

In considering the effect of language as a cultural marketing challenge, there are two aspects to focus on: verbal and nonverbal.

When communicating verbally, it is important to realize that words or phrases in the United States do not always have the same meaning in other countries. Being told your offer was being "tabled" in Britain, for instance, means action would be taken on it immediately. In the United States it would mean the matter would be delayed and brought up at a future meeting.

Since English has become the *lingua franca,* so to speak, of the international business community, many people you will be dealing with will be proficient in the language or at least somewhat exposed to it. Some steps to take to make yourself better understood include:

■ Speak slowly. Pause between sentences because often the other party will not fully understand or digest one sentence until you are halfway through the next.

■ Speak simply. Avoid acronyms, unnecessarily long words, contractions, idioms, slang, sarcasm, innuendoes, and colorful phrases such as "You bet" and "It's Greek to me."

■ Whenever possible, rely on practical examples to explain abstract concepts.

■ Review technical terms in advance.

■ Use gestures and show emotion. Your body language will help convey your thoughts.

■ Listen. Most misunderstandings result from one or both parties not paying attention to what is being said.

■ Be careful about using humor, especially the kind that relies on word plays or U.S. events. It is better that you smile often and display a happy, pleasant disposition.

■ Numbers are often misunderstood. To be sure your counterpart understands completely, write them out.

■ Repeat important statements several times and in several ways, if you can.

■ Confirm all in-person and telephone discussions in writing.

Nonverbal communication involves unspoken messages between people. In the Middle East, for example, it is offensive to look away and not maintain direct eye contact at all times. The Japanese, however, consider direct eye contact rude and intrusive. In many Asian countries, nodding one's head indicates an understanding of what was said, not agreement with what was said.

Many of these problems can be overcome through training and experience. However, there is a limit to the amount of effort that should be invested in learning all the cultural peculiarities of another country. It's a myth that in order to do business in Japan you have to be more Japanese than the Japanese. Here are some tips to consider:

- Rather than being overly concerned with how long to hold a bow, for instance, you should practice presenting yourself politely and considerately. If the other parties sense a genuineness in you, they will be more comfortable.

- Learn and respect local traditions, ways of doing business, and social values and find a mix that's sustainable for you and your counterpart.

- Do not try to change another's values.

- If the other party suggests that for you to do business in that country you are required to do something unethical or illegal or if the price of doing business is too high, take a pass and move on to another source or another country.

- Develop local people as quickly as possible to represent your interests. It can't hurt to have someone who knows the language and customs with you when you have business meetings or at least have someone explain a few expressions common in a particular country and pepper them into the conversation.

- Never assume you understand something implied during a communication. "I thought you meant . . ." is probably the most used international business phrase of all.

- Be patient. Americans believe time is money, but this philosophy is not shared by other cultures. For example, in Latin America and parts of southern Europe lunch breaks can last several hours and people regularly work into the night. In Islamic countries, employees take several prayer breaks throughout the course of the workday.

## MISTAKE 733

**Failure to print directions, uses, and other important product information in clearly understood language of the country you are in.**

## How to Avoid It

While your distributor's staff may speak and understand English, it is unlikely that all sales and service personnel, or customers overseas will have this capability. Without a clear understanding of sales messages, service instructions, warranty and guarantee information, your efforts to succeed in that market will be greatly diminished. See Chapter 19, Mistake 527 for more about mistakes made in translating information.

## MISTAKE 734

**Failure to modify or reengineer products and services to comply with regulations or local cultural preferences.**

## How to Avoid It

Part of doing business in a foreign country involves abiding by that country's safety and security regulations and import restrictions. If product modifications are called for, they should be made at the factory, otherwise, the distributor will have to take care of the problem, probably at greater cost. Or worse, your shipment may be held up indefinitely in customs until rules are complied with.

## MISTAKE 735

**Not certifying the quality of your products or services.**

## How to Avoid It

One of the critical factors determining product acceptance in many foreign countries is product quality. Quality can give your exported product a competitive edge over similar products produced in that country. For this and other reasons, a growing number of U.S. firms are qualifying for ISO 9000 standards.

The Geneva-based ISO, or International Organization for Standardization, got its impetus in the 1980s, during the move toward a unified European Community. The objective was to create voluntary standards that would promote global trade.

ISO 9000 evolved over the years, establishing rules that companies should follow to assure quality. It is a written standard that defines basic elements of the system companies should use to ensure that their products and services meet or exceed customer expectations. It requires companies to document procedures, train employees, assign responsibility for quality results, check vendor quality methods, keep records, and continually correct errors.

Widely used by manufacturing companies, variations in the 9000 series exist for product-development firms and for distribution and service companies as well. In many countries, prospective customers will refuse even to discuss a contract unless the product or service has ISO certification.

Information about ISO 9000 certification can be obtained from most foreign trade specialists at local DoC International Trade Administration offices.

## MISTAKE 736

**Not establishing a policy to deal with foreign inquiries.**

## MISTAKE 737

**Not getting inquiries translated by competent translators.**

## MISTAKE 738

**Disregarding inquiries because of grammatical or typographical errors or because the stationary, printing, or general appearance of the inquiry is not impressive.**

## MISTAKE 739

**Not separating the legitimate inquiries from the frivolous.**

### How to Avoid Them

You want to sell your product or service in other markets, so you send out feelers with letters to distributors, you take ads in trade and consumer publications, you exhibit at trade shows.

Before you know it, inquiries are coming in asking for product information such as specifications, prices, delivery schedules, shipping costs, terms, and exclusivity arrangements. Some foreign firms want information on purchasing a product for their own internal use, others, such as distributors and agents, want to sell the product or service in their market. Some may even know the product and want to place a sample order.

Regardless of what the inquiries ask for, your company should establish a policy or system to deal with them. Steps to take:

■ Reply to all inquiries except those that are obviously not potential customers.

■ Have all inquiries that are not in English translated by a competent, qualified commercial translating service. Some banks and many freight-forwarding firms, as well as colleges and universities also provide translation services.

■ Do not disregard inquiries because of badly broken English, typographical errors, or unimpressive stationary. The inquiry may be from a reputable, well-established company even though the writer probably knows English only as a second or third language and the printing standards in the country it is coming from may be below our standards.

■ Reply promptly, clearly, and completely. Give details that show the credibility of your company and products, bank references, and other sources that confirm your reliability as a supplier. Include information concerning your export policy, costs, terms, and delivery schedule.

■ Enclose details on your products or services.

■ Reply via airmail rather than surface mail, which can take weeks or months. If a foreign firm's letter shows both a street address and a post office box, address your reply to the P.O. box. If your reply can be sent by fax, that is the fastest and safest method of responding. Most companies keep their fax machines on all the time, so differences in time zones will not be a problem. It is advisable to call the party before sending your fax to alert them to watch for it.

■ Set up a file for all foreign inquiries.

■ Obtain whatever information you can about inquiring foreign firms. Several publications list and qualify international firms, including Jane's Major Companies of Europe, Dun & Bradstreet's Principal International Business, and others, available at most business libraries. Information may also be obtained through international banks, foreign embassies, the DoC, and private sources of credit information such as Dun & Bradstreet.

## MISTAKE 740

**Going it on your own without considering a licensing or joint-venture arrangement.**

## How to Avoid It

If you're just testing the overseas waters and don't have a firm long-range commitment, or your product line is very limited and international trade is not feasible, you can still compete effectively in foreign markets by licensing your product or service or joint venturing with companies in the various countries you are interested in.

Before making such arrangements, you should thoroughly research the companies you are considering. Though you may not find such alliances as profitable as doing it all yourself, you will be saving yourself the aggravation and difficulties that come as a result of various import, personnel, and marketing problems.

## MISTAKE 741

**Not preclearing product samples through customs.**

## How to Avoid It

If you carry samples of your products to all the countries you market in, you can avoid difficulties in customs by obtaining an ATA carnet. An ATA carnet is an international customs document that is valid for one year from the date of issuance and can be used for the temporary admission of commercial samples, advertising materials, and professional equipment into foreign countries.

In lieu of formal entry requirements, many countries accept the ATA carnet as a guarantee against the payment of customs duties that may eventually become due on goods that enter using a carnet but that are subsequently not reexported. ATA carnets are issued by the U.S. Council for International Business under the direction of the U.S. Customs Service. The council charges a fee for the service. If the goods listed on the carnet are not reexported from a participating country, the holder is responsible to pay for all duties that would have been due to the foreign country under normal importing circumstances.

Although a carnet can make life much easier for U.S. firms doing business overseas, the holder must still follow all export control requirements, obtain any export licenses, and must file a shipper's export declaration.

## MISTAKE 742

**Not taking advantage of duty refunds (duty-drawback) on imports because you are either not informed or have fear of a Customs Service audit.**

## How to Avoid It

As much as $2 billion in U.S. Customs Service payments are lost every year by American manufacturing, exporting, and importing firms that are either not aware that many duty payments are recoverable through duty-drawback or are reluctant to apply for refunds for fear of a U.S. Customs audit.

Duty-drawback resembles the refund individuals receive on income tax payments, except that duty-drawback requires careful record keeping and some advance planning to qualify.

Companies must identify each stage of the import and production process or report on the age and use of imported items if duty has been paid. Raw materials have to be specifically listed from the time of purchase to the time they end up in a finished product.

The first step is filing a drawback proposal, a document that must be approved by the Customs Service before your company can file a claim. If you qualify, you can start by claiming a refund for a particular shipment and prove that you are the importer of record. There are software programs to assist your company in duty-drawback reporting. These programs will track materials through the manufacturing or inventory stages and calculate the amount of duty that can be reclaimed.

Many small companies let customs brokers handle the paperwork and pay as much as 35 percent commission for the effort. But if mistakes are made, you—not the broker—are responsible for any audit or payments due. It is the possibility of a time consuming and expensive Customs Service audit that scares many companies away from applying for drawback, and sometimes the time and expense of an audit can outweigh the investment in the drawback plan.

But the fact remains, in many cases, the refunds realized through drawback can be the competitive edge a U.S. exporter needs to make bids lower than foreign domestic producers. Income from refunds also may pay for more than the freight, depending on the value of the merchandise.

## MISTAKE 743

**Overlooking "unused" duty-drawback on import-exports.**

## How to Avoid It

Suppose, for example, you are a distributor of dry cleaning equipment. You import a hotel-sized dry-cleaning machine from abroad and pay the duty. Now, without opening the boxes, without testing or using the product, you export it to a hotel outside the United States where you will install it. Because the equipment was unused in the United States, you qualify for a drawback. The Customs Service allows you three years to file for a drawback on unused goods.

Drawback plans are worthwhile mostly for companies that can recover $10,000 or more. A single application can cover a company's entire import-export operation no matter which ports are used.

# POSTSCRIPT

We have covered a lot of territory together since Chapter 1. We've identified hundreds of common mistakes managers make in managing their employees, customers, vendors, professionals and government agencies and we've shown you how to avoid them. Now we present some examples of the common personal mistakes managers make in communicating and dealing with who they are and what they stand for.

## SEVEN COMMON MISTAKES MANAGERS MAKE MANAGING THEMSELVES

### MISTAKE 744

**Assuming that past success ensures future success.**

#### HOW TO AVOID IT

Because we live and work in a time of discontinuities where there are fewer meaningful ways to relate the past to the present and the future, it's becoming more difficult to use the past to plan ahead. Only by disregarding past victories and defeats can the future be fully embraced. What is done is done and tomorrow will be what you make of it.

### MISTAKE 745

**Not taking complete responsibility for your life.**

#### HOW TO AVOID IT

Those who accept success as their due, must also accept responsibility for mistakes. Don't blame others for your pressures or your slacking off. Be in control of your schedule. Don't let the needs of others distract you from your course. By accepting responsibility you show commitment and concern.

## MISTAKE 746

**Not reframing mistakes into challenges.**

### How to Avoid It

Life won't always deal you a great hand of cards, but how you play the cards you are dealt is up to you. Most superachievers have one characteristic in common—they see mistakes and setbacks as opportunities to grow instead of using them as excuses to fail. There's always a good reason why a mistake happens. Find that reason and use it as a lesson that will prepare you for future challenges. Condition yourself to react positively to negative occurances. Understand that setbacks are chances to reassess your situation. Tell yourself, "So what? Big deal. Nothing is worth getting me upset." Then ask yourself, "How can this make me stronger?" In time you may find yourself becoming a supermanager laughing in the face of adversity and undaunted by obstacles.

## MISTAKE 747

**Spreading yourself too thin or indulging yourself in excess.**

### How to Avoid It

Balancing your priorities in most endeavors is an important key to success. It helps you maintain a sense of proportion at and away from work. Excess, for example, can turn even positive qualities such as self-discipline into tragic flaws. Pay close attention to your life and what is most important to you in it. Set aside enough time for your work, your family and yourself. Applying moderation and balance in everything you do also gives you the opportunity to observe and participate in life from a much healthier perspective.

## MISTAKE 748

**Not using positive visualization to get what you want from life.**

## How to Avoid It

Successful people visualize what they want from life, then go out and get it. Make a habit of seeing things as you want them to be. For example, picture yourself advancing to your boss's position. Then develop a strategy and take the action to make that vision reality.

---

## MISTAKE 749 ˋ

**Not being prepared to do whatever it takes for as long as it takes to reach your goals or giving up because you're burned-out.**

## How to Avoid It

Persistence may be the single most important quality you can have to help ensure your chance for success. If you simply throw in the towel anytime there's a setback, you forfeit that chance. When the going gets tough, the superachievers keep going—and don't stop short of their goals.

    Like the soles of a favorite pair of shoes can wear thin, so can the souls of managers. And when they do, they too have to be rejuvenated. You may feel exhausted and burned-out, but you can breathe new life into yourself with the right revamping strategy. For instance, when your body tells you to get some sleep, listen to it. Lack of sleep can make you feel worse mentally and physically and lead to reduced productivity. Chapter 8 covers other methods managers can use to reduce stress which would also apply to burn-out.

    You'd be surprised at the power you possess to turn things around. With a little effort and a positive attitude, you'll recharge your body, mind, and spirit.

---

## MISTAKE 750

**Not moving with the times.**

## How to Avoid It

Never forget that we live in a throw-away world and every business is disposable. The day after you install the latest computer, it's already obsolete. Products, services, customers, strategies, timetables, cycles and attitudes cannot be taken for granted. Survival and success depends on looking ahead, recognizing opportunities when they present themselves, and being flexible enough to make moves unencumbered by old ideas that inhibit change. In other words, if you don't move with the times, the times will move you out.

# AFTERWORD

I'm sure you have heard the expression, "You live and you learn." Well, all of us in business have lived, learned, and are still learning. And we've all made mistakes, too. I'll be the first to admit that I made more than my share.

As work on this book progressed, we discovered some curious facts about mistakes. For instance, it doesn't take much to make one happen, and they don't happen on schedule. Often, some of the smartest people make some of the most foolish and costly mistakes. And we also discovered that many times mistakes can lead to positive results. Alexander Graham Bell might not have invented the telephone if he hadn't made a mistake in trying to improve the telegraph.

In his book, *The Way I See It,* the late, great entertainer Eddie Cantor wrote, "It is better to be in the wrong than never in the running." That philosophy is especially true when it comes to business management. Those in management should not be afraid to ask questions, look for answers, weigh this, measure that, and—right or wrong—make a decision. And if that decision turns out to be a mistake—whether it be an honest error, lack of knowledge, or simply rushing to judgment—they should be willing to learn why and communicate that information so others can avoid making the same mistake.

Someday, perhaps all the businesspeople on earth will communicate in a common language and no one will ever make mistakes again. In the meantime, I hope this book will help you avoid at least 750 of them.

*Allan Krieff*
Hollywood, Florida